ECLIPSE

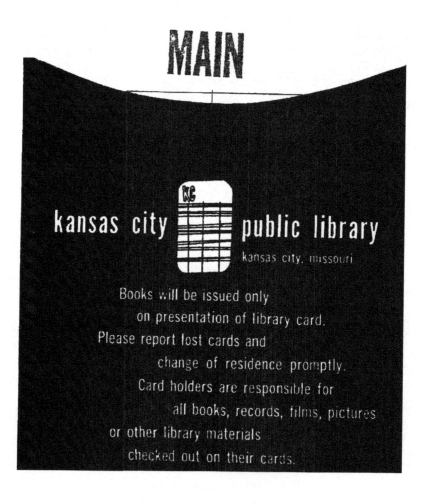

ECLIPSE

DATE DUE

5-22-68		

ECLIPSE

ALAN MOOREHEAD

HARPER & ROW, PUBLISHERS

NEW YORK AND EVANSTON

1817

FIRST HARPER & ROW EDITION, 1968

LIBRARY OF CONGRESS CATALOG CARD NUMBER: 68-15966

To Caroline

Contents

Total Eclipse: COLLAPSE IN THE CENTRE: GERMANY

MAPS

Acknowledgments

We are grateful to the following for permission to reproduce photographs: The Trustees of the Imperial War Museum, for pages 18, 20, 23, 26, 29, 37, 47 top and bottom, 56, 62, 72, 76, 78, 80, 86, 102, 127, 128, 139, 149, 185, 190, 193, 206, 208, 236, 241, 265, 287; Wide World Photos, for pages 96, 168, 171, 225 right and left, 249, 251, 254; The Department of Defense, for pages 28, 106, 112 top and bottom, 243, 245; United Press International, for pages 111, 119, 131, 143; U.S. National Archives and Record Service, for page 110; La Direction de la Documentation Française, for page 167; Keystone Press Agency, Inc., for pages 15, 90 right, 130 top, 212; The Sun, Odhams Press Ltd., for page 135; The Mansell Collection, for page 252; Pictorial Press Ltd., for page 278; Radio Times Hulton Picture Library, for page 303.

The maps on pages 25, 74, 115 and 223 are by Brian Adnams; those on pages 148 and 276 by H. J. Blackman.

Foreword

Eclipse was the code name given by the Allies to their last operation of the war in Europe; the occupation of Germany. I take the word for the title of my book with all acknowledgment to the men who made it possible.

In the beginning it was my intention not to write another war book, but to try an experiment: merely to sketch in the military details and tell the story of the collapse of German Europe sociologically and politically, psychologically and even emotionally. I was after atmosphere more than fact. I wanted to convey what the Italians and the French and the Germans had been thinking through the long five years, how they reacted to the final collapse and what it was like to be there and talk to them at that special moment. A book of hopes and fears and miseries: the truths underneath the more obvious noises and movement of the war. A book that was a half-way house to fiction.

I had not written fifty pages before I realized that my fine Tolstoyan scheme was entirely out of reach. You cannot write a book about war like that—not at least while you are still living in the war or immediately after it. You can write a novel, you can write a straight history which, at so short a perspective, is not much more than a catalogue of events, or you can write a book of your own personal thoughts and adventures.

And so as I went on I found that I was falling between two—or rather three—stools. More and more I was forced to hang my story on the framework of the actual military events; all my ideas and impressions, all my atmospherics, could never make a pattern of themselves. The story itself was too big. But having gone so far one had to persist, and now that the thing is finished and done with I am not sure what you would call it. A commentary, possibly.

All this can be of no possible interest except that it allows me to take out a certain insurance against the reader. This is not a war book, nor a history, nor a social treatise or a novel. You cannot expect accuracy or completeness or education and there is precious little romance. I have not said nearly enough about the preponderant part played by the American and Russian forces, and this for the sole reason that I was not with them.

Those who have been hurt by this war may think I have put Germany in a far too lenient light throughout the book. Whether this be so or not, my underlying object has been throughout to make it clear that there are no solutions to be found for the future of Europe in the conduct of the war itself. Savagery fed on savagery. The sinking of passenger liners, the concentration camps, the bombing—all these were the outward and vicious expression of something that ought to have been foreseen long before 1939. All the world is culpable for the indifference and timidity of the nineteen-thirties. However cynically we may approach the peace, at least we can admit that it might be a good thing to be vigilant in the years ahead.

One can never write a book like this entirely alone, and I must put down here with gratitude a few of the names of the people who helped me. There were Major-General Sir Francis de Guingand, the Chief of Staff of 21st Army Group, and Brigadier E. T. Williams and Colonel J. O. Ewart, the two senior intelligence officers attached to Montgomery. They toiled through many of these pages in search of grosser errors and gave me much information. Lieutenant-General Harding kindly supplied me with a document on the Italian campaign. I had the fortune to hear Field Marshal Montgomery, General Dempsey and other commanders discussing their battles. And a very great deal of work was done on this book by my wife.

Finally, there were the main companions of my travels, the people with whom, day in and day out, in many countries, I experienced and talked over most of the events here described—usually without reaching the slightest agreement: Alexander Clifford, Christopher Buckley, Geoffrey Keating, Edward Gilling and David Woodward. This book is published almost in defiance of them.

ALAN MOOREHEAD

Jevington, Sussex, 1945

The First Quarter

COLLAPSE IN THE SOUTH:
ITALY

1. Taormina

In the summer towards the middle of August the three of us began walking up the road to Taormina. I cannot remember the date exactly, but that day remains astonishingly clear in the mind, like the day of a marriage or a death. Even at the time I believe we were conscious that this was the end of one set of experiences, and the beginning of something quite unexplored and different.

The army, as I remember, had stopped a little short of the village of Giardini, on the eastern coast of Sicily, just above Catania. It was a broken bridge or a minefield on the road or something of that sort; at all events the vehicles could not get through, and the soldiers lay about in the shade accepting grapes from the peasants and awaiting the order to go on again. It was hot. There was a clear leaping brilliance in the sea, and at midday everything had turned into strident color, red rocks, green vineyards, a blaring cobalt blue in the sky and then all the bright colors of the tumbledown houses along the shore. A gunboat, keeping close to the beach, ran on ahead of the front line, and was aimlessly turning circles in the bay below Taormina.

We left the car and walked knee deep across the Torrente Rapido, then across the Fiumefreddo, and then we went squelching on with our wet boots until we got to the forward platoon. They too were resting and eating grapes. There were no Germans about and no Italians, but Giardini, the village just ahead, was on fire. Two officers had gone on afoot, and now we three, after some argument, decided to follow. It seemed to be the thing to do.

The Sicilian campaign was over, or almost over. Catania had fallen. In the North the Americans were advancing upon the Straits of Messina, and from Messina itself the enemy were streaming across the narrow waterway back into the toe of Italy. Only a rear guard was left behind. Of all the lovely towns of Sicily only Taormina remained untaken—the loveliest of all. As we stood with the forward platoon and argued we could see the great hotels on the heights above. They stood a sheer thousand feet above the sea upon an immense red cliff; the hotels where the tourists used to go before the war, a place that looked like a holiday poster, "drenched in sunshine and remote." This was the last important point we had to take in Sicily, and the taking of the town would be the last gesture of the campaign before we set out upon the invasion of Europe.

We had about eight or nine miles to walk along the shore before we got to the bottom of the cliff. At first there was nothing much to see, just the laden vineyards and the fruit trees, the wayside villas with their endless Fascist slogans painted on the walls. *Mussolini ha sempre ragione.* Do not question—Obey. Fascist Italy goes forward to a greater tomorrow. *Credere—Obedire—Combattere.* The letters were a foot thick and two feet high on the crumbling villa walls, a persistent stream of sounding phrases that lost all meaning and after a while even ceased to be ridiculous. They jarred the eyes in this peaceful landscape, just as one is jarred by a persistent tiny noise in a quiet room.

The village of Giardini must be a mile long. A main road and a line of houses on either side. Then the sea and the mined beach. Here and there a house was burning. The villagers had fled into the hills, and those who had stayed behind looked at us incredulously and with that sort of fear you see sometimes in animals—the fear that prevents them from running away. Only the very old or the very crazy were left behind. They were half-mad from hunger. They waved, but when we stopped it was a long time before they would answer coherently. "Yes, yes. The Germans have gone. The soldiers have gone. There are no soldiers in the village." And then: "*Pane. Biscotti. Caramelle.*" Bread. Biscuits. Sweets. All the way through Sicily the peasants had been crying out for food, and the cry had been reduced to this three-word formula and had been repeated so often that now it began to take on the meaningless persistence of the Fascist slogans on the walls.

A little group of Italian soldiers in dirty green uniforms were standing on the beach waving a white flag at the British gunboat. When they saw us on the road they ran forward calling: "We surrender." There was something essentially childish in their dark and troubled faces. Much later, after the war perhaps, they would posture again and make a show in the village street. But not now. All that was gone entirely. They were tired and hurt and frightened and it was embarrassing to feel their deflation. Wanting to please, they said eagerly, "Two British officers have already gone down the road." They added: "No. There are no Germans. The last of them left this morning."

Although this information was quite probably inaccurate it was reassuring to hear. The vineyards came up very thickly to the road, and one was almost entirely dependent on the information of the villagers that no ambush had been laid. That and a "sense" of the atmosphere, a sort of feeling that was more emotional than mental. Either you felt it was secure to go on or not. At all events the other two were in front. One of these men we knew very well. We had not inquired on starting out whether it was he or not, but we knew that at every moment in a campaign when a goal like Taormina lay ahead this officer was certain to go on reconnoitering on his own. For three years it had been like that. We had known him in Syria and Greece and many times in the desert, and it had become a sort of compact between us that we should meet at these moments of the campaign, when the big fighting was done and it was therefore possible to move on to the prize that the soldiers had won but not yet possessed. Although we never expressed it we felt like jackals after the kill.

There was the usual hush over this gap between the advancing army and the retreating enemy. Everything goes to earth. The road is clear and it is a little adventure to turn each corner. You smell the enemy. Here and there, for no explained reason, a house burns quietly and there is no one to quench it; it burns in a vacuum with not anyone to watch. The discarded helmets and webbing of the enemy lie about. You never take your eyes off the road. Twice we saw the usual pattern of square holes in the macadam, and picked our way past the teller mines lying just below the surface. We kept to the middle of the road and walked on into the center of Giardini. The gunboat came steaming back along the beach and disappeared around the bend. At the railway station there was a great deal of disorder. The bombing had carried black debris across the road and a stationary train full of some chemical threw out a strange sickly smell. There were craters in the highway, and these appeared to have been mined with the smaller type of mine, which is quite concealed and is designed to kill single men on foot.

We turned off the road and struck straight up the face of the cliff along a twisting bridle-path. The ramparts of the town were directly above us, but one had neither the breath nor the energy to look upward. Many little groups of Italians were lying concealed at their machine-guns at the bend in the track. They waited till we came abreast of their dugouts and then they came out and called to us: "We surrender. What shall we do? Do you want our weapons?"

"Throw them down the cliff."

They ran to the edge of the track and threw their guns and cartridges into the ravine. They did this very solemnly and with childish dignity, wanting to make a formal act of surrender.

We were now half-way up the cliff, and I for one was sobbing for breath. The sweat ran down the open neck of one's shirt and even one's shorts were becoming sodden with it. We still wore the desert clothes; but here on this cliff everything appeared to draw up the heat from the red rock. The sea was now a pond below. Directly above, the people were gathering on the stone ramparts, and they were making a queer staccato ululation that might have been a warning or a welcome. They could see us clearly as we crept slowly up the goat track.

When I got to the top the others were already there, surrounded by a mob of Italians, all chattering, many of them waving white flags. More and more were running down the hill. They waved their rifles in the air. The children kept plucking at our clothes as we sat on the parapet trying to regain our breath. *Biscotti. Caramelle.* There was a long broken story of how they had fought the Germans in the night, and of how the Germans had looted the villas and the hotels before they left. We sat drinking beer in a little cafe, and presently the chief of the carabinieri arrived to lead us down to the Hotel Beauséjour. "An English tea," they kept saying. "We will prepare an English tea."

Far below lay the Mediterranean, so vitreous that all the green formations of the sea bed showed clearly through the water. A great shoulder of rock butted out to the north, and there beyond it, over a stretch of water no wider than a river-mouth, lay Italy itself. One was hardly prepared for its nearness. There was no boat on the Straits, nothing between us and the unknown enemy country, a great high stretch of coastline that grew up quietly out of the water. It was so close that you could discern the roads and the occasional houses among the olive groves. It needed no great imagination to find German trucks passing along the roads and German guns pointing from the rocks. This was the country towards which the Eighth Army had been fighting for three years, and so this first vision of the shore came as a naturally dramatic moment. All of us had many times lost hope, or at least the immediate sense of hope; and now that we had arrived in sight of Italy it was an unaffected joy merely to stand and look and look.

I imagine this moment had the same effect upon all of us. As we looked, the feeling of urgency which carries everyone through a campaign began to drain away. There it was: Italy. No need to do anything more now. Not at any rate for the time being. No more fighting. No need to move. The invasion was still to come, but that was a long way off; perhaps next week, perhaps next month. It did not matter much exactly when. There would be an infinity of days here in the sun, drinking wine, swimming from the beach, meeting the women.

Far back along the road the army was slowly winding forward to fill in this gap between them and the enemy. They would filter through the villages and along the coast until they reached the tip of Sicily. Then they would sit down and gather strength. It would be a time of holiday for everyone, a time to forget the fighting on the Primasole Bridge and across the Catania Plain. They were tired, and now just for a little time they would be suspended between this campaign and the next, between what they had done and the indefinite future.

The five of us who had come into Taormina were well used to the ways of seizing a holiday at a moment like this. One man went off to find a villa. Another took a truck for wine. A third engaged Italian servants. We gathered fruit and vegetables, eggs and fresh fish from the beach. For the rest there were our cases of army rations, cigarettes, soap and chocolate; all the things that had grown as precious as life in Europe.

Within three days the villa was a home. It perched on the heights of Taormina, above the hotels, below the pinnacled village on the new and higher height beyond. A *petit salon* with leather chairs. A kitchen of hilarious glazed tiles. Then up the stairs to a landing where one dined surrounded by Roman plaques. A bedroom giving on to a great square-tiled terrace under an awning of dried palm leaves, and all the Straits of Messina and the toe of Italy spread out below. Another floor and another bedroom or two. Ten yards of steep path and then the studio. The villa straggled up the mountainside and fitted its rooms into each step of each ladder of the rock. And always through every hour of day and night the light poured in from the garden, a fabulous blinding yellow-white at midday, a theatrical march of sea-greens and rose in the morning and the quick evening, and then the yellow lamps at night.

All this is so long ago that I keep forgetting the usual mechanical details. The cook's name, for example. It may have been Sofia or Sophia. At any rate something beginning with S. But she herself, the woman, is quite clear. She cooked with wine. Wine for the rabbit casserole. Wine in the stew. Army margarine for the eggs. A thin compact mother of a cook desperately trying to adjust her habits to the utter strangeness of the foreigners. She bunched herself up tensely to try to understand our Italian, and when the message got through and she was sure of what we meant she burst into delighted smiles. "Yes, yes, yes. Onions in the soup. Of course." An indeterminate boy, probably her son, kept carrying things in and out of the kitchen, and there were others, too numerous to identify, who called and tidied up the bedrooms and went away carrying packages.

There was an Italian architect in the villa across the road who called with his magnificent wife. She was scented and poised, and she had that bulbous, blooming autumnal beauty of the Latin women who have had their children and lead a life half-way between their responsibility to their family and their intuitive desire to be gay. She spoke French with the harsh Italian accent, and just managed to restrain herself from putting a vowel on the end of every word. The architect sat. La Signora bloomed and smiled and was very gay and witty on the terrace. Then there was Anna Maria, the elder daughter, the urgent reason of the friendship between their villa and ours. Anna Maria was a backward projection of her mother, an early photograph of her mother; slim, jet black hair, brilliantly defined lips and an entire consciousness of the English soldiers dancing round her.

The night we repaid their call Anna Maria played the gramophone while her mother sat watching the soldiers in the dusk. Presently an album of photographs was brought out, the usual thing of bathing parties and babies on the lawn. There was one girl in the pictures of such lush Italian beauty that everyone demanded who she was.

"That," said Anna Maria, "is my sister Mariella."

Mariella in her bathing-suit was a girl of bursting vitality. She was frankly and consciously sexual. She made an aggressive innocence of her body that had become too early ripe in the Sicilian sun.

"Alas," said Anna Maria, "we have no news of her. She went to stay with our relatives near Palermo when the invasion began, and now it is impossible to reach her."

We sent a Ford truck for Mariella in the morning.

It was an easy life. I slept on the terrace in a camp-bed, and at this height above the sea there was no need for a mosquito net. The sun came up through a green light over the Straits, leaving Italy in shadow and hitting Taormina full in the face. Everything—the ravines that tumbled down to the sea, the houses perching on the crests, the pine trees outside, and even the wine bottles left on the terrace from the previous night—was cast either into full light or full shadow.

At nine the batman came with a chipped enamel mug full of the thick sticky tea he had learned to make in the desert. There was no really serious bathroom in the villa, nor any serious need to wash. Breakfast drifted idly forward until ten or half-past, and then we took a jeep and drove down the long precipitous road to a special beach we knew about just to the north of Taormina. A sunken schooner lay in the bay, and it was pleasant to swim naked through the masts and watch the fish passing through the portholes and the rigging. Italy and the enemy lay across the water, and one after another the headlands over there caught the rising sunlight. Time was of no consequence. One made of it a deliberate luxury. On the beach Pietro sat waiting with the fish. It was always red mullet. Tomorrow, he said, he would have the langoustina, the little crayfish that we liked so well fried in bread crumbs soaked in wine and garlic.

The fish were laid in rows on fresh vine leaves at the bottom of a wicker basket, and then, with the windscreen down and the warm wind on our faces, we drove back at speed to the villa. Mariella and Anna Maria were allowed to come across to us alone at midday—their mother was watching from across the street. We sat on the terrace underneath the dried palm leaves and drank the drier of the white wines, especially an Orvieto which we had in the half-fiasco, a round bottle trussed up with straw.

There were always guests for lunch, young soldiers we had known for months or years in Africa. In half an hour they came under the spell of the sun and the wine and the food. We experimented each day with a new wine, mainly the white wines with lunch. All the desire for talk, talk for its own sake, that had been bottled up through the campaign, began to come out. We liked one another. It would have been difficult to have been a bore. Nearly every sentence was given spontaneously and laughing, and some of it may have been good talk and all of it was natural. The fish, taken so quickly from the sea, had that flavor that vanishes within three or four hours. We had a tide of fruit, mostly grapes and melons and apricots. It was presumed that the guests would stay for a siesta and tea.

After this there were two or three hours in the late afternoon when we drove back into the hills behind the town in search of eggs and cheese, goat's milk and wine. In Taormina itself there was a place to which we often went, an antique shop that had been hit directly by a bomb. The junk and the treasure of fifty generations were spilled about among the debris. There were Venetian decanters no thicker than parchment which had taken no harm from the explosion, and these lay among marble busts and mediaeval banners and books and paintings. *Wanderings in Calabria* by Lear, in English, a drawer full of silver spoons, a coat of chain mail and bales of silks from Northern Italy. Only the antique shop had been hit in this part of the town, and one felt acutely about it because this was 1943 and at that time we who had been away from England were still unused to senseless destruction.

It was towards the end of dinner at the villa that the real arguments used to rage. The atmosphere was more than a little undergraduate. Topics began with violent generalizations and ran quickly into abstracts. Something prevented anyone from talking about the war for very long. Every materialistic attachment such as one's job and one's immediate plans and worries drifted away in a cloud of ideas and imagined sensibilities. Taste was infinitely more important than form. Manners became everything and behavior nothing. We made a hundred extravagant sublimations on any theme—food and chess, painting and gambling, books and wine, music and clothes.

It did not matter much who was at the table. Apart from us five there would often be boys who had come in directly from the fighting, or commandos who were crossing into Italy that night, or others again who had arrived by air from London and New York and Cairo. Most of us had had a continuous series of little adventures in many different campaigns and had been grossly uncomfortable. And now this villa, full of wine and talk and comfort, became an unreal and child-like fantasy, and its warm and excited atmosphere was that which children feel at the height of Christmas or a birthday party. It was an intimacy created by three years of the war, but well apart from the war.

The discussions would reach the point where several people were trying to interject at once, and then the Italian architect and his family would knock on the black iron ring on the front door. The mother sailed in first, richly scented, then Anna Maria and Mariella in their party dresses, then the architect. Everyone rose and shook hands with a good deal of ceremony. Chairs were placed on the terrace. We spoke bad French. Brandy and Benedictine went round. Some of the guests, still exercised by their argument over dinner, would go off into a corner to continue it. Others, stirred by the arrival of the women, would begin fussing round Anna Maria and Mariella. La Signora sat superbly in an angle of the terrace making such animated conversation that she gathered most of the men away from her daughters. But not for one instant did she lose sight of Anna Maria and Mariella. No sooner had Mariella been lured out into the garden than La Signora would rise in the most natural way in the world. *"Scusi. Momentino. J'ai oublié mon sac"*—or her scarf or her coat—and she would trot across the terrace. A moment later Mariella would be back in circulation with a balked young officer in tow. And then her mother would take up the conversation gaily again. The architect sat.

The moon coming over Italy turned Taormina into a series of tossing crests and rocky spikes, and here we sat on our own crest, nothing but the lighted empty space around us and the bright yellow sea below. On the right Etna rose up, an immense and sinister black cone. The volcano dominated everything on this side of Sicily. Its cold lava had that strange quality of utter blackness and savagery which I suppose you only see on volcanoes. Nothing would grow on it. For the most part it was unscalable. Nothing could live up there. Here and there great runnels of lava had flowed around Taormina until they had reached the sea and gone hissing and boiling into the water. Despite the complete deadness and savagery of the mountain you never had the impression that it was still, and in fact a white glow and a plume of smoke often showed from the summit. Some of the peasants were convinced that God would visit some new horror on the island in punishment for the war, and they openly expressed the fear that Etna would start retching and vomiting up filthy gobbets from the earth's belly once again. The moonlight, for some reason, made all this seem more probable. Etna was a huge dark backcloth for all the gay colors of the flowers and the houses round Taormina; an effect such as you have when a jeweler spreads out sapphires and diamonds and emeralds on a velvet cloth.

On some nights, when it was a special occasion, the orchestra, a three-man mandolin affair, came up the village street playing and singing as it came. Having bowed and shaken hands they found a place in the corner of the terrace and the dancing began. Because they imagined we expected it, and they felt they owed it to us, the band played "Santa Lucia," "The Isle of Capri," "Funiculi, Funicula" and "Aie, Aie, Aie." The tenor was an extrovert of some power. He gave it everything. He flung his mandolin aside in a passion of uncontrollable grief at the end of each stanza.

"Niente. Niente. Grazie. Grazie mille, signore." The maestro had a way of mopping his streaming face as he bowed. And then they played their own music from the villages, the music the people

composed themselves and sang spontaneously at their fiestas. The maestro protested it was "too simple." Surely we should prefer something rich and splendid like "Santa Lucia"?

There was one Sicilian lament, so soft and gentle and sincere that no one spoke when it was ended. The musicians sat very quietly as they played, played much better than they did before. No one moved or spoke. And then when the spell was broken, someone knocking over a glass or coughing, the musicians would blink and rush into "Santa Lucia." They were a little embarrassed, as though they had been too intimate and naive and lacking in showmanship. At midnight they went away singing down the hill. Mariella and Anna Maria were firmly led back home across the street.

One day merged into another. More and more soldiers poured through the town and took up positions along the coast. Invasion barges began to drift into all the little anchorages along the shore. General Montgomery took up his headquarters in the big villa just below ours, and there was a procession of staff cars coming up the driveway all through the day. Messina fell in ruins. The last German crossed the Straits into Italy, and when one looked across at that other shore, the mainland of Europe, the vineyards and village houses were utterly quiet and all the coast seemed to be gripped in a sense of dread at what inevitably was going to happen. The invasion.

One could not drag one's mind down to the invasion. It had to come. But not yet. Not today or tomorrow. One needed just a little more time.

The truth was that we were very tired. We were suspended in the very middle of the war at a point where we could neither remember the beginning nor see the end. Only lately, in the past year, had we grown used to advancing. Alamein, Tripoli, Tunis, Sicily. All victories. But the way seemed endless. No matter how far you advanced—a thousand, two thousand miles—there was always the enemy in front of you, always another thousand miles to go. And still we had not invaded the mainland of Europe. Still Italy was in the war. Still we appeared to make no appreciable hole in the German armor.

One night the commandos with whom I used to swim below Taormina came back with a prisoner. They had nipped across the Straits in the darkness and scooped up this little man as he was walking down the highway towards Reggio on his way to work. He was a railway clerk, a quaint and pathetic little figure with a black tie and a black hat and an attaché case under his arm. He sat in the stern of the invasion barge as it came back from Italy and he was completely unnerved by the hideous fate that had overtaken him in the night. At one moment he had been walking down the village street quite alone. Then suddenly he was surrounded by enormous rough men who spoke a strange language and hustled him into a boat. And now here he was far from home and probably about to die. Someone on the beach gave him a tin of bully beef.

I asked him how many Germans were waiting to repel our invasion. "None," he cried, "none. Absolutely none. They have all gone away. You can land on Italy this afternoon if you want to."

Was it possible then that we were going to have an easy time? A dry landing? A barrage across the Straits and then a quick rush across the beach? Not too many mines?

Abruptly one began to realize how far one had shrunk from the prospect of making the invasion, how far one had retreated into this brief hedonism in the villa. The morning swim. The certainty of the aperitif waiting on the terrace. Lunch and the siesta. All the characterless talk; the talk without responsibility for what was said. A kind of boy-scoutery began to invade the mind. One was a little ashamed that a piece of incidental intelligence from an Italian clerk, a piece of information which said, "It's all right. It will be easier than you thought," should have been the gently graded path that led one back to austerity and reality.

Once begun the process of resuming interest in the war was very quick indeed. Snowball fashion it fed on itself. The studied fabric of the army, the business of uniforms and ranks that assures the soldier, "It's all right, you are at home with your own people," began to exert itself. It required no great effort to slip into the habits of three years. "Let us now study the form, gentlemen. Let us see what we have to do." ,

The form was not simple, but it could be reduced to a few immediate simplicities. The Italian empire was broken. In all Africa no enemy soldier remained. The enemy fleet in the Mediterranean was broken. But Italy was still in the war, shaky but still there.

In the previous winter when Churchill and Roosevelt and their generals had met in Casablanca three broad alternatives had presented themselves. To invade directly through Sardinia and Corsica and on to the mainland in southern France—the quick route. To invade through Sicily to Italy and thus throw Italy out of the war— the obvious route. To invade through Greece and the Balkans—the attractive route. Or perhaps a combination of two or more of these alternatives.

Number One, the French route, went out. Too dangerous. Not

enough air cover. Number Three, the Balkan route, went out. Too involved, and in any case it could be tried later on. Number Two was chosen because of its very obviousness. We wanted the Mediterranean. The only way to open the Mediterranean was to conquer Sicily. Sicily was near. We could have a dress rehearsal on the island of Pantellaria. We had already made a landing—in North Africa—but that was against very little opposition. The naval planners estimated that we could land seven or more divisions abreast in Sicily. It was the rational thing to do. There would be two commanders under Eisenhower: Patton and Montgomery, both tried leaders, and Alexander would carry out the co-ordination of the armies in the field.

Now, in the late summer, we had done it, done it in one month. True we had failed to catch the German garrison. It had simply fled out of the net that neither Patton in the north nor Montgomery in the south could draw quite tight enough. But we had conquered Sicily and brought Italy to the edge of surrender.

All through August Italy had been striving to find a means of getting out of the war. Mussolini and Fascism were finished. The formula had been wrong. The people had been made slaves and then they had been asked to become masters. It was too much. Mussolini had run up to Fiorli to tell Hitler: "It's no good; we are finished unless you give us help. The Italians are exhausted. They cannot do any more." The rebuff from Hitler meant only one thing; a showdown in the Grand Fascist Council, a vote of confidence or else. . . . Mussolini called the meeting and got his vote: 17 to 5 against. He was out.

Already by this time the dissidents were negotiating with the Allies. British and American air forces and gunners were ordered to give free passage to any aircraft with Italian markings that flew over Sicily to Eisenhower's headquarters at Algiers. An Italian general arrived at neutral Lisbon to sound out the ground. Unconditional surrender, the Casablanca formula. What did it mean? What guarantees would be given for the protection of Italy against the vindictive Germans?

When the general who was sent to Lisbon was late in bringing back the answers, the Italian negotiators became anxious. They released the British general, Carton de Wiart, from prison and sent him off to hasten the negotiations. There were only four German divisions in Italy. Now was the time to get out of the war—quickly, before the Germans did something.

More conferences. Italy would mobilize her troops to fight on the Allied side. Just name the day of the invasion and the Italian

Mussolini and Hitler.

legions would stand ready to stab the Germans in the back. On the Allied side this new proposition caused much doubt and hesitation. Could you trust the Italians? If you named the day and the place would they not reveal these things to the Germans? No. It was too great a risk.

But at least we could try a little sounding out. The American general Taylor was sent by sea to Gaeta, the port just outside Rome. He was met by arrangement and taken in secret to the capital. Already Mussolini had been evacuated. He had been taken first to the island of Ponza, then to Marguerita in northern Sardinia, and now he was being brought back to a skiing hamlet in the Abruzzi—the place from which he was eventually kidnapped by the Germans. Badoglio remained behind to treat with the Allies— Badoglio the elder statesman, the friend of the king, the man who had refrained from actively serving Mussolini for two years past. Badoglio was old, he had no longer any ambition. He wanted to serve Italy, nurture her through the black hour. Not so very much unlike Pétain in France, *le vieux maréchal*. Maybe he had fought the Abyssinians in Abyssinia and the Greeks in Greece; but that, they said, was no more than his duty as a soldier. At all events here he was at the head of an Italian government that was prepared to deal. He met Taylor in Rome. He discussed whether his Italian garrison could help to defend Rome while the Allies made an airborne landing there. At the very moment when the two men were talking the Germans were sending troops into the city. There was fighting in the suburbs. Badoglio fled. The king fled with him. Taylor came back to the Allied lines; the parachute landing was off.

By now we were thoroughly committed to our plans. Route Number Two: Italy. Indeed, such plans have to be made at least three or four months previously in order to get the troops and ships and aircraft into position. We deployed an army in Sicily ready to invade, a British army. We had another army, American, in North Africa. Where should they land? Obviously there should be one landing across the Straits of Messina. That was the easy one. But where else? The journey up through the toe of Italy was long and mountainous with many bridges. One had to strike nearer to Rome than that. After arguing carefully it was decided: "We cannot land without air cover." In the end that proposition dominated the planning. There must be air cover. We would land at the extreme limit of our air cover and as near to a major port as possible. And so, inevitably, the choice fell on Salerno.

And then? Then the larger project. The capture of Foggia, Foggia with its dozen airfields. Given those airfields we could mount a thousand bombers for the assault on the untouched parts of southern Europe, and moreover keep flying when the weather was bad in that other major air-base, England. Foggia was the ultimate aim of the campaign.

Gradually the plan took shape. First object: make good the landing in Europe and throw Italy out of the war. Second: capture a port—Naples. Third: start a new air-base at Foggia. Given these three things, who knew what would happen? Rome might fall, and all the rest. There was reason to believe that the Germans might get clear out of Italy. We could make a junction with the partisans in Jugoslavia, prepare springboards into France. The Italian fleet lay in Taranto. Suppose it surrendered? Why then we could develop a third landing on Italy's heel and make a quick seizure of Foggia by crossing those broad plains around Bari on the Adriatic coast.

That then was the plan that was worked out while some of us were drinking wine in Taormina. It was a plan that took no note, or very little note, of the capacity of the partisans in Jugoslavia. (We could not make up our minds on whom to support in Jugoslavia anyway, and over Greece we were more puzzled still.) It was a plan based upon the defection of the Italians, or at least their neutrality. And it was a plan based on the necessity for air cover. At every point, from the long-range selection of Italy as the route, down to the tactics of landing at Salerno, imagination and risk had been sacrificed to security. We were not sure of ourselves, either politically or militarily. We did not know whether or not to trust Badoglio; or Tito; or the Evzones in Greece. No questioning on our policy from Algiers could get a clear answer from either the Foreign Office or the State Department. In the summer of 1943 they simply did not know. Militarily we were worried about all the many difficulties of an amphibious operation, the weather, the greenness of the troops, the newness of the ships and their crews.

So in this surrounding atmosphere of hesitation and doubt and uncertainty the planners of Algiers fell back on a plan in which they felt they had some element of security. A quick close landing. Limited objectives. Air cover all the way. Wait and see.

Alexander was again given command in the field. Under him again two armies—one the Eighth under Montgomery, with Empire and British troops; the other the Fifth under the American command of General Clark, and composed of equal numbers of British and Americans.[1]

The Eighth was to carry out the smaller operation of landing in Italy's foot. The Fifth would make the big landing on the ankle at Salerno.

I suspect—although I do not know for certain—that Montgomery was not altogether in favor of these plans. He was given only minor objectives. He was not even being asked to make a link-up with the Fifth. It was essentially a diversionary role. But whatever his private views, Montgomery showed nothing of them to his troops. His personal popularity among them had by now gone to fantastic lengths. There was an almost passionate belief in him. The whole army had a sense of oneness with the general.

[1] General Patton had gravely prejudiced his position about this time by walking into an American hospital in Sicily and striking a soldier because he said he was suffering from shell-shock. It was a curiously revealing little incident, one of those minor happenings which suddenly set fire to many dark hopes and fears in the mind of the public. In America especially the incident had all the ingredients of a national scandal. Eisenhower, placed in a very embarrassing position, suspended Patton and hushed up the matter until a columnist in Washington let it out. Much later Eisenhower explained to us that after several sleepless nights he had determined not to lose Patton's talents indefinitely. He regarded the incident as reprehensible, but he still felt that Patton "had a great deal to give the Allied cause."

This was demonstrably true. We had grinned a bit, Americans and British alike, at Patton's swashbuckling manner in the field, his personal truculence towards fear. At the very moment of landing in Sicily he had asked a colleague of mine to write an article saying that it was unnecessary for soldiers to take cover in slit trenches or foxholes. Yet beyond all this one essential thing stood out—George Patton wanted to fight. His was the attitude of mind that was eventually going to destroy the Germans.

Alexander and Eisenhower.

I had not realized how far this thing had gone until a couple of days before the landing, when Montgomery made a visit to the English Malta Brigade. As we went along the roads there was a continuous series of cheers from every vehicle. The men looked up excitedly. They waved their hats. "Good old Monty!"

At the first stopping-place the soldiers were drawn up in an open square. Montgomery handed out a few medals, then jumped on his jeep and called on the men to come and sit round him. They rushed forward. There was nothing very remarkable in the speech. It evoked a direct and simple response. He had the trick of repeating phrases three or four times, so that you were left with a feeling of absolute certainty. The theme was: (a) You are good troops. (b) The landing will not be so difficult after all when you think of the many other forces that will be engaged as well. (c) The operation is part of a world plan including Russia and the bombing operations.

You would have found nothing in the speech but guileless simplicity and conviction, except for one little passage. "You have already done so well," Montgomery said, "that everybody is asking for you. That is a great honor; a great honor [pause]; a very great honor indeed. I myself would like to have this brigade with me wherever I go."

Now the effect of this was exactly the reverse of what the general had intended. There was an open muttering among the men. They thought: "He's going to drag us into every battle from here to Berlin."

It took Montgomery five seconds to see the change of atmosphere. Then he added blithely: "Ah, but you don't know where I am going to go. I may go home on leave." At once there was a roar of laughter.

Deliberately, as with a practiced politician, Montgomery made the same point again at the next meeting he addressed half an hour later. He got the same gust of laughter. His critics said that such devices—like the black beret—were a conscious attempt to win personal popularity. His friends said that he was concerned only to get his points across to the men. To Montgomery himself I believe the matter was different. He frankly enjoyed popularity among the men. And he felt that as long as he had it the men would fight better. If he was ambitious for himself, he was ambitious for the army as well.

At all events, the Eighth Army went forward to this invasion in an aggressive and hopeful frame of mind. They felt sure of themselves. As the last days of August ran out more and more guns were dragged to the heights above Messina overlooking Reggio on the mainland. Zero hour was announced at an hour before dawn on September 3rd, the anniversary of Britain's entry into the war. It was to be preceded by a five hundred gun barrage across the Straits.

Up at the villa we had just enough wine for one more soirée with Anna Maria and Mariella. The parting did not seem especially sad. Most of us were genuinely eager to go. The mood of defeatism and tiredness had been only a temporary thing, a holiday from reality. As we drove up to the gun positions in the hills on the night of September 2nd one felt a curious sense of lightness and expectation.

2. Salerno

The barrage lasted only half an hour. It was night, and we could see little except the yellow flame. Here we sat in the Sicilian hills above Messina, and the guns fired out of the olive groves. We fired out of Italian farms on this side of the Straits, and the shells made the short passage of a mile or two across the sea and landed on other Italian farms on the mainland. The peasants on the Sicilian side were told: "You must leave your cottages because the blast is going to break your windows and would cause you injury." They would not move until the first rounds were fired, and then they ran screaming into the open.

On the other side of the Straits the civilians expected the barrage, and they went into caves in the hills while their homes were destroyed. There were no Germans to hit. The enemy rear guard was retreating up the toe of Italy exploding bridges as it went. British commandos had already lodged themselves in the Calabrian village, and there they sat decorated with flowers awaiting the arrival of the main army. No gun fired back at the British.

There may have been military reasons for making this barrage, but even at the time it was difficult to see that the shells accomplished anything more than a gesture and an insurance.

A number of monitors and destroyers ran close to the Italian shore and advanced the destruction from Reggio to San Giovanni. A little before dawn the rocket-ships sent out a series of immense tearing broadsides to pulverize the beaches. The rockets were an extraordinary sight, a kind of upward flowing yellow waterfall, and the noise was monstrous, even worse than the barrage. Then at last many hundreds of boats and little ships filled with men arrived off

A wrecked German troop carrier upside down on the waterfront at Messina.

the beaches. They tumbled ashore in the half-light, finding no enemy to fight, not even serious minefields on the beaches. There were two or three casualties caused by men slipping and falling as they got off.

Toward nine o'clock I drove down to Montgomery's headquarters a little below Messina. He was in a brisk and amiable mood. In his caravan, drawn up beside the road, everything was in order, pens, papers, maps. "We have landed here and here and here," he said. "Tonight I shall move troops here and here. Tomorrow we will advance to there and there and there. Is that clear?" All this on a map with his pencil flicking back and forth.

We walked down to the road and got aboard a duck. This was the first time ducks had been used on a large scale, and already there were excellent reports of them. The Italian peasants on the other side had gazed in horror and fled when they saw the vehicles waddle out of the water.

Montgomery sat in the front seat. Once in the sea we transshipped into a large motor launch. The duck, with one of the general's A.D.C.'s at the wheel, was towed behind.

We could see nothing of Italy. Heavy clouds of smoke started by the barrage rolled over the shore. Around us, dancing and bobbing about in the brilliant sun, were the invasion barges and the troop-carriers, the big transports filled with vehicles, the destroyers and the distant cruisers. Some pressing forward towards Italy; others already coming back. The ducks sailed in V formation—like ducks. The sea had just enough movement to make an occasional white ripple on the surface. On the beach Sicilian girls were offering fruit to the Tommies as they embarked. A few seagulls wheeled about in search of litter in the wake of the ships. Irresistibly the scene was like a regatta; or some yachting carnival perhaps, even Cowes.

We coasted along very placidly. Every few minutes we overtook a shoal of ducks or a flotilla of blunt-nosed barges. The soldiers laughed and waved. Some of them saw Montgomery's red and black pennant on our mast and whistled shrilly across the water. Montgomery himself stood near the prow of the launch looking across to the point where the Italian coast was beginning to break through the clouds of smoke. Messina was on our left now, Reggio on our right; both partly in ruins. Behind Reggio and its many terraces of white houses rose the formidable mountains of Italy, Montalto, the nearest, six thousand feet high. And then, farther north, the whirlpool and the rock, Charybdis and Scylla.

Half-way across we went down into the tiny wardroom for biscuits and coffee. Someone had pinned up a page from *Punch*;

drawings of the historic British generals mounted on chargers, dressed in flowing uniforms and surrounded by their staffs. Then finally a sketch of Montgomery wearing a beret, sitting alone on a camp stool in the desert, directing the troops onward with a backward jerk of his thumb. Montgomery was well pleased with it. A conversation about cartoonists began. It was impossible to feel that this, at least, was the day, the invasion of Europe after three years, the reply to Dunkirk. Outside there was no firing. Just the gentle crowded passage of the boats back and forth.

"You must never let the enemy choose the ground on which you fight," Montgomery was saying. "You must never fight the battle *his* way. You must choose the ground. He must be made to fight the battle according to your plan. Never his plan. Never. You must make a plan and then both sides, you and the enemy, must fight the battle along the lines of that plan. If you have no plan, or you are unable to carry out your plan for one reason or another, then you must abandon the offensive at once. The whole point is that you must never attack until you are absolutely ready and certain of being able to carry out your plan."

The traffic became much thicker as we approached the beach just north of Reggio. Three or four German planes dived out of the sun just ahead of us, and their bombs made waterspouts between the ships, hitting nothing. Then when they came for a second dive Montgomery and all the rest of us except the gunners went down full length on the deck. The Oerlikons on the launch opened up simultaneously, a terrific din when one was only a couple of feet away.

Presently when it was quieter we climbed back into the duck and sailed directly for the beach. An immense commotion of unloading was going on. Half a dozen big landing-ships had already flung open their doors in the bows, and the lorries and tanks were splashing ashore. On the beach itself Italian prisoners and British soldiers were working together pinning wire mesh into the loose sand and digging a track up to the coastal road. The road was blocked with hundreds of vehicles. Little groups of soldiers were making tea on the beach. To the left and right of us hundreds of other boats were making towards the shore. One had the impression that all this had been going on here for months instead of just five hours.

The soldiers caught sight of Montgomery as soon as we touched the sand. None of them could have hoped for such an easy landing as this. They had massed for an assault, and in the darkness each man in these many thousands had had the prospect of being killed or drowned or hurt. The strain of fear which exists in every front-

Montgomery was the full expression of everything the troops felt.

line before attack is probably brought to its highest pitch in a night
sea landing. And now in a few hours all that had gone. The sun
streamed down. They were ashore and safe. All the pent-up feeling
of relief and pride suddenly burst out at the sight of the general.
Montgomery stood beside the driver holding on to the windscreen
of the duck, and the soldiers yelled and waved and whistled at
him.

It was, in a curious way, a heart-breaking scene. Just for a
moment the man with the thin sharp face standing at the windscreen was the full expression of everything the troops had felt in
the night and their elation in the morning. He represented the risk
taken and the success. Young subalterns clinging desperately to
discipline stood rigidly at the salute along the road. The soldiers
themselves gave way to their emotions entirely. They bawled out
anything that came into their heads. As each vehicle passed us on
the road the soldiers inside jumped to their feet. Someone would
shout: "Jesus. There's Monty!" And then the cheering and shouting
would pass along the column.

Montgomery had a pile of ten thousand cigarettes in the back of
the duck, and he kept handing these out every time we stopped. At
each brigade headquarters where he got down for a conference a
crowd gathered. In Reggio a long line of Italian prisoners recognized him and raised a cheer.

It was like this all through the day. It continued in the same way all through the sunny weeks of September as we climbed slowly up the toe of Italy, over the ravines and the broken bridges. Montgomery was back in the sort of command he enjoyed best of all; a private expeditionary force fighting its battles utterly remote from the rest of the world. Locked away here in these mountains he treated his army as a kind of family. He delighted in being with the soldiers, and he drove among them for hours every day. It was the sort of personal and inspirational leadership he liked best; and on their side the troops enjoyed the sense of intimacy. It was an atmosphere that could exist only in a vacuum. It flourished in the empty desert and in these Calabrian mountains, the poorest and least populated part of the peninsula. It began to dissipate as soon as the army entered big towns, as soon as the original force lost its privacy and was merged into the overall command. The more reinforcements that poured in the more Montgomery lost the personal touch, and after this he was never again to regain it in quite the same way. As his command expanded he was pushed back and away from his soldiers. He was forced to co-operate with other generals, to take orders, to plan on higher and higher levels. More and more the war became for him a matter of maps and printed papers; less and less a matter of personal exhortation to the soldiers. The scope of the fighting became too immense and too crowded, the distances too great. In the end, like a composer who has gone deaf, he found he could continue to design battles but not see them.

This process of enlargement and complication—not only in the case of Montgomery but of the whole army, and the war itself—develops into a major theme in the story of the period covered by this book. We can watch it grow as we go along. But you will understand that many of us look back on this early period of the conquest of Europe with affection and regret.

The issues seem almost childishly simple now. Montgomery had landed with just two divisions—the Fifth British and a Canadian division. There were some attached tanks, and on the third day it was arranged that the Malta Brigade should make a second landing a little higher up the toe at Pizzo. This whole force was designed to go no farther than the neighborhood of the town of Nicastro, not half-way up the instep of Italy's foot. Many of the ships supplying it were taken away after the first few days in order to make the major Salerno landing under General Clark a week later, on September 9th. Clark in the first stages was to have over five divisions—the Thirty-sixth and Fourth American, the British Forty-sixth and Fifty-sixth, and about a division of American parachutists and Rangers.

Two armored divisions, the First American and the Seventh British, were to follow up quickly. For the Taranto landing on Italy's heel the British had in reserve their First Airborne Division and the Seventy-eighth.

Against this three-legged invasion the Germans deployed only four divisions in southern Italy. The enemy command was not at all decided during the early days of September on whether or not to hold in the south. A plan for a fighting retreat through Rome to the plain of Lombardy was drawn up. As a first step in the plan the Germans began to pull out of Calabria in the extreme south, leaving only rear guards to impede Montgomery's advance. At the same time, Kesselring, who was in command, suspected that we would make our major landing at Salerno—the obvious place—and he was willing to contest it. His four divisions were therefore grouped about Potenza, in the middle of Italy's ankle, whence they would be ready to move quickly in any direction. One of these divisions was stationed in the Salerno area, and it actually went through an anti-invasion exercise there the day before Clark arrived. In other words, our minor landing on Italy's toe did not for one moment deceive the enemy. They were prepared to write off Calabria anyway. And so the value of the Eighth Army landing was simply this—it

General Mark Clark commanded the Salerno landing

provided a backstop in case things went wrong at Salerno. Even if Clark were thrown back, we would still have our foothold in Europe.

There remained the Italian side of the picture. It was at last agreed that Italy should announce her unconditional surrender at the moment when we disembarked at Salerno. The idea was that the Italian army, and especially that part of it manning the beaches, should lay down their arms and welcome our men at the precise moment they stepped ashore. The Germans not unnaturally saw that one coming. As early as August, well before the invasion, they had discounted the Italians entirely. By September they were taking over the coastal strongpoints themselves—particularly in the Salerno area. Italian coastal guards who demurred were ordered off at the point of a gun. There was still no open breach between Italy and Germany, but the German officers were ordered to shoot any Italians who impeded or resisted them.

There was another point. Since we were unwilling to trust the Italian negotiators with the date of the Salerno landing, it was General Eisenhower and not Badoglio who had to make the armistice announcement. The news was broadcast from Algiers, not from Rome. The troops on the transports heard it the night before they were to go ashore at Salerno. The immediate effect it created was: "Well, this is going to be an easy landing after all. Now that the Wops have packed up we should be able to step ashore and go right ahead."

Nor was the effect on the Italians very happy. They were confused. They had barely received the news when the landing was on top of them. One doubts whether they could have organized any really effective resistance to the Germans even if they had been given the time, but at least something more might have been done in the cities like Naples and Rome, which were already in somewhat of a ferment.

The whole business of the Italian armistice was a fiendishly difficult problem to decide, and even now looking back it is hard to see how Eisenhower might have timed events better. The root of the matter was that never at any time were we able to put our complete trust in the Italians or their new leaders. We underestimated the defeatism inside Italy, and the desire of the people there to get rid of the Germans. And so the Salerno landing went in at a time when all Italy was in a state of utter confusion and powerless to help us. Worse still, the Germans were awaiting our coming.

Only the weather was favorable. The sheer weight of numbers, the impetus of the army itself, carried the first troops ashore along

Salerno: American combat teams make an assault landing.

that stretch of smooth sloping sand from Paestum to the outskirts of Salerno, and the Rangers quickly got into the rough country on the Amalfi peninsula. They were under fire from the moment of disembarking, both from German guns and aircraft. But in those first vital three days Kesselring never had quite enough fire-power to break up the landing. He was able to contain it while his re-inforcements were rushed up, but he was never quite able to drive the troops back into the sea or prevent the Allied build-up.

Nevertheless, the German reaction to the Salerno invasion was definite and immediate. Kesselring decided to abandon not only Calabria but Taranto and Brindisi as well. Along the whole length of the Italian Adriatic coast, from Brindisi to Venice, there was not one fighting German unit. Everything was concentrated on Salerno. From the German point of view it was excellent strategy. By the fourth day they had all but driven a wedge through the Allied bridgehead and cut off the British section of the army from the American. They felt strong enough to launch a series of staggered counter-attacks with one definite object: the annihilation of the whole beachhead.

This situation had an immediate effect upon the south. The Italian fleet had steamed out of Taranto and presented its sur-render to Admiral Cunningham at Malta. Not only had we gained some of the most modern warships in the world but the way was clear for the conquest of Italy's heel. The Seventy-eighth and the

Airborne Division were rushed ashore, and in a trice they mopped up the three key cities of Taranto, Brindisi and Bari. Unlike the southern part of the peninsula, all this territory was flat country, a region of rolling olive groves, ideal for tanks, ideal for quick advance. Unfortunately they were separated by the Apennines from our comrades who were struggling so desperately at Salerno, and in addition enemy rear guards and broken bridges blocked the path westward. In any event they had no supplies with which to advance so far so quickly.

And so the Taranto operation did nothing to help Clark. There remained Montgomery.

Montgomery's original orders to halt at Nicastro were scrapped. He was now told to go full steam ahead to Salerno. This meant an entire alteration in the organization of supplies. Somehow new ports had to be found, and at speed, up the length of the toe. Somehow the boats plying to the base dumps in Sicily had to be accelerated and kept in service at a time when they were becoming unseaworthy. By September the 12th and the 13th very little headway had been made. Everywhere troops were grounded for lack of petrol. It was in fact simply impossible to alter a supply situation overnight. Moreover the few troops Montgomery had ashore were just then straggling over some of the most fantastic mountains in all Europe. They were blocked by immense chasms and gorges. At the time Montgomery was criticized for slowness. There may be something in the charge. Enough supplies might have been got together to send a small token force up the west coast road, which was flat and had no broken bridges. One doubts whether it could have added much to Clark's fire-power, but it would have been an immense moral support. However, it was not done, and Montgomery's men remained wedged in the mountains a good two hundred and fifty miles away from the pitched battle of Salerno. The Fifth Army faced its crisis alone.

For those of us who had to report the war day by day it was a galling thing to be isolated with the minor operation at the tip of Calabria. We knew the crisis was on at Salerno. Owing to a monumental muddle at Algiers we had been forbidden to go in with the Salerno landing, or even report the subsequent battle on the spot. However, there comes a time when army orders ought to be disobeyed. We decided to get through to the Fifth Army by the overland route.

The journey began for us at the extreme tip of Italy. We borrowed a fifteen-hundredweight truck and somehow got it across the Straits on a completely unexplained Turkish ferry full of Arabs who had turned up from Egypt. Just two of us had decided on this trip. We had no driver, no spare wheel, no tools, no rations, no petrol, no oil and no maps. It was a clean start from scratch. However, for three years on and off we had been traveling with the Eighth Army, and I believe that anyone belonging to that club could have obtained anything up to a battleship had he wanted it. It was a mulish brute of a truck, and it took two days to repair it and stock it by running from dump to dump. Then we set off up that fantastic road that clings between the shore and the Apennines on the western coast of Calabria. Walled villages. Grapes dripping in tons from the vines. Shouting peasants. The procession of ducks making white lines on a blue sea thousands of feet below.

We kept behind the front line. It was a sappers' war. Here and there a little group of Germans would stand for an hour or a day, or at any rate just long enough to explode the bridge. Then one waited in a procession of vehicles for the engineers to come up and erect a new bridge or a new detour. They were fabulous villages; Bagnara and Palmi and Rosamo, places that had been sleeping in the sun through centuries and still slept. The landing at Pizzo came in, and we made a rush to join up with them. There had been a savage little skirmish on the shore, but now the army was pushing on again. Filadelfia, the Bivio Mastro Elia, then Nicastro. And with Nicastro a full stop.

We tried the mountain road to Cosenza, but it led into a maze of blown bridges. The trains were still running up there, and British scouting units were actually doing their reconnaissance on the trains. But that got us nowhere and we came back to Nicastro. The coast road was much clearer, but the advanced army units had stopped a short distance north of Nicastro near a fishing hamlet called Cetraro. They had not petrol to proceed. They would be there for days, they said, and in any case they were first going to mop up through the mountains. With every hour now the news of the big battle at Salerno was coming through. Two car-loads of war correspondents even more impatient than ourselves had gone on ahead on their own. Indeed the road looked clear and peaceful enough. We followed gently. It was two hundred miles to Paestum.

Through Belvedere and Diamante and Scalea and all the other seaside villages the road was empty. The bridges were up. The Italians, well pleased with their armistice, cheered madly. *"Si, si, signore.* Your comrades have already gone through. Two cars."

At times we seemed to be getting very close to the others, and it appeared to be a good plan to join them, since we would have to spend the night suspended in this space between the Fifth and the

Eighth Armies. There were still no signs of German patrols, but the villagers kept telling us, "They left here last night," or "An armored car went through this morning," or merely that the German rear guard had withdrawn to the next village inland. It was a strange sensation bowling down the empty highway, mile after mile, the sea on our left, the wild hills on the right, and just this snub-nosed truck that was a friendly island in a region that was at least technically no-man's-land. So long as you are with the army on the march it throws a protective atmosphere round you. One reads the signs leading off to the camps beside the road, the traffic goes by and here and there little groups of soldiers hang about the village houses. It was a scene in which we had lived for years, and it did not matter very much whether you were in Asia or Africa or Europe, you felt at home and secure. But once you left the army behind and penetrated a region where there were no signs and no traffic, the country at once became very definitely foreign. One began to imagine enemy soldiers at every bend in the road.

At Policastro the coast sweeps into a wide bay, and here at last we were halted. Twenty Germans had exploded the village bridge the night before and then driven off. At first we could get no sense out of the villagers. Some thought they had seen our friends in the cars ahead; others not. Finally a man offered to guide us along a cattle track through the swamps on to the other side of the river. We started out into the undergrowth and burst a tire. No mechanics in the village and no tools in the truck. It was the usual kind of hopeless atmosphere that comes with a breakdown, but here the effect was heightened by the nearness of the German patrol and the fact that we were now definitely cut off.

Aircraft flew overhead and some of the villagers began to grow afraid. They saw the helpless truck on the road. It carried no arms. There was no sign of the rest of the British army, and you could see the fear growing in their minds. "Perhaps the Germans will come back."

On our side things did not look very healthy either. The Italian soldiers round us still carried their rifles. Their armistice with us was only three days old. They stood in a group and waited to see what we would do.

Little by little we got them to work. They fetched bayonets and improvised tools from the bicycle shop. They found a pump. I handed out sweets to the children while we worked, and in the end they mended the tire. Twenty minutes groping about through the swamp and we reached the road on the other side. We had telephoned ahead to the Italian railway officials in the next village and they had said that the countryside had been clear of Germans since the day before.

We left the sea now and began climbing up through the inland ranges. Eggs and flowers and fruit were flung towards us in the villages. We used the side roads. The Germans, they said, were patrolling along the main highroad farther inland. And so we kept on hour after hour heading for Vallo del Lucania, where at last we hoped to be within striking distance of the Fifth Army bridgehead at Paestum.

Meanwhile odd experiences had been happening to the two British vehicles ahead of us. They had felt their way forward from village to village by telephoning to the police stations ahead of them. Once they had actually talked to one of the carabinieri when a group of Germans were sitting in his room. He made it clear over the telephone that it would be unwise for the British cars to come on through that particular village. Everywhere the carabinieri had been loyal, and their information good. Our friends had skirted past the danger spots and reached the main road near Vallo. And here they struck trouble. A group of German armored cars appeared on the road. They doubled back fast into a side road and continued for some miles until they judged it safe to pull up and have a conference. As they stood talking beside the road the distant noise of a car engine sounded down the valley. The peasants listened anxiously to the noise as well. It was the Germans coming, they thought. And the unfortunate thing was that the noise was approaching from behind them, which meant that they had no escape route since the main road they had just left was being patrolled.

Our friends had two tommy-guns with them. These they posted with their two drivers about thirty yards off the road, and covering a sharp hairpin bend. The drivers got down on the bend. The rest of the party parceled out three or four revolvers between them and took up positions in the ditches beside the road, a little higher up than the drivers. The remainder got down out of sight behind the trees. The period of waiting must have seemed endless, because the approaching vehicle came very slowly up the twisting mountain road, and the foliage was so thick they could not hope to get a sight of it—or them—until it turned the last bend.

The anti-climax came very quickly. The two drivers sighted on the corner of the road and were about to pull the trigger when they suddenly realized they were aiming at a British truck—with myself and my companion in it. And we on our side were a good deal astonished to see the trees and ditches around us sprouting armed men. For a moment I thought it was a German ambush, and I pulled up the truck with a jerk. And then as our friends came forward, grinning a bit, we realized what had happened. "We had you cold," they said a little regretfully.

All this still did not remove the difficulty of the six German cars that lay on our road ahead. But the incident had stimulated everybody, and we decided to go forward together towards Vallo, hoping to slip through between the enemy patrols. As we mounted up through pine forests the peasants brought more reassuring news, and at length towards evening we coasted down into the town. Here again the atmosphere was a little tense. The people were overjoyed to see us, but at the same time the German cars had gone through a few hours before and were expected back that night. The officer who was now in charge of us was one of those very rare people who really genuinely enjoy fighting. He hurried into the police station and began organizing the defense of the town; all the carabinieri to go on to the rooftops with bottles of petrol and grenades which were to be flung down on the Germans as they came through the town gate; the male villagers to throw up street barricades; the rest of us to lay ambushes down the main street; the police station to be defended with the heavier arms.

The chief of police contemplated all this with sadness and much doubt. "Yes, certainly, if the British officer really wanted it. But was it really necessary? Would it accomplish anything except the destruction of the town? Would it not be much nicer for everyone concerned if we went on to a quiet monastery he knew about, and spent the night there?"

In the end, to my intense relief, he got his way. We loaded up with a barrel of Italian petrol and drove down to the monastery. In the darkness I smashed the truck against a concrete road trap, but somehow it kept going provided one did not wish to make a right-hand turn. At the monastery there was again the atmosphere of mingled welcome and fear. The Germans had been here too that afternoon. They were said to be camping only a kilometer away, and I believe they did in fact come through the village that night while we slept in the monastery courtyard. No one gave us away. It was now barely thirty miles to the haven of the Fifth Army.

But now the real trouble began. On every road the bridges were blown. We tried the coast, the foothills, the winding tracks higher up. Sooner or later on every route we came across a river with the tangled remains of the bridge falling into the water. It was the Americans who had smashed the bridges to protect their southern flank while they fought their main battle north of Paestum. They had destroyed the bridges only the day before and then withdrawn.

Their empty ration boxes were lying beside the road. It was a frustrating business, this probing away at the bridgehead trying to reach our friends. What a difference if they had only known that the road south to the Eighth Army was clear. Our own position moreover was becoming more awkward as the day went on, since sooner or later the German patrols would discover our existence. We made one more attempt far up into the high mountains, and there at last we sighted a little group of American soldiers. They were laying charges in this one remaining southern bridge into the Fifth Army area. An American armored car was covering the road for the sappers while they worked. Expecting only Germans, they took aim on our leading jeep as it approached, but we waved and shouted and then in a minute or two we were shaking hands on the bridge. The Eighth and Fifth Armies had, in principle at least, joined up. But since orders were orders the Americans blew up the bridge as soon as we got across.

The run down to General Clark's headquarters at Paestum was sheer pleasure. One felt like Red Ridinghood after she had escaped the wolf and finally slammed the door safely behind her. The general's officers were a good deal surprised and pleased to see us. In the region we had just crossed between the two armies they had marked on their maps—two German armored divisions. Well, clearly those two divisions did not exist. Orders went out to restore the blown bridges.

We had arrived in the bridgehead at the moment of its peak crisis. Even corps headquarters on the shore, a great barn hung with drying tobacco leaves, was under shell-fire. German bombers kept diving over at the shipping. You could cross the bridgehead in an hour. It was only a few thousand yards deep. In the night a general order for evacuation had been prepared—prepared but not issued. The leading officers of formations had been ordered to stand ready to get what troops they could back to the ships if the position became worse.

At this moment General Alexander, the overall field commander, had flown in from his headquarters in Sicily. He had turned up at just such a moment in the previous winter in Tunisia when the Germans were breaking through at Kasserine. And earlier in Burma. Earlier still at Dunkirk. In a tactical crisis Alexander was probably the most vigorous and clear-sighted leader thrown up by the British in the war. He seemed to have that rare talent of seeing things clearly and wholly at a time when he himself was under fire, and when from all around the most alarming and confusing information was pouring in.

The position here was simply this: the existing small forces could not carry on unaided if the German attack continued and developed. It would simply be a matter of time before the British forces in the north of the bridgehead were entirely cut off from the Americans in the south, and then there would be the vivid danger of both groups being destroyed piecemeal. To secure the position we had to hold on for a least another forty-eight hours while the reinforcements came in by air and sea. There was only one way to get immediate help to the troops fighting on the ground. That day every available strategic bomber in the central Mediterranean was called off its normal target and sent to the Salerno area. Every available warship was ordered up to the invasion coast. Between them the navy and the air force began to lay an explosive wall around the bridgehead.

It was the first really big experiment in the use of naval gunnery in close support of landing operations; an experiment that succeeded brilliantly, and led ultimately to the use of the naval barrages at Anzio and Normandy.

Under this canopy, and protected by an extraordinary outburst of endurance from the soldiers, we drove about the bridgehead for the next two days. The noise at night both from the outgoing and the incoming shells was shattering. Up on the British sector one day we climbed a hill and watched the German vehicles and soldiers moving about in the next village, barely five hundred yards away. Peasant women with bundles on their heads and men with laden donkeys passed back and forth from the German line to ours. Out of mechanical habit, because these were the only things to cling to in the cataclysm, they went on with their normal lives even when their villages were falling to pieces around them. I watched one man ploughing while mortar shells fell about him on the freshly turned earth. We had seen something of the same thing in Tunisia, but here the civilians were mixed up with the fighting in many thousands, and it often turned the battle into a curiously human and pathetic thing. The people could never get used to the sudden arrival of death in a village street they had known for forty years or more. They never accepted it, never comprehended it. They were unable to drag their minds out of the lazy, easy-going past to the violent present. And when a child was killed, perhaps in front of the local tavern, they cried over it with a nameless uncomprehending anguish, blaming no human agency, attributing everything to the implacable will of God. In a way this attunement to blind providence communicated itself to the soldiers. The searing, bursting thing that was the enemy bullet became an abstract evil and not

Troops enter the smashed streets of Salerno.

the result of a German deliberately aiming and pulling a trigger. Or so it seemed to some of the men who endured the worst of that close fighting, when no one knew how the battle was going to end.

But the crisis was passing. You could sense it in the lifting barrage. Shells began to fall farther and farther inland. New troops poured in, long lines of young boys in fresh uniforms came marching in single file along the roads. Fewer and fewer German bombers dived on the ships, and those that had been hit burned down to wet wreckage and the fires went out. An immense dust screen put up by the battle at such places as Battipaglia began to roll slowly on to the foothills. A second airstrip was added to the first along the beach, and the big Dakota supply planes started to come in on a regular rhythm from Sicily and North Africa.

Later on, when we had become veterans at these amphibious invasions, we would be able to separate the operation into different phases: the assault landing, the securing of the beachhead, the "break-in" to the enemy's encircling ring, then the "break-out" and the pursuit. What was happening here was that we were moving on the nursery school of the technique that led to the Anzio landing and its capture of Rome, and finally to the French invasion and its capture of Paris.

But for the moment we could see nothing of these phases and movements. Perhaps Alexander and his generals saw them and assessed them. Even at the pitch of the crisis General McCreary, the commander of the British troops, said to me: "They may take the town of Salerno tonight, or tomorrow. But the tide has turned. You will see it in the next day or two."

For the troops themselves everything was confusion and discomfort and danger, which somehow little by little and with agonizing slowness began to diminish. By the last week of September the bridgehead was secure beyond all prospect of dislodgment, and the Fifth Army was preparing for the "break-in" and the conquest of Naples.

How had it looked to the Germans, this first of our great landings on the European mainland? About this time our intelligence staff became possessed of a diary written by a Lieutenant Rocholl of the 16th Reconnaissance Unit of the 16th Panzer Division of the German Army. Rocholl saw the Salerno landing from the cliffs above, and recorded his impressions in a notebook in pauses of the fighting, and I for one find it one of the most lucid and enthralling reports of the whole campaign. Here it is:

> For many weeks now the Allies had been entrenched in Sicily, and it was apparent to all of us that the long-awaited, threatened and well-prepared invasion of the European mainland by the Allies would shortly have to take place if they wished to avoid the unfavorable October weather. We were ready for anything, and already on 6 Sept. a "Stand-by" alarm had been given.
>
> At 1400 hrs on 7 Sept. a call came through from the G-1 (Ops) of the Regt: "Attention—Operation: FEUERBRUNST." This was alarm No. 1—the "Stand-by," which meant that we could reckon with an early enemy attempt to land. This news, however, made no special impression on us, as we had had similar alarms often enough; consequently we did not interrupt our afternoon siesta.
>
> Suddenly, about 16.30, the G-1 (Ops) of the Regt came through once more: "Attention—Operation: ORKAN." This was Alarm No. 2—the "Get Ready," and meant that an enemy convoy was actually in sight; all preparations to move to be made immediately.
>
> Thereupon began a feverish activity, especially among the

three Rcn Patrols which were to be employed, in the event of an attempted enemy landing, at Salerno, Castellamare and Vietri. Within a short time I was able to announce that my patrol, which was to proceed to Salerno, was ready to move. When I reached the Co. HQ, to obtain from the Co. C.O. my battle instructions and to telephone to the Signals Officer for the Radio ciphers, I learned that Italy had unconditionally surrendered. At first the news came as a shock to me, but afterwards I realized that I had foreseen all this, and, in fact, had expected it.

At last everything was finished. I shook hands with the Co. C.O. and the other Co. Rcn Patrols and went down, my map-case under my arm, to my three arm'd cars, which were stationed in front of the church, awaiting my orders. I called the crews together and explained briefly the military and political situation, our assignment and the Radio cipher. "Mount—Take Positions." I fixed the map-case into place, loosened my revolver in the holster—one could not tell how the Italians would behave now. With a quick glance around to see that everything was in order, I signaled to the C.O.'s of the other two arm'd cars: "Start up Engines"—"Forward." At a very high speed we proceeded down the motor road to Salerno. Everywhere Italians were standing in groups, deep in excited discussions; they had obviously also heard of the capitulation of their country.

Thanks to our fast journey we arrived, as I intended we should, in daylight at the observation point I had chosen, and I was able to make all necessary arrangements before dark. The O.P. was located on the top of a mountain ridge, near the sea, southeast of Salerno. From this point I had a view N.W. towards Salerno—Vietri and S.S.E. along the entire coast and the Faiano plain. I was glad to see that in the neighborhood of the O.P. an Hy machine-gun section of the 3 Co. had taken up position, so that together we formed a small combat force. I contacted the sergeant in charge of the MG section. Now everything was in order with the exception of the arm'd cars. Where should I place them, and in what way to give the best reception for the radio car? I could not leave them all on the road, as this ran along the forward slope of the hill, and the cars would be too open to enemy fire. On the other hand, I did not want them too far away. Consequently I placed the radio car facing back along the road, just round the bend in the road in front of the O.P. In this spot the radio car, even if it meant a high aerial and 80 kw., would have good reception.

Darkness descended, and as, apart from the near-by noisy

Italian post, nothing was to be heard or seen, I ordered a few potatoes to be fried on the Esbit cooker. Scarcely had my lads started to peel them when the Sgt from the Hy. M.G. section came running up to me in great excitement. "Sir, a D.R. has just arrived from Regt HQ. I have been ordered to take over the Italian position. Would you, as an officer, undertake this mission?" Good? I made my arrangements; one half of the section was to give me cover and to open fire if I signaled with a white tracer. I went with the other half of the section and in no time at all had disarmed the personnel of the Italian Hy. M.G. nest. I told them that their country had capitulated and that after being disarmed they could make their way home. It happened just as I had expected. They threw their weapons away, and showed their joy that the war was now over for them, and they could go home.

Much more difficult were the negotiations with the Arty. position, which was under the command of a Lieut. First of all I spoke with a 2/Lieut. who showed great fear and didn't deserve to be an officer. When I requested his revolver, he handed it over without question. I next approached the Btry. CO, and found him quite the opposite—he behaved as an officer and gentleman. I explained the position to him, of which he knew nothing, and demanded the unconditional surrender to me of the Arty. position. He asked permission to contact his superior officer, but I had to refuse him this. He did not seem at all keen to comply with my order, and I was forced to give him a short-term ultimatum—to hand over or be fired on by my men. When the officer realized that it was a case of "either—or" he came to a decision, and handed over his Btry. Some of my men fetched out the Italian personnel, fell them in and disarmed them. Later we sent them home. I gave the Lieut. his revolver, however, without ammunition. The whole thing did not take more than about 45 minutes. It was now about 22.15 when we got back to our fried potatoes, but they tasted wonderful. We were just enjoying this meal when we were surprised by a terrific explosion. We sprang to our feet, to witness a terrifying, yet beautiful spectacle. The mole in the Salerno harbor had been blown up by the engineers. Explosion followed explosion, and soon warehouses and numerous small schooners in the harbor were on fire. The warehouses were apparently empty, as they burnt to the ground in no time; on the other hand a large boat burned the whole night through.

Slowly the time passed. We were all keyed up. Towards midnight we were disturbed by a sound overhead. These weren't British planes. German bombers! Flying out to sea. The moon shone as a weak crescent, very low on the horizon. We could recognize nothing at sea. Suddenly on the horizon terrific A.A. fire opened up: "A convoy." The broad curtain of A.A. fire showed us clearly the full length of the convoy. One could recognize especially the special A.A. ships, with the 4-barrelled guns firing uninterruptedly. The first wave was over. An hour later the second wave flew in from the sea. We could see quite clearly that the entire convoy had advanced far into the bay of Salerno.

Soon afterwards heavy fire (I estimated it to be from cruisers) was opened on the coastal area before Faiano, and then followed a new terrifying picture; the British opened up from the sea with rocket mortars (*Nebelwerfer*). One could hear the whistling and whining shots and the reverberations of the explosions. Soon afterwards we saw that the M.G. along the coast had opened up. "Tommy" with his landing barges must be very close in now. All this time, the heavy ships' guns bombarded the area around Pontecagno-Faiano.

Up till now my reports to Regt were going through so fast that the Radio operator had his hands full, encoding and despatching. But he managed. In this connection I was a bit uncertain: I was using 80 kw and a high aerial. That means, with the strength of a medium sender like Cologne, we could easily be detected, but fortunately the Allies were too busy with their landings to intercept my station. We continued with this luck all the next day.

Now followed a break. One could still hear the sounds of battle from the mainland, but could determine nothing definite, as it was still an hour from daybreak. Shortly after 06.00 hrs it became quickly light. I immediately sent my arm'd cars down below, and remained above with a Sgt and three men as messengers. We moved into the Btry position which the Italians had evacuated. At dawn our astonished eyes witnessed a magnificent spectacle: the entire Allied landing fleet lay in the bay of Salerno. Two ships of about 20,000 tons were lying near the coast near Faiano, unloading under arty fire. Among other things we could see tanks in the distance, which meant that the Allies had succeeded in gaining some ground, as they are usually the last thing to be landed. It wasn't very long before the daylight made things unpleasant for the Allies, which was very understandable, as the entire landing fleet lay before us as on a platter. Consequently numerous destroyers started laying a smoke screen. From 09.00 hrs onwards the main landing point was continually under smoke, so that we could not see what was happening there.

About 10.00 hrs a new convoy appeared from the west, moving

in the direction of the port of Salerno, but it stopped some 7 miles from the shore. A single landing barge with some 12 to 14 men left this convoy, and all alone approached the destroyed mole. Still 100 m. to go, still 50 m., only 25 m. now. Suddenly a shot close to the barge. An 88 mm of an A.A. Btry. located on the rear slope of our mountain has fired, but too short. Another shot, close to the barge. The stern dips into the sea. We wait to see it sink completely, but what happens? The little boat turns sharply around—that caused the deep dip of the stern—and paddles, as if nothing were the matter, back to the main force. These were regular fellows!

Another 15 minutes passed. Suddenly a few shots whistled close over our heads and landed behind our ridge. More shots came over. Had we been spotted and they had fired wide? We did not have to wait long to find the solution. The landing barge had spotted the A.A. position and "Tommy" was shooting it up. The first salvo was 20 m. short, the second was right on the target. The entire Btry was knocked out. Later on the convoy which was lying off Salerno turned towards the main landing point at Faiano.

During the entire day this gigantic landing fleet lay quietly and undisturbed in the bay. In spite of the smoke screen I was able to count, excluding the numerous small landing barges and the stuff already on the beaches, 365 units. This picture remained unchanged during the whole day. Around mid-day, the ships fired a few shots towards Salerno, but apart from that nothing special happened.

About 16.00 hrs, 3 Co. left their positions, in order to occupy the second line of defense at the road block north of Fratte. Why this was done I do not know, seeing that 3 Co. had had no contact with the enemy. At any rate, they were off, and with them our Hy M.G. section. And so I was left on the ridge with my handful of men, armed with revolvers, sending an occasional message down to the arm'd cars. Time went on, and it was already 18.00 hrs. Not anticipating any trouble, we sat there in the grass and ate a few grapes, when suddenly some M.G. shots whistled past our ears. "Take cover." Damnation, what was it? Once again the unpleasant tat-tat-tat, but this time from behind the Btry position. Two men of a British Rcn unit had approached on rubber soles to within 10 meters of our position. There was nothing for us to do but to scurry away to the left and attempt to reach our arm'd cars. This we successfully did. I deliberated: as up till now no orders had been received from Regt to withdraw, but our O.P. had been discovered, I had to establish a new point. If we remained up on the ridge, we would certainly be wiped out in the night.

I drove with my patrol into the now uninhabited town of Salerno. It is a ghastly feeling to drive through a destroyed and dead city, where, however, one may find an AT gun hidden round every corner. I drove through the whole city to the sanatorium, where I intended to set up a new O.P., and from where I would have at least a new road of retreat open. We had been there scarcely five minutes when a priest came up and beseeched us not to shoot, to give thought to the sick. A strange conception of war these Italians have! However, I was able to do him this favor, as an order came through then by radio to drive on to the road block. It was already 20.00 hrs and dark when I drove through Salerno for the second time and was able to establish that it was still free of enemy troops. On the return journey through several small villages the Italians waved to us and threw flowers on our arm'd cars, shouting *"Viva Inglesia!"* These had been our allies and now presumed that the British were already on the march.

Without further incident we reached the road block, behind which I made a halt, in order to contact the AT gun comd, who was standing there beside his weapon. I dispersed my arm'd cars behind the block and drove on a motorcycle to Regtl Battle HQ, but was unable to find it as it had been moved in the meantime. I drove back to the road block and found that the Quartermaster, who had been looking for us, had arrived with rations and post. I drove with him immediately to HQ and reported. It was now 23.00 hrs. The CO was asleep, but the Adj assured me that the CO had been particularly pleased with my messages, and dismissed me. I returned to my quarters and found that my patrol had already come in. I called the crews together and expressed my appreciation, especially to the radio operator, who had really earned the greatest praise. He had remained without break at his set for 32 hrs, and had even gone to the latrine with the earphones on, and his message pad in his hand. Extraordinary willpower on the part of a 36-year-old! Soon after we ate and then slept like the dead.

The next day my patrol was given a well-earned rest. The Allies had advanced to the block, and had liquidated our 75 mm. AT gun. During the night there had been the danger that 3 Co., which were in the neighborhood of the block on the left flank, would be surrounded but the enemy were driven back. On 10 Sept there was heavy fighting round the block, in which the Allies suffered severe casualties, and were finally driven back by a counter-attack. Among other things, an AT gun was captured.

In the night from 10 to 11 Sept, contact with the enemy was lost. As a result, on the morning of the 11 Sept, my patrol was sent out to contact the enemy again. We reached Fratte without hindrance, but on leaving it in the south, we were fired on by infantry weapons. Our mission as such was fulfilled, but I had to await orders at the northern exit of Fratte. I placed my arm'd cars close to the left side of the road (the sea-side) as there was a perpendicular slope here, about 5 m. high. This gave us the necessary cover from the ships' guns which were firing uninterruptedly on a bridge about 50 m. behind us. The spotter for this firing was on a hill about 1 km. away, and could see us clearly and obviously wanted to catch us. Nearer and nearer the shells dropped, with shrapnel flying past uncomfortably close. Involuntarily one ducked together in the car, although that would not have given the slightest protection. Suddenly there was a sharp crack and a deafening explosion—a shell had exploded on the edge of the slope directly over the second arm'd car. All the earth and dirt seemed to drop into our open turrets. This was a bit too much, and I ordered the arm'd cars to withdraw under a bridge about 200 meters in the rear. Here we met a clerk from the Co. office, with orders for us to return.

The following two days were quiet, particularly for us in the Rcn, who are used for three things only:

1. To make contact with the enemy;
2. To make contact with neighboring forces;
3. To secure open flanks.

As a result, I had plenty of opportunity to be in Battle HQ, and to study the situation map. According to this, the following counterattack was planned for the evening of 12 Sept.

One Regt with its two Bns was to take Height 522 in a night attack; following this, one Bn would remain on this height, and the second would take over the neighboring height, lying to the southeast, and hold it. If this succeeded, tanks and Panzergrenadiers would sweep round from the north on Faiano and take it. If this was also successful, Rcn troops would occupy Salerno and then move out towards Vietri, while the H.G. Div would take Vietri from the north and then move eastwards. In this way the entire Allied front would collapse. But the plan failed because the C.O. of the Inf Regt was in charge and had too much confidence in himself and his Regt.

During this time I was in charge of the Co., as the C.O. had to be continually with the commander. The Co. lay more or less quietly although we had to change position several times, as we were often between the Btry positions and unnecessarily exposed to the strong enemy arty fire. For this reason I decided in the end to move the Co. to the old position at Penta, as Penta was beyond the range of the arty fire, and our quarters there were situated at the foot of a hill, standing between us and the enemy. We reached this position about 21.00 hrs and were looking forward to a quiet night. With great care we established our camp on the spot on which we had already spent many weeks. The guards were posted and soon we all lay in the deepest sleep.

I was awakened suddenly by a violent shaking of my arm and found a guard bending over me and pointing towards the sky: "Lieutenant! Lieutenant! Paratroops!" I was still half-asleep, but I forced my eyes open and saw the amazing sight for myself. While in the distance one heard the faint droning of the departing planes, 50–60 paratroops, still at the height of some 150 meters, swung towards the ground. As it was a bright moonlight night, one could recognize every single white fleck in the heavens. I quickly overcame the moment of terror and roused the whole Co.: "To your arms! Prepare to fire!" Like cats the gunners sprang into the turrets, and soon fourteen 20 mm guns and some 20 MG's. were firing on the descending enemy. This continued until the angle of fire became too small, and our men were in danger. "Cease fire!" Now we had to move quickly. I have mentioned before that we had camped at the foot of a thickly-wooded hill. The paratroops were landing all around us, but most of them about half-way up the hill, so that they would be able, under cover of the trees, to approach close to us and place stick-grenades or similar "toys" on our arm'd cars. With this in mind, I ordered all arm'd cars to proceed without delay to the main road and secure it from attack. When this was done, I set off towards Penta with a few men to carry out a Rcn. Nothing was to be seen; we searched a few houses but could find no trace whatever of the paratroops. In this way we reached the last house in Penta, which I also intended to search. I went up to the door and found it locked. Two of my men tried to force it and finally burst it open. At the same moment, three automatic rifles opened up from the house and my men were lucky to escape injury. So that's where they were! One, two, three grenades were our prompt reply. A few bursts with our automatics and we forced our way into the house. Pitch black! I risked it and flashed my torch round the room, calling out, "HANDS UP." There were 8–10 paratroops, apparently wounded, in the hallway. They blinked in the light and hesitantly raised their arms. The remainder had escaped through the back door of the house, but it was too difficult to go after them then. We took the prisoners and all the material we found and started back, heavily laden.

On arrival back at the cars, the prisoners and booty were thoroughly examined. They were American paratroops from Sicily, on their first combat mission, which was to interrupt traffic on the road between Avellino and Salerno, to the rear of the German front. Among the material we found a sack with mines, two AT rifles, two light M.G., two light mortars and two days' rations for 30 men. Each man was excellently equipped: one 12 mm tommy-gun, one 12 mm revolver, three hand-grenades, numerous fuses, knife, compass, maps printed on silk, a brass knuckle-duster-knife, cigarettes and excellent first-aid equipment.

During the next two days I undertook three further patrols on foot, during which I brought in another six prisoners, beating them at their own game. The patrol, which consisted of four men, armed with automatic rifles, revolvers and hand-grenades, had to wrap rags round their boots—we did not have rubber soles like the Americans—and in this way could approach the enemy unnoticed. Every time we were successful.

The diary, which covers the period September 7th to 14th, ends here because the lieutenant was killed. The notebook was found on his body.

3. The Follow-through

By October all the foot of Italy was clear of the enemy. The Eighth Army with many reinforcements was taking up its position on the northern flank of the Apennines. On the southern side the Fifth was bearing down on Pompeii and Naples. One could drive freely back and forth across the mountains from one army to another and, after an interval of two years, see how life was lived in Axis Europe.

In Taranto the shops were open, Italian and British sailors

King Victor Emmanuel moved into Brindisi.

moved about together and the harbor was filled with Allied shipping. Many little piratical raids were going out by night to harass the Germans on the shores of Corfu and Albania and Jugoslavia. The Axis navy in the Mediterranean had been silenced forever.

Brindisi too was normal, and presently King Victor Emmanuel moved in there with his wife and the faithful Badoglio, his prime minister. A skeleton Italian government was set up, but, alas, without records, without funds and without authority. Badoglio met us one day, an old man with all the plausibility and amiability that old age and long years of wealth and authority can bring. He told us the story of Mussolini's fall, of the impoverishment of Italy, of the country's hatred of Fascism. The theme was: "I am loyal to my king. He has called me in to do what I can for Italy, and then I shall resign."

Badoglio was a sympathetic figure in those days, a handsome old man with charm and wit. On both the occasions I saw him he talked logically and freely; he had a kind of *dolce far niente* demeanor, something between deprecation and regret and patriarchal dignity. "The wickedness of Mussolini! What horrors that man had brought on Italy! Italy which had fought heroically on the side of the Allies in the other war." He talked with immense regret. And as he talked one felt that there was something deeply and irrationally wrong in all this, something that just would not do. The whole façade was absurd, the old querulous king in the background, the courtiers frisking elegantly about him, the aged retainer who had come from honorable retirement to his master's side and finally the generals like Ambrosio and Roatta who had done so well in suppressing the Balkan partisans until they saw the wind was blowing the other way.

There was a curious cardboard quality about all these figures, a strange kind of toy-like respectability which was quite unreal and bore no relation towards the original objects or the spirit of the invasion. "Our poor country has sinned grievously because of that wicked man." No. It simply would not do. Each one of these men had thrown in his fortunes with Mussolini and Fascism, had worn its uniforms, accepted its medals and its money. One man had signed the kingdom's declaration of war against England—and that at a time when it was a criminally easy thing to do. Some of the others had actually led the jackal Fascist expeditions in the wake of the Nazis. Others again had worked hard in Fascist politics. They were at the top of affairs in Italy, not because they loved Italy but because they had accepted Mussolini.

Charming men, all of them. Men who were no doubt determined to assist the Allied cause, now that the Allies had a winning cause.

One had to grant them a little altruism, even perhaps a slight sense of responsibility. But the list of events was too long and much too recent. Abyssinia, Spain, Albania, France, Greece and Jugoslavia. Italy had known how to be ruthless when she was winning. And all these men had been Mussolini's agents.

General Eisenhower had set up an Allied Military Mission in Brindisi under Lieut.-General Mason Macfarlane, who was formerly the Governor of Gibraltar. The attitude of the Mission (and therefore presumably of the State Department and the Foreign Office) was this: We deal with Badoglio and the king because they are the only people we have to deal with. Later on we shall have a democratically elected government in Italy, but for the time being we simply must have someone to organize the Italians and raise their resistance to the Germans. Badoglio is the logical leader for the moment.

That was the argument. It had occurred before over Darlan in North Africa. It was going to occur again in different forms over the refugee kings and governments of Greece and Jugoslavia. The presence of de Gaulle had finally settled the issue in North Africa as it was to do later on in France. But in Italy and the Balkans a political vacuum existed. For twenty years Fascism had reigned. The Liberal leaders who had survived were either out of touch or too old. They were without the skill or the means to govern. This was a problem that went right down through society, and into the roots of local government. Wherever we put a young AMGOT[1] officer in charge of a town he found himself overwhelmed with problems and in an impossible position. If he sacked the existing Fascist bosses he found he had no one capable of taking their place. Let him dredge down as far as he liked among the shades of 1920 Liberalism, he still could find no one with enough authority and business sense to put the town on its feet again, to get the bomb damage cleared up, the courts administered, the schools and hospitals working, the banks and business houses operating. And so perforce he had to rehire the Fascist officials in order to get the jobs done. And not unnaturally this puzzled the Italians a good deal, since they had believed we were fighting on the other side. Nor were things very much improved by the fact that some of the AMGOT officials had no knowledge of Italy or of its language. Without staffs or equipment of any kind they were given huge areas to succor and administer. It was probably the carabinieri who saved the situation as much as anything during those early days.

However, there it was. Every official in the country, from the king

---

1 Allied Military Government Occupied Territories.

downwards, was thoroughly compromised. There remained only the people themselves, the unpolitical peasant, the conscript and the factory worker and his wife. Fascism, being a positive thing, requiring aggressive action on the part of the individual, had not entirely contaminated the masses by any means. They stood aside from it. They accepted the new concrete roads and groaned over the taxes and the wars. They were never part of the system. The proof of that we were seeing under our own eyes. Despite the slogans, despite the uniforms and the statues, despite everything, Italy was flinging aside Fascism almost overnight. Within a day of our entering a village you would have thought that Fascism had never existed. One puff and the whole fabric was blown away. It was the same everywhere you went. In twenty long years Mussolini had still not illicited anything out of the real heart of the people.

For the moment they were too utterly crushed to care about politics. They wanted food and peace and their men back home. Yet underneath that immediate and insistent layer of wants the political beliefs were waiting there, as they usually are. Already such of the political feeling as was vocal was expressing itself very strongly against this compromise government, this bridge between Fascism and the curiously benign invader. Badoglio could not last if his fate was left to the Italians. Nor could the king. That was certain. The historical question was simply this—how far did Badoglio organize anything? How far did the king stimulate resistance to the Germans? And how far did we damage our cause not only in Europe but among our own people by dealing with the reformed collaborationists?

General Alexander, as military governor, was technically responsible for the domestic organization of the Italians. But Alexander had his hands full enough with the battle. During the early days when his headquarters was stationed in Sicily he had been too remote to maintain daily control. But now he moved into the village of San Spirito, just north of Bari, and from here he managed the co-operation of the two armies.

On the face of it the situation was not too bad. Naples was about to fall. Bari was untouched and it was being built up rapidly as a subsidiary port. Foggia was captured at a gallop. The airborne troops swarmed across the flat plains meeting very little resistance. It was ideal country for an advance. Mussolini's neat farmhouses, all built to exactly the same pattern, were dotted about a dreary landscape unrelieved by trees or hills or crops. Foggia itself when we got in was a frightful shambles. It was one of those brand-new Fascist towns, full of tall apartment houses and grandiose public buildings, and nearly every one of these was split open by a recent bombing. The population had left. A few gutter rats remained behind to loot the shops and scatter the debris of broken cases knee deep down the pavements. On the airfields, the all-important airfields, there was nothing—no soldiers, no aircraft, no dumps. It merely remained for the Allied air forces to move in.

I remember the day Foggia fell because of a silly but rather revealing prank. A number of flesh-colored tailors' dummies had been flung across the roadway by the looters. I picked up a broken cardboard leg with the idea that I might amuse myself by drawing a map of Italy on it. It was a well-shaped leg, and as it dangled outside the jeep it gave the impression that a naked dead body was lying inside. As we drove back that night to our billet in Bari the Italians in many thousands were gathered on the roadside to cheer us. But at every village when the people caught sight of the leg their cheers froze at once. Women, gazing in horror, clutched their children indoors. Even when they saw that the thing was a tailor's dummy they were still only half convinced. Only the young bloods in the village squares thought the matter amusing. The point was, of course, that there was still mortal fear in the hearts of the Italians. Four years of propaganda had taught them that we were barbarians, and probably quite capable of flinging a naked girl into a jeep and carrying her off.

This over-riding fear of the British was mixed with a most venal determination to make money out of the soldiers, and escape any personal responsibility for the country's defeat. At Bari, for example, we had been unable to find a billet in the town, and eventually we took refuge for the night in an empty villa outside. It was a handsome place, and we were unwilling to break in so long as the rain did not increase. We spent most of next day getting the address of the owner, an immensely wealthy countess with half a dozen such villas at her disposal. She had taken refuge in the country, and we drove out to ask her for the key and permission to remain a few nights in the villa. The woman threw hysterics at the mere suggestion. Encrusted with jewelry, she sat in an armchair and screamed that she would faint, that she would die. We had been ordered to treat the Italians well, more as allies than as the conquered. I pointed out that we could requisition the place but preferred this more friendly way of doing things, and promised that we would do no harm. She answered that with wonderful rolling Italian abuse, and deplored that the Germans had ever left. At that I ordered her servants to give me the key, and told her that she could send two of her retainers back with me to keep an eye on the place. They stayed with us the whole time we were in Bari. In the end we discovered that they were doing a brisk trade in selling our rations to their neighbors.

This kind of dealing did not at all represent the majority of the Italians, especially the country people. You could not judge Italy from the rats in the big cities who sold the soldiers faked and poisonous spirits at exorbitant prices. Yet still there was this universal thing—a complete lack of any sense of responsibility or shame or regret for Italy's part in the war. Everything was blamed upon the Fascists—especially by those who had hidden their uniforms and ceased to be Fascists overnight. There were no morals in Italy any longer. Morally and militarily and economically the country was bankrupt. It seemed that all pride and dignity had gone out of men's minds. However, all this will more aptly come into the story when we reach Naples. For the moment the military issues were paramount, and, as I say, upon the face of it our campaign was prospering.

But was it really doing well? Now that we were inside Europe we were getting a mass of intelligence from the enemy, and it was becoming clear that on three major issues at least our judgments had been hopelessly wrong.

Look for a moment at the German side of the picture. I give it here mostly as I got it from the Italian General Staff Intelligence Summaries for June, July and August—the months immediately before our invasion. These summaries were compiled in co-operation with the German Intelligence Service. They were weekly reports from Axis agents all over the world, and their distribution was limited to 200 senior officers. It took two companions and myself three days to go through those reports, and I am adding to them here from the mass of information we got every day from talking to Italian officials who had been working with the Germans.

In the summer of 1943, when Sicily was falling, the Italians panicked, and for the first time the Germans began to envisage defeat. Stalingrad and Alamein, in the previous autumn, had been the real turning-point in the war, but the effects of those Allied victories did not become apparent until six or eight months later. All Africa fell (with the loss of a quarter of a million German prisoners in Tunisia). The Russians broke out from Stalingrad in a major winter campaign. And still in the spring and summer they came on towards the German border. At this time—July and August of 1943—the Axis Intelligence staffs were reporting to their High Command that Anglo-American invasions on a vast scale were to be expected immediately. They grossly over-estimated our strength. We were given, for example, fifty divisions and ten thousand aircraft in the Mediterranean. The scare began inside Germany, and the heavy bombing stimulated the depression.

It was estimated—I am quoting from the documents—that we were capable of making simultaneously, *and the Germans incapable of withholding*, landings on Greece, Italy and southern France. Other landings on the northern European coast (mainly the Low Countries) and Norway were "to be expected." Plus an increase in the bombing. Plus an intensification of the anti-submarine war. Plus the continued advance of the Russians. And the Italians with their fleet had to be written off entirely.

In these circumstances the Germans were deploying about twelve to fifteen divisions in holding down the Balkans, and perhaps as many more in northern Italy and southern France. In southern Italy and Sicily they maintained virtually nothing—three or four divisions. It did not seem possible either that they could hold their line in Russia, or the immensely long and jagged coast of the northern Mediterranean. Jugoslavia was on the point of boiling over. Every day there were new reports of railways being cut and villages taken by the partisans. In Hungary and Bulgaria the most depressing things were happening. For example, when the Allies bombed Ploesti the Bulgarians repressed the news that their fighters had shot down six of our planes—presumably because Bulgaria was unwilling to anger the Allies. In the same way the Hungarians refused to publish the news that units of their army had fought against Tito in Jugoslavia—even though the news was given in the German communiqué. Strikes in the armament factories were happening all the way from the Black Sea to the Pyrenees, and French resistance was becoming dangerously effective. Attempts to force Frenchmen to work in Germany were being met with persistent obstruction. Sabotage in Czechoslovakia. Riots in Milan. Snipers in Holland. Evasion at Vichy. Unexplained fires in Greece. Wherever the German agents went they were reporting a creaking and a straining away from the Axis. It was the first small series of warnings of the coming collapse. Europe at last was beginning to find herself strong enough to protest, to come out into the open here and there and fight. And all the time the people were breathlessly watching the advance of the Allied armies, waiting and waiting for the day of invasion.

It was a genuine pleasure reading these reports, mostly because of their exciting information but partly too because it was almost the first political reading entirely divorced from propaganda which had come my way since the war began. These were secret and technical reports to the Axis High Command, reports stripped down to the truth, so that military operations could be based upon them.

When the Allied invasion of Italy began in September—at least a month later than they had expected—there was only one rational thing the Germans could do: abandon the Italian peninsula to a rear-guard action, abandon Rome, and mass on the plain of Lombardy. They were encouraged to this decision by the fierce uprising of Tito's partisans in Jugoslavia, and by their fears that other landings would be made. They simply had not enough troops to go round. A pool of reserves would be made in France and Northern Italy, and from this the troops could be fed out to the places east and west and south where they were wanted most.

But then in that vital month of September, and again in October, things began to change very greatly indeed. With growing hope the Germans began to realize that Italy was to be our only landfall, that already it was too late for the Allies to invade across the Channel from England. In Russia the Reds had at last come to the end of their tether. The Germans counter-attacked at Zhitomir and rolled them back. One good thing followed another (I am still writing from the German viewpoint). A feeble attempt upon the Dodecanese islands was turned back with no trouble at all. Turkey stayed out of the war. Marshal Tito was getting no support from the Anglo-Americans, and the German garrison was beginning to hold him. Spalato was retaken, Trieste released, the railway to Belgrade restored. Better still, in Italy the Anglo-Americans were coming on so slowly through the mountains that very soon the winter rains would be upon them. More troops were hastened to southern Italy. Perhaps the south could be held after all: indeed, it began to look like it.

One can imagine the sigh of relief with which the German Command saw these vital weeks slip by one after another and still nothing drastic occurred. By late October it was fairly clear that they were safe for the winter in their fortress of Europe. Six months' grace. And then? Then the flying bomb would be ready. Then they would have new reserves of manpower; manpower that could still be impressed from the unwilling villages of Europe. Then Rommel's defenses would be ready in the north. Then the jet-plane and the rocket. Anything and everything could happen before next summer.

And so in these autumn weeks the whole character of the Mediterranean war and the Italian campaign was changed. All possibility of a quick run through Italy and the release of the Balkans vanished. It vanished because the Germans found themselves strong enough to send reinforcements down to the south. And once those reinforcements arrived they had only to hold until the winter and then decisive fighting in the mountains would be impossible. For us now there was no escape: a war of the rivers and the mountains, a war in the bitter icy rain, a winter campaign along some of the highest ranges in Europe. No army will willingly engage in such conditions, and it has since been admitted by our High Command that we had hoped and planned to avoid such a deadlock in Italy.

From this misjudgment flowed two other mistakes. We never envisaged that Tito's uprising would spread and increase the way it did. We did not even understand Tito's place in the war during the autumn. The attitude of the Foreign Office and the State Department was confused. Officially we were still supporting Mihailovitch. The Russians had long ago thrown over Mihailovitch for the very good reason that Mihailovitch was co-operating with the Germans and the puppet government in Belgrade. He was assisting the Germans in fighting the partisans under Tito. That is to say we were deliberately supporting our enemy, who was exterminating our friends. King Peter of Jugoslavia was in England and we supported him too. Peter's position (like that of George of Greece) was isolated and obscure, but one thing was fairly certain—Peter was having no dealings with Tito. Tito was a Red. Tito did not acknowledge either Peter or his refugee government in England. There were a lot of other people too in England and America who feared Communism more than they feared the Germans, especially the Germans in so remote a place as Jugoslavia.

Quite apart from our policy, our information upon what was really going on in Jugoslavia was grotesquely inadequate. We had sent across by submarine a few technicians and advisers—sent them to Mihailovitch of course. Very soon these British officers realized that they had been attached to the wrong army, that Mihailovitch was using the weapons we sent him to fight our real allies, the partisans. They reported upon this with the radio sets they had brought in. No answer. No result. An acquaintance of mine, Terence Atherton, was among those sent across by submarine. Atherton had lived in Jugoslavia for years, and spoke Serbian. He and his friends, the other British officers, saw clearly their duty. They decamped to Tito, the only man who was fighting the Germans. They ran fantastic risks and hardships in doing this. When the news of their action came through they were declared to be traitors, renegades, deserters from the Allies. Atherton's pay to his wife was stopped. Atherton persisted in what he thought to be right. Then one day when he was with Tito in the field the German planes got him. Tito was injured and Atherton was killed. When we have a few monuments to spare for the British soldiers and agents who fought, isolated and alone, behind the enemy lines, we might remember Atherton and his friends. Not all of them had lived long enough to find themselves completely vindicated.

I am not attempting here to elucidate the jungle of Jugoslav politics. Possibly I over-simplify. But the fact remains that there was a reversal of our policy about this time, autumn 1943. Mihailovitch was at last discredited. We continued our support of King Peter but at least we acknowledged Tito. And negotiations were begun for bringing Tito and the king together.

Unhappily all this was too late. The vital moment when Tito needed supplies, bombers above all, had passed. He was pushed off the offensive on to the defensive. And yet fantastic things had been done by the partisans. Lest anyone should think that Tito's rising was a flash in the pan, of no real consequence to the global war, let us have this here in print: through these months Tito held down more German divisions than the entire Anglo-American forces in Italy. He continued to engage more divisions for months after we had landed in Italy. He won more ground, took more towns, killed more Germans, than the whole of Alexander's armies. This was admitted in Alexander's headquarters. And all was done with the merest fraction of the equipment which we wielded in Italy.

What had happened in Jugoslavia—all unknown, possibly deliberately unknown, to the outside world—was this. An immense revolt had swept the country at the announcement of the Italian armistice. In a thousand villages the Serbs and the Croats had

Tito won more ground than all Alexander's armies.

banded themselves into guerilla groups to throw out the enemy. It was a spontaneous movement, something coming directly out of the passion and the hatred of the people. They had no uniforms, so they wrenched them off the Italians and the Germans. They had no weapons, so they rushed upon the disordered enemy garrisons along the Adriatic coast and seized trucks and rifles and bullets. They seized Spalato and the neighboring islands. They engaged the Germans in pitched battles around Trieste.

This was the flame of revolution burning about as purely as you can get it. The women quite naturally and simply joined the ranks. For them the conditions of service were just the same as for the men. Before you could join a partisan band you had to get a weapon. To get a weapon you had to ambush an enemy vehicle on the roads, kill the occupants somehow, take their clothes and weapons, and then report back for duty. Fighting of an unparalleled savagery broke out in twenty different places at once. On both sides prisoners were interrogated, stripped and shot. It did not matter if the prisoner was a child or a woman. Automatically they were shot. To the desperate German garrisons the red star and the clenched fist became symbols of utter barbarity—a barbarity they themselves had practiced all too easily from the days when Belgrade was suddenly betrayed and bombed, and all Jugoslavia over-run.

Presently the ammunition which the Partisans had seized from the Italian garrisons began to run out. No help came from Italy or North Africa. They began to retreat into the hills. Little by little, with their planes and artillery, the Germans regained the Adriatic ports and the islands offshore. Tito went up into the rough Montenegrin mountains and set up a kind of brigand headquarters there. He was becoming acknowledged throughout Jugoslavia as the partisan leader. The same maddening tribal disputes went on inside his own ranks, Serbs and Croats killing one another. But in general Germany now was regarded as the common enemy.

A phase of intense guerilla warfare began. The partisans would swoop on a town, hold it for a few days, and then retreat. They had mobility. They were everywhere. Surprise was on their side. Even if the Germans sent a punitive expedition it usually found the countryside empty as it advanced. And then as it turned to retire, burning the villages as it went, the partisans crept back to attack on the flanks.

About this time—the end of September—the first partisan wounded were secretly brought across by boat to Bari in Italy. They were girls of twenty or less, a few children who had been acting as runners. All were seriously wounded. In Jugoslavia there were no drugs, no means of operating. A doctor's wife, a little nut-brown woman known as Tina, smuggled her patients across at night, feeling sure that the Allies would help her. But in Bari no one was quite prepared for them. The Jugoslav girls were turned over to their old enemies the Italians. The Italians bundled them into a civilian hospital outside Bari. They were given a thin soup, a few vegetables, nothing else. They lay on dirty beds.

That was where I first saw them. It was nothing particularly new to them that they were hungry and unwashed. All these girls had been marching in the mountains, sleeping round fires in the open at night. They had all killed and killed frequently in the past few weeks. They had all been hit in the body by machine-gun fire. There were four of them in the first ward, and one was quite unprepared to find them beautiful. They were big girls, students of their local universities but from peasant stock. A wave of dark brown hair. Good white teeth. Unusually large brown steady eyes. High breasts. Long thin fingers. Then the less obvious things. A curiously composed, clear, steady gaze in the eyes: a most unexpected spirituality and gentleness. They were completely without affectation or toughness. They seemed to be entirely sure of themselves. It was the quality you see in animals; simply a state of unconscious being. They accepted their existence and their behavior as inevitable, something requiring no embellishment or explanation. And most of the time I was with them they were laughing. I think they were probably the most innocent women I have ever seen. It was impossible not to feel indignant and angry at their treatment. They lay neglected at this miserable hospital for another week, and then at last the effect of our changed policy and better conscience began to work. Doctors were found. The amputations were carried out with proper drugs. The Italians were compelled to disgorge decent food.

Meanwhile refugees in thousands were beginning to gather in a camp outside Bari. These were the vanguard of that immense army of drifting people who had been thrown out of their homes by the war—Russian conscripts forced by the Germans to work in Italy, Jews, Poles, even Letts and Finns. They stood like cattle waiting to be fed. They were helpless. They were the beginning of a problem as big as the war itself.

But now at last Tito's army was being organized and given its right status. Soon after this arms began to flow across the Adriatic, pathetically small consignments but still of immense moral value to the partisans, enough to enable them to halt their retreat.

Apart from all this, but connected, was the matter of the British prisoners in Italy. Or you might choose to call it the tragedy of the British prisoners. When we invaded there were seventy-five intern-ment camps and prisoners' hospitals in Italy containing seventy thousand men, taken mostly in Africa and the Aegean. By various means the senior British officers in the camps were given orders along these lines: "When the war ends you will stand fast and await the arrival of the Allied army. Do not allow your men to escape and roam about running unnecessary risks." The orders came from London. They were official. Indeed they represented a considered plan. At the end of the last war many thousands of our men im-prisoned in Germany broke from their camps and became lost. Many died. This time it was determined that we should avoid that error and so the "stand fast" orders were sent out.

The plan seems to have been based on the belief that once we set foot on Italy the Italians would collapse (which was accurate) and the Germans would clear out of the country leaving our prisoners behind (which was grossly inaccurate). At all events most of the larger camps in Italy were contacted many months before our invasion and when we landed the men sat down to wait.

At the time of the Italian armistice Italian guards were posted on these camps. On hearing the news of the armistice, guards in many cases presumed that their duties were finished, and they invited the British to escape. At some places they even offered rations and weapons to the prisoners. For the first time in many weary months the British found the gates open and no obstacle to their departure. But the senior British officer in each camp had his instructions. In the majority of cases those orders were passed on to the men: "Stay where you are. Wait." And so they waited while the Italian guards looked on incredulously. A few bold spirits saw the craziness of the instructions. They disobeyed and got away either to Sicily or south to the invading Allied forces. The majority stayed put. Within a few days German guards arrived and quickly took charge. One after another the camps were again sealed off. And then in batches of thousands the British in southern and central Italy were put in trains and taken off to new and securer camps in Germany. Of the original seventy thousand only twelve thousand got away before the Germans arrived.

That is the story. The interesting thing is to know who judged the Italian campaign so confidently that he thought we would over-run Italy and release the prisoners within a week or two.

There were many heartbreaking scenes as the prisoners began to realize that they had been tricked. One officer I remember came in across the hills and insisted on going back to lead out the rest of the men still interned in his camp. When he got back he found the Germans had already arrived and the prisoners were being entrained. In another camp only a few miles north of our front-line on the Adriatic, twenty thousand British soldiers were taken off in a body. Probably most of them could have got away. One of those who escaped by walking at this time was General Klopper, the South African who had commanded at the surrender of Tobruk. He had written a full explanation of the Tobruk story in his camp, and buried it on his escape. Klopper, like the others who got away, said that he had been given immense help by the Italian peasants. Indeed everything—this matter of the prisoners, the treatment of the Jugoslav partisans, the failure to exploit the Italian resistance to the Germans—seemed to indicate that we had come into Europe with very muddled ideas of what we were going to find.

It is all too easy now to see the mistakes and write about them. It is all too easy to forget the risks and puzzling alternatives that lay before the planners, especially as they had to do the planning six months before the invasion took place. This book makes no attempt to judge the competence of the Allied generals. I am simply trying to explain this most puzzling and, at first, most disappointing campaign.

Many will still argue that the whole plan of the invasion might have been different. Suppose for example we had taken the risk of being temporarily without air cover and landed the bulk of our forces on Italy's unprotected heel. Suppose we had carried them on across the Adriatic to the coast of Albania and Jugoslavia, which was already falling into Tito's hands. Might we not then have carried Jugoslavia, and with it Greece? Might we not have made an early junction with the tremendous Russian drive along the Black Sea to Rumania, and at once thrown the Balkans out of the war? Even the invasion of Hungary might have been possible as early as the end of 1943.

There were other possibilities, many others. One presumes they were studied and rejected. But probably one main criticism can be made: the Allies went into Europe on a plan that was distinctly conservative and lacking in imagination. And so in October we found ourselves committed to a series of the bitterest and most difficult mountain battles of the whole war. Naples fell on the heels of Foggia, and so we got our airfields as well as the port necessary to supply the army. But in order to guarantee Foggia and Naples we had to have defense in depth. We had to advance farther, say to an east-west line running across the peninsula from Pescara to Rome. Rome itself began to fascinate and psychologize all of us. Rome—

the first Axis capital. Rome—the symbol of Italy, the most famous city in the world. Yes, certainly we must have Rome. That was the feeling even among some commanders who were not blind to the fact that Rome, apart from being a crossroads, was of very little military use whatever. Little by little the conquest of Rome began to color the conduct of the campaign from this time forward.

Unhappily before Rome lay a series of obstacles: the Volturno river just north of Naples. Then the Garigliano. Then Cassino, the natural fortress which was used even in peace-time military maneuvers. Beyond that all the wild hills reaching north through Frosinone. The Adriatic side was just as difficult. The Biferno river, then the Trigno, then the Moro, then the Sangro, and heaven knew what else in the way of mountain valleys and naturally defensive positions.

A period of hacking and thrusting began, a period of trying one thing, then another, of regrouping troops and swapping artillery about. And with every day the weather grew colder, the mountains whiter under heavy snow; and in the valleys the slimy deepening mud that follows every army into Europe.

To win the Biferno the Eighth Army tried a small landing at Termoli at the river's mouth, and they got away with it. Carefully Montgomery wound up the spring and uncoiled it again at the Trigno. Another mile or two was gained. But the roads were in a hopeless condition. I lived at this time at the little town of Lucera, near Foggia, and it soon became impossible to visit the front and return in one day. A solid mass of transport blocked the roads all day and all night, and things got steadily worse when we moved with Montgomery's camp into Vasto. Traffic would be one way for six hours at a time, and no overtaking. As the New Year turned we were still a long way from Pescara. An immense effort was made to carry the Sangro River, and fling across a bridge. It was done, but then—nothing. A few more Germans killed. Every one of these battles seemed merely to open up new obstacles ahead. When Montgomery came to leave early in January to take charge of the invasion in France it was clear that the Eighth Army was going to be stuck all winter more or less where it was. Immense sacrifices had been made. Men had put up with conditions that made the desert seem a paradise.

In Vasto's little theater, Montgomery took an emotional farewell of his desert followers. He had been just over eighteen months with the Eighth Army, and had made of it one of the most successful instruments in British military history. Nor, despite all the setbacks, could one overlook that it had advanced some six hundred miles up the Italian peninsula. But now for the time being there was a pause in its march. Germans alone the Eighth could defeat. When the mountains and the winter were added it was just too much. Over on the Fifth Army side it was much the same thing. At first the projected date for the capture of Rome was November, then it was Christmas, then January or February.

There was a fierce encounter on the Volturno and through the neighboring canals. At one moment both sides were attacking simultaneously across the river. Boats and rafts met in mid-stream and engaged. Germans reached the southern bank only to find that the British and Americans had landed on the northern bank behind them. Down at the mouth of the river another group of German boats was picked off from the southern bank, and the drowning wounded men were washed away by the current into the sea. A party of British ducks attempting to make a sea landing above the river fouled a sandbank. Everywhere machine-gunning and sniping was going on through the reeds along the canal banks. Anything served to get the men across the water. They lashed boards to empty petrol cans and paddled over. Waterproofed tanks plunged down to their turrets in the yellow water, and were hauled by cranes up the slippery banks on the other side. The rain poured steadily. Soon the river was in flood, and as the British infantry floundered about in

The slimy, deepening mud that follows every army into Europe.

the mud the Germans fired down on them with mortars from the inland hills. Every valley was a stronghold and had to be assaulted with artillery fire and flanking attacks.

Large numbers of tanks had been landed in Italy, but these became increasingly useless. It was impossible country for armored fighting: excellent country for concealing anti-tank guns. The tanks in scores lay idle under the olive trees.

An extraordinarily polyglot army had now come under Alexander's command. Driving out from Naples toward the front you would pass Frenchmen and dark Moroccans, British and Americans. There were even American Japanese troops, and many Negroes. Russian and Brazilian deputations arrived. Then towards the Adriatic there were Canadians and Poles, New Zealanders and Indians wedged among the English. An Italian brigade was put in the line. Everyone was prepared to scoff at it. In point of fact the Italians took four hundred casualties in their first rush, and brought back two 88-millimeter guns.

But this was a situation in which bravery alone could never bring a decision. The Volturno crossed, there was still the Garigliano and the Pontine Marshes to the north which had now been flooded by the Germans. One of our forward divisional headquarters was set up in the stone castle at Sessa. Looking out from the ramparts one saw all the battlefield below: the gray sea on the left, the German entrenchments on the other side of the river, and then the Cassino monastery and the fabulous blackcloth of the Apennines rising tier on tier into the snow-line and the heavy sky.

Before we could get at Cassino we had to take a nearer height, Monte Camino, which also had a monastery on its crest. The Monte Camino battle was typical of all this fighting, an ominous warning of what was going to happen at Cassino. The Guards got half-way up and were thrown off. In December they tried again. The guns fired out of the hidden valleys to the south. You could watch the shells bursting up the mountainside until everything appeared to be engulfed in drifting smoke; and then the bombers came in. One was able to sit on the opposite mountain and watch it all with the same impersonal feeling with which one goes to the races or a theater. It was when they went down into the valley directly below Camino monastery that the whole thing became startlingly personal, and you were confronted with the horror behind the vivid spectacle.

An earthen track zig-zagged up the sheer face of the mountain to the monastery. There were no trees, only coarse grass, and so the enemy on top had a perfect field of fire. Rain water was cascading down the track at such a pace that it unseated boulders and loose rocks, and these went careering to the bottom. There were two processions on the track, one going up, the other coming down, and the whole of this moving human frieze was under shell-fire. You could see it all from the bottom if you arched your neck. The upward travelers were mostly Italian mule teams carrying blankets and boxes of ammunition. Then there were single soldiers, each one with a heavy box of rations on his back, and they were bent double by the incline. As they lifted themselves upward step by step their faces were only a few inches from the mud. And then there were the reinforcements, the infantry in their camouflaged waterproof gas-capes, the rain streaming off their steel helmets, their hands gone blue with cold. They climbed numbly, contemplating each step, each few yards in front of them, since no one there could compre-hend the whole battle or the worse discomforts that were to be added. Each man found it enough merely to contain himself, to keep himself alive and moving.

The stretcher bearers were on the downward journey, eight men to a stretcher. They carried the stretchers on their shoulders and they slithered rather than walked. Often they dislodged a boulder, and the whole party wobbled uneasily. For the most part the patients, their blood mixing with the pools of water on the canvas stretchers, would be held at an angle just short of overbalancing.

Every minute or two a shell came down. They hit first on one side of the track, then the other, then in the angles of the sharp bends. Whenever a shell hit the track itself a gap would open up in the procession. At first this gap was filled with smoke. Then as the smoke cleared you would see the fallen men scattered about on the steep grass and the mules stampeding. And then the gap would close again as others came down and others came up. At the top on the exposed slopes in front of the monastery the men lay in slit trenches and these were half-filled with water. There comes a time when the mind will react no more to cold and danger. Those who had been exposed up there for two days and nights slept waist deep in the water. In utter weariness they lost all sense of time and place and even perhaps the sense of hope. Only the sense of pain re-mained, of constantly reiterated pain that invaded sleep and waited for the end of sleep to increase. For these soldiers the risk of war had passed out of consciousness and was replaced by the misery and discomfort of war, which in the end is worse than anything. Fear is not the worst thing. You recover quickly from it. It leaves no scar.

To many of us who have been merely observers of war it has seemed that risk is often no bad thing. I have seen soldiers going up to the front-line for the first time, and they were afraid. They had no direct fear of being wounded. They were afraid of the unknown, the mystery represented by the front-line. This you could read clearly enough in the dread in their faces. It is a dread of going up to the abyss and looking over into the unknown, and of risking the chance of falling over into the unknown. As he goes up to the front the man has to say: "Now I gamble everything. I put all my life and everything I hope to do and all that part of everyone I love—I put all this in the way of death. I stake it all."

Then later when you see the man return safely he appears to have gained in stature. He has been up to the edge and looked over and come away. There is tide upon tide of happiness as he takes back his life and all the things he hopes to do with it. And having regained what he staked he seems to be a more considerable being, and to have gathered some profit from the risks he took.

It is the sort of experience that possibly women have when they voluntarily risk themselves to bear children, and having been up to the unknown, having faced the mystery, they come away immeasurably comforted. You might even argue that in peace time men are too seldom obliged to take risks, and that their lives might be clarified if from time to time they gambled everything.

In the war that we had seen leading up to this moment on Monte Camino it was quite different. Men were too often asked to risk their lives in sudden sharp moments and usually for no clearly comprehended reason. The pilot who went out again and again over enemy country was too much in the way of death, and the intervals between his risk were too narrow. It was a constant wonder to see men keep their normality and go back again and again. The thing that finally broke them was not the risk but experiences such as this at Camino. Exposure. Cold. The overstraining of the body over long periods. Bad food. Lack of sleep. These things did the damage. It was when the men were put to do too much that they suffered. Here at Camino a few soldiers, just for a short period, were put to do too much. And yet they won the hill. And presently they went on again, the ones that survived, to do the same thing all over again at Cassino.

4. Naples to Rome

Naples was the reverse side of the picture, the peace behind the war. It was the first great city of German Europe to fall into the hands of the Allies. Here was the prelude to Athens and Paris and Brussels and all the other capitals. Here at last we could discover what life had been like under the rule of the Axis.

As we drove over the Sorrento peninsula and caught sight of the city for the first time it appeared that nothing had changed. The black cone of Vesuvius smoking gracefully on the right. The island of Capri serenely floating beyond the mouth of the bay. The crenelated city spilled along the shore, and that same mesmerizing blueness in the water. Sunshine and orange groves. Brilliant creepers on the tumbling walls. The enervating atmosphere of a long lazy summer's afternoon.

As we drove through Castellamare and Pompeii the crowd thickened steadily along the road. On the outskirts of Naples itself it was one tumultuous mob of screaming, hysterical people, and this continued all the way into the center of the city. They had been cruelly bombed. There had been spasmodic street fighting for a week. And now they stood on the pavement and leaned out of their balcony windows screaming at the Allied soldiers and the passing trucks. They screamed in relief and in pure hysteria. In tens of thousands the dirty ragged children kept crying for biscuits and sweets. When we stopped the jeep we were immediately surrounded and overwhelmed. Thrusting hands plucked at our clothing. *Pane. Biscotti. Sigarette.* In every direction there was a wall of emaciated, hungry, dirty faces.

I had had the notion that the people would be hostile, or resentful, or perhaps reserved. I had expected that they would indicate in some way the feelings they had had as enemies in the past three years.

But there was no question of war or enmity here. Hunger governed all. There were some who in their need fawned and groveled. They thrust their dribbling children forward to whine and plead. When a soldier threw out a handful of sweets there was a mad rush to the pavement, and women and men and children beat at each other as they scrambled on the cobblestones.

Day by day the pimps and the black marketeers multiplied along the Via Roma. "You want nice girl?" "Biftek, spaghetti. Verra cheap." "Good brandy. Only fife hundred lire." "Beautiful *signorina*." Every ten yards down the street a dark little man would slide up to you and pluck you by the sleeve. Children of ten and twelve were being offered in the brothels. Raw spirit mixed with flavoring was sold in dirty bottles with fake labels. Every form of imitation jewelry came out on the pavements. Six-year-old boys were pressed into the business of selling obscene postcards; of selling their sisters, themselves, anything. Army cigarettes and chocolates were stolen by the hundredweight and resold at fantastic prices. Vehicles were stolen at the rate of something like sixty or seventy a night (not always by the Italians). The looting of especially precious things like tires became an established business. Knifing skirmishes in the back streets became a nightly affair. In the whole list of sordid human vices none I think were overlooked in Naples during those first few months.

What we were witnessing in fact was the moral collapse of a people. They had no pride any more, or any dignity. The animal struggle for existence governed everything. Food. That was the only thing that mattered. Food for the children. Food for yourself. Food at the cost of any abasement and depravity. And after food a little warmth and shelter.

I am writing here of the mob in Naples. It would be grossly unfair to say that all Italians, especially the peasants, had fallen so far. Nevertheless a rottenness ran through the country. Under Fascism a vast black market, and an incredible network of bribery, had been erected into an economic system. This rickety structure now began to collapse. Had not the Allies backed the currency there would have been instant inflation, and even as things were the lira was bust on the international market. It was pegged at four hundred to the pound, but in actual fact it was worth nothing like that. Only goods mattered—mattered more than human life—and now the means of distributing the goods was being battered to pieces by the war. All over Italy railways and bridges, ports and cities, factories and dumps were being destroyed. And this process of disintegration was going to get steadily worse the longer the Germans fought in Italy.

Side by side with all this corruption and mismanagement the luxury trade had been flourishing in the country right through the war. It was astonishing to see the Naples shops stocked with gloves and jewelry and non-essential gadgets of every kind. Italy had never begun to organize for war with one-quarter or one-tenth of the seriousness of England. You could still buy radio sets and electric equipment and all manner of articles built of material like rubber which is essential for war production. Silk stockings cost a pound and they could be bought freely along with scent and cosmetics. As for the rationing system, it was simply chaotic. You might be able to obtain your tickets all right. But it was quite another matter to try and make your legitimate purchases with them. To live you had to deal on the black market.

As for the usual social services and facilities—the buses and the trains, the hospitals and the sewage, the water and fuel supplies, the telephone and the post offices—all these had been getting steadily more inefficient and hopeless since the day Italy turned on France. Corrupt little officials strutted about in every government building, and all the Italian genius for invention could not rescue the people from increasing hardship.

It had not needed the Allied invasion to throw the social economy of the country out of gear; it was steadily decaying of its own accord. And yet this was an Axis partner, not a country beaten and occupied by the Germans. For three years Mussolini had been on the winning side. He was lord of the Balkans. He even occupied part of France. Italy had every reason to fare better than any country in Europe save Germany. Its government had been in office for two decades. And now here was Naples broken and half-starving. In addition, something more precious than buildings and bridges was gone; the spirit of the people themselves. They had no will any more. They were reduced to the final humiliation of begging from the people they had tried to kill.

For anyone who loved Italy it was a bitter experience to come to Naples. The traditional talents of the people, their charm and generosity, seemed for a little to have vanished in the savage and abject struggle for existence. I met quite a number of distinguished and honorable Italians in Naples, good haters of Fascism for many years, and the thing that they saw clearly at last was this: "We failed to revolt. Everything had derived from that. Nothing we could have suffered in a revolt against Fascism would have been as bad as this."

For the victor, of course, life in Naples was fine, even downright gay. One of the loveliest theaters in the world, the San Carlo Opera House, was untouched by the bombing. A really good company was playing *The Barber of Seville, Lucia di Lammermoor and Il Trovatore*. The sun streamed down. As one lunched at the black market restaurants on the quays below the Excelsior Hotel musicians roamed from table to table. You could drive up to the crest of Vesuvius or see an American movie in the city. A regular steamer service took soldiers on leave across to Capri.

Capri had remained a curious little nodule of lotus-eating through the war. The same international society, a little diminished, had continued somehow through the trouble, although with the slightly beaten air of a worn-out roué. On the island I met British residents who had continued in their villas unmolested. The good old traditions survived. A copy of *South Wind* in every tourist's knapsack and genuine coral in the shops. The horses with the nodding plumes to run you up to Anacapri or down to the Piccola Marina. The Quisisana. The Funicular. It was as though someone had placed a glass bowl over the whole confection in 1939, and now that the bowl was lifted again the people came out, a little jaded, like a railway sandwich, but quite genuine Capri stock.

One day we sailed on an apple boat across to Ischia, the other Neapolitan island, which produces the better wine of the region, labeled Lacrima Christi, or possibly Orvieto, according to the caprice of the dealer. From Ischia we saw the German planes come in to raid the Allied ships packed in Naples harbor. These were probably the most pictorial raids of the whole war. Every ship opened up with its guns until there were a hundred necklaces of red tracer bullets over Naples bay. They mounted in a cone, and the German bombers, with the Allied fighters in pursuit, dived in and out of the barrage and the searchlights. In the background Vesuvius flamed soberly.

In Naples music ran through every restaurant. A huge pulsing crowd moved up and down the Via Roma among the bright silks and the flowers and the pimps. The whole motif was that of a gaudy tropical flower that springs out of decay and smells rotten in its heart. Seen from Sorrento or the heights of Policeto the place seemed to grow more beautiful hour by hour. Every night a sunset of breathless theatrical color broke over Capri. Every morning there were the same flamboyant banners of light. Vesuvius was never still. Sometimes it lay in purple mists, and you could see nothing of the freshly ruined ruins of Pompeii in the foothills. The volcano indeed was working furiously towards its great outbreak in the spring, when red streams of lava overwhelmed the houses on the upper slopes. Already on Christmas night it was erupting. Two separate runnels of lava pouring out of opposite sides of the crater ran together a little farther down the mountain and made a brilliant red V in the night sky. And always that constantly renewed plume of smoke was washed back and forth by the wind across the summit, taking its color from the changing color of the sky.

In Naples typhus broke out. Through November and December the disease took hold and began to develop into an epidemic. The unwashed, cold and hungry people died very quickly. One hundred cases. Then two hundred. The carts came round at night and took the bodies away. The American army medical staff rushed drugs to Naples. They visited the people in the air-raid shelters and sprayed them with anti-typhus powder. Stations for giving injections were set up all over the city. You could not get the people washed, since the water supply had broken down among the ruins where many people were living. In January at last the epidemic began to come under control. One good thing had emerged from the scare. No British or American soldier was infected, although they rubbed shoulders with the Neapolitans every day. The typhus injection which every soldier had received was proved effective.

Then a thing much more serious visited the army. Gonorrhea in a new and most virulent form began to spread at alarming speed. Even the new drugs like M & B appeared to be incapable of resisting it. The Americans had set up prophylactic stations throughout the city, but not all the soldiers could be induced to visit them. Several hundred new cases were reported every week, and before Christmas we were taking more casualties in Naples through gonorrhea than we were through enemy action on the whole of the front-line.

All the roads leading into the city were plastered with notices warning the soldiers against the disease. At length the epidemic became so serious that only those men who had jobs in the city were allowed to enter. And so in the end the thing was brought under control.

The German time bombs brought still another horror to the city. They mined all places like the telephone exchange and the post office, where considerable numbers of people were likely to be hurt or killed. The explosions went off without the slightest warning as a rule, and there were very few safeguards which could be taken, as most of the mines were laid secretly at night by the last enemy soldiers to leave the city. In effect the explosions were rather like the V.2's which fell on London and northern Europe much later in the war.

I remember the gardener in our villa above the town reported to us that he had been hearing a constant ticking noise at the foot of the cliff beneath the bridge that carried the main road round the coast. One of our officers jumped into a car and called on the bomb disposal squad. "You will have to wait," they told him. "We will put you on the list of suspicious noises. We have a hundred and fifty jobs on hand already." Eventually they came and took two big charges away from under the bridge.

It was the impersonality, the cold pre-calculation of the mining that so astonished one at first. Many of us had only known the German army in Africa, where the war had been reduced to a straight military contest between the forces in the field. In general the Germans had behaved very well. There had been no Gestapo. But now something quite different was happening behind the German lines. One could easily understand their mining the roads and ports on their way of retreat, since that was a military device. But now for the first time in our experience they were killing civilians for no military advantage but out of a simple desire for killing, and possibly for revenge.

A hundred atrocity stories were reported, most of them greatly exaggerated, some quite true. At the announcement of the Italian armistice the German soldiers had, quite understandably, reacted strongly against their former allies. Houses and shops were entered and looted. Watches and jewelry were seized from women in the streets. Italians were impressed into labor gangs. None of all this is very remarkable in an operational zone. You cannot submit men to the brutality of war and then expect them to come out of the line and behave like little gentlemen. But the German command deliberately fostered the hatred of the Italians. The soldiers found they could go to further and further extremes without any official reprimand. If an Italian peasant refused to give you a chicken you simply shot him and took the chicken. If someone sniped at you from a village you simply lined up the inhabitants and shot them. And then if you felt like it you burned the village. I do not say that at this stage the German army in the west was entirely committed to this savagery, but here and there quite definitely the assassin complex began to break out. And there was a special viciousness in it since the Italians had once purported to be their friends. The senseless burning of books in Naples was part of the same thing.

All through the war up to this point the reactions of the Allied soldiers towards the enemy, and the reactions of his people at home, had been developing on broadly different lines. The divergence was particularly marked among the British. Every time any of us went home to England we were struck by the intensity of the hatred of the enemy. A number of things seemed to have contributed to this feeling—the bombing, the endless difficulties of life occasioned by the war like the blackout, the anxiety for the safety of the men abroad. Then too the people were under a daily barrage of propaganda. Since they had no direct physical contact with the Germans, the German soldier was little by little invested with a monstrosity and savagery that was almost inhuman.

The experiences of the soldier in the field up to this point were,

A marble bed for the night; a soldier sleeps in an old Roman amphitheater.

in the main, quite different. As soon as he met a German prisoner he observed that to all outward appearances he was a normal human being. A bit pompous perhaps, and wooden, but still just another man. It was rather gratifying to have fought him and caught him. Owing to a very thorough lack of newspapers and radio sets the average soldier viewed the enemy freshly and at first hand, and also in a very limited way. The war for the soldier was not a thing of imagined fears but a very simple mechanical process. The enemy was a defined and exact animal who had to be beaten by certain physical means.

Then too it was a very different thing being bombed in the field to being bombed at home. In the field you did not care much, and you certainly hated the Germans no more, if a bomb fell over the hill and destroyed a foreign village. The main thing was that it had not hit you personally or the others in your platoon. At home every bomb counted. It was a bomb on England. It expanded the hatred.

I am not speaking now of the soldier's feelings at the height of a battle (the mixture of desperation, fear, anger and hatred is quite definite on the firing-line), but of the average overall reaction to the Germans, up to this time. In a word, it had none of the acidity and passion which one found at home. It was usually a waste of time for an officer to bluster to his men about the "Boches," and call them murderers. He got far better results by simply referring to the enemy as though he were an abstract evil which had to be destroyed. And after the fight was over the reaction of the average soldier on seeing the prisoners was to think: "Well, the poor dumb beggars, they certainly bought it. They've had it." And he would hand out his cigarettes.

As we went into Europe we found more and more that it was the civilians who hated the Germans most, not the soldiers. But about this time the men in Alexander's armies began to notice a difference in some sections of the German army. Whenever they over-ran areas where the young SS, the Hitler Youth or the Gestapo had been they found the unmistakable evidence of atrocities—rooms where civilians had been tortured, the courtyards where firing squads operated, the houses looted and bodies lying about. The number of atrocities was in direct proportion to the condition of the German army; where its situation was desperate the atrocities increased. This developed into a general rule during the whole retreat of the enemy through Europe.

The effect of it upon the soldier was to bring his attitude round towards that of his people at home. It was a slow process, but it began here in Italy and accelerated. The soldier began to hate the Gestapo in the same vicarious and violent way as the people in England did. The sight of the civilian bodies in a Naples street after a time-bomb explosion made him angry. The old feeling "We have got to fight for liberty and honor and all the rest of it" was replaced for short intervals by the more animal reaction that demanded revenge.

All through this period the front-line was only an hour or two away from Naples by car. The generals had settled their head-quarters in the vast and ugly palace at Caserta, and just beyond that were the Germans. Flowers and songs and women in Naples. Men in their last extremity on the Garigliano. The contrast was almost too much to be comprehended. And now to make the contrast more extreme the winter settled down in full earnest. Half the modern, elaborate devices of war became useless: the burden fell on the infantry, the men crawling in the mud.

The generals gave up all prospect of Rome by January. They hatched instead a plan for February. Eisenhower, meeting us one day at Caserta, said: "We must go on through the winter. There will be no lull. Whenever we see a chance of using some new tactic, or taking the enemy by surprise, then we will put it into effect." The Anzio landing was to be the new tactic. Instead of smashing head-on interminably against the mountains we were going to take the enemy in the rear. We would land several divisions at Anzio, a

Cassino and the Anzio Bridgehead

gently graded and unflooded stretch of country just south of Rome. The troops would advance *not northward to capture Rome* but east, in order to cut the Frosinone and the coastal roads behind the German army. At the same time a massed frontal attack would be launched on Cassino by the main bulk of the Fifth Army. The Germans would be caught in a nutcracker. They would retreat from Cassino only to find themselves blocked in the rear. Somewhere round Frosinone they would be destroyed. Then would follow the march on Rome, the pursuit northward. That was the plan. Those were the hopes. Some eighty miles divided the Anzio landing from the Cassino front, but things would go rapidly once Cassino fell. It was important to get a link-up of the two Allied forces within a week, so that the Anzio troops could be supplied. Lorries and dumps were held ready to get supplies through to them as soon as the road was clear.

The First German Parachute Division was garrisoned at Cassino. Upon their insensate bravery the whole plan foundered. Other things helped to set back the operation, but essentially it was the fanatical morale of those youths who from infancy had believed their lives to be dedicated to Adolf Hitler. The depth and passion of that feeling was something that was never quite understood among the Allies. Nevertheless it prevented the necessary junction of General Clark's two forces, and condemned the army to four bitter and unavailing months of exposure. Some of the very finest of our troops, like the New Zealanders, battered uselessly against positions that normally would have fallen.

Cassino was bombed and shelled into rubble. The German parachutists remained underground while the barrage was on, and emerged to fight as soon as it was over. We had not quite realized in advance the effect of heavy bombing. When the tanks tried to support the infantry attack they found themselves blocked by great craters and piles of rubble. Then too the infantry had been withdrawn well behind the bomb-line, and by the time they came up to it after the barrage the Germans were already waiting for them with sighted machine-guns. Day after day the battle went on, and the Germans continued their act of blind faith. They lived underground, and emerged in packets to die.

At Anzio nothing at all went wrong at first. Indeed it went far better than one could have hoped. The coast was not heavily mined, and the Germans had stationed barely a brigade of second-rate troops to garrison that spot. The landing was almost bloodless. Surprise was complete, so complete indeed that there is some justification for saying that we surprised ourselves. The first scheduled

Monte Cassino.

stage was won so easily that the local commander might have been justified in thinking that it would go on being easy. At all events the first day appears to have been given up merely to consolidation, and little attempt was made to run ahead of schedule by crossing at once to the Alban hills and getting astride the Frosinone Road. Against all our hopes, Kesselring was not stampeded by the threat in his rear. He appears to have seen all along that the Anzio landing was never intended to take Rome by storm, and that the real issues had to be fought out at Cassino. *He immediately reinforced the Cassino area,* instead of adopting the more obvious and safer course of ordering a withdrawal. At the same time he brought down part of his Rome garrison and sealed off the Anzio bridgehead. Even the landing-vessels came under gun-fire from the Alban hills, and during the whole of the Anzio period the soldiers were overlooked by the enemy. Once their original landing impetus was gone, and the prospect of a link-up with Cassino began to fade away, they never had a real chance to break out. They had to be supplied for months on end by sea, and this put an immense strain upon the Allied shipping which was already wanted for the French invasion. The bridgehead had its early hours of crisis more or less on the lines of Salerno. The troops were forced to draw back, and once more the naval gunnery came in to tide them through the worst moments. For a while the Luftwaffe with its shorter distances was matching our own air force over Anzio.

And so it went, right through the spring, while Alexander regrouped and drew in the best of the Eighth Army to buttress the Fifth for one more decisive battle. His May attack finally went in with immense weight. The parachutists at last were steam-rollered out of their rubble fortress. Cassino dominated the whole valley. Once it fell two things had to happen immediately—the link-up with Anzio and the fall of Rome, which never was and probably never will be defensible, since it can be by-passed on either side.

With nice timing Alexander entered the city on June 4th—two days before the event which most people on earth were awaiting—the landing on France. And then began the process which Winston Churchill once described as "dragging the hot rake of war up the length of the Italian peninsula."

Phase one of the collapse of western Europe was over. Corsica and Sardinia had fallen in the process to the Fighting French, without a struggle. Allied ships could ply freely through the Mediterranean. There were many loose ends, many unsatisfactory complications. Still, we had shaken loose the western peg of the Balkans, and they were ripe for collapse when the Russians swept through Rumania

Bagpipes in the Piazza Venizia, Rome.

and Hungary in the autumn. The eventual British return to Athens and Greece was scarcely opposed.

The story of that lamentable and bitter skirmish between the British and the Greeks in Athens in the following winter has no place in this book. It was essentially a forerunner of the problems of the post-war years. But here again with the Greek crisis one notes our appalling political ignorance of the countries we were liberating. To those of us who were living abroad it seemed that the heads of the Allied governments in London were incapable of grasping the fact that time had not stood still during the four years of the German occupation in western and southern Europe.

In point of fact, new political leaders had sprung up all over Europe; underground fighters, underground politicians. A huge and complicated network of political tendencies was developing, and neither the exiled governments in London and Cairo, nor the Foreign Office and the State Department were fully in touch. Indeed, it seemed that there was a kind of "king complex" in London. Zog of Albania, Victor Emmanuel of Italy, Peter of Jugoslavia, George of Greece; all these were jostling for position, and getting a good hearing in an unreal world, which had very little connection with the helpless human beings living in Hitler's Europe. Already in the summer of 1943 most of these pre-war rulers and their courts were hopelessly out of date. It was not that the peoples opposed them so much personally, but the whole idea of kingship in Europe had become associated with defeatism and corruption and instability. In the occupied democracies too, Poland and France especially, it was obvious that new currents had been set in motion by the underground forces. The leaders of these forces were clearly going to demand a place in the post-war governments. Yet except in the case of France this point seemed to have been neglected in London. And so it was only under the overwhelming pressure of military events—and riots and street fights and demonstrations—that Britain and America were forced to drop the outmoded kings one by one. Victor Emmanuel went easily enough, although it took several months' struggle to get him out. After all he was the ruler of an enemy country and so presumably we did not care so much about him. But the bitter and confused debate over George of Greece and Peter of Jugoslavia dragged on and on.

Mr. Eden had declared that he was going to reform the Foreign Office, so that its representatives abroad would be better fitted to send information to Whitehall. But there was no evidence of this. Wherever the Allied troops went British diplomats of the old school came in behind them. There were only one or two notable exceptions—Mr. Harold Macmillan, a newcomer to diplomacy, was given a roving commission through the Mediterranean, and showed a most unusual vigor and freshness. Duff Cooper was making a favorable start with the French. Possibly this point is not of great importance, since the development of transport makes it possible for cabinet ministers to travel quickly to any point of crisis, and the function of the ambassador becomes less and less.

No one can pretend that our early attempts to establish government in Italy were a great success. It is true that Count Sforza had more or less ruined his own position in Italy, but no one enjoyed the spectacle of his being tipped ruthlessly overboard on the orders of London. The Bonomi government was a government of exhaustion, a cohesion that came out of weakness, a thing that could never be permanent. And so, with the war slowly ravishing the peninsula, and Italy at the bottom of the list for food priorities, the country began to suffer the cruelest sort of revenge for its fatal weakness in allowing Mussolini to have ruled for so long. Before the winter of 1944 set in it was apparent that Italy was going to become one of

View from the Ponte Vecchio, Florence; the Santa Trinita bridge, perhaps the most beautiful bridge in the world, lies shattered in the foreground.

the worst sufferers of Europe, second only to Holland and Germany. It was not the war, it was the aftermath of war that destroyed Italy. Hunger and the lack of housing did more damage than high explosive.

Many of us who followed the Italian campaign still think it was wasteful, and the insensate battering of the Gothic Line in the north appears to have been especially futile. It was a campaign which never had a definite and reasonable military object in view. It could end only in the Alps, the worst possible place. Still, you could not say that the campaign was a failure by any means, and apart from human lives and the Italian cities the only major loss was that of time.

Four countries which had declared war on the Allies—Italy, Hungary, Bulgaria and Rumania—succumbed about this time and all of them revealed one common thing: their peoples had not wanted to fight. They had been committed to the war by their governments, and their sole desire was to reverse their governments' decision and escape the consequences of it. Only the Turks, in virtue of their geographical position, had been clever enough to keep out. And now only one prospect lay before the Balkans, and that was something quite new: the domination of Russia. Everywhere one went in Italy and the Mediterranean one found a profound fear of the Russians, usually based on religious grounds. But now there was no alternative. The Russians had arrived and were in possession. They showed every sign of coming on farther. Even if they withdrew their troops after the war it was apparent that the Russians were going to have a strong zone of influence west of the Black Sea and round the vital oil wells of Ploesti. And there was just a chance that they might prevent the otherwise inevitable landslide of the Balkans into mass hunger and misery and outright civil war.

The Second Quarter

COLLAPSE IN THE NORTH: FRANCE

5. England

Autumn 1943. Teheran. Stalin, Churchill and Roosevelt meeting together agreed that the Anglo-American forces should invade northern Europe in the summer of 1944. This was to be co-incidental with a further series of Russian attacks from the east.

Zones of operation were discussed at this and later meetings. Russia was to have all the eastern approaches to Germany (Finland, the Baltic States, Poland, Rumania), and eventually occupy the eastern half of the Reich. Britain as a naval power was to have the northern seaboard of Europe, a stretch of coast running from Normandy through Belgium, Holland and Germany to Denmark. To the United States fell the central regions of France and Germany. Berlin was to be international.

In addition to this the British and Americans divided their joint zones into two halves. The British commander, General Maitland Wilson, was to control the Mediterranean basin, with the British General Alexander as his chief executive officer in the field. The American General Eisenhower would command the invasion in the north, with the British General Montgomery as his field commander during the opening stages. The commands were closely interlocked. British and Americans alternated in the high offices. French, Polish and other Allied forces were fitted into the scheme.

The predominant strength was to come from America. Already she had recruited, equipped and partly shipped to England four separate armies, the First, Third, Seventh and Ninth, with attendant naval and air forces. In addition she was sending vast dumps of food, fuel and ammunition, great quantities of rolling stock. A political and propaganda group was attached to Eisenhower's command. America was prepared to move into Europe on a scale that

Conference at Teheran, autumn 1943; Stalin, Roosevelt and Churchill planned the Second Front.

completely eclipsed her intervention earlier in the century. Something like three million Americans were earmarked for the conquest, and they were being built up into the most effective striking force the world had ever known. For the first time since the beginning of the war the United States' contribution in the field would exceed the British, and very greatly.

This American invasion, following upon the rise of the U.S.S.R., completely upset the balance of power as Europe had known it for the past two centuries. The old tripartite balance—Germany, France and England—had gone, or at least was about to go. Britain now took her place in the new triangular command, with Russia and the U.S.A., and it was evident that these three would not only conduct the final battles of the war but settle the future of Europe and the world as well. Teheran had begun something of incalculable importance, and was one of the really significant conferences of the century. It was also significant that it should have been conducted by three statesmen who enjoyed immense, almost dictatorial, powers inside their own countries. All three were very much stronger figures than their predecessors in the last war. Stalin and Churchill were firmly seated in indefinite command, and there was good reason to believe that Roosevelt would carry his November elections. The world was about to be dominated not only by three nations but by three personalities, a thing that had scarcely happened since the time of the Roman triumvirs.

For the moment both the U.S.A. and Britain were militarily in a weaker position than Russia. As a sort of entrance examination to the new triumvirate they had first to carry their invasion of northern Europe. Every priority was now given to that adventure.

When the conference broke up, Eisenhower and his chief of staff, Bedell Smith, were in Algiers, and Montgomery and his chief of staff, de Guingand, were at Vasto on the Italian Adriatic coast. It was decided that Smith and de Guingand should travel ahead of their two chiefs to England in order to study the invasion plans and be in a position to report on Eisenhower's and Montgomery's arrival. The British General Morgan and a staff had already been at work on a plan for several years. When they got to England the two chiefs of staff took copies of this plan and went off to separate offices to study it. After a preliminary survey, both de Guingand and Smith quite independently reached the same conclusion: the Morgan plan would have to be greatly intensified.

The conferences began. Instantly the navy rejected the idea that we should land on both sides of the Cherbourg peninsula, since the small invasion craft would be exposed to the Atlantic gales as well as the Atlantic tides. Other alternatives and combinations of alternatives were discussed. It was indeed the most difficult and complicated problem which any commander could be asked to face. In that spring the coming invasion loomed as the most hazardous adventure in all military history. Quite apart from the imponderable and capricious conditions of nature—the tides and the moon and the weather—there were all the considerations of the air force and the navy, the questions of supply, the defensive measures of the enemy. The broad essentials were easily forced upon the conference. It had to be France. It had to be the summer. One after another the other imperatives were grouped around that time and place. And in the end it was decided that the landing would take place on one side of the Cherbourg peninsula, directly across the Channel from England. An indefinite week in May or June was decided upon as a provisional date: the actual day would be known as D Day.

Once ashore and through the Atlantic Wall, the soldiers would fan out into a bridgehead roughly eighty miles long and twenty miles deep, running from the neighborhood of Caen to the base of the Cherbourg peninsula; the Americans on the right, the British on the left, in roughly equal numbers. Then while the British held Caen against the expected enemy counter-attack the Americans would wheel north to capture Cherbourg, and the build-up of supplies would begin. Once Cherbourg was working and the flow of supplies across the beaches was deemed adequate, the whole force would pivot on to a north-south line reaching inland from Caen. This would give the American follow-up army, the Third under Patton, a chance to slip round the corner westward into Brittany and seize the vital port of Brest and its satellites. Then with these ports in operation the combined armies would wheel round Caen once more, and advance north-eastward upon Paris and the Seine. It was expected that a battle would be fought on the Seine, and then again the Allies would surge forward through northern France until they reached the German border in Belgium and Luxembourg. A schedule of dates or "phase lines" was worked out for each stage of the campaign. It was expected that we would touch the Rhine about one hundred and twenty-five days after the original landing—sometime in October. During this period the American Seventh Army (including French troops) would land in southern France in the neighborhood of Toulon, and proceed northward up the Rhône valley to the Swiss border.

This was planning on a cosmic scale, and the key to the whole thing of course was—ports. The proposition that we should directly storm the northern ports like Calais on D Day was rejected on the grounds that they were too strongly defended. Nevertheless, we had to have ports: temporary ports for the first few weeks, permanent ports for the autumn and winter. As everybody knows, there are big tides in the English Channel, and on the flat portions of the Normandy and Brittany coast the sea runs out for hundreds of yards. It was therefore necessary to construct artificial ports (known by the code name of "Mulberry"), and tow them across the Channel from England: huge chains of linked pontoons which would be protected by sinking lines of ships and concrete blocks about them. The seaside hamlet of Arromanches, just north of Bayeux, was selected as the site for this extraordinary engineering adventure, and other sites for the American landing were chosen farther west. It was judged possible to get some thirty or forty thousand tons across the beaches in this way every day.

For the assault landing the hours of daybreak were obviously best. It was also necessary for the troops to be put ashore at high tide, so that they would not have to cross a long exposed stretch of beach under fire. The first week in June offered these conditions of semi-darkness and high tide. Gradually the planners began to work towards that definite date. The vast business was begun of getting the men and supplies across from America and distributing them along with the British at the English ports opposite France. Secrecy was all. Bit by bit England was sealed off from the world. Diplomatic bags going out of the country were searched. Plane services to neutral countries were stopped. The traffic to Ireland was rigidly controlled. But secrecy could not be complete. We could have tactical but not strategical surprise. On a pure basis of common sense the Germans were able to calculate that we were coming during the spring or the summer, and probably to northern France or the Low Countries. They had also to take in the possibility of subsidiary landings at such places as Norway, Denmark, the Bay of Biscay and the Gulf of Lion, even on northern Germany itself.

Let us just for a moment look at things from the German side. They had already made their disposition of forces for 1944: some forty divisions for France, about the same number for central, northern and southern Europe; the rest, about 200 divisions, for the Russian front. What should they do to meet the critical summer? How should they retract their line so that they could meet the main Allied thrusts with the greatest possible strength? Clearly they could not guard all Europe. They had to retrench somewhere. The most obvious places to give up were Finland, the Balkans, Norway, Italy, the Baltic States and Poland, more or less in that order. This scheme of retrenchment would leave them two main lines to defend —one in the east in central Poland, and the other in the west in northern France, Holland and Belgium.

Having accepted this appreciation, the German High Command had next to decide which front needed most of the troops and supplies. Clearly again it was Russia. The bulk of the Wehrmacht had to keep back the Red tidal wave. And just as clearly the priorities in reinforcements had now to go to the west to meet the invasion menace. It was arguable in Berlin in the late winter of 1943 that if the Anglo-American invasion could be repelled, then the chances of stalemate were certain and even the prospects of victory might grow bright again. Roosevelt might lose his election. Americans might grow tired of the European war and turn to the Pacific (the American people were more interested in that anyway). Lend-lease to Russia and Britain might dwindle. America might abandon Europe to her own mess. England was very tired. The flying bomb and the rocket were being secretly prepared, and there was some prospect that they might render southern England uninhabitable. And while Goebbels presented a version of this optimism on the radio, the German High Command laid its plans. Hold in the east. Throw back the invasion in the west. Then turn back for a decisive battle with the Russians.

For some years France had been used as a sort of pool and training camp for the German army. Tired divisions were sent there for rest and re-grouping and re-equipment. There was a continuous convexion current of soldiers around Europe: battered divisions coming out of the line in Russia, re-fitting in France and then returning east. In the early spring of 1944 the Germans halted this current. The soldiers continued to flow into France; but there they stayed. They rested, re-equipped and then took up positions to ward off the expected Anglo-American invasion.

Marshal Rundstedt was in command of the vital defenses of northern France. His view of the situation was this: we cannot hope to prevent a landing. And once ashore, the Anglo-American build-up under their immense air cover will be so rapid that they will force their way across France. We must be prepared to give up France, and conserve our army for a major battle on the Rhine. In this way our army will be fresh for the crisis, and will be fighting on short lines of supply. If we fight around the perimeter of Europe, we will have long supply lines constantly exposed to air attack. That was the opinion of Rundstedt, the regular army general, the man who had a contempt for the Nazis which he often expressed.

Rommel, "a man with a magnificent record." Von Rundstedt, "a great professional."

Rundstedt was retired from his field command. He had committed the heresy of suggesting that German soldiers should retreat. In Hitler's mind German soldiers never retreated. They stood on what they had won, and they died rather than go back. Everything the Reich had conquered must be held. That was Hitler's opinion, and he found at hand a man who was precisely of his views.

Rommel had recovered from his desert ulcers. An aggressive general who had risen through the party; a man with a magnificent record in Africa. Rommel was the man to defend France and defeat his old enemy Montgomery once and for all. To be on the safe side Rundstedt, who was after all a great professional, was kept in the overall command in the west. But Rommel was to be the instrument of Hitler's will; he would command in the field and check this nonsense about allowing the Allies to land and conquer France.

Time was getting short, and Rommel got to work. The heavy German defenses, he noted, were placed well back from the French coast—part of Rundstedt's defeatist philosophy. He collected an army of laborers. He plucked up the road blocks and the anti-tank traps and moved them on to the coast. The invasion was to be defeated on the beaches. Millions of trees were sawed down and erected on all the seaside strips that offered a chance of glider landings. The minefields were redoubled on the beaches, and heavily laced with barbed wire. Stakes were driven into the sea bed, and shells and mines placed on top of them, in the hope of stopping the landing-barges. Heavy steel spikes were set down under the high-water level with the same object. All this was in addition to the encircling concrete pillboxes and the systems of trenches and tank traps.

By the end of May the Atlantic Wall was a very formidable thing indeed. Every beach and cove was defended. Every seaside town was a fortress, with its seaward roads bricked up and guns sprouting out of the hotel cellars. The Germans apparently expected the invasion to fall most heavily on the Belgian and Dutch coast, and here the wall was made continuous and deep. Even the sand dunes were tunneled, and guns were spaced along the railway. Into this system of entrenchments Rommel placed his secondary divisions, units with large numbers of foreign conscripts. Their job was simply to hold for an hour or a day until the SS and the Panzer troops arrived. These last were grouped some miles inland at points where they could rapidly advance to any danger spot along the coast.

Two armies were under Rommel's command; the Seventh, distributed west of Paris, and the Fifteenth, which was holding the coast in the Pas de Calais area north of the Seine. In addition,

Blaskowitz had another army defending southern France. It seemed not impossible that they could hold. Morale was fairly high. Food for the army was plentiful in France. There was wine. Through the end of May one fine day went by after another. One had only to look at those millions of tons of concrete, those many millions of stakes, to be reassured. The only unsettling thing was the constant waiting and waiting.

Things were not much easier in England. The delay began to oppress both the civilians and the soldiers. Montgomery had set up his headquarters at his old school in Kensington, St. Paul's. From here he toured England in his special train, addressing the troops, talking to the officers. As usual he took no part in the detailed planning. He believed that morale was everything at this stage, and he set out on a policy of deliberately selling himself to the troops who were going on the assault.

I traveled with him one week. Each morning we got out of the train towards nine o'clock and drove to a village green, or a clearing in the forest, where a brigade of soldiers would be drawn up in a hollow square, with their senior officers standing out in front. Montgomery talked to each of the officers. Then with a band playing, and the troops turned inward so that they could see him closely, he walked between the ranks. Often it was a matter of half a mile. He walked slowly, peering sharply at the men, face to face. They were ordered to stand at ease, but this they found difficult to do when the commander was looking directly at them. Often it took us twenty minutes or half an hour to get round the parade. Except for the distant band there was complete silence, an atmosphere of theatrical tension. At the end of the inspection Montgomery would get on to a jeep in front of a loudspeaker and tell the soldiers to break ranks and gather round him.

This was always an astonishing moment. Five thousand men in heavy boots would charge together towards the jeep like stampeding buffaloes. It caused a heavy rumbling in the earth, and often the jeep would be nearly overwhelmed. And then Montgomery's speech would go like this: "I wanted to come here today so that we could get to know one another: so that I could have a look at you and you could have a look at me—if you think that's worth doing. We have got to go off and do a job together very soon now, you and I, and we must have confidence in one another. And now that I have seen you I have complete confidence . . . complete confidence . . . absolutely complete confidence. And you must have confidence in me."

That was the beginning. For a hundred yards all round him row after row of young upturned faces, an atmosphere of adolescent innocence and simplicity. They sat on the grass keeping utterly still lest they should lose a word. The uniforms and the years of army life had already reduced these youths to an outward pattern, but now it was evident that something else had intervened, a community of simple emotion, a curiously childish monasticism. They were committed to the assault. Everything in their lives, for month after month, had been shaped to that end: the assault landing on the beaches. Nothing else was of any interest any longer, nothing except this simple proposition: the assault. To run, to shoot, to kill. And not to be killed. All the usual decoration of life was stripped away from these children; the normal life of playing football and going out with girls and visiting the movies. All the usual peacetime manners and affectations were gone. Even the most intelligent showed no glimmer of irony or sarcasm or criticism in their faces. The atmosphere was completely subjective and unself-conscious. They were to run and shoot and kill, and here was the expert, the man who knew all about it. It was vital not to miss a word he said, vital not to miss a clue.

"We have been fighting the Germans a long time now," Montgomery went on. "A very long time . . . a good deal too long. I expect like me you are beginning to get a bit tired of it . . . beginning to feel it's about time we finished the thing off. And we can do it. We can do it. No doubt about that. No doubt about that whatever. The well-trained British soldier will beat the German every time. We saw it in Africa. We chased him into the sea in Tunisia . . . then we went over to Sicily and chased him into the sea again. . . . I don't know if there are any more seas . . ."

This was the point where the soldiers relaxed and laughed. Well, it was true, wasn't it? The Germans *had* been beaten in Africa. They weren't so wonderful.

"The newspapers keep calling it the Second Front," Montgomery continued. "I don't know why they call it the Second Front. I myself have been fighting the Germans on a number of fronts, and I expect a good few of you have too. They should call it Front Number Six or Front Number Seven. As long as they don't want us to fight on Front Number Thirteen. . . ."

Most of the tenseness had gone out of the soldiers now. Monty was all right. He didn't talk a lot of cock about courage and liberty. He knew what it was like. And perhaps one had been taking the whole thing a bit too seriously. It wouldn't be so bad.

Then—"We don't want to forget the German is a good soldier . . . a very good soldier indeed. But when I look around this morning and see the magnificent soldiers here . . . some of the finest soldiers I have seen in my lifetime . . . I have no doubt in my mind about the outcome . . . no doubt whatever. No doubt at all that you and I will see this thing through, together."

Finally—"Now I can't stay any longer. I expect some of you have come a long way to get here this morning and you want to get back." (Some of them had been traveling since 4 A.M.) "I just want to say good-by and very good luck to each one of you."

That was the speech, followed by three cheers for the general. I listened to it four and sometimes five times a day for nearly a week. We went from camp to camp over southern England, sometimes standing on wet hill-tops, sometimes surrounded by civilians in city parks, sometimes on a football field or under the shelter of a wood. Always the same rush to the jeep, the same tense attention. It fascinated me every time. Long after one knew the words by heart and had ceased to listen to them one was swept into the contagious and breathless interest of each new audience.

I suppose I have heard fifty generals addressing their soldiers, most of them with much better speeches than this. Indeed I suppose this speech in print is just about as bad as one could hope to read, outside the hearty naïveté of the kindergarten. Spoken by Montgomery to the soldiers who were about to run into the Atlantic Wall it had magic. No mention of God, of divine assistance. No mention of England. Not a single eternal verity. No hate. No question of revenge. But I doubt whether the soldiers remembered the words. The words were the least of it. The whole performance succeeded because it was the expression of a wanted emotion. Without their consciously knowing it, the speech adopted an attitude which the soldiers wanted to have. At the end of it they felt they knew Montgomery as he believed he knew them. They felt that they were thinking on the same plane as he was, that they would indeed go into the assault together.

In the end Montgomery had made that speech to every British, American and Allied soldier who was to go on the landing; he must have talked to at least a million men. His energy was enormous. Every day on his tours he would speak personally with a hundred people; the engine driver of his train, the station master at each station, the local mayors. Once on my trip with him he made a detour to talk to a public school. ("I don't know what I am supposed to say to you. I am more used to talking to soldiers. Perhaps the best way to begin is to ask the headmaster to give you all a half-holiday." Roar of delight from the worshipping boys. Montgomery: "Obviously that is a good way to begin a speech.") Another time he opened an ice hockey match. He lunched each day at a different mess with at least fifty officers hanging on every word he said. At night on the train we would talk. For the most part Montgomery's conversation consists of either asking questions or making flat statements of fact. A little after nine he would go off to his cabin on the train, write his diary and go to bed.

He had no fear of the future, no doubts about the success of the landing. He would say slowly: "It will succeed. It will certainly succeed provided we make no mistakes. We must make no mistakes."

In England there was no such certainty. The waiting had gone on so long. The mystery and secrecy of the operation made it seem more difficult. Although there was a general certainty that the landing would occur, people were without any technical knowledge of how it would be done; they had no means of estimating the chances; and as the talk and conjecture continued the fears increased. All that one could see ahead was a deliberately planned massacre. It would have been much easier if they could have watched the preparations: the submarines stealing in to chart the coast and the sea bed; the commandos landing on the beaches to gather information; the hundreds of boats collecting in the ports; the five thousand aircraft preparing for the day. They knew nothing of the organization of the French Maquis, and were unwilling to believe that the French could be of much assistance anyhow.

A dead, heavy mood settled over the country, and this was communicated to the army. Having prepared so long, so thoroughly, so intimately, it seemed on some black days that one thing would be lacking—the spirit to put the plan into operation. There had again been raids on London. May turned into June. Surely it could not be much longer now. Standing on the South Downs one could see the Channel, bright and clear and calm. It was a hot midsummer sun. The country never looked more calm and beautiful. One felt only an emptiness and a mental weariness, an overburdening ennui.

One June 3rd, unknown to nearly everyone in the world, General Eisenhower called his senior commanders to the country house he was using as a headquarters in southern England. There were present Air Chief Marshal Tedder, the deputy commander-in-chief, Admiral Ramsay of the Allied navies, Air Marshal Trafford Leigh-Mallory of the air, Montgomery with his chief of staff, de Guingand, Eisenhower's chief of staff, Bedell Smith, and one or two others. Of that company two, Ramsay and Leigh-Mallory, were soon to die, but for the moment they were met to decide on the fate of a million other men. Although it was already past nine

Eisenhower and Churchill; the mood of the country was heavy.

o'clock the gentle light of the long English summer day was still coming through the windows. Coffee was poured out, and there was desultory conversation round the room until Eisenhower called them down to business. Three men, the best weather experts England and America could provide, came in, and one of them, a Scot, acted as spokesman. He was gloomy. A series of depressions was approaching the Channel. Wind, waves and cloud, that was the prospect. And the invasion fleet was due to sail on the following afternoon. One by one Eisenhower questioned his three chief commanders. Could the navy manage it? Ramsay thought not. The assault might go ashore all right, but if the weather worsened there could be no adequate build-up. Same thing with Leigh-Mallory. Plan "B" would have to go into operation, the lesser plan. His crews would have to bomb on instruments through the clouds without seeing what they were hitting. No. The weather was not good enough for the air. Montgomery? Montgomery alone was favorable. "I'm ready," he said. But just for the moment this was more of a decision for the navy and the air force.

It was an immense undertaking to postpone D Day. The troops and tanks and guns were embarked and waiting at scores of secret ports around the coast of England. The bombers were waiting on the airfields. The whole elaborate machine was poised to move on this day, and to upset it now, to let some ships put to sea and then bring them back, to retard the immense and exact program of the build-up, to alter the schedule of the trains and the convoys and the loading, to keep the waiting millions of men strung at high tension —all this was a fearfully dangerous prospect. Worse still, the meteorologists warned the meeting that if these next few days were lost in inaction then a week or a fortnight might go by before the channel tides would again be suitable for the landing.

"We will meet again tomorrow morning at 4:30," Eisenhower said. As the commanders went off to their rooms in the building already the machine was beginning to turn over. Already some of the assault gunboats were putting out to sea, the glider troops and the parachutists were waiting with their harness. The early hours of the following morning were the latest possible moment when a decision could be taken. After that the thing would roll on inevitably and nothing could stop it short of a victory or a disaster on a scale that would eclipse anything that had passed in the war. The history of Europe depended entirely on the rising and falling of the wind.

At 4:30 A.M., June 4th, the same scene again. The same room. The coffee. The men feeling gray and a little unsteady. The meteorologists came in and it was seen at once that they had no better news. Again Eisenhower questioned his commanders. The navy? No. The air? No. The army? Yes. "We will postpone it twenty-four hours," Eisenhower said. Officers ran to send the signals to the ports and the airfields. All over England the machine sighed down into a standstill. There was nothing now to do except wait.

On the evening of June 4th, the third meeting was called. From the meteorologists this time there was a definite flicker of hope. Most unexpectedly the weather had not worsened. It was dark, it was far from favorable, but it was no worse. And there was a hope that it would continue evenly like this for a few days.

Admiral Ramsay was not enthusiastic. He was still worried about the build-up. And yet—the chance was there. It could be done. Things could easily go wrong on the beaches, but still the landing was possible. Leigh-Mallory, too, thought that he could manage to put up his bombers and fighters. But they would have to go in on a modified plan. Montgomery again was all for sailing. The men sat round the table going through the possibilities over again, trying desperately to bring the facts to the point where they would produce a hard inevitable decision. But that was not possible. The element of luck remained.

Suddenly Eisenhower came forward. "This is a decision which I must take alone," he said. "After all that is what I am here for." The meeting waited. Then the commander-in-chief said: "We will sail tomorrow."

6. The Landing

This was a camp near Southampton like all the other camps. A ring of barbed wire round a forest. Earthen footpaths leading up to the tents and the wooden huts among the trees. Notices stuck into the ground: "A" Mess. "B" Mess. Camp Cinema. Officers' Showers. Camp Commandant. Naafi. Paymaster.

When you arrived at the gate of the camp the sentries looked at your identification papers. Then you went inside and the gate closed behind you; and that, without any ceremony, was the act of renunciation. Once the gate was closed you could no longer return to the normal world outside, not even to buy a packet of cigarettes at the shop on the corner of the street, nor have a haircut, nor telephone your friends. You were committed irrevocably to the landing, perhaps tomorrow, perhaps the day after; no one knew for certain. It was all very carefully arranged. Each man had a place and a number. Each camp had a certain complement of soldiers, and presently they would be drafted to their corresponding places on the ships waiting in the harbor. Everything was prescribed and exactly ordered.

I found my place in one of the tents and set up my camp bed. There was nothing to do, so I lay down on the bed and stared through the open flap of the tent at a field where the soldiers were playing football. On the opposite bed a young naval officer was trying on his harness. There was a rucksack full of explosives, a trenching tool, pistol, ammunition, a butcher's knife, gas-cape, helmet, a small sack that looked as though it contained hand grenades, a tin of rations. He strapped all this gear on himself and began making alterations so as to distribute the weight more evenly. Then he practiced slipping the bundles on and off until he found he could do it in the space of thirty seconds or so. I tried to think what his job was. To wade ashore and plant explosives on the sea-wall? He was a boy of twenty-one or twenty-two, and he went about this buckling and unbuckling of his kit quite oblivious of his surroundings. Presently he too lay down on his bed and began watching the footballers outside.

"It looks as though we are going to have good weather."

"Yes."

He did not want to talk. After an hour I got up and began walking round the camp. Some of the soldiers were lying on the grass near the recreation tent. They were talking and listening to a radio loudspeaker hanging from one of the trees. A disembodied dialogue was coming out of the marquee marked Camp Cinema, and occasionally there was a burst of laughter from the audience inside. At the paymaster's tent I asked how much money I could change.

"Ten pounds if you like."

"Into what currency?"

"Francs."

So it was going to be France then; that was definite. The same flimsy notes with their pastel shades, the bundles of wheat and the buxom woman in the corner, Banque de France. Five years ago, when I shut up my home in Paris, I had changed the last of those notes at the Gare de l'Est, and these were the first I had seen since then, and they were the first clear passport for my return. But it was not going to be the same. I stood outside the tent looking at the notes and expecting a nostalgia for the things that had made France a better country to live in than anywhere else on earth. But it was no good. The mind projected itself forward as far as the embarkation, as far as the landing. Then there was a blank, a kind of wall over which the mind would not travel.

In the mess tent the food was very bad. We sat at rickety trestle tables, eating slices of cold bully beef and cold white cabbage. Then there were army biscuits, margarine, a mug of tea. A few made some attempt to talk, but most of the officers sat eating silently, and brushing the flies away from their plates. Every few minutes a loudspeaker outside the tent began calling numbers. These were the numbers of units which were to prepare themselves to go down to their ships and invasion barges. As the numbers were called the men at the table cocked their heads slightly to listen. One or two men got up and left the tent. The rest went on eating the cold cabbage.

I went back to the tent and got down on the bed again. There was nothing to do. My driver had packed the jeep. The kit was stowed on board, chains, petrol cans, blankets. The engine had been plastered with waterproofing glue so that the vehicle could travel through water. A long flexible hose ran up from the exhaust and was tied to the top of the windscreen. He too, the driver, showed that he was feeling the strain of waiting. Everybody felt it. Over all the camp, over a hundred other such camps, over all the army at that moment there was this same dead weight, this same oppressive feeling that the delay might continue indefinitely, growing more and more unbearable as the days went by. The invasion was already like an overrehearsed play.

I got up and walked around the edge of the camp, where civilians were passing by in the streets outside, on the other side of the wire. On the telegraph poles there were notices saying: "Do not loiter. Civilians must not talk to army personnel." They hurried by without looking into the camp. More and more the feeling grew that one was cut off, that all the normal things would go on, the tramcars and the shops, but they were, for you, of no consequence any longer. In some strange way you had been committed to the landing, to the blank space ahead. You had not chosen it and you were not resentful about it. But how had it happened, at what point had it been decided that you should be separated from the other people on the earth? Who made this fantastic and widening gulf between you standing here behind the wire and those others going by in the tram? It was absurd to try and rationalize the thing that had to happen in a day or two. Yet (one argued) it was a monstrous contradiction of reason. You cannot present fear and death and risk in this cold way, with all this calculation. You can accept these things vicariously in a theater. You accept them when you are angry. But cold cabbage. A lot of numbers shouted on a loudspeaker. A tent with a number on it. A number even on *you*. What sort of preparation was this? And to let it go on hour after hour. To try and tabulate a thing that was essentially a matter of passion and excitement. It simply drove the mind into a fixed apathy. It made you reluctant to walk, to talk, to eat, to sleep. There was no taste in anything any longer. Not even in drinks, and there were no drinks in the camp anyway. Just waiting, waiting until your number turned up. And meanwhile no loose talk. What you had to do, your job, your place in the machine, was everything, but you must not talk about it. You were not even told where you were going. You were given no idea of your place in the plan. You had no method of assessing the black space ahead. You had to be suspicious even of the other soldiers in the camp. Everything had to be secret. You were driven back into yourself to the point where you lacked even a normal companionship with the others, who after all were in exactly the same situation. It was not fear that oppressed you, but loneliness. A sense of implacable helplessness. You were without identity, a number projected in unrelated space among a million other numbers.

On June 3rd these were the ideas that made this camp the most cheerless place that had come my way since the war began. And all around, in the mess, and along the earthen tracks, one could read the same ideas in the heavy sullen faces of the soldiers going by. No wonder another twenty men had deserted in the night.

That evening the soldiers were told the plan and what they had to do. The change was electric. The suspense was snapped. A wave of relief succeeded it. Now that the future was known and proscribed everything would be easier. We were to embark the following afternoon. We would sail during the night. H Hour was the following morning. An immense aerial and naval bombardment would precede the landing. Ten thousand tons of bombs would fall along the coast on which we had to land. The naval guns would silence the shore batteries. The brigade had been given a small strip of beach on which to land, a strip marked on the map as "King Beach." Other brigades would be landing to the right and left of us. Airborne divisions would be arriving by glider and parachute to clear the way inland.

All this was an immense reassurance. As the men stood in their

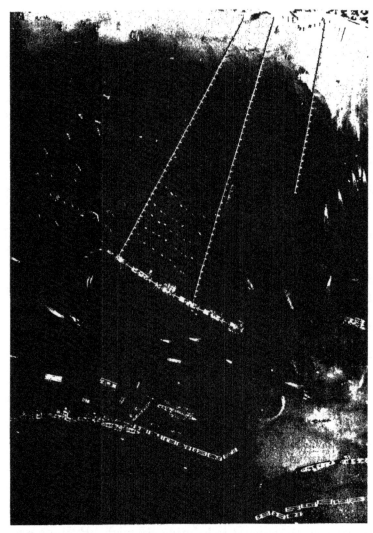

Mulberry Harbor—a prefabricated port as big as Gibraltar—was towed across the Channel and set down off Normandy.

ranks listening to the colonel you could feel the confidence growing. Here at last was something practical and definite. Something to which one could adjust oneself.

We were not yet told exactly where we would land, but maps with false names were issued. They showed every German position down to the last gun. Here a machine-gun nest. Here a minefield. Here a pillbox and a fortified wall. The defenses did not appear nearly so formidable now that one knew the extent of them. Each company was given its objective, the distance it had to go, the obstacles in its way. And all the time continuous air cover, a continuous barrage of guns from the sea.

Dinner was almost cheerful that night. And in the morning there was the cheerful noise of the soldiers packing their kits, wheeling their handcarts down to the entrance of the camp. Outside in the suburban streets long lines of vehicles were drawn up ready to take the men on board.

At three o'clock we were standing in a line on the path leading up to the gate. The young naval officer came by festooned with his explosives and rather surprisingly took up a position behind me. As each new group of troops turned up they exchanged wisecracks with the others already arrived. "Blimey, 'ere's the Arsenal." . . . " 'Ome for the 'olidays." . . . "Wot's that, Arthur?" "Them's me water-wings, dearie." Even after waiting another hour there was still optimism in the ranks. Then we marched out through the gate and got on to the vehicles. An officer was running down the line making sure everyone was on board. He blew a whistle and we started off. Five miles an hour. Down Acacia Avenue. Round the park into High Street; a mile-long column of ducks and three-ton lorries, of jeeps and tanks and bulldozers. On the sidewalk one or two people waved vaguely. An old man stopped and mumbled, "Good luck." But for the most part the people stared silently and made no sign. They knew we were going. There had been rehearsals before but they were not deceived. There was something in the way the soldiers carried themselves that said all too clearly "This is it. This is the invasion." And yet they were cheerful still. It was a relief to be out of the camp and moving freely in the streets again. Every now and again the column halted. Then we crept on slowly again towards the hards.

About four o'clock the procession came to a very definite halt in front of a cricket field. Standing on our vehicles we could see the game going on, two suburban teams who shuffled a little nervously under the eyes of this unexpected audience. The soldiers watched quietly for a minute. Then they began to applaud ironically and shout wisecracks over the fence. It was something to pass the time. The first team was dismissed under a barrage of cat-calls.

Two hours went by and the soldiers began to grow bored. They seized on anything for amusement. When a girl came by on a bicycle she was cheered with salacious enthusiasm from one end of the column to the other. An athlete dressed in a pink suit began to pace round the cricket field. The soldiers watched him with relish for a minute. Then, "Hyah, Pinkie." "Careful, dearie." Derisive shouting followed him round the ground. Towards the end of the column a soldier who was trained as a sniper took down his rifle with its telescopic sights and fixed them upon two lovers who were embracing at the farther end of the park. His friends gathered round him while he gave them a lewd commentary on what he saw. The soldiers were becoming very bored. It grew dark and the cricket match ended. Every hour or so a tea-wagon came round and the men ran towards it with their enamel mugs. One after another the lights in the houses were blacked out and the soldiers, left alone in the empty street, lapsed into complete listlessness and tiredness. Rumors kept passing back and forth from vehicle to vehicle. "Our ship has fouled its anchor." "There has been a collision in the harbor." Or more spectacularly, "We have already made a landing on the Channel Islands."

Towards ten o'clock the officers began running down the column shouting for the drivers to start. We began to edge forward slowly and presently came out on the dark promenade along the sea. There were many ships, both those moving in the sound and those which had brought their bows up on to the hard and had opened their gates to receive the vehicles. We were marked down for the Landing Ship Tank 816. A clamor of light and noise was coming out of its open bows. One after another the vehicles crept down the ramp and on to the great lift that took them to the upper deck. The sailors kept shouting to one another as they lashed down the trucks on the upper deck. All night the thump of army boots against the metal deck went on.

When I woke in the morning we were far out in the sound, surrounded by many hundreds of ships such as this, each one under its silver anti-aircraft balloon that wallowed and bucketed in the wind. The sea was rising. We walked about the deck with our rubber lifejackets, waiting for 15.00, the time of sailing. At 16.00 hours we were still at anchor. None of the other ships had moved. Then it was given out to the soldiers: postponement for another twenty-four hours.

Up to this point the morale had been steady. Everyone's spirits had risen as we had come on board, although this act of embarking had been the final irrevocable break with England. But now with this renewed delay there was time to think again. And this at a moment when one had no desire to think or to write letters or engage on any distraction from the inevitable thing ahead.

L.S.T. 816 was an American ship which had already made three assault landings: North Africa, Sicily and Salerno. On this their fourth landing the sailors showed no excitement or emotions. Their attitude was summed up by, "Another dirty job." The captain had sailed for twenty years. The crew had seen the sea for the first time at New York a year or two before. The captain himself had taken the wheel since he had no wheelman as they left New York. He himself had trained his officers on the voyage to Europe, during the actual assaults. He was gloomy. "This will be a bad one." It was perhaps more superstition than gloom. For eight or ten hours through the day inconsequent American swing music poured out of the ship's loudspeakers. The American sailors liked to work to the music. They went about, loose-limbed, chewing gum, not mixing much with the soldiers. One of them sat in the stern peeling potatoes endlessly.

There was a party that night in the gunboat moored alongside. It was a little cockleshell with nothing much on board but two big guns. The idea was that she should run ahead of the bulk of the invasion fleet and engage the shore batteries pretty well at point-blank range as soon as it was light. There was a great number of these little ships, and they were expendable. It did not matter much if they were sunk, provided the first and second wave of troops were got ashore. The captain was a bearded little man. He spent most of the evening complaining about income tax.

That night the waves were smacking so heavily upon the ship that the Rhino ferry was only with great difficulty got into a position for towing. This was a big metal pontoon equipped with two motors. The idea was that as soon as we got off the invasion beach the Rhino would come round to the open bows of the ship and take the vehicles on board, and then run them to the shore. This meant that the ship need not beach and could return at once to England for reinforcements. We were due ashore in France six hours after the first infantry.

When the actual moment of sailing arrived the next afternoon the water was still full of movement. All around us the other ships were heaving in the gray waves, and these increased as the land at last slid away. And now that we were in the open sea the men were falling into a settled depression. It was cold on deck, and stuffy to

The build-up: American ships load up at the port of Brixham, in Devonshire.

the point of nausea below. Many were sea-sick. It made no difference that we were surrounded by the other ships, destroyers and
cruisers passing by, and great convoys sailing out to the horizon. As
the night closed in the men were oppressed by a sense of strangeness
and insecurity. In the darkness the dangers of the voyage became
magnified and unbearable, and the rising sea alone seemed a
sufficient terror, without the unthinkable climax of the assault at
the other end. Unexplained lights flared up in the distance, and
towards morning the drone of heavy bombers sounded above the
continuous whining of the engines of the ship.

The men were called up at 4 A.M., and they came on deck gray-
faced and cold, their uniforms tumbled about by the night's sleeping. One after another the surrounding vessels disengaged themselves from the darkness, became black silhouettes and then finally
resolved themselves into the shapes of ships. The men moved
clumsily in a queue along the deck to get their breakfast. A German
mine, shaped like a top, came floating by and we turned to let it
pass astern. Far out on either side gunboats were darting about
shooting tracer bullets at other mines on the surface. We sailed in
line astern. In the night buoys with flags had been dropped across
the Channel to mark the way.

There was still no sign of the French coast, no sound of the battle
which now must be breaking there as the first assault troops went
ashore. Overhead the last of the night bombers flew home. On the
sea our tow-rope broke, and the Rhino ferry was washed astern with
its stranded crew on board. No ship was allowed to delay in that
danger area in the open Channel, and we sailed on.

At nine o'clock the captain shouted down from the bridge. He
had a signal form in his hand, but I could not hear what he was
saying and I clambered up to him. "Two companies ashore and
reached their first objectives with only slight enemy resistance." It
was scrawled in pencil on a pink slip of paper. One was not able to
comprehend it. We stood in the wind looking at the paper, re-
reading the scrawling handwriting. One had nothing but a sense of
confused anti-climax. This signal bore no relation whatever to the
long, hard expectation of this day. It was almost an impudent
comment on all the dread of the past week. It punctured all the
unending imaginings, all the lurid apprehensions. The tremendous
shelling and the sunken ships. The men drowning in the water and
crawling bleeding on the beach. Where was all that? There was
nothing around us but the gray sea and the peaceful passage of the
other ships, nothing to illustrate this perfunctory message that had
come from somewhere out ahead, from someone actually standing

on the French shore, someone who had made the landing and lived.

And then when finally we came up to the invasion beach and stared across the water there was a second and deeper anti-climax. There it was, France after five years. It was incredibly and inexplicably the same. A stretch of seashore. The ugly little seaside villas. The lovely gentle slopes behind running into green copses and straggling farmyards. A windmill on the hill. Yellow cliffs on the right. No rolling battle clouds. No diving bombers. No noise like the monstrous noise one had imagined. All one's memory of France rushed up to meet this positive visual proof that it was the same. Yes, of course. This was the place to which one took the children for the summer holidays. There should be colored parasols down there on the *plage,* an ice-cream man on the promenade. *Demandez de la glace. Un franc la coupe.* Governesses. Little Frenchmen with spiky beards and straw boaters. Baskets of crayfish. The *pension* on the hill.

Nothing in all one's experience could have been a preparation for this picture postcard, this unbelievable quietude; a French beach by the sea. This was the focus of the world, the cataclysm behind the headlines and the urgent radio bulletin. And look at it: a French beach on a summer morning. As we looked and looked a tremendous tide of relief came into the mind, as though we had suddenly woken after a long fever with a normal temperature, and all the pain had drained away.

Yet there was a battle going on. As we crept closer one could pick up the detail. In the six hours since dawn something like a thousand ships had arrived on this stretch of beach. Cruisers and battleships were standing off-shore and firing on to the heights above the cliffs, presumably against the unseen German batteries. Perhaps a hundred of the larger landing-ships like the 816 were rolling in the waves a few hundred yards off-shore, vainly trying to unload their tanks and vehicles on to the Rhino ferries. Each time the ferries came up to the open mouths of the ships they were dashed back by the waves and drifted away. Those ducks which had been got into the water were either struggling towards the shore or swamping and sinking outright with their crews on board. The tide had already receded, and upon the shore itself many landing-barges were beached or awash and rapidly sinking into the sand. Four or five ships were alight and burned brightly, throwing out shells and explosives over the debris at the water's edge. German shells were falling in little puffs of gray smoke, but the whole scene looked at from this distance was toy-like and unreal. It lacked the element of danger or excitement, even of movement. Behind us more and more ships were coasting in, until the whole horizon towards England was blocked by a jagged line of tossing silhouettes. Occasional aircraft flew by, but aimlessly and apparently without obvious direction. We put out a motor-boat from the 816 and it filled and sank. Our ferry arrived and shot upward past the open bows like a huge electric lift. As it subsided it slewed round and drifted away. All the rest of that day passed like this. The ferry smashing up against the side of the ship and drifting away; the curious toy-like scene on the beach, the battle without explanation and without movement. It was agonizing not to get ashore, only five hundred yards away. There was nothing to do but stay there in the unreal and unwanted comfort of the American ship, taking hot baths, eating grilled steak, listening to the infuriating swing music through the loudspeakers.

In the morning nothing had changed very much except that there were more ships in the sea, more wreckage on the beach, more fires burning inland. A few of us at last managed to drop on to the ferry, and like a bull running amok it ran for the shore on the incoming tide. We smashed against the next ship and wrecked a longboat. Then the ungainly thing, with only one engine working, veered in the opposite direction and smashed its dead weight through a shoal of ammunition barges. All around us ducks were sinking and soldiers splashing about in the water. Our actual landfall was perfect. The ferry, long since out of control, lunged up against a wreck at the water's edge, and we jumped for the shore. A six-foot soldier for no reason except generosity yanked me on top of his shoulders and set me down on the dry sand with my typewriter dry and intact.

The beach was an extraordinary shambles. So much had happened here in the past twenty-four hours; wreckage piled on wreckage, that one had the impression that the battle had been going on a long time, for weeks, even for months, and that the soldiers who came to meet us on the shore were natives of the place. At the spot where we landed two Sherman tanks had already sunk up to their turrets in the quicksand. A sharp wind was blowing over the sand-dunes, and now that one was close at hand one saw that this was no normal French beach but a wasteland pitted with thousands of craters and shell-holes. The villas were only shells, with their insides blown out. The roofs of the farmhouses had tumbled in. The pillboxes and the concrete trenches had been wrenched about by the fantastic violence of the barrage of the day before. The first companies on shore had found the enemy broken and dazed by the bombardment, but there had been bitter skir-

The beach already looked as if the battle had been going on for months.

A tank trap on a Normandy beach, 15 feet deep, flooded and mined.

mishing, and the dead lay about the blackened entrances of the pillboxes. A stream of ducks was making directly up the hill towards the village of Crepon. Following them one traveled quickly through the belt of utter destruction on the seashore, and came out into the clean countryside beyond. The first hamlet was inexpressibly French. The St. Raphael advertisement with the picture of the two hurrying waiters. Then painted on a wall: "Dubo . . . Dubonn . . . Dubonnet." Two peasants in blue drill boiler-suits, old men, stood looking with a kind of peasant acceptance at the fabulous stream of military vehicles going by.

"Ça va?"

"*Mais oui. Tout va bien, monsieur. Sommes très contents de vous voir.*" And then the older of them in a high-pitched quaver: "*Vive l'Angleterre!*"

In the wheatfield beyond a platoon of German soldiers had held out for a little. They lay dead now in the positions in which they had been firing. But then beyond this no sign of the enemy anywhere, not even the sound of continuous firing. There were other experiences in other sectors, harder fighting. The parachutists, for example, were under continuous fire on the Orne canal, and the Americans to our right were engaged in pitched battle on the beach. But here after the first assault it was a clean break-through. A breach had been driven clear through the Atlantic Wall, and be-

A German soldier, buried up to his neck by a shell explosion, fights his way out of the mud.

A German gun position looked Martian.

wildered German soldiers were running for cover through the open countryside.

We went on into the town of Bayeux. For a moment a few German officers had fired from the post office, but the town had fallen intact. It remained exactly as it had been through the past four years; the soaring cathedral, the Camembert cheeses in the shops, the wine carts going up the Rue St. Jean; the evening gowns in the shop marked *"haute couture."* The Lion d'Or was a bright little provincial hotel, set back from the road round a courtyard, colored canvas awnings over the windows, a bar on one side and on the other the long dining-room giving on to the terrace.

Yes, certainly we could have lunch. The proprietress was a round little woman dressed in black, and she accepted our arrival with aplomb. With astonishment we watched the lunch arrive. Soup, omelettes, steak, vegetables, cheese. There was gritty brown bread, *café nationale*. The wine was a dry Sauterne, fifteen shillings a bottle. The Armagnac was genuine Armagnac. While we ate there was a commotion in the square outside. A crowd came yelling up the Rue St. Jean, driving an old man in front of them. His shirt was torn off to the waist. There was blood running down his face, his eyes were wide with fright. Every now and then a man or a woman would run forward to beat him or scratch him. They did this viciously, with an evident sense of gratifying some pent-up desire for revenge. It was difficult to get much sense out of the crowd. They merely shouted, *"Collaborateur."* Presently more victims were brought out and beaten in the square in front of the hotel. Excited young Frenchmen were running about carrying tommy-guns.

Inside the hotel a little group of luncheon guests were watching all this. They watched without surprise and comprehended it, but at the same time they were frightened. This was a Wednesday, and Wednesday was the day on which the woman who ran the brothel above the hotel brought her girls down to lunch. It was absurdly like a scene from de Maupassant's *Boule de Suif*. By an understanding with the hotel manageress (who had her reputation to maintain), the girls were forbidden to glance about them in the luncheon room seeking clients. They sat primly, making no conversation except giggling and waiting intently for each course to arrive. But on this day with English soldiers coming into the hotel they found it impossible to observe the rules. They turned and smiled, and Madame kept calling them sharply to attention. A man with a round oily face was lunching at the next table to mine, with a girl.

"Have you any need for a motor-car?" he said. "You must certainly take mine. I have petrol. The car is outside; everything is ready."

As we drove through the suburbs, the man and the girl sitting in front, people shouted at us: *"Les deux. Collaborateurs."*

"What does that mean?" I asked them.

"They're crazy," the man said. "The whole town has gone mad. They're completely unable to understand affairs. I run a garage in the town. Naturally I was obliged by the Germans to keep my cars running. It was not my pleasure. Still, it was better for a Frenchman to have his own cars on the road rather than the dirty Boches. And so I accepted a miserable ration of petrol. Many times my cars brought food into the town. And now they turn on me."

It was the first of many such incidents we were going to see through France and Belgium. Everywhere the collaborators attempted to ingratiate themselves with the Allied soldiers as soon as we arrived.

It was impossible to find the front-line, since at that moment it did not exist. At nearly every point incredible, unbelievable success had attended the landings. Despite the millions of stakes set up along the coast, the gliders had set down with the parachutists and seized the bridges on the lower Orne canal. At every major landing-point—Courseulles, Asnelles, Port-en-Bessin and Grandcamp—the German outer perimeter had cracked. The best part of six divisions was already ashore, Americans, British and Canadians. The Atlantic Wall was broken on a front of sixty miles. Rommel's attempt to hold and smash the assault on the beaches had completely failed. The original impetus had already carried the Allies fifteen miles inland, and now their vehicles were beginning to flow ashore. Only at two points—in the American sector and around Caen—were the Germans regrouping themselves for resistance, and still after forty-eight hours they were incapable of counter-attack. Utter confusion had spread through the German coastal command. Their forward brigade and divisional headquarters were either over-run or in a state of rout. Every one of their coastal batteries had either been smashed by the bombing or put out of action by some of the most superb naval gunnery seen in the whole war. The German coastal troops, which had taken the first shock, included many Poles and recently conscripted Russians. These men became demoralized as soon as they lost their officers and N.C.O.'s. They either gave themselves up at once, or drifted aimlessly about the countryside waiting for a chance to surrender. When, on the evening of the third day, Rommel bunched his tanks for counter-attacks in the direction of Bayeux and Douvres it was already too late. Enough stores and

The Normandy Bridgehead

weapons had been got ashore to keep the Allies going for several days. Having made their original penetration, it was simply a matter of sitting down, of digging in and holding what they had won. That was the plan—not to continue inland at once at the same pace, but simply to consolidate the first break-through.

The front was only ten minutes' drive by jeep outside Bayeux. We had come to the end of a six-course dinner the night the German tanks tried to break into the town. We jumped into our cars and drove down to the forward platoons, but already it was all over. The German squadrons had been broken up with anti-tank guns among the hedges and the orchards. Now too the Americans had got their foothold securely. Even when a storm of unseasonable violence hit the coast it did not alter things greatly. For several days the landing of reinforcements was delayed. Concrete ships and barges which had been sunk to make harbors along the beach were uprooted by the waves and smashed. All this might have become serious, but at the end of the week the weather abated and the invasion began to take on a rhythm that could never have been interrupted. Our losses in ships and men and tanks were barely a fifth of the forces engaged. There had been no blood bath, no massacre on the beaches. Even among the shock troops, those who came in aboard amphibious tanks and flame-throwers, and the infantry who waded ashore and tackled the pillboxes point-blank, the casualties were far less than we had expected. The sheer imagination and daring of the whole enterprise had been its best guarantee. The risk taken began to bear an immense return.

7. The French

What was France really like? How did the French receive us when we got ashore? These were the questions that began to agitate people's minds very soon after the landing, and the whole matter was hopelessly complicated by prejudice and the lack of information. The average British soldier had been taught to believe that the French had "let us down" in 1940. At home there was a general disposition to think that the French were a weak and venal people, but that they had suffered deeply by the German occupation. They remained foreigners, but they had learned their lesson.

To the average American, France was simply another untidy foreign country, another obstacle to his return home. He compared France to his own sane and much-desired world, where there was decent plumbing and ice cream and movies and a language you could understand. As for the French themselves, they were simply more problem children in the general unsavory mess of Europe.

Both the British and the Americans in fact were on guard against the French. They were watching closely to see how the French would behave. The suspicion was eagerly exploited by one or two journalists who came ashore and, with a good sense of news value, reported that the French in Normandy were "sullen," "resentful" and even downright enemies. The story about the women snipers had a particularly good run. One correspondent reported blithely: "Every French woman here is a potential sniper. The French are against us."

The facts of course were exactly the reverse, but still the many trends of feeling among the Normandy people were immensely complicated. Physically they had not suffered very much. Normandy is France's great supplier of beef and cheese and cider and other staples. No German occupation could destroy the natural fertility of the soil. With the arrival of the Allies, the foodstuffs that would normally have gone to Paris and the industrial areas were blocked, and accumulated in the shops and on the farms, making a great display. The people were only too ready to sell the stuff to the Allies. Then again, as in Italy, it was at once apparent that France had never been organized for war with one quarter of the efficiency of England. The luxury trades went on. True the stuff was mostly ersatz and fantastically expensive, but it was well designed and gay. There was a facade of sprightliness over all the goods in the shops. The black market governed everything. It was the acknowledged system of social economy, and the only ration tickets that were taken at all seriously were those relating to bread and wine.

The bread was very coarse and poor. Also very scarce. As for the wine, the Germans had seized most of the crops normally used for *vin ordinaire* and turned them into power alcohol. They had, however, allowed the vintage wine growers to continue, and if you were willing to pay three or four times the normal price it was still easy enough to get a bottle or two. As in any country which has been growing grapes for centuries, France still had vast reserves of good wine. In any case the Normandy peasant grew and drank his own tart cider.

And so it was not hunger that made him detest the Germans. It was something else; a very ordinary sense of pride. We shall have to wait until we get to Paris to see the full effect of this, but it was strongly apparent here in Normandy. The mere presence of the Germans in the role of overlords grated on these country people in a surprising way. It was not that the Germans behaved very badly. It was simply that they had the power to behave badly or any other way they chose. This was the third time in two generations that they had come to France and rubbed the Frenchman's nose in the dust. Normandy, it is true, had escaped on the two previous occasions, but that somehow made it seem all the worse this time. And so the Normandy peasant had settled down to a policy of cheating the Germans, of swindling and opposing the Germans, all of which was good business. It was a sort of passive resistance which yielded good dividends. It helped them to preserve at least a vestige of their pride. Your cider-drinking Norman is a dour, unemotional, intensely parochial man. He lives in a cold climate not conducive to blood heats one way or the other. He did not hate the German *per se*, but simply what the German represented, the abasement of France.

His real hate was aimed in quite another direction. It was aimed at the collaborationist. Since this was a narrow farming community, the collaborationist was not in the main hated for the obvious reasons—because he was a traitor, because he supported a foreign ideology. Frenchmen tend to be liberal about other people's ideologies. He was hated principally because he used his German connections to score off his neighbors. That was the crime. He inflated himself above his rivals. He got more money, more privileges. That was the unforgivable thing. He did good business, while the others trudged along in the hard old way scraping their sous together.

All this may seem intensely materialistic. But there it was; that materialism existed and not only in France either. Apart from the adolescents, the genuine enthusiasts, and apart from private altruistic love inside a family or a circle of acquaintances, the French were no different from anyone else. This materialistic basis of their lives had to be settled first. After that one spared time for the patriotism, the loyalties and enthusiasms. So the collaborationist angered the mass of Frenchmen on two planes: he threatened his neighbors' essential materialistic existence and he ran counter to the general loyalty which was love of France and hatred of her invaders.

The French guerilla fighters, the Maquis who sacrificed everything to their loyalty and enthusiasm, were loved in direct ratio to the hatred directed on the collaborationists. The Maquis were a minority of Frenchmen, but everyone admired them and was willing to hide them and assist them. They were the expression of the best side of France, of France revived, France non-materialist. So long as the Maquis existed and were ready to risk torture and death at the hands of the Germans, every Frenchman could say: "France is not dead. She is still a country of heroes." Not unnaturally then, when a collaborationist gave away a Maquis to the German Gestapo he was hated with a passion which the incoming Allied soldiers were quite unable to understand. The doughboy and the Tommy were disgusted at the way the French mistresses of German soldiers were dragged out into the village squares to have their heads shaved. It seemed indecent and vicious. Often they intervened. All this became much more intense when we got to Paris and Brussels, where the flame of revenge burned very brightly indeed. But the basis of the anti-collaborationism was the same in Normandy as everywhere else. After four years of pinpricks and favoritism, the average Frenchman's first desire was to get his own back on the minority of their own men and women who had done well out of the Germans.

The Allies were welcomed in Normandy mainly because of this;

Women of the Resistance, ready to risk torture and death.

because it enabled the collaborationist to be dealt with, because it led to the expulsion of the Germans. We were not welcomed for our own sakes, for the friendly smile on our faces. We were welcomed because of what we came to do, to clear France. That is why the Norman accepted the smashing of his towns in the first assault. To me it was a staggering thing to be met with cheering and waving in the ruined villages. I used to stop and argue with the people. "Why do you welcome us? We have destroyed everything you possess." They would reply: "You don't understand"; and in various ways out would come the arguments I have given above. It never altered. It was always the same argument, and in the end one had to presume it was genuine.

Here and there this general good will was wanting. The French could not understand a great deal of our bombing. Time and again they watched a town go down in ruins when there was not a single German near the place. This they simply could not understand, and they resented it. God knows one can forgive them that. Then too our soldiers did not behave like angels. They seldom do; nor can you expect them to be gentle creatures if you are going to pitchfork them into the brutality of war. Vegetables and fruit were stolen. There were other misdemeanors. The reaction of the Norman was to become a bit sullen.

One other thing has to be understood. Our propaganda had suggested that food and good times would follow in the wake of the invasion. What we had forgotten to tell the people was that there would be a delay in the arrival of the good things, and during this period conditions would be very much worse than they were under the German occupation. With the collapse of the black market and the destruction of the railways and ports it was very difficult to resume the distribution of foodstuffs and goods. Nearly everywhere the arrival of the Allied army was followed by a sharp decline in the civilian standard of living, and often by hunger and disease and cold and death itself. The mails broke down. So did the electric light and the gas. Liberation usually meant excessive hardship for the first few months. In these circumstances you could not always expect the people of Europe to continue to rush about with glad cries and shouts after they had experienced a few months of downright misery.

There was one slight trend which one noticed at first in the French reception of the Allies, especially the British. They were a little afraid that we might be resentful of their country's collapse in 1940. They feared that our reaction might be something like that of the Germans towards Italy when Italy collapsed. In point of fact no such attitude was expressed, and whatever the troops said and felt among themselves I heard no British soldier flinging recriminations at the French in the whole march through France.

There remained the attitude of the French towards General de Gaulle. De Gaulle was a household word in France. Day in and day out the people had been listening to the French radio from North Africa and England. De Gaulle became the symbol of resistance. The people did not know him. They had no notion of what he was like as a man, as a politician or even as a general. All they knew was that he was the chief Frenchman carrying on the struggle from abroad, and would therefore naturally lead the nation as soon as the Allies arrived. There was no question of any opposition party. The only really organized underground group in France was the Community party. The Communists suffered most and worked hardest. They accepted de Gaulle. So did the Socialists and the other left-wing groups. There was therefore no possibility of de Gaulle being disowned. He was simply accepted. His position was not discussed. He was the leader.

Of de Gaulle's personal unpopularity with the leaders in Whitehall and Washington the French people had no knowledge whatever. They presumed that de Gaulle was hand in glove with Roosevelt and Churchill all the way through. Moreover, de Gaulle's intransigent attitude was by no means unpopular with Frenchmen who had been living and fighting abroad. They liked the way he stood up to the President and the Prime Minister. They liked his determination that France should not surrender a foot of her empire. As Henri Bernstein, the playwright, said in New York: "Believe me, this will not make him unpopular with Frenchmen."

I was on the beach when de Gaulle arrived, a week or two after the landing. He was due to arrive in a British destroyer at eleven o'clock, lunch with Montgomery at his headquarters at Creully, and then re-embark for England at 4 P.M. It was no secret that Montgomery, intent on his battle, was finding the stream of visitors from England a little irksome. But this was no tourist jaunt. De Gaulle had a big game to play, and he played it on this day superbly, whether you agree with his tactics or not.

He arrived, not on a British destroyer but on the French *La Combattante;* and late. The first duck that set out to take him off the destroyer was swamped and sunk. Eventually he arrived, not alone but with half a dozen high officials of his staff. There was no emotional scene as the general jumped down on to the sand and thus set foot for the first time in four years on the France that had outlawed him. No French citizen saw him arrive. There were no cheers, no guard of honor. Two A.D.C.'s alone met him. The lunch with Montgomery passed off quickly. Next thing de Gaulle turned up in Bayeux. A jeep ran ahead carrying a young Frenchman who shouted to the crowd, *"de Gaulle vient d'arriver."*

The general got down from his car in the outskirts of the town and walked the length of the Rue St. Jean on foot. He came ambling down the street, a stiff, lugubrious figure, and the people stared curiously. Presently all gathered in the central park, where a rostrum had been erected, and from here de Gaulle delivered a simple and sincere and quite unnotable speech, winding up with everyone singing the Marseillaise. Then he went on to Isigny and other towns in the bridgehead.

Meanwhile it was after four o'clock, and it was suddenly realized at Montgomery's headquarters that de Gaulle was loose in the bridgehead and doing God knew what. A search party set out, and it was appalled to find a banqueting table spread out in the Lion d'Or Hotel. Madame explained that the general had decided to stay the night. This was by no means in the program, and finally de Gaulle was found and conducted back to his destroyer.

A day or two passed before it was realized that a *coup d' état* had been carried out. At Bayeux and the other places he had visited de Gaulle had dropped off his officials, one by one. These officials quickly got in touch with the local resistance movement, and began to assume executive powers. They fired collaborationists. They supervised the local courts. They appointed new men. They began the rounding-up of suspects, and the organization of supplies and housing for the refugees. In short, they began to govern.

These facts were reported to Montgomery, and he was asked what he was going to do about it. Montgomery's attitude was typical. "Are they doing a good job?" Our Civil Affairs officers who had been sent to assist in running the local government were forced to admit that de Gaulle's appointees were doing a very good job indeed. Things of real assistance to the troops were being done. It was decided that the men should stay. De Gaulle's little coup had succeeded.

From this time forward de Gaulle's men were always about two jumps ahead. Their attitude was simply this: France is going to govern herself. More and more they took over the work that the Civil Affairs branch of SHAEF[1] was designed to do. They short-circuited the SHAEF propaganda plans; indeed, the French people had little need of conversion, and were perfectly capable of running

[1] Supreme Headquarters Allied Expeditionary Force.

their own liberation newspapers and radio stations. And so it continued until de Gaulle and le Clerc between them carried off their master-stroke of seizing Paris both politically and militarily before the American army arrived.

But none of this was yet apparent in the early days of the bridgehead. All one knew was that the French were very well disposed indeed. Each day we took our rations into a farmhouse to be cooked, and at once we would be offered cider and meat and fruit. Each day at the front the people gave information to our forward troops on the movements of the Germans directly ahead. Some of the information was a little woolly, but it was always an attempt to be helpful, and often they risked being shot by the Germans. Whenever our patrols or our airmen got cut off, they were sure of finding someone to hide them in the first farmhouse they visited. And eventually the peasants would pass them back into our lines. In places like Bayeux the recruiting of young Frenchmen went on at so hot a pace that it had to be delayed because there were insufficient arms and uniforms.

Meanwhile in the interior the Maquis had risen in strength. At different times they cut all the railways leading into Paris. Enemy divisions crossing France were forced to proceed as though through hostile country, with armed reconnaissance units on either flank. Pitched battles involving ten thousand men were being fought in the south. All over France German ammunition dumps were being exploded, bridges blown up, telegraph lines cut and German convoys waylaid. It was no longer safe for German vehicles to travel through forests without escort. Hundreds of miles behind the front the enemy garrisons found they had to mount guard at night. Sabotage spread through the factories and the workshops like a disease. Within a few weeks the Maquis were holding areas of France three or four times the size of our bridgehead in Normandy. France was in a state of open rebellion.

Very little of all this was known to the outside world at the time, partly because the facts were largely secret, and partly because attention was focussed on the more definite and understandable front in Normandy. It was not until the Allies broke out and began to run through France that it was realized how much the way had been prepared for us by the French themselves. From the moment of our landing the Germans were forced to fight a secondary battle against the Maquis in their rearward lines, and that fight increased and continued right up to and after the fall of Paris.

This then was the first essential difference between what we found in southern and in northern Europe, between Italy and

France. Both countries wanted the expulsion of the Germans, wanted it with an intensity that amounted to a mania and a passion. The Italians in the mass were entirely passive about it; they simply wanted food and peace in a non-German world. The French were prepared to fight for peace. They were sickened of passivity. They now said that anything was better than surrender to the Germans, and that no tragedy that could have befallen France in the war was equal to the misery of the four years' occupation. I will not say that all Frenchmen were prepared to act upon these lines; but I must report from my own observation that a genuine renaissance had taken place among the young men, especially since 1940.

In the two years I lived in Paris before the war, life for the average young Frenchman was a thing of *apéritifs* and political arguments, of little intrigues and maneuverings to make more money, of less and less work, less and less willingness to take responsibility for a family or a cause or anything. An effete and chirrupy cynicism was the vogue. War at any price was regarded as a meaningless suicide, and (when it actually began) an unbearable horror.

A great deal of all that had now completely vanished. Somehow the Germans had accomplished the impossible; they had made themselves so detested that a whole nation was ready to rise against them. This movement was entirely spontaneous. The young men who had been so reluctantly dragged down to the Maginot Line in 1940 were now running underground arsenals, and deliberately starting skirmishes in the streets. The terms now were no fixed rate of pay, no pension, torture if you were caught. They volunteered in tens of thousands from Marseilles to Cherbourg. They had no uniforms, and precious few arms. When you met them in the streets they were full of excitement and enthusiasm. They had all the martial confidence and eagerness one used to see in Mussolini's young Fascists when they came home from their victories in Spain and Abyssinia. What had made the change in the two countries? In Italy the people cringed and whined when we arrived. Here the French held up their heads. Even the children did not beg. Yet Italy had been the victor; France the defeated.

In the end, as one went round the *bistros* of Bayeux and the villages of Normandy, one could find only one answer—that it was an affair of the spirit. Italy had suffered no more than France, but something in the character of the Italians had collapsed. They had made a throw for a series of mean little victories, and then when the luck began to run against them they found the stakes were too high, and they had no heart to sustain the game. In reality the Italians had had twenty years of surrender. They surrendered first to the Fascists, then to the Germans. When finally they came to surrender to us they were utterly broken. Since the days of Cavour and Garibaldi there had been no real spirit of rebellion in Italy; she simply went the way of least resistance, and the brief Fascist hour in Africa and France only made things seem worse.

In France the people were not used to surrender. In 1940 they knew war far better than either England or America knew it,[1] and on being exposed to 2000 German tanks they collapsed. They had no real heart for the struggle. Then before the end of 1940 they began to realize that there was something worse than war, and that was the humiliation and injury to the spirit in defeat. This was the soil of the resistance movement. It was first of all a revolt, not so much against the Germans, but against the concept of defeat, *against themselves as they were* in 1940. Most of France did not see this to begin with. The people were bewildered. But by 1942 they began to feel the profound necessity for revolt. By 1944 it had developed into a national revival, a revival of pride. And since they found themselves willing to die they saw no need to apologize to the Allies or to anyone. This was the basis of de Gaullism, or more particularly de Gaulle's unsubtle refusal to compromise. I do not say it spread very far and wide against that broad platform of materialism. But it was an accepted and increasing part of France's life, this desire for revolt, by the time we came to land. It was stimulated by the Gestapo, by the dragging absence of three million Frenchmen in Germany, and by some of the bitterest memories a people had ever known.

The question then of whether or not the French welcomed us was really hopelessly out of date. They had gone a long way beyond that: they wanted to fight the Germans. They had found themselves in defeat, just as Italy had lost herself in years of seeming victory.

.

1 CASUALTIES OF LAST WAR

	Killed	Wounded
British Empire (including India) . .	947,023	2,121,906
United States	115,660	205,690
France (incomplete) dead and missing	1,385,300	2,000,000

8. Caen-Cherbourg Battles

(The information contained in the footnotes to this and subsequent chapters was gathered from captured German documents.)

Rommel by the middle of June had taken his decision. Or rather the decision began to be forced on him, partly by his own impetuous aggressiveness and partly by the dreams of Hitler. The Allies had won the first "battle of the beaches." Well and good. They could still be driven off. They could be contained in the narrow bridgehead. They could be continually harassed and attacked. Then at the first signs of weakness the panzers would make their drive through to the sea. The battle of France was going to be fought in Normandy. And the order was: "Attack. Keep on attacking."[1]

It was a policy the end of which no one could see, a bull-at-a-gate policy, a short range policy, a gambler's policy that might eventually suck up every German reserve in France. And it was the policy which we could most nearly have wished for. There were still two strong German armies in northern France; the Fifteenth, north of the Seine, and the Seventh, grouped round the bridgehead. In addition there were still the forces in the south. Even at this early date the Germans decided to abandon southern France. All troops down there which were capable of movement were directed northward on to the bridgehead. At the same time several panzer divisions were brought across from Russia, and Rommel began to milk the Fifteenth Army. Bit by bit the reinforcements were brought up to the line in Normandy and put directly into battle. A series of chiseling attacks were developed along the line; principally around Caen.

This is the point at which the flying bomb enters the story. The launching sites were established north of the Seine, largely in the area between Amiens and Dunkirk. They were designed to destroy London. It was also hoped that they would break up the invasion by smashing the embarkation ports in southern England. But the program for the flying bomb was much delayed. First there had

[1] June 6th, the day of the landing, General Jodl ordered from Hitler's headquarters that the Allied bridgehead must be "cleaned up by midnight." He was told that this was impossible.

In Northern France the bombs were launched from huge ramps.

been that fantastically lucky and successful raid of the R.A.F. on the experimental station at Peenemünde, when so many of the German scientists had been killed. Then when some two hundred launching sites had been established the R.A.F. had blotted them out. The opening barrage of flying bombs, which was planned for the autumn of 1943, was only ready to come into operation on a limited scale in the summer of 1944: nine months late.

With some reason Germany placed tremendous hopes in the flying bomb. Vast underground factories were at work. There was a reasonable chance that by October of 1944 they would be able to increase by five times the number of missiles in their original barrage. One can imagine that Rommel was therefore instructed with some urgency that the launching sites north of the Seine were to be protected at all costs. It was reasonable to suppose that the Allies might attempt another landing in the Calais area in order to silence the flying bomb. How far then could Rommel milk the Calais garrison, the Fifteenth Army, in order to reinforce his troops in Normandy? He needed the troops badly at the bridgehead. He was running round the outside of a perimeter, while the Allies sat compactly inside. Given the whole of the Fifteenth Army he might smash the invasion, or at least contain it until the rains came and he had thrown up a defensive line. But could he take the risk of entirely denuding the flying bomb sites of their garrison?

In the end it was a compromise. He took divisions away from the

The bombs were stored in great underground cellars.

Fifteenth Army one by one. As the German position round the bridgehead became more and more critical he accelerated the process. At length only a skeleton army remained north of the Seine. Some forty divisions were committed to the Normandy battle, and when they were out-maneuvered and beaten there was nothing left in all France; not even enough men to defend the flying bomb sites for a few weeks.

The whole battle of Normandy becomes clear if this point is understood; the fact that one by one the German divisions were lured on to the Allied lines round the bridgehead, and there cut up one by one. Had they all been committed together the Allies might well have been contained in Normandy for another six months or a year. It might have been another, larger Anzio. Alternatively, had Rommel abandoned the Normandy battle in June, and withdrawn his forces to stand on the Seine or even back on the Rhine, the war might have been still further prolonged. As it was, he suited our purposes perfectly. Three-quarters of our troops were green. Since the Germans never mounted a major counter-attack we were able to "blood" these green troops carefully. They were not put to do too much too quickly. They had a chance to learn. At the same time we were able to build up supplies against the day when we would be ready to break out of the bridgehead. And all the time, in one futile attack after another, the German divisions were being worn down. They were often tired before they even got to the front. The Allied air forces bombed them all the way up to Normandy. With the bridges down, and movement only really safe by night, it often took a division a week or more to make the short journey from the German border to the front-line.

You must conceive the Normandy battle in three phases: first the assault, lasting over a period of about forty-eight hours. Then from the end of the first week in June until the last week in July, the period of building up supplies and of wearing down the enemy: then the break-out. Perhaps it is early yet to judge, but the whole operation (from our point of view) seems to me to have been classic both in its planning and in its execution. There were many tactical errors and, as always, the imponderables like luck and the spirit of the soldiers were the deciding factors. Yet the plan was there before we ever started out, and credit must be given for it.

Let us return to the moment at the end of the first week in June, when nothing was certain except that we had got ashore. Caen was to have been captured on the first or the second day. The Germans saw its importance as a pivot just as well as we did, and as soon as they recovered from their original shock they rushed to protect the place. The battle for Caen continued thereafter for a solid month. That was the extreme left flank. On the extreme right we needed Cherbourg. The Germans foresaw that danger too. But Cherbourg was stuck out on a limb at the end of a peninsula, and there was nothing much they could do about it except tell the garrison to hang on for (and until) grim death. In the center, just below Bayeux, was Mount Pinçon. We wanted Mount Pinçon. It was a height that dominated the whole of the bridgehead. And the Germans knew that too.[1]

From first to last during the whole six weeks battle this central

---

[1] On June 8th the Germans picked up from the water in the Channel an Allied operational order revealing that we intended to take Cherbourg from the land with American troops, while the British seized Bayeux and Caen and ultimately effected a junction with the U.S. contingent at Carentan.

June 9th: Rommel ordered Cherbourg must be held at all costs, and the U.S. and British forces prevented from linking up. Rommel at this time had lost contact with his disordered coastal units and his forward commands were everywhere appealing for air protection.

June 11th: The Panzer Group West headquarters were knocked out by a direct hit.

June 12th: General Marchs, one of the most seasoned German commanders, was killed.

Defenses line up: rocket guns in action.

Londoners slept in the underground stations.

By freak chance a flying bomb hit the Guards Chapel in London at 11 o'clock on a Sunday morning, when the church was full.

sector of the line hardly moved. When either side attempted to do anything spectacular in the center they ran into trouble. This we began to learn in the first week. Someone found an empty road leading down from Bayeux through Villers-Bocage to the bottom of the mountain, and the tanks made a bolt along it. At first there was no opposition. The advance began in the hot afternoon sun, and it was like the old desert days again, especially as the men engaged were the Desert Rats, the men of the Seventh Armored Division. Thick fine dust smothered us all. Like most of the Normandy roads, this was enclosed by steep banks and hedges, and even in the surrounding fields you could not see more than a couple of hundred yards ahead; a hedge in full leaf invariably blocked the view. By any standard it was extremely unsound country for tanks—especially our tanks. Our tanks were Shermans, Churchills and Cromwells. None of them was the equal of the German Mark Five (the Panther), or the Mark Six (the Tiger); nor could all the ministerial statements in the House of Commons make them equal. It was after all solely a matter of plain figures, and the tank being a fairly out-of-date weapon it is not difficult to define.

The German tanks had 88-millimeter guns. We had 75-millimeter guns. The Germans had much thicker armor than we had. Their tanks were effective at a thousand yards or more: ours at ranges around five hundred yards. We had a tank known as the Firefly which was a Sherman with a 17-pounder gun. We also had a new type of ammunition. But both the Firefly and the new ammunition scarcely existed in France during the vital battles of the bridgehead. In the end we used rocket-firing Typhoon aircraft with which to fight the German tanks, and they were a great success. Whenever we sighted German tanks we called up the Typhoons. Our own tanks were unequal to the job because they were not good enough. There may be various ways of dodging this plain truth, but anyone who wishes to do so will find himself arguing with the crews of more than three British armored divisions which fought in France. A destroyer does not engage a cruiser on equal terms. In fairness it must be admitted that neither Tigers nor Panthers could have exploited the break-through in the way the Shermans and the Cromwells did. I am simply asserting here that in battle our tanks were inferior to the German models.

However, here we were in this first week of the battle exploiting a possible break-through with very little opposition, an armored brigade in front and the infantry coming along behind in lorries. It was exciting to be on the move at such a pace. We by-passed Tilly-Bocage, where the Germans were still holding out, and early the following morning the tanks ran through to Villers-Bocage. It was a neat little crossroad town. The central square. The church. The restaurant called Vieux Puits which was famous for its tripe and its *Escalope à la Normande*. Just over a thousand inhabitants. The tanks roared through to the slopes beyond. The infantry followed in single file along the side of the road, and presently we were all standing in the central square together.

Then began the battle of Villers-Bocage which was typical of all the fighting in central Normandy. The Germans opened fire on the town, and while we ran for cover the Vieux Puits, with the chef inside, began tumbling down. Then our tanks were engaged. They were dispersed hull down behind the hedges, but every time they moved the Germans sighted them and hit them. Eventually the whole squadron was cut off, and while the German infantry began pressing in on the flanks the rest of us drew back out of Villers-Bocage. You could never be sure of where the fire was coming from. Every time a tank turned the corner of a road it ran the danger of being ambushed by an anti-tank gun. When the infantry went forward through the breast-high wheat to get at the enemy gun they found themselves enfiladed. At this stage the Germans were far ahead of us in using the country. Their infantry smothered themselves in leaves and branches. They crawled up to the forward positions on their bellies. They never showed themselves. Whole platoons of snipers would tie themselves into the leafy branches of the trees, and there they would wait silently for hours, even days, until they got a chance of a shot. The snipers were something new in our experience. They were deadly. First the British officers were picked off; then the N.C.O.'s. No road was safe. Even when you were well behind the front you had to expect a sudden burst of bullets through the jeep. You had to be ready to jump for the ditches at every daylight hour of the day. I for one found this sniping unnerving. It was so sudden. So secret. There was so little you could do to protect yourself. And the Germans were experts at it. It was a kind of Red Indian warfare, with no defined front. One day, for example, I drove up to a deserted railway siding, and found the station master standing about in a bemused way. He had just been bombed.

"What's happening?"

"I don't know," he answered dazedly. "All I know is that there have been no trains through since Tuesday." And even as we talked a Spandau machine-gun began firing. We were miles behind the line, but the Germans had crept back through the grass in the night.

And so with our tanks out-gunned and our infantry running into ambushes we abandoned our thrust to Mount Pinçon and called up the bombers instead. The plan was: "Let us bomb the crossroads town of Villers-Bocage. Let us knock the houses into the streets, and then the Germans will not be able to get their supplies through to their forward troops."

(It was early in the campaign; much too early for the commanders to pause and remember Cassino, and all the useless battering down of the villages in Sicily and Italy.)

The bombers came low over the bridgehead from England. They were a majestic sight as they came past the spires of Bayeux Cathedral in the evening light, and headed for a rift in the clouds above Villers-Bocage. There was just this channel of clear pale-blue sky, flanked by great banks of white cumulus clouds, and as soon as the bombers, wave on wave, entered the clear space they came into ack-ack fire. Then they dropped their bombs and wheeled away round the western cloud bank for England. It was all over in twenty minutes. In went the ground attack and came under precisely the same opposition as it had struck before. The Germans had simply withdrawn out of Villers-Bocage and taken cover in the surrounding fields. Eventually, after many days, when we got into Villers-Bocage there was nothing you could really recognize any more. The bulldozers arrived and drove new roads through the twenty-foot deep rubble. It was like an archeological excavation into a lost world. As one stood in the cuttings and looked up at the walls of debris, one saw perhaps the fender of a car lying on a baby's pram, or other odd thing like a bathroom tap or a wine basket or a painting. But for the most part it was unrecognizable dust. The Germans had not bothered to try and open up the roads. They simply made detours round the many side-tracks. The bombing of Villers-Bocage accomplished nothing unless you count the delay caused to our subsequent advance.

One after another the Normandy villages were obliterated like this, until there was a pretty continuous belt of destruction round the bridgehead. In some cases the bombing and shelling of built-up areas was fruitful; often it was simply the use of power because the power was available. The Germans, as we saw from captured documents, very quickly developed a technique of fighting without the aid of aircraft and with one-half the number of guns the Allies deployed. As soon as we were about to attack they withdrew the bulk of their troops to the rear, leaving only a light screen in front. When the bombing and the barrage were over, the main German forces were quickly moved forward into their old positions. They preferred a system of staggered defenses rather than a continuous line. If an Allied tank was missed by the first platoon it was tackled farther back. When Allied tanks pressed forward down a road, the Germans chose to shoot first at the third or fourth tank, so that when wrecked and burning it would block the retreat of the others.

Little by little our green troops learned. The progress of the Americans was astonishing. I remember their advance on Cherbourg chiefly as a series of fast loops and detours along the side-roads. One or two really skilled divisions like the Ninth were in the van. As soon as they struck opposition on the road they dodged round it, and pushed ahead, leaving the artillery to clear up the blockage later on. Very soon they had crossed the base of the Cherbourg peninsula and cut the German forces in two. Those of

One after another the Normandy villages were obliterated.

the enemy who were in the north turned and ran for the garrison at Cherbourg, and Cherbourg itself was invested on three sides. It was all done with remarkable speed, and with a kind of buccaneering spirit which you only find among troops who are entirely fresh, entirely confident.[1]

1 June 15th: Rommel expressed to his staff officers the opinion that the German front would have to be withdrawn and Normandy given up.

June 16th: Hitler personally ordered that NO troops were to be taken out of the Cherbourg garrison and that the present line had to be held at all costs. Hearing this Rommel telephoned Rundstedt and said: "If the troops stay where they are the enemy will enter Cherbourg today." And he asked for "freedom of movement."

June 17th: Rundstedt got through to Hitler and extracted a new order: "The line can be withdrawn on Cherbourg, but there must be no general retreat." Hitler was also insisting that a large perimeter must be thrown up round the fort.

One's memory of that blitz falls into a series of unrelated little incidents. There was the day when we lay in a sunken lane in the sunshine above Cherbourg. German bullets kept smacking against the far bank of the lane, but it was quite safe if you kept low down. The soldiers slept. They slept like tired-out children who had played very hard and now for a few hours were weary of the game; and if the others wanted to go on playing, well then, that was their affair. The Bocage country opens out into rich green slopes around Cherbourg, and now we could look down on the retreating Germans and see the town burning. There were many unburied bodies along the road, and much loot to be had from the abandoned German camps. Army horses were roaming about or lying dead among the dead cattle and the dead men. We must have seen a thousand dead cows in Normandy, perhaps two thousand, and one could never get used to that appalling sweet sickly stench. There was only one thing worse, the sweet smell of dead men. But all this for the moment was of no consequence to these children lying asleep in the sun. Up to now this had been for them a fine clean war, with plenty of excitement and movement. They had had the pleasure of moving on to a new place every day, the stimulation of the hunt. They were fighting on the run, which is probably the best kind of fighting; just as static trench warfare is probably the worst kind of fighting. Even the tearing screaming wail of the nebelwerfers coming up the valley—one of the most eerie noises of the war—did not wake them. As yet they had not been touched either by fear of war or the squalor of war or by the consequences of war. They were not yet bored by it. For all these reasons, plus the fact of their superb physique, they were probably at that moment the finest soldiers in France. Nothing was more certain than that they would presently wake up and go down the hill to the conquest of Cherbourg.

Traveling with these buoyant soldiers one was quite unconsciously gathered into their enthusiasm. There was a good deal of street fighting in Cherbourg. The arsenal on the western side of the town was burning furiously, and in all the surrounding streets the shots were passing up and down. It rained, and nobody appeared to care either about the rain or the shooting. Something was happening every two minutes—a batch of German officers coming in with their hands up, a landmine going up in the next street, a team of mortar gunners running down the pavement to a new position in the schoolhouse. Often the skirmishing went on at a distance of barely a hundred yards. A Frenchman who could not wait until the end of the battle to express his joy drew us into his parlor. Out came the usual bottle of liberation champagne; the calvados and the cognac. The women ran about the kitchen making omelettes for the victors. A stream of Spandau bullets hit the wall, and still the Frenchman raised his glass: *"À la Victoire!" "Aux Alliés!" "À la France!"* He was not drunk, merely intoxicated with excitement. And so, I imagine, were we. A soldier clamored at the door: "Get out of here quick. There's a German with a machine-gun coming through the garden."

"Entrez! Entrez!" shouted the patron. *"Prenez un verre."* Another round of bullets hit the wall.

One of the women spoke English. "You must have a little more omelette," she said. "Dear, dear, what a day it is for us. You cannot imagine how we have waited for you."

And the patron: *"Vive la Libération!"*

The soldier banged at the door again. "He's getting over the garden wall. You better get out of here."

"Away, away!" roared the patron. "You are spoiling the lunch. These gentlemen are my guests."

I do not clearly remember the upshot of it all, except that there was some confusion in the garden, and after that the meal went on more peacefully.

Over the opposite side of the town a group of German gunners bricked themselves up in one of the underground passages of Fort Roule for a suicide stand. Eighty thousand cases of brandy were found in a Wehrmacht storehouse there. Genuine drunkenness began to succeed the drunkenness of excitement. Haphazard fighting was going on in a dozen different places at once. And eventually the German commander came out for the surrender.[1]

The prisoners were most unusual. It was in a little village called Bricquebec that I finally got a chance to see them close at hand. A series of wooden sheds had been wired off as a prisoners' cage, and there were five separate compartments. German officers. German N.C.O.'s. German soldiers. A mixture of Russian, Polish and Czech conscripts. And then an indeterminate collection of Todt workers in civilian clothes, mostly Italian and Spanish. A French crowd stood outside looking through the wire.

[1] June 27th: Urgent inquiries were being made in the German High Command to discover if the BBC statement that von Schieben, the commander of Cherbourg garrison, was a prisoner was correct or not. For some days von Schieben's only communication with the outside world had been radio and now this had failed. A message did come through to Rommel from one of the last German outposts at the tip of the peninsula several days later. It related that the Americans had released eight captured German nurses to tend the wounded in this final stronghold. The commander wanted to know whether or not he had the permission of the High Command to thank the Americans.

In the midst of this babel each nationality behaved exactly as you would have expected. The German officers and N.C.O.'s sat in taut and rigid little groups. They looked across the heads of their guards and the other prisoners, saying nothing. They did not even speak to each other. What they wished to convey was perfectly clear: dignity, pride, contempt, indifference. Strength in defeat. On the whole they succeeded in this attitude. Or at least they succeeded in convincing themselves. The guards were bored with it, and the other prisoners indifferent.

The German privates were sleeping in rows, striking no attitudes, simply resting. When a new truck-load of prisoners arrived, and they were ordered to make room for them, the Germans rose in a body. They moved three paces to the right. Then they lay down again in rows. Quite possibly they would all have gone to sleep simultaneously if someone had given the order.

Then the Russians and the Poles. They stood like cattle. Dumb, slow and heavy. One man sang a lament. The rest simply stood and waited. They were given biscuits and meat, and they showed no reaction except to reach out and take the food. Had they been led out and shot one by one they would probably have shown no surprise. In every way the situation was entirely beyond their comprehension.

Then the Italians. They came clamoring at the wire, ten of them talking together. "You speak Italian? Ah, Merciful God, he speaks Italian. Excuse. Excuse. A great service! The very greatest service! Will you explain to the American soldiers that we did not fight? We did not fight at all. We were prisoners of the Germans. They made us work. We are nothing whatever to do with the Germans. We wish to fight the Germans. We wish to be free and go home. Mario and Giuseppe here must return to Cherbourg to collect our things. We had no time to collect our clothes. They will be gone only a short time. Have you any cigarettes, any chocolate?"

Outside the cage the French had been shaving the heads of two village girls who had slept with the Germans. And now in the dusk they had come up to the gates to jeer and spit at the Germans inside. They began thinking up new lines of invective and the noise was considerable.

The American private on the gate was a good head and shoulders above the crowd. "Aw. Git the hell out of it," he said at last, waving his gun.

That was the outward scene in the prisoners' cage, and it made no sense at all. A dozen different nationalities. All of them reacting in different ways, pulling in different directions, speaking different

German prisoners in Cherbourg.

languages. And yet an hour or two since they had all been fighting with a suicidal ferocity. Pillboxes were being held long after their eventual destruction was a certainty. The Russians had been firing right up to the last few yards before they threw up their hands. And now here in the prisoners' cage there was complete disintegration, an evident hatred of the Germans. As one group had marched in, a German officer had stooped to pick up a fallen cigarette. Before his hand could reach it a Pole ran forward and ground the butt into the mud. Then he turned and laughed in the German's face.

I found an American soldier who spoke Polish, and we began to talk to the prisoners, especially one man who was more intelligent than the others. "Why did I fight for the Germans? Like to see my back? It's got scars across it from the neck down to the arse. They hit me there with a sword. Either you obeyed orders or you got no food. Certainly I went on firing from the trench. There was a German N.C.O. standing behind me with a revolver. It wasn't enough just to shoot. You had to shoot straight. If you didn't you got a bullet in the back. Don't believe me. Ask the others. Like the Germans? I'd like to tear their guts out."[1]

Little by little the story came out. The Turkestan carpenter, the clerk from Lvov. The mechanic from Barcelona and the farmer's boy who was born in Gorizia. These were the children of occupied Europe, and it suddenly became apparent that to ascribe to them the name of "enemy," or indeed the name of anything, was a ridiculous over-simplification. The word "conscript" came nearest to their condition. But conscription in what circumstances? Nothing had been seen like it in Europe since the Napoleonic wars. Even that parallel was not complete enough. One began to have a vision of the dark ages in Europe, of a period infinitely less moral than the time of the Roman Empire. This was less than a mercenary army. It was an impressed army. The soldier fought not out of the voluntary desire for money, but out of fear for what the Germans would do to him if he did not fight. He avoided the certainty of immediate punishment from the Germans by accepting the chance of being hit by the Allies on the battlefield.

One began to follow the stages of Nazi conscription. They, the Germans, the master race, the men with all the modern engines of war, had over-run the villages of Europe. France, Belgium, Holland, Norway, Denmark, the Baltic States, Poland, White Russia,

---

[1] June 28th: The commander of the Wolga Tat Battalion, a foreign unit, reported to the German army headquarters that he (the commander) had been shot at by his own men and one hundred of them had deserted. The battalion was withdrawn from the line.

the Ukraine, Jugoslavia, Czechoslovakia, Hungary, Austria, Rumania and the rest. They came into the villages in uniform, riding in armored cars. They were the overlords, the new feudal masters. They made a great show in front of the unpolitical village boy. They said: "This is the new epoch. This is the era of the new god Adolf Hitler. A new uniform and a gun for everyone who wants to follow." It was easy enough to dazzle the villager. Instead of milking cows every night he could swing along behind a military band. He got a new rifle all to himself. There were sports and competitions. Adolf Hitler wanted to build young healthy bodies. Up at dawn. Exercises. Plenty of good· fresh food. Solemn and stirring parades. The boy was one of a team now, an heroic team, a crusader against bolshevism. And off he went to the front.

Quite a few Letts and Croats and White Russians had been gathered in this way. All volunteers. Germany was on the way to victory, and they were marching with her. But as the war went on more men were needed. It became necessary to visit the villages again. There were a certain number of able-bodied men in every place. Now they were told: "You must play your part in the great revolution. We want workers and fighters. We will pay good wages." And then, when the volunteers did not come forward, the threats. The unpolitical boy did not have much choice. Either go with the Nazis or run away and hide. It needed courage to do the latter. Food was becoming more and more difficult to get in the village. Life was getting duller and more constricted. Reluctantly many went off to the labor gangs and the new regiments. Still it was not enough. More men were needed. This time they were taken by force. You got a ticket saying you must report for duty. There was no alternative. From one end of Europe to the other the conscripts were forced into the machine. And finally you arrived at the ludicrous anomaly of the Russian peasant firing at the American doughboy in Normandy—a Russian peasant who knew nothing of Stalinism or Hitlerism, who knew only that somehow he had been led into a pillbox and told to fire.

In this village of Bricquebec there was a shrewd little French lawyer who said: "You cannot understand it yet, because you have not experienced these past four years as we have. As you go forward into France you will begin to understand. In the end you will see that the important thing is not what the Nazis have done to Europe, but what they have done to themselves. The real tragedy is not this mercenary army, but the perverse superiority complex in the mind of the German boy. He really believes in his superiority—at any rate on a physical plane. For four years he has run around

Europe, the master of everything. Whenever he has given an order the people have to run to obey him. He really believes that he is a superior being, and that he is unconquerable. The idea of defeat, of obeying someone else's orders, is unthinkable to him. He cannot adjust his mind to it. Even here at Cherbourg when he sees himself retreating he says: 'This is only a local thing. The Führer will prevail in the end.' And so he makes one last triumphant gesture, the gesture that will finally prove his superiority. He elects to stand and fight until he is killed. To you and me, my friend, it is Wagnerian. It is pathological. It is ridiculous. But I assure you that the German adolescent regards suicide on the battlefield as the final defiant act of the superior being, the final gesture of his overlordship. And later on, when it is apparent to the Nazis that they are going to lose, they will continue to indulge in this hara-kiri for its own sake."

The argument seemed extravagant. And yet the prisoners seemed to support it. Everywhere we went it was apparent that as soon as the conscripts got free of the German control they turned on their masters. They hated them. Even the Germans themselves, people like the Austrians, turned on the Nazis as soon as they were captured. They would give any information they were asked for. Except among the outright Nazis the Germans were already convinced that they would lose the war. Even the Hitler Youth began to be doubtful of the outcome as the days went by. But their attitude—just as my little French lawyer had indicated—became that of the gangster who is determined to shoot it out long after all chance of escape has gone.

The more one saw of these German problem children—the sixteen- and seventeen- and eighteen-year-olds—the more one lost hope for the future of Germany. They were barely coming out of the kindergarten when the Nazis got hold of them. Steadily, year by year, life had been represented to them merely as a preparation for battle and death for the Führer. Side by side with this was a gangsterish lack of ordinary morals. Every SS boy we captured appeared to be having affairs with several girls at once. They carried love letters of an extraordinary lewdness, and many of these letters were written by German girls of barely sixteen. This pornography went hand in hand with a superstitious revival of religion. Many of the youths carried printed prayers and charms and lucky favors. Their chain of reactions was simple enough. It was the fevered and masturbatic little boy who grabbed at his pleasures and then suddenly in a fit of depression and remorse turned to religion for support and forgiveness. Among his comrades he had all the

A 16-year-old German prisoner taken at Cherbourg; for him, life had been nothing but a preparation for battle.

obvious virtues; physical courage, honesty, cleanliness, a sense of method. But if he was dealing outside the master race then any excess was condoned. In every French village it was the accepted thing that the SS boy got drunk and smashed things. For the first time we came on the evidence of rape. And then again, as in Italy, the atrocities began. There was one incident in particular, concerning a number of Canadians who were herded together and shot in reprisal for the raid on Dieppe. It was at Dieppe the Germans alleged that the Canadians had handcuffed some of their prisoners, and that they had shot others.

All this viciousness increased rather than diminished as the campaign went on, but it is essential to make a difference between the ordinary German and conscript on the one hand, and the Hitler Youth and SS and the Gestapo on the other. What I have written above refers to the minority, the Nazi boy and the Gestapo agent.

Among our own men the most interesting thing that was coming to light was the success of the green soldier and the green division. They tended to make a number of obvious mistakes to begin with, and then almost overnight they became veterans. In the end the new divisions probably did better than the old ones. Formations like the Fifteenth Scottish, the Forty-third, the Eleventh Armored and the Guards Armored were in the main without battle experience before D Day, and they all did brilliantly at different times. So did the Third and the Forty-ninth and some of the independent brigades. If I do not write of the others it is simply because I did not have the opportunity of seeing them in action.

It is probably invidious to single out special units. Three of the greatest divisions in the British desert army—the Fiftieth, and Fifty-first and the Seventh Armored—took part in the Normandy assault. Elsewhere in other books and in many dispatches I have tried to report their exploits. The Fiftieth landed at H Hour on D Day. Partly because I myself came ashore with its rearward elements and partly because I have known that division since its first engagement at Gazala in 1941, I must confess I have a warm bias towards its men and its commanders—a bias which I will try to keep out of this book. All I would like to say here is that the Fiftieth was in the frontline almost without a day's respite throughout the Battle of Normandy and again in Belgium and Holland. Eventually it had to be retired to England.

When the crisis came to the bridgehead, it was the new divisions which bore the first full weight of the shock. This was in the first week of July. We had made some progress across the Orne and the Odon watershed just below Caen when suddenly Montgomery's intelligence staff reported that two German panzer divisions, newly arrived from Russia, were forming up for counter-attack.[1] The Fifteenth Scottish and the Eleventh Armored, who were going ahead steadily, were a little balked when they got urgent orders from the commander-in-chief to cease all offensive operations at once and to retire on to defensive positions. The maneuver was barely completed when the German attack began. The attack continued in waves for nearly a week. Again and again the Fifteenth Scottish came under fire. It was the German intention to break through to the sea if they could. When at last the panzers drew off, leaving their tanks on the field, and their infantry utterly broken, it was seen that the Scots had not budged a foot. To many of us this has seemed the turning point of the whole bridgehead. General Dempsey, the commander of the British Second Army, at once

[1] June 28th: General Hauser was appointed to the command of the Seventh German Army. As a result of the loss of Cherbourg there was a crisis in the enemy High Command about this time. Rundstedt and others had gone to Hitler's headquarters to straighten things out. Hauser's first instinct on getting command was to attack.

advanced upon Caen. On Sunday, July 9th, what was left of the city fell to the Canadians and the British troops. It had been an untidy and in some ways an unsatisfactory action. The final assault was preceded by an immense aerial bombardment, which wrecked large areas of the town without hitting the Germans or discommoding them seriously.

Those of us who were on Livisy Ridge, which runs down into the city from the north, came under shellfire from the Germans who were retiring on the opposite bank of the Orne. We bolted for the uncertain cover of the outer suburbs, and came at once upon such a desolation that one could think only of the surface of the moon. Where three- and four-story houses had been, there were now merely hollows in the ground. Row after row of immense craters. New hills and valleys wherever you looked. The very earth was reduced to its original dust. House after house had been dragged down into the ground and there disintegrated, so that there were no longer streets or footpaths or any decided evidence that human beings had once been here and lived. There was a kind of anarchy in this waste, a thing against which the mind rebelled; an unreasoning and futile violence. We hid in the gray dust and waited for the shelling to stop. There seemed to be no point in going on. This was the end of the world, the end of the war, the final expression of man's desire to destroy. There was nothing more to see, only more dust. Quite possibly one was in a slightly fevered condition to let these ideas run through the mind. One of my companions said: "It's four o'clock. We've just got time to catch the last edition." Catch it with what? With this dust? That was no story.

We walked up the hill very incautiously, exposing ourselves on the skyline. The German 88-millimeter gunsights were very powerful. They shelled us all the way up the hill. Every time there was a lull we ran on for another twenty or thirty yards, and then lay still while the next salvo came over. All the soil in this area had been so shattered by explosives in the past few weeks that the walls of the slit trenches tended to crumple and fall in. Our dog had already been killed by a passing tank that afternoon, our jeep hit by shrapnel. And then there had been this dust. One after another the little despairing events of the day ran through one's head as we lay on the ground, waiting to be hit or not to be hit. Eventually we collected ourselves in the cellar of the farmhouse on the hill, and the barrage went on and on. This, compared with the average barrage we fired at the enemy, was a trifling thing. How did they stand it?

When it slackened a little we decided to run, one by one at

intervals of fifty yards, until we got over the crest of the hill. I was
the last out and I was puffing comfortably along the road at a jog-
trot when suddenly a voice hailed me across the field. "Hey you. Are
you from SHAEF?"

"No. Why?"

"Well, do you mind not running like that? It makes my men
wonder what's happening when they see people running."

I was much too frightened to be angry. Just the same I wanted to
kill that officer. It was a pretty dirty crack at SHAEF at that. However, we caught the edition and got back to our beds in the Lion
d'Or in Bayeux. The officer and his platoon stayed out on Livisy
Ridge.

Caen was relatively quiet the next day. There was much to see.
The best of the delicate tracery on St. Peter's had survived somehow, although the building was only a shell. St. Etienne was intact,
and in the belief that God would protect them from bombs about
five thousand people were living there. Children were racing about
between the chapels. Each family took up about twenty feet of floor
space, and there were more in the crypt. The stench was appalling.
A little crowd gathered in front of the Lycée next door to see the
ceremony of liberation. They put up the French flag. Then the
Marseillaise. The Marseillaise sung among the ruins and the inter-
mittent shellfire, the most triumphant cry yet allowed to the human
spirit, a thing beyond tears when there were so many dead.

Aux armes, citoyens!

Six French youths, looking theatrically serious, with tommy-guns
under their arms, marched down towards the canal where German
snipers were holding out. The lieutenant in front was trying to
keep them in step. *Aux armes, citoyens!* They were not very skillful.
The lieutenant got shot dead before he had gone two blocks.

9. The Break-out

Towards the end of July nearly a million American and
British troops were either ashore in Normandy, or about to come
ashore. The bridgehead was stretched like a drum. Even though a
completely new system of roads and ports had been built, the traffic
blocks sometimes extended for ten or fifteen miles. We were ap-

proaching the crisis of the campaign, the crucial moment for the whole of western Europe. Montgomery remained Allied commander in the field, working from a headquarters near Bayeux, midway between the American and the British armies.

Rommel lay on a hospital bed fighting for his own life. The long personal struggle between him and Montgomery was over. Allied fighters, little knowing what they were doing, had swooped on the German commander's car near Lisieux. Rommel was sitting in the front seat beside the driver, and the smashed corner of the wind-screen had splintered against his temple. A chemist from the neighboring French village looked at the unconscious figure on the road, and said he could do nothing. After that Rommel lay for a long time in the field hospital without regaining consciousness. At last, when he had sufficiently recovered to be removed to Paris, it was seen that it would be months at least before he could return to active command, and indeed his death followed soon afterwards in Germany. His place was taken by von Kluge, a Nazi.[1]

Everywhere the Allies were moving into position for the great battle: the Americans at St. Lô, the British towards Pinçon and the southwest of Caen. It is quite true to say that the bulk of the German armor and some of their best divisions were spaced round Caen, opposite the British; it is quite untrue to suggest that because of this the Americans had no serious opposition at St. Lô. Both armies had immense battles to fight; the British a static battle, the Americans a break-out battle. In neither sector were the opening stages particularly brilliant; many mistakes were made. These errors were followed by a most memorable stroke of arms, when the American First and Third Armies fanned out through Brittany and western France; and still another extraordinary feat when the British took up the running and headed straight for Belgium. These vast and fast pursuits took the headlines. Being easily explicable operations, and in themselves the proof of victory, they engaged the public's attention, and no doubt will remain longest in everyone's mind. In actual fact, they were no more than the intelligent and courageous exploitation of a *fait accompli*. The real decisive issues were fought out on the bridgehead perimeter, and

1 July 4th until July 17th (the date of Rommel's injury) : There were constant upheavals inside the enemy command. On the 4th Rommel told Hauser there was an express order from Hitler he "must not withdraw an inch." Hauser replied the enemy had already broken through. "In that case," Rommel answered, "the enemy will be in St. Germain tomorrow." It is interesting to see the steady disintegration of Rommel's morale right up to the moment of his wounding; it is almost as if he knew that both he and his army were doomed.

The Normandy Campaign

later round the Falaise pocket. It was here in Normandy that the German army was defeated, and in military history the battles of St. Lô and Caen will take precedence over the subsequent rush to the Rhine.

It was already late in July when Montgomery decided to try and smash the German hinge at Caen. Caen, though occupied by the Allies, was still under fire. We now wanted to push beyond the town, and run out over the flatter wheatfields of the Falaise plain, which was said to be excellent tank country. All this time Caen had been in the position of the hinge of a door which stretched out westward towards St. Lô. The plan was for the Americans to keep pushing the door open until General Patton and his fresh Third Army could slip round the corner at Avranches, and over-run Brittany. At the same time the British were to try and unseat the door at its hinge.

Then, when the whole structure was wobbling, the Americans would run round behind the open door and pin against the British such Germans as were left on the spot.

General Dempsey, the commander of the combined British and Canadian forces, now had three full armored divisions—the Seventh, the Eleventh and the Guards—plus several independent armored brigades. He decided to move these in secret to the extreme eastern part of the bridgehead. Bridges were to be thrown up at night across the Orne canal north of Caen. The armor, some five or six hundred tanks, would then cross and charge due south through the German lines in the general direction of Falaise. Some three divisions of infantry would follow to consolidate. The bombers would prepare the way for the tanks.

At this moment the whole question of the use of heavy four-engined bombers was in debate. One school believed that they should be used exclusively for the strategical bombing of Germany; the other school argued that every available weapon should be thrown into this Normandy crisis. The latter school won. We were committed to the use of a new and immensely powerful weapon in

Montgomery with Bradley and Dempsey.

circumstances for which the personnel had had no proper training. When you fly over a battlefield you can very rarely see where the front-line runs. For the most part, nothing shows on the ground except a few indeterminate puffs of smoke. Since all the Normandy countryside looked alike it was extremely difficult to pin-point targets. And now the four-engined bombers were asked to bomb not clearly defined targets like towns and bridges but the open country-side where, unseen to the crews, the Germans were hiding. Further-more, they were asked to bomb targets within a thousand yards or less of our own troops. There had already been a series of mistakes. British and Americans alike had been hit by their own bombs.

By the time Dempsey came to make his tank drive there had been some advance in technique. It was now at last accepted that you do not necessarily hit armies in the field by knocking down towns, and you do frequently retard your own advance because of the craters and the piles of debris. And so this time it was resolved that we should bomb in "strips." The four-engined planes would lay a path of bombs along either side of the projected tank run. This was designed to silence the anti-tank guns and infantry on the flanks. Then the lighter machines would scatter non-cratering anti-personnel bombs along the central strip, where the tanks had to travel. In addition, as soon as the tanks started their run the artil-lery would commence a creeping barrage. The shells would fall just ahead of the oncoming tanks, and the barrage would advance about the same rate—five miles an hour. In other words, the armor would go into action surrounded by a wall of our own explosive. It was a plan that depended on perfect timing. It went wrong. The bombs failed to silence the German gunners. The gunners simply stayed underground until the bombing was over, and then they emerged and opened up at very close range on the hundreds of vehicles deployed across the plain. Two hundred British tanks were lost within a few hours. A number of villages were destroyed by the Lancasters, but the Germans were sheltering outside. And now the enemy rushed his Panthers and Tigers with their superior guns to the front. Only three bridges had been laid across the Orne canal; blockages quickly occurred. The Luftwaffe managed to catch a number of replacement crews while they were sheltering for the night. And so the advance faltered and stopped after a few miles.

We tried again a few days later, using new devices. Pink smoke was put up to blind the enemy to our movements. Searchlights were shone against the clouds at night to give the effect of moonlight. Colored lights were fired into the enemy lines to direct our bombers. All these maneuvers were countered by one means or another. The enemy, for instance, quickly seized on the idea of firing colored guiding lights into *our* lines as soon as aircraft appeared.

It was decided to bomb still more closely to our own infantry, and then we really began to take casualties. It was impossible to strike the targets accurately. I watched one great salvo fall five or six miles inside our own lines. It wiped out a headquarters and caused hundreds of Canadian casualties. Exactly the same thing was happening on the American sector at the opening of the battle of St. Lô. The army was growing distinctly nervous about its own air force, and although much more good than harm was done by the bombing the effect upon morale was becoming serious. A senior American general had been killed, and in the forward platoons the soldiers became just as apprehensive about the bombing as the Germans were. There is always something particularly unnerving about being hit by your own side.

Fortunately the need for heavy, close-support bombing vanished soon after this, and subsequently the technique was greatly improved. One brilliant exception all through had been the British Typhoon rocket planes. They had by now developed such accuracy that they were diving upon single tanks and even if they did not get one-hundred-per-cent results, they often succeeded in scaring the crews into hiding.

All through this period, too, our artillery was increasing and increasing until it reached fantastic proportions. It was an unsettling thing to drive anywhere near the front. Hundreds of guns would suddenly erupt out of the bushes on either side of the road, and the blast would make your eardrums ache for hours on end. In numbers of tanks also we had immense superiority. Provided the crews had been saved, it was no great tragedy to find a hundred wrecked Shermans lying about the fields; one knew that another couple of hundred had just been put ashore. The whole plan was to keep attacking, never to let the enemy rest; to bomb him all the way to the Seine, to shell him all night, to submit him to infantry rushes day after day. We now had overwhelming fire-power, and at the end of July it was in continuous operation for a hundred miles along the front.[1]

1 Conditions in the enemy lines were going in just the opposite direction: towards disintegration. At the end of June German coastal commanders were complaining "the fire of enemy naval guns is unimaginable." On July 5th there was much discussion at German headquarters about the possibility of new Allied sea and air landings. On the same day Seventh Army headquarters was reporting that all their counter-attacks were "suffocated" by the Allied air force. The

There was little enough to show on the map. Villages were won and lost by the dozen, and still the front-line did not move. All the way down the Odon river to Pinçon and thence to St. Lô the German line bulged under an intolerable weight, and still somehow it was patched up and kept together. When prisoners were taken they came out of the line with gray lined faces, suffering not so much from wounds as from shock. Their pocket diaries told the story of the gradual crumbling of the will under persistent fire. The belt of destruction thickened and lengthened every day, until all the area of the perimeter began to assume that beaten, worn-out appearance of the French battlefields in the last war. Great stretches of forest were uprooted. One after another the villages went down into dust. Hundreds of bulldozers struggled to keep pace with the wreckage of the bombing. It did not matter in what direction you turned; within an hour's run by jeep from the beaches you found yourself involved in a battle, and the incessant aching noise of gunfire never ceased. One began to marvel at the German endurance. Somewhere surely the line had to break.

It broke at last at St. Lô. General Bradley, who controlled the American armies under Montgomery, was rapidly developing into one of the ablest field commanders of the war. At St. Lô he was determined to force the issue one way or another. Old friends like the American Ninth Division were being cut to pieces, but still he persisted. On July 24th St. Lô collapsed, a heap of ruins. Patton raced through the gap. He was round the corner at Avranches, a bloodhound in full cry. Aircraft patrolled ahead of the armored columns. At the slightest opposition the tanks and armored cars

---

Chief of Staff added: "Our ground forces will be simply slaughtered if it goes on." July 7th: General Jodl, back at supreme headquarters, told Rundstedt that he "could not" put up to Hitler proposals for new withdrawals. But on July 15th the Germans were describing the battle as "one tremendous blood bath." Appeal after appeal went out for more fuel, more tanks, more aircraft, more men; and above all, permission to withdraw.

Hitler followed the battle very closely, village by village, unit by unit. His occasional direct orders were treated with the utmost reverence even by such seasoned professionals as Rundstedt. "The Führer says"—that was enough to make every German soldier spring to obey. All through this period one has a picture of Hitler, tormented, harassed and blindly angry as the appalling news kept coming in. Even his closest advisers like Jodl were balking at the job of acquainting him with the worst disasters. Possibly there were moments when Hitler was not sane. In the midst of his passionate megalomania one can conceive the bitter personal struggle in trying to force down his mind to the humiliating facts. And the final bitter awakening must have come when the attempt was made upon his life by his own people in the middle of July.

raced round, attacked on the flanks and pressed on. Prisoners who were completely bewildered began to come in by the thousand.[1]

And now the whole line began to give way. Bit by bit the door was pushed wide open. On August 7th the British at last surged up to the crest of Mount Pinçon, and for the first time since D Day looked down over the bridgehead and out across the Loire valley, where the Americans were already beginning their great encircling movement. Village after village collapsed on the Falaise plain, and the Canadians battled their way into the burning ruins of Falaise itself. The trap was being laid.

The German Seventh Army and all its reinforcements now found itself in a rough rectangle bounded by Falaise, Vire, Mortain and Argentan. Since the Americans had passed right round the south of their position, one escape route remained: the area between Falaise and Argentan. But they were not yet thinking of retreat. Rommel's successor, von Kluge, sitting in his underground headquarters at St. Germain, outside Paris, was on the telephone to Hitler every night. And always he received the same order: Resist. Counter-attack. No retreat. It did not matter that corps commanders were reporting that they could not hold, that their lines were already breaking, that the chances of re-grouping on a better line were diminishing every day. They had to hold. They were ordered to a counter-attack at Mortain.

On paper it was an attractive idea. Here were the Americans strung out all over Brittany and the Loire valley on a very thin line. Everything had to pass through Avranches, since we still had no ports in Brittany. The Germans at Mortain were only twenty miles from Avranches. Once break through to the sea there and the bulk of the two American armies were cut off.[2] Two panzer divisions led the attack. For a while things were locally critical. If there was any deficiency at all in the American equipment it was in anti-tank guns. Then at the height of the battle the rocket-firing Typhoons arrived. They continued throughout the entire day, remaining only long enough on the ground between trips to reload. Nearly a hundred German tanks were destroyed. Their entire striking front was broken up, and the attack turned abruptly into defeat. What-

[1] July 31st: The German Seventh Army headquarters informed the High Command, "The left flank has collapsed."

[2] July 31st: Von Kluge's appreciation of the position was: "The whole western front has been ripped open. Avranches is the anchor of Brittany. It must be recaptured." And he himself came down to the battle area to supervise the operation.

ever Hitler ordered now, only one course remained for the Seventh Army: retreat. But could they retreat?

A revolutionary change had overtaken the situation while the Germans were wasting time round Mortain. Rennes had fallen. So had Laval and Le Mans, Angers and Tours on the Loire. Orléans was falling. So was Chartres. Paris itself was in immediate danger. The Americans raced on and on through the unguarded south. Their tanks roared through one city after another, leaving behind great empty stretches of road, great regions of open countryside; and still they kept on. It had the effect of an octopus laying tentacle on tentacle round a victim, and now the grip began to tighten. Everywhere the French Resistance was rising. Little groups of Maquis ambushed the German garrisons along the path of the American advance. Snipers were surprised, road blocks cleared, mines torn up. It became unnecessary for us to occupy the country we took; the French were doing that for us.

In Brittany the scattered remnants of the enemy army gathered themselves into the coastal fortresses, chiefly at St. Malo, Dinard, Brest, St. Nazaire and Lorient. Here at least they could stand aside from the general route and take refuge behind concrete and mine-fields. The German policy of denying us the ports was started in good earnest. A series of sieges began, and this was later to develop into the only coherent line of action the Germans were able to adopt to the west of the Rhine valley. For the moment, however, the battle for the ports was secondary, just as the fall of Paris was secondary. Everything was focused upon that Homeric scene round Falaise, where the German armies in the west were about to fall headlong into one of the greatest military defeats in history.

Even those of us who were visiting different sectors of the front every day were unable to grasp the enormity of the thing that was happening. All we knew was that somewhere to the south of Falaise, in an ever-dwindling pocket of rolling countryside, there was a horde of broken and bewildered men, the survivors of some thirty or forty divisions. And now they were being killed and captured and maimed at the rate of several thousand every day.

It had been a dull and indifferent summer. Since D Day we had never been able to rely on the weather for two days at a time. But now the sun shone out day after day. The trampled corn turned brilliant yellow. The dust rose up with the smoke of the explosions. And through this hot August sun the Allied aircraft streamed down on to the trapped German armies with such a blitz of bombing as western Europe had never seen. No German convoy could take the roads in safety before nightfall. But now in their extremity they were forced out into the open, and the carnage along the roads was horrible. Unable to stay where they were, unable to go into hiding, little groups of enemy began feeling their way blindly towards the east. They used side-roads. They traveled as much as they could by night. It made no difference. Sooner or later they found the forests on fire around them, and Allied troops cutting in from the flanks. The pressure on the western end of the pocket became unbearable. Condé and Tinchebray fell, and with them all the villages of the upper Orne.

The Germans now abandoned all pretense of keeping up a continuous or coherent line. Their regular units lost all identity. Little battle groups were formed, given a sector and told to look after themselves as best they could. In one day alone we captured men belonging to thirty different German formations. As the refugees streamed back they were grabbed at the mouth of the pocket, re-formed, and put into the crumpling line. Cooks and signalers were fighting side by side with gunless gunners and grounded airmen. Tank fitters became infantry, along with butchers and staff officers and road menders. Then presently, towards the concluding stages, the battle groups lost contact with one another. In a blind instinct for self-preservation the Germans were either surrendering or deserting in little companies, in the hope of reaching the Seine on foot. There were no drugs for their wounded; no time to bury their dead. One after another their field hospitals were over-run. The time when half or even a third of the diminishing army could retreat had long since disappeared. Nearly all their vehicles had been lost. The horse-drawn traffic was utterly disorganized. Those who had struggled back to the Seine came under a new and still fiercer blitz from the air on the river itself. Barges and ferries were shot up in scores. The bridges were already down.[1]

A little group of surviving German generals met in the forest of Chambois for a conference. What should they do? General surrender? One last effort to get the best of their men away? They took a vote, and by a narrow margin decided on the latter course. Foreign troops, raw and second-rate troops, wounded men and men who had got themselves isolated—all these were abandoned. The surviving panzers and SS troops climbed on to what was left of their

[1] August 8th: The Seventh Army reported: "A break-through has occurred at Caen the like of which we have never seen." August 10th: The order at last came down from Hitler: "Disengage." In the opinion of the army staff it was already too late.

tanks and vehicles and headed northeast for the Seine. Already the British and American armies had locked the gate. But this last desperate column determined to smash it open again for a few hours; for just sufficient time to enable them to get away. They struck through a village called Trun, outside Falaise. A Polish division in the Canadian army took the first blow. Then for the next thirty-six hours all this sector of the battlefield disappeared under continuous smoke and explosion. Broken staccato reports came out of the arena. A few German tanks were getting through. Canadian reinforcements were rushed in. There was a final head-long onslaught round the hamlet of St. Lambert. I do not think I can do better than to describe the scene in the same words I used in a message to my newspaper at the time:

If I were to be allowed just one more dispatch from this front this would be it; not because the dispatch itself is important, but because we have begun to see the end of Germany here in this village of St. Lambert today.

The best of von Kluge's army came here *en masse* forty-eight hours ago. They converged upon the village to fight their way out; long caravans of horses and gun-carts, tanks and half-tracks, hospitals and workshops, artillery and infantry. It was the sort of panzer battle array that the Germans have used to terrorize Europe for four years. We knew no combination to stand against it.

And now, here in the apple orchards and in the village streets one turns sick to see what has happened to them. They met the British and the Allied troops head on, and they were just obliter-ated. Until now I had no conception of what trained artillerymen and infantry can do, and certainly this is the most awful sight that has come my way since the war began.

It begins in the back streets of St. Lambert, where the German columns first came in range of the British fire. The horses stampeded. Not half a dozen, but perhaps three hundred or more. They lashed down the fences and the hedges with their hooves, and dragged their carriages through the farmyards. Many gal-loped for the banks of the river Dives, and plunged headlong with all their trappings down the twelve-foot banks into the stream below, which at once turned red with blood. Those animals that did not drown under the dragging weight of their harness, or die in falling, kept plunging about among the broken gun-carriages, and trampled to death the Germans hiding under the bank. The drivers of the lorries panicked in the same way. As more and more shells kept ripping through the apple trees, they collided their vehicles one against the other, and with such force that some of the lighter cars were telescoped with their occupants inside.

At some places for stretches of fifty yards vehicles, horses and men became jammed together in one struggling shrieking mass. Engines and broken petrol tanks took fire, and the wounded pinned in the wreckage were suffocated, burned and lost. Those who were lucky enough to get out of the first collisions scrambled up the ditches and ran for cover across the open fields. They were picked off as they ran. One belt of shell fire fell on the Dives river bridge at the moment when two closely packed columns were converging upon it. Those vehicles and beasts and men on the center of the bridge were all pitchforked into space at once. But so many fell that soon the wreckage piled up level with the bridge itself, and made a dam across the river.

At the far entrance to the bridge, where a number of heavy guns were attempting a crossing, a blockage was caused and took fire. Those in front apparently tried to struggle back. Those behind, being utterly bewildered, tried to push on. And so the whole column was wedged immovably until it was reduced to flames.

I suppose there were about a thousand German vehicles of every sort lying out in the fields behind. All these came under fire. The Germans made no attempt to man their guns. They either huddled beneath them, or ran blindly for the futile cover of the hedges.

They ran in the direction of the fire, shouting that they had surrendered. They gave up in hundreds upon hundreds. There was no fight left in them any more, and now, here, you can see what is left by the battle in the warm midday sunlight. It is exactly like one of those crowded battle paintings of Waterloo or Borodino—except of course the wreckage is different. Every staff car—and I suppose I have seen a hundred—is packed with French loot and German equipment. There is a profusion of everything: field-glasses and typewriters, pistols and small arms by the hundred, cases of wine, truck-loads of food and medical stores, a vast mass of leather harness. Every car is full of clothing, and every officer seems to have possessed a pair of corsets to take home.

If you want a car you walk up and take your pick—anything from a baby tourer to a Volkswagen or a ten-ton half-track. The

Tommies start them up and go off through the orchards. Two Russians in German uniform stand stupidly on the river bank, and they timidly hold out cigarettes to anyone who comes by. They stand in the middle of piled-up riches they never dreamed of before; purses crammed with notes that have fallen from dead men's bodies, radio sets and dumps of rich clothing looted from the French. I have just picked my way across the wreckage to the house on the far side of the orchard. It is full of Germans— Germans beaten and numbed into senselessness. Like animals, they seem to have no will of their own. They are all armed with machine-pistols and rifles, but no one takes the slightest notice of them. It would be absurd to think that they would fire, and nobody has time to take their arms from them and lead them into captivity.

Over at the hospital it is far worse. The dead and the wounded lie together. Living or dead there is not much difference in the appearance of the men. Many hours ago life ceased to count for anything at all. The wounded keep dying, but quietly, so that one is not aware at any given moment of just how many are surviving. They are all jumbled on top of one another, and the stench makes it difficult for one to refrain from being sick. Outside a Canadian soldier is mercifully going round shooting wounded horses with a Luger pistol. It would be equally merciful if he did the same for some of these enemy patients who are beyond hope and too weak to cry any more. At any rate, I have just directed this mercy-killer down to the river, where there are about thirty horses wounded and unable to get up the steep banks. Long ago they stopped trying, and they stand patiently in the water waiting unconsciously to die.

I do not know the limits of this battlefield, since I have been here only four hours. It stretches I know for about a mile up the Falaise road, because for a good part of that distance you see the line of many hundreds of German helmets flung away by the enemy at the moment of their surrender. A young Canadian lieutenant explains: "They kept coming up the road in bursts every three minutes. We shot the leaders of each group and captured the others."

I have just selected a Volkswagen to get me back to my billet. The back seat is piled with the belongings of the man who now lies dead by the front wheels. He had taken the precaution, I note, of procuring a civilian suit, which is always a good thing to use if you are going to desert.

Well, there it is; there could be no reason in this ghastly scene.

I say again I think I see the end of Germany here. This was their best in weapons and men, their strongest barrier before the Rhine. It has been brushed aside, shattered into bits. The beaten Wehrmacht is a pitiable thing.

10. Paris

The Volkswagen ran very well. The dial on the dashboard showed that it had covered only five hundred kilometers when its owner, a German captain, had been shot dead. The motor, placed in the rear where you normally expect to find the luggage carrier, was often capable of outstripping an American jeep on the road. And now I was determined to drive it into Paris on the day the city fell. On August 24th we set out from the Lion d'Or in Bayeux, which had been our bridgehead home for two and a half months.

An unbelievable change had come over the battlefield. The road blocks had vanished. The guns were silent. Everything was in movement, and that claustrophobic feeling we had had in the narrow bridgehead was now suddenly and completely dissipated. We ran on through the powdered wreckage of Caen, and out into the exhausted plain of Falaise, into Falaise itself, where the cathedral altar was still burning quietly; then across the mouth of the extinct pocket, where all the side-roads were piled with the debris of dead carcasses and carts and tanks. Then into the American sector at Argentan and Alençon. We were now part of an enormous hue and cry along the roads. In tens of thousands of vehicles the American colossus was rushing forward, on to Paris and the Seine. The railway line had been opened up from Cherbourg to Le Mans, a fabulous achievement. When trains stuck along the line they were simply pushed over the embankment to let the rest of the traffic flow through. On the road the truck drivers had orders to blow up their vehicles if they had a breakdown, so that the route should be kept clear for the oncoming convoys.

We darted in and out of the rubber-tracked Shermans traveling forty miles an hour. As we went past each tank a fetid blast of hot air nearly blew the Volkswagen off the road. The rain poured down and it made no difference. The whole army had gathered itself into an irrepressible momentum, and it stretched back along the roads for two hundred miles, gargantuan, frightening, thunderous, forever renewing itself and rearing forward. Upon the villagers it had the effect of a tempest, something uncontrollable, beyond any human jurisdiction. The soldiers themselves riding in the tanks were seized with an excitement that urged them on and on, so that they forgot or disregarded the normal routine of life, the need for rest and sleep, and everything in their consciousness was directed into this one desire to go forward, faster and faster, farther and farther.

For nine hours we never for a moment left this continuous roaring of the traffic. If there chanced to be an empty dip in the road you came immediately upon another line of vehicles that stretched ahead without end, a convulsive column of discolored steel that lay over the green countryside with the appearance of some monstrous dragon.

In the afternoon we ran on to Chartres, still pretty well untouched, life going on fairly normally in the streets, the two spires still soaring upward with the same majestic placidity and indifference. Some exuberant patriot had climbed to the pinnacles with clusters of flags, the tricolor, the Stars and Stripes, the Union Jack.

We found friends inside that good restaurant at the foot of the cathedral, where the German officers had lately been taking the best of the wine and the black-market food.

Had Paris fallen?

No, not yet. There was fighting round Versailles. Fighting inside Paris between the German garrison and the Resistance. Le Clerc's French division had been pushed to the front to try and break into the city from the south. Everybody was gathered at Rambouillet for the latest news. We plunged into the traffic again and came out at Rambouillet. About two hundred journalists were frisking round the hotel. Rumors by the hundred, but no definite news. Tomorrow perhaps, or the day after. Everyone was venting their irritation and impatience on the BBC, which had been broadcasting that Paris had already fallen.

In the morning we were told to go on to Longjumeau, about fifteen kilometers to the south of Paris. A fever now began to seize the villages. As soon as a vehicle stopped the people rushed to decorate it with flags. The women, especially the larger and less personable women, flung their arms round the soldiers, plastering them with lipstick. Once we got out ahead of the column in a forest, and we turned back. There were many Maquis roaming in the woods, and they were shooting on all German cars. Even with its load of flags the Volkswagen looked aggressively German. But then we were swept into the stream again, and it carried us on through Longjumeau, and straight on towards the Port d'Orléans and Paris.

And then before it was yet midday the Eiffel Tower suddenly soared up over the plain, and one knew with certainty that Paris was falling, and here at last was the end of a four years' voyage round the world.

A young French lieutenant stood in the center of the roadway, blocking all traffic except that of le Clerc's division. He spoke English well in a clipped and resolute way.

"No one can pass this point."

"But we are British and Americans."

"I have my orders."

Over on the left a long line of civilian lorries and cars was drawn up beside the road, refugees who had fled Paris during the fighting, and who now wanted to get back. A little group stood round the lieutenant arguing fiercely.

"But there is no fighting. The road is clear."

"I'm sorry, but you cannot go on."

"We have passes from Eisenhower's headquarters."

"That may be. But I take my orders from General le Clerc."

The situation was clear enough. The pride of the Fighting French was at its peak that morning. They and they alone were going to occupy their own capital without anyone else, American or British, interfering. There was going to be one liberator of Paris, and that was General de Gaulle. When the rest of the Allies arrived they were going to find the strategic parts of the city occupied by le Clerc's men.

An American colonel drove up in a jeep and was stopped.

"But I am the Corps Commander's liaison officer with General le Clerc," he protested.

"Sorry sir, but you must have a special pass."

"I'm going on," said the colonel.

"I have orders to shoot."

"Then shoot," said the colonel, and he drove on.

Everyone was feeling a little excited at that moment. No one dared to shoot the colonel, and some of the rest of us decided that we too were going to get by. We found a side-road, slipped along it, and presently we were back on the highway traveling fast into the southern suburbs. A warm and brilliant sunshine had succeeded the rain. At the Port d'Orléans the crowd was out in the streets. Nothing was changed, nothing really altered. The cobblestones. The flapping signs in red and gold over the pavement cafés. *Patisserie.*

Charcuterie. Three golden horses' heads over the horse butcher. The newspaper kiosk at the corner. *Café des Sports.* The Métro maps with the broad blue lines. The *flics* with their flat blue *képis. Appartements à louer* under the mansard roofs. A battered green bus beside the road. Two priests who stood, gesticulating. A girl with piled-up hair intensely and unnaturally blond. The racing changing colors of the city, the uplift of a Paris street. A woman in a black shawl, incredibly old, her face wizened and monkeyish, pausing uncertainly at the intersection.

"Bonjour, maman."

Had we ever been away? Had it not been just one night, a long sleep? And now good morning; another day. It was not at all the feeling, "I have been here before," but, "I have never been away." Only this long night had intervened. Driving the Volkswagen down the road we used to take so often, the Avenue d'Orléans, I found it impossible to feel any of the expected things; either the sense of accomplishment or triumph, of release or joy, of reverence or excitement; not even any deep feeling of delight. It was even beyond anticlimax. One had been prepared and braced to plunge down to God-knew-what excesses of emotion and hysteria. But here was nothing, absolutely nothing. An utter ordinariness, an acceptance. Jean Sablon used to have a song: *"Paris, tu n'as pas changé, tant mieux."* Idiotically it went racing round my head while I casually noted that such and such a house was still there, and the Métro on the corner unmoved. It had not even been such a long sleep but simply a sleep troubled by bad dreams. The retreat to Belgium. The bombing. The years in the desert. All that time in Tunisia and Sicily and Italy. The smashing and destruction along three thousand miles. All this was completely unrelated in time to life as it had been in Paris before the war. There was no strain upon the memory. Everything was here waiting to be taken up again as though those four years had never existed, and now there was nothing to get excited about, no need to shout.

At the junction of the Raspail and the Boulevard St. Michel the big green lion still pranced triumphant. All round the crowd surged and scurried and ran among the vehicles. They had now given way entirely to delirium. There was a pressing wall of faces round the car. Again and again the phrase, *"Nous vous avons attendus si longtemps."*

Sometimes when you got a moment to sit back and take a breath you saw nothing but fifty or a hundred hands stretched out to take your own. After so much kissing, the soldiers in self-defense were seeking out the prettier girls. The column was halted, and for the next twenty minutes events went by in a blurred and confused whirl of light and sound and movement. It was like watching a distorted motion picture. and that phrase, *"Nous vous avons attendus si longtemps,"* went on and on until it sounded like a damaged gramophone record on which the needle keeps jumping back on to the same three bars of music. There was something heartbreaking in this welcome. It had an undertone of exhausted relief. We were made to feel that we were not only welcome but a necessity to life itself. The people of Paris had had their bad dreams too; but of that we knew nothing as yet as we stood on the edge of the city at the Place Denfert Rochereau.

Already General le Clerc had advanced as far as the Gare Montparnasse, and he was conducting armistice negotiations there with General Scholtz, the commander of the German garrison of Paris. Scholtz, a regular soldier, had been holding out at his headquarters in the Hotel Meurice, in the Rue de Rivoli. But now, seeing it was hopeless, he had emerged under a white flag to make his surrender. Germans and Vichy sharp-shooters were still resisting at a dozen strong points through the city.

"Very well," le Clerc said. "We will write out a dozen orders to the commanders of these strong points, instructing them to surrender. You, General Scholtz, will sign the orders. Then one of your officers and one of my officers will jointly take the orders to each of the strong points." Scholtz signed. Except at one place where ·a Frenchman and the German with him were shot dead, this device worked perfectly. But here and there the fighting was still going on.

One of these combat zones lay directly in front of us: the Luxembourg. It was a scene that bore no relation to anything I can remember in modern war. Here in the Denfert Rochereau were the crowds and the music and the delirious shouting. Bottles of wine were being passed up to the soldiers on the trucks. Girls with flowers in their hair were clambering over the tanks or riding in the jeeps with their arms round the soldiers' necks. Women were lifting their babies to be kissed. Old men were embracing. Others were sitting weeping in the gutters. Others again just standing and crying aloud with joy.

We walked a hundred yards down the street to the Boulevard Montparnasse, and all the celebration was there cut off with the same abruptness with which a cliff falls into the sea. Out beyond the corner of the Boulevard Montparnasse there was simply empty space; first the wide empty crossroads, then the empty gardens, then the sinister façade of the Senate buildings, where the enemy snipers were holding out. Every few minutes a fusillade of shots came out of one of the upper windows, and they smacked sharply against the walls of the houses looking on to the gardens. Occasionally one of the French tanks drawn up under the trees spat out a stream of tracers that ran like fireworks up the face of the Senate. Here on this side was the wild rejoicing; there on that side the empty space and the war. There was no liaison between these two scenes; they might have been separate sets at a movie studio. But occasionally some unknowing cyclist or perhaps a woman hurrying home from her shopping would walk out into the empty space. At once the gendarmes and the Resistance boys blew madly on their whistles. Frantically they beckoned the trespassers back into the cover of the walls. Then for a little there would be nothing but the empty space again, and the bursts of machine-gun fire.

It was the same wherever you turned. Along all the streets where the army had penetrated the snipers had drawn back, and the people had rushed into the open to express their joy. Then when you got to the head of the column the crowds and the exultation died away together. People crept from door to door along the walls, furtively and silently. Odd shots burst down from the roof-tops.

This was the high moment in the lives of the boys of the Forces Françaises Intérieures, the Maquis of the streets, the youths who had plotted in the secret cellars against the Germans through all these years. Now they were out in the open, shooting with their hoarded arms. Many of them were half-mad with passionate excitement. They had long since passed the stage where they recognized any risk at all. At this tense crisis of their revolution they had seized every workable car from the city garages, and now they were careering hectically through the streets, five or ten men to a car, all armed, trying to draw the fire of the snipers on the roof-tops.

For a full week before we had arrived, this street fighting had been going on. Already three-quarters of Paris had fallen to the Resistance movement. The whole city had been secretly divided into resistance zones, little underground cells that might be in a garage or a back-street hotel.

I was looking round for someone to guide me down towards the left bank of the river when one of the boys with an FFI arm-band stopped me. "Come on," he said. "I'll take you to our head-quarters."

"You speak English?"

"I'm in the R.A.F."

"But how . . .?"

It was the sort of story that is impossible to absorb. Shot down over the Channel, the rescue and the escape, three years wandering round Europe, the fight in the Warsaw ghetto and then Paris.

"I'm Australian," he said. "In our group we have Spanish, Dutch, Poles and Portuguese as well as the French."

They lived in a rambling garage-cum-workshop. At the gate the young Spaniard was piling half a dozen wooden-handled German grenades into his car.

"I can't make out how you work them," he said. "Do you pull this or this or what do you do?"

They had about twenty prisoners, men and women, locked in a back room. All of them stood up when we entered the room, and it was fairly clear that they expected to die. More than half were French snipers. The attitude of the FFI youths towards them was that of a workman in a butchery, who will presently take such animals as he is directed to take, and kill them. Within the hour they had received an order that all prisoners must be handed over to the incoming Allied authorities. It neither pleased nor displeased them. To kill or not to kill. It was all the same so long as these pieces were taken off the chessboard of Paris. The prisoners were without identity any more. To the FFI youths who had captured them they were merely abstract evil; so many capsules of poison which were pleasant to display as the measure of their success in the fighting.

The Dutchman said in English: "We have been conducting our court-martial in the next room. Last night we had a dentist who used to give his patients away to the Gestapo. We took evidence on his behalf before we shot him."

They had captured a quantity of liquor in their raids on the snipers. We drank brandy. There was some trouble in getting enough glasses. They wanted to follow the brandy with Benedictine and Grand Marnier, and when we refused they put the bottles in the Volkswagen. Three of them jumped on the back to guide us down to the river. The Australian had already patrolled as far as the Hôtel de Ville that day, and so we headed in that direction. It was necessary to take a detour through the back streets to the east. The Boulevard Arago. The Boulevard de Port-Royal. The Rue St. Jacques and on across the St. Germain. Every now and then the Australian shouted from the back seat: "Rush the next two blocks. . . . Sharp right and keep to the left-hand side . . . rush the next intersection." The Volkswagen was going beautifully. We had the windscreen down and the hood down, and with the engine in the rear it was possible to grip the road and turn abruptly left or right as he directed.

Unawares we came out on the left bank, and headed straight across on to the Île de la Cité. Notre Dame. The bridges over the Seine. The Tuileries and the Louvre. How beautiful was Paris. One more bridge. Then we went directly into a sea of human beings. They were swarming like ants across the square in front of the Hôtel de Ville. The color red on the women, red for revolution. They opened up a passage for the Volkswagen. Then they rushed it. I could not tell exactly what they were doing; they seemed to be trying to pick it up and carry it forward. At any rate, the wheels were half off the ground, and as we were borne along to the gates of the Hôtel de Ville the gendarmes stood back and pushed us through.

Then up the staircase and into the reception hall, a place of vast Rubensian murals and mirrors that had been lately splintered by the bullets coming up from the river bank. For a week the Hôtel de Ville had been a stronghold barricaded against the Nazis. The prefect was immaculate. He was one of those sparrow-like Frenchmen described by the French word *mince*. He bowed. He smiled and made one of those measured and polished little Parisian speeches. "May I offer all my felicitations on your arrival, and assure you of the warmest possible reception from the people who have been looking forward to this day of liberation with a fervor matched only by their admiration for your feat of arms in Normandy." Or something along those lines. It was elegance in the midst of hysteria, a strange mixture.

Three people together started telling us of the uprising which had begun a week before. Some ten thousand German troops had been left to garrison Paris. All through August soldiers had been appearing from the west and passing eastward through the city; columns of horse-drawn vehicles, men on bicycles, men wheeling prams and handcarts. More and more kept passing through. The tide had turned, and everybody in Paris knew it, the Nazis and the FFI and the people. The strikes began in the factories, then incidents in the streets. It became unsafe for single Germans to go about at night. In the workers' districts they were completely unsafe.

For the most part the Nazis had taken over the West End of Paris: the Senate and the Quai d'Orsay and the Chambre des Députés (where Goering had a suite), the Hôtel Crillon and the Ministries and the hotels round the Rue de Rivoli, the Place Vendôme and the Rue Royale. They were clustered thickly round the Arc de Triomphe, in the Avenue Kléber (which had been partly wired off for four years) and down the Avenue Foch, where the main Gestapo headquarters operated, and the millionaires' flats were taken over, especially those belonging to the Jews. About five hundred hotels in all had been requisitioned. The German garrison

Paris, 1940: The Germans parade in triumph down the Champs Élysées.

now began to retire into these places for their last stand. At the same time the "gray mice" were evacuated. These were the German women wearing gray uniforms who were working as clerks and secretaries for the army of occupation. Venomously the Parisians watched them going off at the Gare de l'Est, with their food supplies and their trunks of dresses and materials. The atmosphere of the city grew more and more tense and overcast.

On Friday, August 18th, the FFI began to strike. They over-ran the workers' districts at once. The Parisian police rose with the FFI. They barricaded themselves in their big barracks on the Île de la Cité, and from there they had a field of fire across both banks of the Seine, and the traffic stopped. From the Hôtel de Ville too the FFI blocked the eastern exits to the city.

This *coup de main* threw the Germans temporarily off balance. Uncertain of how far the revolution would spread, and urgently needing to keep the roads open for the retreating troops, they sued for an armistice. There was a confused series of negotiations through the Swedish minister, and on the Saturday it was agreed that firing should cease on condition that the Germans withdrew from the capital.

Paris, 1940: German officers at ease in a Paris sidewalk cafe.

On the Sunday the Germans began to bring tanks into Paris. They had quickly re-grouped their outlying strong points. In the evening the FFI saw clearly that they were being cheated and opened fire again. The Germans at once sent tanks along the boulevards, and attacked the Préfecture where the police were holding out. Spasmodic street fighting continued all through Monday, Tuesday, Wednesday and Thursday, while all Paris breathlessly waited for the arrival of Eisenhower's forces. The skirmishing was continuous in the green belt round the city. FFI sharpshooters were racing through the forests at night with their headlights full on. When they drew fire they shot back from the open luggage carriers at the rear of their vehicles.

Through this period half a dozen liberation newspapers like the *Figaro* were printed and sold openly in the streets. One after another the houses put out French flags. There were bitter gun duels with Darnand's *Milice:* the young Frenchmen who had thrown in their lot with the Germans.

On Thursday night one of le Clerc's officers got into the city as far as the Hôtel de Ville, and announced his news: "The French division is about to arrive."

And now here we were on the morrow, Friday, August 25th, and all Paris was rising to breathe again.

At the Ritz, the last of the German officers were running out of the front door and jumping into their cars. At the Ministry of

Marine another group was trapped, and they came out carrying their luggage. The bags were torn open, and the contents scattered over the street; priceless unbuyable things like soap and chocolate and cigarettes. At that moment the Paris mob made one of its superb gestures. The people drew back from these luxury things. Then they trampled them underfoot. Fifty such incidents were going on all over Paris; at the Hôtel Crillon, up the Champs Élysées, down the Avenue Kléber. No one knew exactly what was happening, what streets were safe. Towards evening things were a little calmer. Exhausted by a day of mad excitement the crowds were drawing back to their homes. The Rue de Rivoli looked fairly clear, and we put the Volkswagen down it at speed. French tanks were arriving in the Tuileries. At the corner of the Rue Castiglione a heap of German staff cars burned, but it was quiet in the Place Vendôme and the Place de l'Opéra.

At this moment there were no Allied troops in Paris except the leading squadrons of the le Clerc division. The rest of us who had come in—censors and correspondents and the other camp followers —had all been instructed to gather at the Hôtel Scribe. There must have been a hundred cars drawn up outside the entrance, and twice as many men clamoring for rooms in the foyer inside. The staff of the Scribe, utterly baffled by this invasion, were crying out in despair: "We have no more rooms. Why don't you try somewhere else?"

And then the correspondents: "But we *must* have rooms here."

"I tell you we are full up."

Perhaps James Thurber could have handled that dialogue. All over Paris there were huge hotels, luxury hotels, simply dying to take in the first Allied troops. But all the vehicles headed straight by them for the Scribe. You could almost feel the managers of the Ritz and the Vendôme and the other hotels saying to themselves: "Now what has the Scribe got that we haven't got?"

It seemed sensible to disobey orders and head for somewhere comfortable like the Ritz. As we turned back into the Place Vendôme it even began to seem possible that we were going to liberate the place. With precision and great aplomb the staff booked us in: "Perhaps we can waive the usual formality of seeing your identity card. Will you go up to your rooms now or have dinner at once?"

It was a little galling to find Ernest Hemingway sitting in the dining-room over a bottle of Heidsieck. At that time he was acting as the commander of a company of Maquis who had fought their way in through Versailles. He had liberated the Ritz just an hour before.

Through that night there was spasmodic gun-fire in the northern suburbs, but in the morning Paris was calm again, de Gaulle had arrived, and every able-bodied Parisian in the center of the city was hurrying to the Champs Élysées. The people had now settled into their exhilaration. They had composed themselves for pleasure, just as previously they had had to compose themselves for the misery of the arrival of the Germans. In June 1940 they had rushed for their homes; now they rushed into the streets. Both moves were spontaneous, subjective, unpremeditated.

The last time the Champs Élysées had filled with a crowd like this was on July 14th, 1939, for the Bastille celebrations, during that last summer of peace when people, despairing of the future, were determined to seize what pleasure they could. And now the colors were the same, the immense tricolor floating from the Arc, the girls with flowers in their hair, the red, white and blue dresses, the flags hanging from the window boxes. They stood in the same places under the trees on either side of the road, in all the windows and the balconies, and they perched like flies on the house-tops. Some things were missing from that other day: Daladier with his Cabinet on the wooden stand in front of the Café Coupole, the diplomats, the top hats and the ceremonial dress. But the real difference lay in the intangible emotion of the people, this sense of utter relief. It had the glow and freshness of an adolescent love affair.

If it is true that the greatest joy humanity can experience is release from pain, then this was it. Here it was in tens of thousands of faces, a thing beyond cynicism or excitement, a consuming well-being more like gratitude than pleasure. Given the meanest sensitivity you could feel this atmosphere coming out from the crowd, wave upon wave, a sense of complete content.

I did not yet understand it. Tomorrow or the day after I would perhaps begin to understand. As yet I had not been able to find anyone who was able to explain what had happened in those four years in Paris, when she was cut off not only from the outside world but from herself as well. At this moment people were too engrossed in their revolution to talk. They simply stood and, as it were, savored the new atmosphere in a Paris that was their own again. Not knowing what had happened, not being part of the dark experience, it was difficult as yet to see anything more than an outward Paris that was itself, a place of great open spaces, of statues and trees and graceful buildings along the river. Nothing bombed. All intact, and as it was. If anything more beautiful than ever because it was so invested with memory.

De Gaulle got out of his car and began to inspect the ring of

Paris, 1944: The city is liberated.

French armored cars drawn up in a circle round the Arc. Ten thousand people looked at him as he walked along, stiff, ungainly, a heavy lugubrious face under his *képi*, an air of school-masterish tautness, an imposing and unattractive figure, General de Gaulle, *le libérateur*. More than ever he was the remote symbol of resistance, an undefinable man representing an idea, and now personifying an idea. His lieutenants, great figures of the Resistance, walked behind: Koenig, *le vainqueur de Bir Hacheim*, le Clerc of Lake Chad, and those who fought in Paris. Then the cameramen, the police, the officials.

They moved in a body up to the central arch and the eternal flame. As de Gaulle saluted, the Marseillaise began. The people sang it quietly and falteringly, as though it were a prayer of thanksgiving rather than a triumph. They were a little out of tune. They missed a beat and hurried to catch up again. They were facing one another, and they kept staring through one another as they sang, apparently seeing nothing with their eyes, and evidently unconscious of tears. They sang as though the words had come quite freshly into mind, as though they were singing the music for the first time. It spread and expanded, bar after bar, down the Champs Élysées, a contagion of emotional feeling; and soon everyone was engulfed, all those who were hemmed in by the crowd and could see nothing, and those on the roof-tops who could not hear and those who had expected nothing from this day beyond a celebration.

It was a little difficult to follow de Gaulle as he turned and began to walk down the Élysées, with his men spread out in a line on either side of him; we ran for the cars. I edged the Volkswagen into a position in the center directly behind the general. A hundred other cars came swerving forward through the crowd and soon we were locked together, twenty cars abreast, the mud-guards touching, another row of cars behind, and then another and another, a solid block of vehicles moving at walking pace and hemmed in on either side by the vast crowds. It was difficult driving. Three inches from the car in front; three inches from the car behind. One was conscious only of repeated waves of noise from the people. Once when I got a moment to look up from the driving I turned and saw with astonishment that everyone in my car was crying.

From somewhere a young poilu had jumped aboard, and he was sitting bolt upright in the back seat, with his rifle between his knees, staring ahead, weeping. From somewhere flowers were raining down on us. From somewhere odd people kept jumping on and jumping off. Faces went by, livid and shouting, and then disappeared. It was hot. People seemed to be yelling anything that came into their heads. The congestion got steadily worse as we turned into the Place de la Concorde; then a brief clear moment in the Rue de Rivoli, then back into the dense masses of people again outside the Hôtel de Ville.

The first shots of the snipers came from the row of buildings on the opposite side of the street, but they were too unexpected for anyone to know exactly what was happening. The crowd rocked dazedly. Then a second volley came down. One or two people round us dropped screaming on to the asphalt. At once like a house of cards the whole crowd went down and fumbled blindly and instinctively for the ground. Some crawled under the armored cars. Others attempted to rush for the cover of the pavement, tripped and fell, in shouting and convulsive groups. In the windows people slammed their shutters. There must have been five or six thousand people in front of the Hôtel de Ville, and it was like a field of wheat suddenly struck by a strong gust of wind.

After the first blank moment of shock everyone who had a gun began blazing away at the house-tops. If a man saw a stream of bullets hitting a window he aimed in the same direction himself without in the least knowing what he was firing at. Some of the armored cars began opening up with their machine-guns, and the bullets passed a few inches over the heads of the people. The firing was now spreading up and down the Rue de Rivoli, and indeed all over central Paris. In the Champs Élysées; in the Place de la Concorde. On the Île de la Cité. Through the back streets.

It had begun at an obviously pre-arranged hour. German snipers and the French *Milice* had secreted themselves at twenty or thirty vantage-points on the roof-tops, and now they were simply firing point-blank into the crowd below. They were even in Notre Dame. As de Gaulle walked in the congregation was suddenly horrified by a volley of rifle shots which were fired, it seemed, from the crypt and directly towards the General. Officers jumped forward to drag de Gaulle back behind the pillars. He shook them off and walked forward down the aisle. After that there was no more firing in the cathedral, but outside the skirmishing went on. The *Milice* had chosen rows of flat-topped buildings where they could unloose a volley and then run to a new point on the roofs to open up again.

These were the young men who had been carried by the war out of all normal relationship with mankind. They shot, not out of a desire for revenge, not out of anger or hatred, or in self-defense, but out of a sheer desire to kill. They had turned traitor. They knew they would be massacred by the crowd if they were caught. They knew they could not escape, and that their freedom was measured only by the number of bullets in their pouches. They shot coolly and deliberately into the unprotected crowd. It was a last defiant gesture against society, the instinct of the gangster at bay. One man was brought down from the roof-tops in the Rue de Rivoli, and I watched the mob rush him. He was already half-naked when they got him on the ground.

French nurses kept bicycling by with bandages. The FFI patrols reached a state of animation that was unbelievable, and their erratic firing became really dangerous for everybody. I touched one lad on the arm as he was blazing away at an empty window, but he was too far gone in excitement to listen to reason. Other officials were running round shouting at the people either to open or close their shutters. But it was impossible to understand what they were saying, and consequently half the shutters remained closed, half flung back. Oblivious to it all, two lovers clung to one another beside my car. The boy was a soldier in an armored car, and he was forced to reach down awkwardly to the girl standing on the pavement. Stretcher bearers hurrying into the *bistro* behind kept breaking them apart. There were many women with babies in their arms, their faces streaming with perspiration and white with anxiety. They scurried into the shops and the cafes and sat down panting.

It seemed unbearably sad that all this happiness had been turned so quickly into fear. Not many people were killed or hurt, but the shock was intense. No one had been prepared for so swift a return to the danger of the past week. They had no mental reserves for the ordeal, and they stood about on the pavements, white-faced and pathetic. Presently as the firing died away they began to drift homeward, leaving the streets to the FFI and the soldiers and all the furtive things that were happening just then in Paris by night. Too much had happened too quickly. Paris that night lay prostrate in nervous exhaustion.

11. The Four Years in Paris

Clearly the Paris of the day of liberation was not the Paris of the past four years. The Parisians hated the Germans, that was evident. And yet when one began to move round the streets a mystery intervened, something that was not at all explicable.

The city had not starved. The people were by no means in rags. Except for the first winter there had been heating of a sort and at least enough gas on which to cook one meal a day, enough electricity to keep a household going. They had not been severely bombed. The Métro ran. Most people had a bicycle. The rationing system had been a farce, but then there was a black market for every income. The cinema was working. So were the theaters and the night-clubs (though mostly for Germans). The shops were selling things that had not been seen in most of England for years, things like cosmetics, silks, champagne. Paris was a working and a workable proposition, a capital full of business and industry, a place of restaurants and football matches, of hospitals and schools and churches. The Germans had not killed it. Under German rule life was possible, even profitable if you collaborated a little.

Why had they hated the Germans?

Was there some point one had missed in the catalogue? The question of food perhaps, always the most important thing. The bread was blackish and gritty and remarkably scarce; but it did arrive. A slice per day per person. Meat too was so scarce that for the most part people were thrown back on vegetable dishes. But they had many other things lacking in England, like fruit, a certain amount of *vin ordinaire*. There were macaroni and cheese dishes, the *café nationale,* which was drinkable. True you had to pay up to five pounds a head at a first-class restaurant, but the majority of Parisians did not go to those places. They used all their genius for living *en famille* with gifts from the country and little extras from the market. They were far from living normally. They had much less than the people in England. But it was not starvation and they could have continued on those standards. There was milk for the children, not enough, not always good milk, but still the tuberculosis figures were not surprisingly high. There was no serious epidemic through these four years. No. The food situation, though difficult, was not enough to explain the horror and aversion of the people in even discussing the occupation.

What was it? The behavior of the German troops? Hardly that. They were *trés corrects*. Incidents, of course, but on the whole very correct. There had been a rush of tourists to Paris at first; but they had paid for everything. Naïvely the *Hausfrau* and the German country boy had asked for the perfumes which had been fashionable ten years ago. They had not heard of the new brands. They were indeed a little shocked by Paris. When the petrol supply stopped, every girl rode a bicycle in a skirt that billowed round her waist. It scandalized the Nazi soldier no little—or so the Parisians said. And then in dealing with their French *employés* the Germans paid good wages. There were no complaints on that score. Then why hate them?

It would have been different had they destroyed Paris. But Paris was still the loveliest inhabitable place on earth. One had forgotten how beautiful it was. One could not have believed it would remain the same; the bookstalls on the quays, Montmartre, the radiance along the Champs Élysées as you looked up towards the Concorde in the autumn evening. The only damage done here was by the Allied bombers. The Germans had kept the city beautiful. And when they left they were loathed.

Was it the matter of the prisoners then? This was getting nearer it. Over a million prisoners were still in Germany. There was hardly a family which did not have some relative who was taken away. The return of those men to their homes was a burning thing in the French mind. If you added the political prisoners and the men who had gone either voluntarily or under compulsion to work in Germany the total was nearly three million. It was a grievous lacuna in the family life. But the Germans offered good houses and living conditions to the women who would follow their men to Germany. And was the matter of the prisoners enough to explain the bitter deadly violence of the hatred of *les Boches, les sales Boches*? Did it explain why the FFI boys were shooting the Germans out of hand, treating them like cattle, taking a ferocious enjoyment in the meanest prisoner they caught? Much more important still, a catch in the breath when you urged a very ordinary working woman to talk about the *Boches*, the way she burst out with: "Why talk about it? It's finished. They've gone."

Paris is a venal city. It has a floating population of a million or more foreigners. It has a vast and extremely cynical tourist trade. It is used to invasion whether at the point of a gun or at the point of a dollar. It sells gaiety and hospitality to all comers. Underneath that profitable business it has a life of its own not immediately apparent to the week-end visitor escaping from his wife and from his own dreary existence. This interior life which has nothing to do with the Bal Tabarin or the Folies Bergéres was profoundly and spiritually uprooted by the occupation. Yet their *amour propre* was not excessively disturbed by the fact that the Germans had conquered them. Many residents of France had grown to believe that physical force does not necessarily establish superiority. They hated the idea of Germans as conquerors in the Paris streets, but this I believe they could have borne. It was the final thing they could have accepted and yet it might not have been too much. Many Parisians placed their standards elsewhere than on the scale of material prowess. The right to laugh, to criticize—that was very valuable. The right to laugh. The right to criticize. As I hunted about in the city and talked to old friends trying to get to the bottom of this mystery of the hatred of the Germans that phrase suddenly began to recur. It came up in every conversation rather like an obscure clue in a detective novel, a novel by Simenon for example. The right to criticize. The right to say what they pleased about the people who came to Paris. Very well, one said. They had lost that. Did they genuinely mind? Then they began to talk about the Gestapo.

By the end of August 1944 the total number of people who had been seized by the Gestapo in Paris was greater than the total number of air-raid deaths in London. Plus this: a large percentage of those taken by the Gestapo were tortured. They were arrested because the Germans were frightened of what the French people were saying. The Germans were never very much afraid of facts during this war. You have only to study the broadcasts of Goebbels and General Dittmar to establish that point. At every moment of crisis they exploited the morbid Teutonic desire for self-immolation. When they failed at Stalingrad the country went into mourning for three days. When we broke through in the west Dittmar was piling on horror after horror in his weekly broadcasts. At the blackest moments of the Russian fighting Goebbels did not hesitate to say: "We have suffered heavy defeats. You must expect more bombing, bigger discomforts, worse danger." Whenever there was a German disaster Goebbels was first out with the news. Germany, the methodical planner, was never afraid of facts. They were afraid of ideas. The Gestapo was sent into Europe to crush ideas. They concentrated upon Paris.

They set spies in every cafe. They collected the venal little harpies of the Paris streets and set them on to their own countrymen. There were men listening in every railway station, in every food queue, in every cinema. The waiter in the hotel might be an informer. Or your own servant. They were paid. Once paid they were threatened by the Gestapo: "If you do not continue in our service we will expose you to your own people." A reckless word in the Métro and an arrest followed the next day. In the end no one spoke freely on the telephone. No one wrote a frank letter. No one discussed politics in a restaurant. You did not even talk inside your own flat lest the people next door could hear, or perhaps the liftman was at the door. If you had something vital to exchange with a friend you met him in the street and waited until you came to an empty stretch of pavement. And then you opened your mouth with always just this doubt—could you really trust your friend?

You could not believe your radio. You could not believe your newspaper. You could not believe the ordinary gossip at the fish-monger's. People found themselves going crazy. What in the name of God could you believe in? The whole fabric of normal society which in the end is based on trust began to give way.

And if you were arrested? No doubt the stories of the torture were exaggerated. But you had only to go into the Gestapo headquarters in Paris to see that torture was torture for those who were taken there. One torture for the women consisted in forcing them to sit naked on ice. You had only to go into the Paris asylums and see the people who did not regain their reason after the Gestapo had finished. When members of the underground and agents who had been dropped by parachute were captured they were automatically tortured to force them to reveal their confederates.

As time went on the Gestapo were arresting on any sort of infor-mation. All Paris knew what the Gestapo were capable of. What then do you imagine were the feelings of a father whose son was taken? How do you weigh up the anguish of the boy's mother?

These arrests were continuous. After the arrest, silence. No information. If the victim came back, again silence. They did not speak of what had happened. They had been told that worse would follow if they spoke. Very, very few men came out of torture proud of their behavior.

Knowing all this, living with all this, the Parisians fell into a fearful and hateful silence with one another. It was not that you could not laugh. Not that you could not criticize. You could not even speak. There was no family which had not fallen under the shadow, no family that had not listened with sudden choking doubt to someone's footstep on the stairs.

A man summed it all up to me in one revealing trenchant phrase: "I'll tell you what liberation is. It's hearing a knock on my door at six o'clock in the morning and knowing it's the milkman."

And then again another phrase: "You Americans and British will never understand. I will tell you why. You have never heard the boots of foreign soldiers in the street outside your own home."

Out of fear, hatred. All Paris, being afraid of the Gestapo, hated them, and through them all Germans. And in the end the thing that Paris and most of Europe revolted against was this; the fact that the people could not speak freely.

We, the conscious or unconscious propagandists on the Allied side, had been writing and broadcasting this sort of stuff for years. Freedom of speech. Liberty for the press. Now suddenly it was come true. In the last resort the people of German-occupied Europe had minded this more than anything else: the right to speak. Or more intricately, the luxury of trusting your neighbor. This was the whole basis of the Parisian revolution. Not the food. Not the withholding of the prisoners or the wounds to *amour propre*.

It is when one grasps this point—a point round which I am trying to bind the theme of this book—that I imagine one begins to see some hope for the future. Whatever the alternatives may be about the positive reconstruction of Europe—and for that matter the rest of the world—the thing that people *won't* have is exactly prescribed. They will not, so long as they have any strength, put up with an arbitrarily enforced censorship, a censorship imposed from outside. And the converse probably holds good: they will put up with any censorship, any stricture upon their liberty, which is of their own making.

The very naïveté of this argument had blinded a good few of us to its force. We were astonished by the facts as they were presented to us in Paris. It was difficult to believe that the issues could have become so primitive. And yet here it was. At the end of the first week after we arrived twenty newspapers had been rushed into the street. *La France Libre. L'Aube. Libération.* All Paris began to talk. And now when one came to think of it the people of Italy had begun to talk too as soon as we had invaded.

Out of this passionate determination to talk freely Paris and the rest of France had found their strength again. Young Frenchmen who had lived a life of outright hedonism and materialism before the war were now willing to risk torture and imprisonment and death itself on this score alone: to obtain the sensation of freedom. Every underground conference in a Paris cellar made him feel free. Every time he helped an American or a British airman to escape he felt free. The workman felt free when he sabotaged an engine in the factory. He felt free when he risked imprisonment by tuning in to the BBC, when he read a clandestine newspaper. The risk itself contributed to the sensation of freedom. It made a special appeal to the adolescent and the more risk he took the better he began to feel.

Once one accepted this point—the fact that the ordinary human desire for the sense of freedom always in the end triumphs over laziness and venality and ennui—then the events of the four dark years in Paris immediately fall into a lucid and logical pattern.

Nineteen hundred and forty and nineteen hundred and forty-one were the great years for the German garrison in Paris. Everywhere in Europe their success continued undiminished. It indeed appeared that they were about to start a new era on the continent. The French, broken, bewildered and cold, gave little trouble; there was little need for the Gestapo. The Germans argued: "You must face facts. Here we are. France and Germany must collaborate. If we work together we really can erect a new social order in Europe which will give everyone a chance of a decent peaceful life. You can leave it to us to finish off the English and the Bolsheviks. All we ask you to do is to help us get an efficient social economy running in Europe." Life was not too difficult. It was possible to pursue one's business, to work one's farm more or less on pre-war lines. The occupation was irksome, but you could live under it. In any case where was the sense of resisting since there was no hope whatever of breaking the Germans? Paris was plastered with anti-British posters: "Remember Oran." "Did the English help you in 1940?" "Do you Christians want Bolsheviks in your homes?" "What do you think of the English terror-bombing of your cities?" A wave of antagonism towards England ran through France. It helped to heal the humiliation of France's defeat. It put Germany in a new light. Many Frenchmen were persuaded. These sober hard-working Germans really had an ideal for establishing peace once England, the persistent mischief-maker, was silenced. Many took jobs with the Germans. Many—even most—were apathetic, simply wanting the war to end. Marshal Pétain was loyally upheld from one end of France to the other. He was the nurse for these sick days, *le vieux maréchal* who was going to make France healthy again. He knew what war was. He knew when the moment had come to say: "This is enough. We must rest and build up our strength again or we will die. France suffered too much in the last war. She lost a million of her young men. She is exhausted." Nineteen hundred and forty and nineteen hundred and forty-one were great years for the Germans.

But the war did not stop as everyone had expected in 1941. It expanded. England did not collapse. Moscow did not fall. America came in on the wrong side. It was rather thrilling to hear about the stand of the Free French at Bir Hacheim in the desert. There was a strange restless stirring in France like the stirring of the vines in the spring. As 1941 ran on into 1942 the people were still sick of the war, still convinced that Germany would win, still faithful to the program of the Vichy government. But they were getting pretty sick of the Germans too. Why were the prisoners not brought home? Why were men being taken off to labor camps in Germany?

Here and there Frenchmen began to protest. The Gestapo made arrests. The more protests the more arrests. And vice versa. The spiral climbed upward. The Parisians began to take another view of their jailers. A German officer was shot. Then the business of taking hostages began. All France was appalled at this ruthlessness and viciousness. Students parading in the Champs Élysées were charged by German soldiers. The ringleaders were arrested, tortured. It seemed a monstrous reprisal. The German character began to take on a Jekyll and Hyde role, and as far as the Parisians could see it was going to be straight Hyde from now on. The tolerant good-looking Nazi nation-builder became a man with a whip. The citizens were learning, moreover, that he was not above taking bribes.

Then the Allied landing in North Africa in November 1942, the turning-point in the whole bitter story. Few, if anyone, outside France could have realized at the time what that news meant to the French. Those of us who were down in Tunisia certainly had no idea. And yet in point of fact you will discover that for many, many Frenchmen it was the moment of their real awakening. From this moment the whole general character of the French scene begins to change. Up to now everything had been heavily weighted on the German side. How could they lose? How could France be rescued? Now, suddenly, in one blinding flash, it was brought home to every Frenchman that the Allies were on the march. And to make it all the more significant the Americans were committing their troops as well. They were not going to be tied up by the Japanese. It would next be the turn of France herself. The Allies would certainly land at Marseilles in 1943.

There remained waverers in France, people who were only half-convinced, people who were still apathetic or deeply involved with the Germans. But the vast majority now began to look forward with tremendous hope. And their anger towards the Germans mounted still higher when Hitler marched in to take over the unoccupied zone in the south. The Resistance movement took flame from the news that the French admirals had scuttled the fleet at Toulon. Everywhere—in every suburb and every village—guerilla groups began to take in volunteers. The sap now had mounted in the vines and nothing could stop its bursting growth—not even the Gestapo.

The Gestapo hacked savagely into the French people and especially the people of Paris. This was the beginning of the period of wholesale arrests and the taking of hostages. And still the resistance mounted. By the beginning of 1943 it was a fairly clear-cut issue. It was the French people versus the Germans. The dream of collaboration was over.

There was disappointment in the summer when the Mediterranean invasion fell not on France but on Sicily and Italy. But it lasted very briefly. It was seen that the general movement was strong and constantly directed towards the inevitable end, the liberation of France. The people found they could wait a little longer. Meanwhile they got ready.

The Vichy government was now altogether discredited. Not

Pétain. He remained the old man who was doing the best he could for France. But Laval and Darnand were utterly divorced from the mass of the French people and their government was a paper government without authority or backing except from the Germans.

The early months of 1944 were a time of breathless whispered hopes in Paris. Rumors swept the city. Surely it would be in March. Then April. Surely then next month. At the end of May everyone was certain the invasion was about to fall. There was immense tension throughout Paris in the first few days of June. Then the invasion burst like a thunderclap.

All through midsummer Paris seethed and fermented. In mid-August the people broke their bonds and rose in the streets.

That was the inner psychological record of the four dark years as I came to gather it immediately after we entered Paris. My informants were the people I lived and worked with there before the war and many others, collaborationists among them. It is not essentially an heroic story. A skein of materialism runs through it. It is basically a story of the effect of *force majeure*, first from the Germans, then from the Allies. Before one accuses France of swinging by turns to the winning side it is only fair to remember that she was the anvil of these events just as she was in the last war, and Paris was the spot where the hammer fell very heavily. They escaped the worst of the bombing, but they knew the sound of foreign soldiers' boots in the street outside. They lost something the people of London never lost—their pride. They had to live with their conquerors. Until a country has done that I do not believe it will ever know how intense hatred can be. Not even the bombing of England created the passion which the Gestapo excited in France.

Why did the Germans do it? Why did they give rein to their specially trained and brutalized young men? I believed the answer is that they lost their nerve in 1941 and 1942. I am convinced that they lost the war in that period not so much through their military defeats in the field but because they grew afraid in their domestic administration of Europe. They feared ideas. When a few students paraded in the Champs Élysées they could not bring themselves to stand aside and laugh. Had they merely ignored the demonstration, that students' movement might well have stopped there and then. But something in the German nature forced them to shoot. The result: the students took fire, the resistance doubled. All through this early period there was no serious revolt in occupied Europe. More than half the continent was persuaded that the German occupation in the end might turn out to be a good thing. *Europe was a workable proposition under Nazi rule.* That was the main thing, the thing that impressed itself on people's minds. They found they could live fairly normal, comfortable lives under Nazi rule. Up to 1942 three-quarters of the Allied propaganda about starving Europe, Europe under the Nazi boot, was purest nonsense. Europe was doing very well. The Germans supported the local systems of government and law. They advanced law and order. They kept the railways working and they got the food and coal distributed. They did not interfere unduly with the village life. Their economy was undoubtedly rotten since it increasingly drew the arts and practices of peace into the business of making war; but that was not immediately apparent to the Frenchman and the Croat and the Czech. All he could see was that if the war ended *now*—in 1941 or early in 1942—then the Germans had a reasonably good chance of setting up their New Order in Europe. And possibly they argued it might be a better order. The Germans were zealous. They wanted to govern well.

Look where this state of mind might have led. It might have led to general good will right through Europe, general acceptance of the German cause. Instead of conscript armies and conscript workers Hitler might have had volunteers. It is obvious of course that neither Russia nor Britain nor America was going to accept this state of affairs and that their aggressive return to Europe would have smashed the Nazi New Order anyway. But might we not have been faced with vigorous national and pro-German resistance in France and Belgium and everywhere else? Might we not have found on landing in Normandy that we were opposed to a powerful French army? Is that so fantastic? Even as things turned out Hitler was able to raise a certain number of foreign volunteers. He had no difficulty in conscripting an immense foreign mercenary army.

At all events the chance was there. The Nazis might have had many more friends in Europe but for that one fatal act: the putting in of the Gestapo. The Gestapo crushed the one thing that people in the last resort really cared about, their sense of liberty. And the Gestapo failed dismally because it was pitted against something intangible and uncrushable.

There remains the figure of General de Gaulle in this complicated Parisian scene. As in Normandy so in Paris; so everywhere in France—de Gaulle was accepted from the start. Unlike Italy, waking like Rip Van Winkle from her Fascist sleep, there was no political vacuum in France. The void was filled at once and completely by de Gaulle. The Communists and Socialists accepted him at once. The extreme right wingers who had collaborated were much too frightened to raise a voice—yet. They may have disliked his left-wing tendencies, but they lurked deep in hiding, in the autumn of 1944.

With tact and decision de Gaulle embraced the Forces Françaises Intérieures. Their best men were brought into his cabinet. General Koenig, an acknowledged hero, quietened the over-exuberant FFI boys who still wanted to go on with the shooting now that the party was over. Little by little he disarmed them and drafted them into the regular army. The Press and the Radio were taken over. The hunt for scalps among the collaborationists was allowed to proceed just far enough to satisfy most loyal Frenchmen without degenerating into a regime of terror. Many escaped. There was a great deal of muddle and maneuvering for position. But one thing remained quite clear: the French people were going to support de Gaulle just so long as he devoted himself to the expulsion of the Germans and the revival of the position of France in the world.

Having made his gesture in the Champs Élysées and Notre Dame de Gaulle with minimum fuss took up his residence in the city. He established his government by simply carrying on from the point where his successful *coup d'état* in Normandy had left him. First le Clerc was got into the city ahead of the Americans. The vital keypoints were seized. The de Gaullists and the FFI administrators moved into the vacant offices behind the soldiers. Within a few hours they had control.

It was an astonishingly slick bit of work, something that could only have been carried out with a good deal of revolutionary fervor. Tremendous plans had been made in America and Britain to nurture France back to health, to disengage her from the Nazis. At SHAEF a large Civil Affairs staff had been set up complete with American or British mayors who were to move into the cities as they fell. There was a film section, all ready to show the healthy Allied films to the Nazi-drugged French. A newspaper section that was going to publish new newspapers which were to put the French on the right track again. Radio announcers, food controllers, medical officers—a whole military government designed to put the French back on their feet.

Most of these people suddenly found themselves without a job. Their work was already done for them by the French themselves. Surprisingly the French were found to hold very strong views about the Germans already. Their own radio stations and newspapers were at work long before the SHAEF officials arrived. Their law courts and departmental administrations were operating at full blast. And now de Gaulle arrived in Paris to cement the whole thing together.

Paris, 1944: From the Hôtel Crillon guards look down on an American infantry division crossing the Place de la Concorde.

All was done so smoothly that one felt that somewhere, somehow, one had lost track of the situation. At one moment France had been utterly crushed, her capital occupied, her army and navy scattered, her colonies over-run and her government in captivity. In 1940 it was a fair bet that France was finished as a great power in our time.

Now in the autumn of 1944 the whole situation seemed to have been completely reversed overnight. With bewilderment one suddenly saw that France was about to become the strongest power on the mainland of western Europe. She deployed a large army in the field and it was getting steadily larger. The French fleet was at sea. Vast tracts of the country—the richest in Europe—were unscathed by the war. Her capital was intact. The Germans were not only in flight from France but they faced the certain prospect of being a great deal weaker than France in post-war Europe. Italy, the other enemy, was ruined. The French gold reserve was waiting to hand in America, the paper currency fixed at the excellent rate of fifty to the dollar and two hundred to the pound. The French Empire—the second largest and richest empire in the world—was ninety per cent liberated and already under the control of the mother country. The people at home, moreover, were not exhausted by the war and it was reasonable to presume that she would get back large numbers of her men from Germany.

Certainly there was trouble waiting in the post-war years. Something would have to be done about the surplus paper notes and the black market. The country's industrial system of ports, factories, railways and fuel supplies was in an appalling mess, and with the lack of incoming raw materials unemployment was a certainty. But basically the nation was sound; the means of revival existed.

All this was an immense, an unbelievable change from 1940. But there was one thing more. France had at her head the strongest figure since Clémenceau. He was uncontested. For the first time in a generation the country was completely united under one government, and this was the government that was going to look after France's interests at the peace conference. Indeed General de Gaulle had come a long way since he struggled back to England a penniless refugee, an outlaw from his own country, without authority, without an army, without even the backing of his own countrymen.

Whether or not they approved of this electric change in the general's fortunes, there was only one thing the British and American governments could do in the face of a *fait accompli;* they had to recognize him and his government. This was belatedly done in October. By November France was admitted to an equal place on the European Advisory Council. History had turned a full cycle. In theory at least France was back among the great nations. Barely four years had passed since her defeat. It was the most astonishing come-back in modern history.

Paris, however, was not going to reap the benefits just yet. She had a cold and hungry winter before her in 1944. She remained suspended on the edge of an over-long war. She was largely without light or gas or heat. There were still no buses in the streets, no taxis. Every boulevard was a river of bicycles. The shops remained half-empty. The Allies requisitioned not five hundred but seven hundred hotels. All priorities went to the war. The black market increased, and there seemed little immediate hope of getting a new and more equitable distribution of food over the broken railway system.

But the outward city remained, glowing and dignified and beautiful, ready to take up her place again as the most graceful capital in the world.

12. Brussels

When the Allies broke out of their bridgehead at the end of July two major alternatives lay before General Eisenhower and his senior commanders. They could either attempt to bounce Germany out of the war by rushing a flying column directly into the Reich. Or they could take all their armies more slowly up to the Rhine together and then cross into Germany on a broad front.

The first project required great imagination, great daring and great good luck. In other words a gamble. The second project (which had already been planned in some detail) was the sound· and certain way of doing things.

As matters stood in August there were seven Allied armies either already in France or about to arrive. The landing in the south on the Riviera had already been carried out against light opposition and the soldiers were proceeding at a good pace up the Rhône valley towards the Swiss border. Thus in descending order from the English Channel to the Gulf of Lion on the Mediterranean these armies were about to be deployed across France: the First Canadian, the Second British, the First, Ninth, Third and Seventh American and the First French.

General Eisenhower took over from Field Marshal Montgomery the command of all the armies in the field, leaving Montgomery in control of the Canadian and British troops in the north and General Bradley and General Devers in charge of the United States and French troops in the center and south. All moved on to the Rhine.

Yet there were some lingering regrets about that possible piratical dash into Germany. The enemy armies in France were in a state of rout. The Siegfried Line was not manned. The German home defenses were not organized. The attempt on Hitler's life had made a division in the High Command and for a moment left all Germany apprehensive and uncertain. Already since D Day the enemy had taken nearly half a million casualties in the west. Could we not have struck while the iron was as hot as all this?

There were two claimants for the honor of trying to rush Germany with a narrow spearhead: Montgomery and General Patton. On paper Montgomery was the obvious choice. One glance at a relief map shows that the way into Germany is along the flat northern coast of Europe through Belgium and Holland and then across the northern Ruhr to Berlin. The left flank is secured by the sea. The ports are convenient, the distance from the English air-bases small. One rather important matter remained: if Montgomery ran ahead of the rest of the armies what was going to happen to his right flank? It was going to be exposed over a distance of several hundred miles. Even suppose he was given all priorities in supply, how far could he get into Germany leaving three-quarters of France unconquered behind him? Far enough to precipitate a collapse? Or would he be simply cut off? In the High Command no one cared to take that risk.

In fact (but not on paper) General Patton's chances looked brighter. He had made a prodigious and dramatic march to Verdun. True he was headed for some nasty country, but there appeared to be no serious opposition in front of him for the moment. Had he been given the bridging and the petrol could he have gate-crashed the Ruhr and spun on into Germany? There seems to be no doubt that he could have gone on. There equally appears to be no doubt that all the resources of the Allies could not have kept him going for very long. The spirit and the heart were there. Only the dull weight of logistics dragged him back. The trouble with old "Blood and Guts" Patton was not that you could not hold him back but that with all the good will in the world you could not give him the supplies to go on.

For a month perhaps—the month of August-September—the gamble was there and the rosy hope on everyone's mind. Expose the methodical Montgomery to one flank; expose the headstrong Patton to two. Could either of them have made it? That was the question for Eisenhower to decide.[1]

The general was a genius in a conference, making men feel at ease and show the best side of themselves. He sat long over the problem with men like Bedell Smith and de Guingand and Tedder. And, as with every other major decision of the war, he adopted the course which it was obvious he must adopt, the course which was the consensus of the best minds at his disposal. He decided to wait until the odds had shortened a bit.

[1] Russia's tremendous onslaught in January 1945 failed to break the enemy. In view of this it seems unlikely that had half a dozen American and British divisions crossed the Rhine the previous autumn it would have been sufficient to throw Germany out of the war.

The seven armies came at their several paces up to the Rhine. When the flank was sufficiently guarded he put Montgomery in to make his attack by flying column. He was to cross the Rhine if he could. He was to pierce the Fortress of Germany at Arnhem. The risks had diminished a good deal by this time. So had the prospects of a gambler's glowing success. It was part of the steady advance to the end of the war.

A good deal had happened to Montgomery's armies since the break-out in Normandy. After that long static battle they had spread their wings. I remember it really began one wet Sunday in early August in the lower Orne sector which had remained fixed since the invasion. A battle of attrition had been going on. Trench warfare. The kind of fighting in which you eventually got picked off because you were forced to stay in the front-line. Gradually the surrounding earth was reduced to mud or dust according to the weather. The minefields had grown thicker and thicker, the dugouts deeper. Day in and day out the mortar shells passed back and forth until eventually, you, the soldier in the line, were hit. And never for an instant did the front-line budge.

Now, suddenly, everything had changed. You drove through the barbed wire that once made the German line. You could drive on into the seaside resort of Cabourg. And then to Houlgate from which the big enemy gun had been shooting for two months. Then to Deauville with its hotels all intact, but its *plage* a sad entanglement of barbed wire and concrete. Already this front was stale. Without its normal tourist life, without the animation of battle it had the dreariness of a cabaret in the morning. The places were deserted and the smell of battle hung about like the stale smell of cigars in an over-used room.

The big drive was on the Seine, through Rouen. While Paris fell General Dempsey made his crossing into the midst of the beaten and retreating enemy. The Eleventh Armored Division under one of the best of our desert commanders shot northeastward at incredible speed; they covered something like sixty or seventy miles in a single day. This was the reward of the decisive battle of Normandy. Wherever they went the tanks found the enemy in a state of bewildered rout. A string of big inland towns fell to the infantry pushing on behind: Rouen and Beauvais, Abbeville and Amiens, Arras and Cambrai. The American First Army performing great swoops and circles to the south kept smashing up the broken groups of enemy in the same way. Once the tanks were warned that a German troop train was approaching. They lay in wait under the embankment until the train arrived, packed with Germans. Then they opened fire and silenced the locomotive. Four German tanks aboard the train tried to shoot back but the Americans ran in under the cover of the embankment and demolished them one by one and soon the whole train was ablaze. It was the great period of the hue and cry when everything seemed possible and the men at the front wanted only petrol to carry them on into the Reich.

And now the Guards Armored Division with picked infantry took up the running and headed straight for Belgium. They at once entered the region where the British Expeditionary Force had held the line in 1940; a rolling open countryside dotted with the British graveyards of the other war. On Sunday, September 3rd, the fifth anniversary of the start of the war against Germany, they crossed the Belgian border and entered Brussels.

The Americans meanwhile, wheeling right, rushed on to Luxembourg and the German border.

The taking of Brussels was a crazy headlong skirmish. Nearly all the Germans had decamped and those that remained at the southern approaches found themselves overwhelmed with a tank charge that burst through the streets into the center of the capital. Mad

"The million people of Brussels rushed out into the open."

with excitement the million people of Brussels rushed out into the open, screaming and shouting and waving flags. The joy of Paris was a pallid thing compared to this extravaganza. At one moment women would be spitting and kicking at the German prisoners: the next day they would rush at the British soldiers with bottles of wine and cakes and flowers. Someone discovered the German wine dump —some eighty thousand bottles of a remarkable claret. A kind of frenzy, utterly uncontrollable, seized the people. They danced wildly all night through the streets, the hotels and the cafes. They scrawled their names over the tanks and trucks. They carried off the autographs of the soldiers as though they were precious manuscripts. One girl I knew unwrapped a bottle of dry champagne she had kept for four years and simply poured it on the head of the first British soldier she saw. Every house was flung open and every passing soldier—even though he might be engaged on a mopping-up operation—was dragged inside and given a meal, a bed, anything he wanted. Effigies of Hitler were paraded through the streets. Tunes like "Tipperary" and "We'll Hang out the Washing on the Siegfried Line" became the steady monotonous background of the wild shouts and screams in every street. When a German was routed out of a house the crowd surged toward him, and then, being held off, they hissed and booed and spat. It was the same with the German wounded. None would raise a finger to help them; the Belgians tried instead to trample on them. Viciousness and the extremes of gaiety ran side by side. There seemed to be no end to the excesses of hate and the excesses of delight. And Brussels continued with this madhouse atmosphere for ten long days and nights on end.

Of the five of us who had started on this invasion of Europe at Taormina, four were together in Brussels. The major who was still in charge of us had perhaps the most remarkable adventure of all. His job at that time was to get the correspondents' dispatches back to the censors and the transmitters many miles behind the front. As Brussels was falling he and his pilot took a tiny Piper Cub aircraft and flew over the German lines so as to be ready to drop down on the city as soon as the leading tanks entered. They could find no landing-place at first as they circled through the enemy ack-ack and when eventually they put down on a racecourse they came under two lines of cross fire. Civilians came running out to them with bicycles and they pedaled off towards the center of the city.

Our major judged that the correspondents would head for the leading hotel to type their messages, but this was some miles away. At length as he and the pilot cycled along they saw a large tramshed and a man standing at the front door wearing a bowler hat. He turned out to be the director of tramways.

Yes, certainly, the manager said, the electric power was on although no trams were running on account of the fighting at certain sections along the line. Yes, certainly he would be pleased to place a tram at the disposal of the gallant Allies. He would drive it himself.

The major, the pilot and the manager in his bowler hat jumped into the driving cabin together and proceeded through a storm of applause along the street. Every so often when they ran into a quarter held by the Germans they ceased bowing and accepting flowers, crouched down on the floor and put the tram at its maximum speed. Once safely through these difficult stretches, they rose and again received the salutes of the crowd; and in this way they arrived at the Hotel Metropole.

The return journey with the dispatches was equally exciting. As soon as the aircraft took off it was shot at so fiercely it was almost blown to the ground behind the cathedral. Then by roof-hopping over the suburbs they got back to the British lines where the petrol ran out. Somehow they found another aircraft and flew the messages on for transmission to London and New York.

By staying a day too long in Paris I had missed this opening frenzy, but managed to meet our major as he stepped off his aircraft at Arras. That night he piloted me back along the German line in a jeep and we entered Brussels at midnight without much trouble.

Antwerp and its vital port lay next in the line of advance and the army ran into it on September 5th, two days after the fall of Brussels. There was a more subdued commotion here because there were still many enemy snipers about. A collaborationist hunt was on. We were still unused to the violence of the Belgian reaction towards the traitors, the unreasoning passion for revenge. Then when we got to the lion house in the Antwerp zoo we began to understand. The Antwerp lion house is very much like the one at Regent's Park in London, a broad high building with a promenade down the center and the barred cages on either side. A large crowd was baying at the entrance to the zoo, trying to get inside past the Belgian guards. They had divined that the lion house was being used as a prison for collaborationists and they wanted to get inside and lynch them.

I can only compare the scene to the Colosseum in Rome about the time of the Emperor Caligula. The lions had been turned out and now the cages were full of human beings. A cage for German officers. A cage for German privates. Then the cages for Belgian

The zoo in Antwerp was used as a prison; it was like the Colosseum in Rome.

traitors. There was a special cage at the end for the mistresses of Germans and the wives and daughters of collaborationists. These human animals sat on the straw staring through the bars. Every few minutes another victim, much bruised by the crowd, was brought in; the iron gate was raised and he was flung inside among the other prisoners. Two pretty Belgian girls sat at a table in the center of the hall checking-in the prisoners as they arrived. They were laughing a good deal at their quaint position.

"These," explained the Belgian officer in charge, indicating the Germans, "we will turn over to the British authorities. These," indicating the collaborationists, "will be shot this evening after a fair trial."

The men prisoners had long since lost all hope. The whites of their eyes had gone bluish and they lay in the straw twitching nervously. A couple of photographers had gone into the cage and were arranging the condemned men in convenient and artistic groups to have their pictures taken. Having been placed in a position, the models stayed rigid like wax figures. Another man was going among them taking their money and wrist watches.

The captured women were more expressive. They stood up for the most part. Some reached their hands through the bars at the guards. Others, especially the younger girls, simply stood and wept and they had long since become unconscious of their tears. One girl had frozen her face into a completely waxen rigidity. She merely stared and stared, seeing nothing.

This scene was giving a good deal of satisfaction to the Belgian guards. "This lot," explained the officer, "handed over about fifty of our White Army boys to the Gestapo. They were taken to the camp at Breendonck and tortured. Ten days was the usual length of the torture. That is to say the special torture used to get members of the Resistance to give away the names of their comrades. It was very severe.

"You have not been to Breendonck? Then you must certainly go and see it. When the Gestapo constructed the place they made special runnels in the cement floors for the blood."

He was very precise and lucid. He spoke about torture and death as though it were a mathematical problem exactly prescribed and defined. His whole approach to the war was utterly different from ours, utterly different from that of the American or the British soldier. There was something surgical and inhuman about it. Kill Germans. Kill collaborationists. The procedure was very simple. Kill them. There need be no passion or excitement. Just perform a surgical operation.

I went round Brussels from home to home where the hospitality was abounding. Sooner or later in every conversation the subject of the Gestapo came up. And then you would hear of incidents that made the blood run cold. Brussels is probably still the most bourgeois capital in Europe. Its normal values lie rather less in the region of the human spirit, rather more in the field of trade and money and possessions. The city was unscathed by bombing. On the whole they had fed and lived a good deal better than the people of France. And now their hatred of the Germans was psychopathic. Indeed everything we had learned in Paris was underlined and emphasized here in Belgium. Being shrewd businessmen they had made a great deal of money out of the Germans. The black market for them was not only profitable; it was a way of withholding food-stuffs from the invader. And still their hatred knew no bounds.

One fact went a long way to explain it: this was the second time this century that the Germans had marched across Belgium. They had endured not four years' occupation but nearly nine. Everyone had grown up under the shadow of foreign rule and the revulsion against it was therefore historic. Liberation came to Belgium with a double force and their desire for revenge was doubly savage.

Like France, Belgium too was undergoing a spectacular revival. Her empire in Africa was also intact. So was much of her gold reserve. This time the war had passed across the country so quickly there was relatively little damage: the great industrial centers like Charleroi, Mons and even most of Liège were untouched. Bruges and Ghent were intact. The guerilla bands known as the White Army had kept up the heart of the people. The Belgian government arrived from England and it was able to call together the national assembly more quickly than any other liberated country in Europe. The factional disputes between the Walloons and the Flemings were not yet serious. The monarchy was not gravely discredited. If Leopold was disliked at all it was largely on the score of his second morganatic marriage. His first wife, Queen Astrid, had been loved and her photograph was now in every shop window. At all events the issue was not a live one since Leopold was still a prisoner of the Germans and his brother slipped into the regency easily enough.

What was serious was the financial situation. Far too many paper notes printed by the Germans were circulating. Prices were at a fantastic peak and inflation was on its way. The official rate on the English pound was one hundred and seventy-six Belgian francs. Actually the pound brought anything up to eight hundred francs on the unofficial exchange. The first act of the re-established Belgian government was one of the most drastic financial decrees in the history of Europe. It was announced that new notes would be issued. Temporarily no one would be allowed to change more than two thousand francs of the old money into the new. Thereafter all citizens who possessed more than two thousand francs of the old money would be obliged to explain how they came by it. This of course was a move to crush the black market and expose the war profiteer. A financial panic started at once. Many people who had made fortunes out of black marketeering took fright. Some of them actually burned their notes rather than face discovery. The decree fell very heavily on the peasant who was in the habit of hoarding his cash at home instead of putting it in the bank. He now began to rush about offering fantastic quantities of the old notes for anything he could buy—one hundred pounds for a bicycle for example. Liquors like gin and brandy with which Belgium was better stocked than any other country in Europe vanished like magic from the shops. The bulk of the black market collapsed. All restaurants shut. The coal miners being unable to buy food came out on strike. Brussels and the other big cities began to face a winter without heating, without gas and precious little electricity. It was a bitter anti-climax to the liberation. The standard of living temporarily fell far below what it had been during the occupation. This was the price of liberty, the inevitable result of the false economy which the Germans had imposed on the country.

It really had been childishly simple for the Nazis. They simply went on paying higher and higher wages with notes taken directly from the printing press. Half Europe had been hoodwinked the same way. No one paused to ask what was the backing for the franc, no one dared to consider the inevitable collapse. Workers and peasants were induced to go on and on parting with their goods and their labor in return for more and more notes. Always the prices kept pace with the wages. Now suddenly the bottom fell out of the market. The worker saw that in some strange way he had been defrauded. His paper savings were almost worthless. And so he went on strike. The farmer refused to part with his produce. And so the country began its winter of hunger. The rosy and ruthless economy of the Nazis had crashed at last. The echoes reached as far as Greece.

The Belgian government showed great courage in clapping on its drastic remedy. With every little businessman roaring that he was ruined the government stuck to its guns. Gradually the healing process began. The black market was reduced. The ruinous surplus of notes was called in. Inflation was halted. Belgium had looked over into the pit of financial collapse and was jerked back just in time. Little by little the food distribution was improved; the miners returned to work. The country was safe at least until the peace, and possibly after that.

Here, as in France and Italy, there was a powerful and wholly ignorant fear of Russia. I dined at many a little bourgeois home where they shook their heads apprehensively over the advances of the Red Army. Ces gens-là; they were bad for business. Bad for the Church too, if it came to that. It was the one part of Goebbels' propaganda that had sunk home. The little doctor had an instant success whenever he broadcast, as he did so well, a line like this: "You will not listen. We know you will not listen, you Christian peoples of Europe. But one day you will have to listen. You say you are opposed to Nazi Germany. Very well. What is the alternative? The Bolsheviks. Don't believe the Americans and the British will come and save you. The Red wave is breaking towards you from the east. One man and one man alone stands against it: the German grenadier at Kiev (or Warsaw or Odessa according to the news). If he fails then everything goes. You can take your choice, you Christians."

It sounded pretty good stuff to a lot of people at home in America and England as well.

The truth was of course that what the people feared was not so much Russia but the rise of their own Communists. In Belgium as in France and Italy the swing to the left was very marked. Since the war had placed the emphasis less on money and more on human energy the labor organizations had grown greatly in power. There was no unemployment in Europe during the occupation. The demand for man-power grew stronger and stronger. And with it the strength of the left. Presumably as soon as the war was over good old peace-time unemployment would start again and the influence of the left diminish. But the little Belgian and French capitalist by no means felt sure of this happy issue of affairs. He feared that in some way the local worker would join hands with the terrible Bolsheviks who were, as the good doctor said, surging on from the east. And then where were you? What happened to business then? A minor stockbroker cried hotly to me over the blackmarket oysters one night: "These strikers in the Belgian mines. I would put a machine-gun at the pithead and force them to go down."

We learned a good deal (mostly by inversion) at these little *soirées* in Brussels. One of my colleagues had coined a cynical misquotation of the old saying "Dine with the right and vote with the left." Clearly, he said, we must dine with the collaborationists and fight with the patriots.

The main trouble probably was that none of these people had received one iota of reliable information about Russia for more than five years. When one told them that Russia was now probably one of the most nationalistic and conservative countries in the world, that class distinctions were being rapidly revived under Stalin and private ownership well on its way back, they regarded this as a joke.

On the whole Brussels was a queer mixture, much more materialist than Paris, more violent in its loathing of the Nazis, more divided against itself, more apprehensive about the future, more friendly to the British.

Both capitals had contained German headquarters which were to have been used for the invasion of England. Von Kluge had an impressive place at St. Germain outside Paris dug into the living rock. It was rather like going into a transatlantic liner; a place of endless passageways and caverns enclosed behind steel bomb-proof doors. From here the central German telephone exchange extended throughout France, and there was a private line to Hitler's headquarters in Germany. During an air raid it was von Kluge's habit to lock his staff indoors while he himself paced about the nursery garden defying the high explosives. He used to work until three o'clock every morning, and it was during these early hours that he took his nightly call from Hitler. In the end, the strain became too much. He collapsed through nervous exhaustion on his way back in the train to Germany, where he was relieved of his command.

Falkenhausen's headquarters in Brussels were much less pretentious. It was from here that the Germans plotted the incoming air raids from England on a lighted glass panel. There was a huge store of detailed maps of England, showing how it was proposed to invade in 1940 by crossing quickly on to Salisbury Plain; and then performing an encircling movement on London. Both these headquarters were seized by local guerilla bands and partly wrecked before Eisenhower's armies arrived.

With the flying-bomb sites it was different. These lay mostly in the coastal area between the rivers Seine and the Scheldt, and they had to be overwhelmed one by one. For the most part the crews had packed up and left for Germany before the advanced elements of Montgomery's army attacked. There was never very much to see—a concrete runway; a circle of sheds, the ordinary litter of a soldiers' encampment. The local people said they had been rigidly excluded from the neighborhood of the sites, and their clearest memories were of prodigious explosions which used to break the windows of the houses half a mile away. The flying bombs were brought up to the launching sites by railway from underground factories in the Reich. Throughout the summer of 1944 all priorities in manpower and materials had been taken away from the ordinary Luftwaffe and given to the men working on the V.1, the V.2 and the jet-propelled fighter. Experts who have studied the factories which ran for several stories underground say that production methods were in advance of anything in the United States. It was clear that had we not over-run northern France and Belgium until the spring of the following year, the Germans would have had a very good chance of rendering London uninhabitable. General Dempsey told me when we were still in the bridgehead at the end of July that he had taken a bet that he would capture the French flying-bomb sites by the end of September. He did it in August.

The Germans, however, were still in possession of parts of the coast, and they now embarked on a definite considered policy of holding their garrisons in the ports until they were wiped out. Despite this Le Havre and Dieppe fell quickly enough to the Canadians, but at Le Havre especially the German demolitions had rendered the port unusable on a large scale for months to come. In Boulogne, Calais, Dunkirk, Ostend and on the approaches to Antwerp the German garrisons stuck fast. This meant that the bulk of Eisenhower's armies had still to rely on what they could get across the beaches and through Cherbourg in Normandy several hundred miles away. The effect of this was felt more and more through September. Patton was stopped dead through lack of petrol. General Hodges, commanding the American First Army, could get no farther on his march to Aachen, the first big German city in the enemy's line of retreat. Both of Montgomery's British armies were using up every shell and every case of rations as soon as they could be got to the front. The whole Canadian army was switched on to the job of opening up the ports at any cost. On the German side, the port garrison commanders got their orders directly from Hitler—"You'll stand till you are wiped out." The matter was put on an emotional level for the German soldier. He was told: "This is your homeland you are defending. Unless you hold here until your death the Anglo-Americans will enter your home in the Reich." They were presented with written pledges saying that they would never surrender, and these they were obliged to sign. All through September and October, while the armies were famished for want of supplies, bitter unrewarding skirmishing went on along the coast. Ostend fell, with its railway running into northern Belgium, but it yielded only 4,000 tons a day. Then Boulogne; then Calais, but they too were not the answer to the problem. As the weather began to turn cold and rain set in the question of supply began to dominate the whole battle. We had to open up Antwerp.

In the south things were not so bad. Liberty ships were arriving directly from New York at Marseilles. They carried enough to keep the Seventh United States Army going, but that was all. A route was cleared right across France from the German border to Normandy, and 10,000 trucks ran along it carrying nothing but petrol. Drivers were put on a charge if they traveled less than forty miles an hour. Still it was not enough. An army of engineers were sent to reopen the railways and bring a pipe-line across the battle-front from the base ports in Normandy. Some thousands of Dakota transport planes began to ply out of England to the French and Belgian air-fields carrying the most urgent supplies. Even with these and many other expedients Eisenhower found that his rate of build-up was not sufficient to launch all his armies into Germany before the winter set in.

It was a most dangerous period of delay. Every hour, every day, the German morale was hardening. As the broken remnants of the Fifteenth and Seventh Armies struggled back to the Reich they were regrouped into new formations. Anything and everything served at this desperate moment. Submarine crews were put into the line as infantry; the German water-police were mobilized; there was a brigade of deaf men who presumably received their orders in deaf-and-dumb language. There was a whole division of men who suffered from stomach ailments and had to be served with special bread. Throughout the Reich every officer and man on leave was summoned back to his post. We began to collect extraordinary prisoners—near-sighted clerks who had left their city offices three weeks before; men with half-healed wounds, even cripples and children of fifteen and sixteen. It was a makeshift hotch-potch army, an emergency army put in simply to hold the gap, simply to fight for time while the German generals reorganized on a sounder basis. Little by little a crust was formed, reaching along the valley of the Rhine from the Swiss border to the Zuider Zee. It was useless now to regret that we had headed straight for the Dutch border in early September instead of cleaning up the approaches to Antwerp. Along the city docksides everything was intact, but the cranes stood idle. The Germans were deeply entrenched all the way down the Scheldt, especially on Walcheren Island and on the mainland south of Flushing. Their guns entirely commanded the estuary, which in any event was now heavily mined. The Luftwaffe at last appeared to tide Germany over the crisis, and the jet-propelled fighter was seen along the front. V.2's as well as V.1's began to land on Antwerp.

In Montgomery's headquarters it was judged that the approaches to Antwerp would take a full month to clear—most of the month of September. Antwerp was nearly big enough to supply the whole of the Allied armies, but clearly they could not stand idle indefinitely while the German crust every day grew thicker, their morale more sure. Eisenhower judged that the time had come for him to make his strike with a flying column into Germany. Its immediate object was to bounce the Germans out of their half-formed line and clear the way into the Ruhr. Two American and one British airborne divisions, with an attached brigade of Poles, had been standing by impatiently in England since midsummer. Eisenhower now decided to commit them at the traditional gateway to Germany—the lower Rhine where it splits into three streams near the border of Holland and Germany. All three divisions would drop simultaneously. They were to capture the irreplaceable bridges at Arnhem, Nijmegen and Grave, and at the same time secure the roads leading to the south into Belgium. The British ground forces were on the Belgian-Dutch border, where they had been fighting a cold and desultory battle for the canal crossings. They were now to select a corps of their finest infantry, tanks and engineers and send them ahead in a narrow spearhead to link up with the airborne troops on the Rhine bridges —a distance of about seventy miles. Every priority in supplies, and especially bridging materials, was to be given to this flying column, and it was hoped that it would relieve the airborne troops within three days. The flanks of our ground spearhead were to be protected by one of the parachute divisions. The starting-line was the Belgian border: the route Eindhoven, Veghel, Grave, Nijmegen, Arnhem. Montgomery was given the overall command of the operation. General Horrocks, the ablest and most spirited of our corps commanders, was given control of the ground troops. The airborne corps was in the charge of Lieut.-General Browning who proposed to land with his men. By mid-September everything was ready. From one day to another it was put off because of weather and last-minute adjustments to the program. On September 20th the attack went in.

13. Arnhem

It's a grim, unlovely corner of Europe on the border of Belgium and Holland. Flat land under a gray sky. Dingy and dark villages that remind you of the industrial north of England; a common slate-color over the landscape; clogs; the throaty Flemish language. Somewhere on the way through Belgium you lose the lightness and uplift of the Latins and now you are in a country where the world moves heavily. It was no setting for an adventure. The troopers sat in their tanks and looked across the mournful slag-heaps. Presently, in the early afternoon, the gliders and the para-chutists would come over: then the attack. Three picked divisions were waiting. The Guards. The Forty-third. The Fiftieth. Across the canal, over into the pine forests of Holland and then northward until they hit the Rhine. It was even a dull zero-hour: 14.00. The minutes went by dully, evenly, without any special drama.

Somewhere on the left a sniper opened up across the bridge, but nobody took much notice. No sign of the airborne divisions. Some-one said he had glimpsed dark smudges in the sky over to the north, but you could not be sure. Then the barrage began, the familiar whip and crack of the twenty-five-pounders. The column began to move into Holland, through the battered customs post, past the circular red-white-and-blue sign with the word *"Douane."* The leading squadron of tanks sped straight up the road for Valkens-waard, the first Dutch town. They burst into the belt of pine trees and out the other side and then the squadron leader turned back and saw with some astonishment that four of his rearward tanks were ablaze. The enemy had opened fire. He was cut off from the rest of the column.

The Typhoons arrived. From his wireless vehicle on the ground the brigadier directed them. "You see that line of trees over there? Do you see three German tanks at the end of the trees? Go on."

They saw the trees, the tanks; they dived. They came out of the low clouds one at a time. Near the climax of their dive with the tanks held in the sights the pilots let the rockets go and then jerked their machines upward. It was like those switchback railways at a fun fair. One after another they performed their swoops in the gray sky. It was not until they were mounting again through the ack-ack into the clear air that the noise reached across to the British on the ground; a rending, tearing, terrifying noise, a disembodied noise that ended at last in the commotion of a more normal explosion. The brigadier was ecstatic. He sent back to his headquarters the warmest praise for the pilots. And now the whole column began to move through the forest to join the stranded remnant of the squadron and carry beyond into Valkenswaard.

Suburbia, rich, lush suburbia, opened up before the British tanks. Fine allotments not a stone's throw from the road and the bus. Garden villas standing in their own grounds with the council's light, heat and water. Central heating. Sewerage. A district noted for its civic pride, its attractive shopping centers, its charming gardens. We were in Holland.

All the Latin untidiness had fallen away. The war flowed between neat privet hedges and mown lawns. Every house was an affair of tricky little casement windows under the newly thatched roofs, of gravel driveways and flower-beds and much freshly painted woodwork.

The Dutch, plump and homely and jolly, flowed out into the streets and danced ring-a-ring-a-roses. Everyone wore something orange; orange aprons and ribbons for the little boys and girls, orange paper caps for the grown-up boys and girls. Everyone danced together. They smiled and smiled. And from every shop window, a fine big lithographed portrait of Princess Juliana smiled back at them.

For a day the Germans shot it out with their eighty-eights among the hedgerows, and then we drove on to the model town of Eindhoven, the center of the great Philips works which supplied a large part of Germany's electrical requirements.

The town had fallen intact and untouched without a battle, and already we had made contact with the first of the American airborne divisions. As the armored column rolled on towards the first great bridge across the Maas at Grave, all Eindhoven gave itself up to holiday. The streets were one long blaze of orange. All the Philips workers were out on the pavements with their wives and children. They blew tin whistles and banged toy drums. They threw their paper caps in the air and made noises with wooden rattles. In the open square they joined hands and danced round in a circle. Sometimes they clapped hands together and sang part-songs and national hymns. They shook hands with all the soldiers and wrote their names on the army vehicles. Some of them formed impromptu bands with whistles and rattles and combs and then arm-in-arm they skipped through the streets together. For Eindhoven, neat, trim, modern Eindhoven, it was one long Christmas party. The children were allowed to stay up long after bedtime.

They were still skipping and dancing when we came back from the head of the column in the late afternoon. Then suddenly, about five o'clock, you could not tell where it started, a rumor went round the town that the Germans were coming back. All smiles stopped together. Mothers with their paper caps awry ran along the streets to gather up their children and carry them home. The tin whistles subsided almost on a note and there was no more dancing. Along every street you could see little crestfallen groups hurrying home. Every one of the fat jolly faces was now full of apprehension and misgiving. The big party had collapsed entirely. The squares and streets were clear and one after another the doors of the homes were banged shut.

The headquarters of the Dutch Resistance movement were in the offices of the Philips works and they seemed to be taking it calmly enough, but very seriously. They showed me the reports. A doctor had telephoned from a village fourteen kilometers to the north that six German tanks had passed by his house in the direction of Eindhoven. A Dutch ganger on the railway had reported that four Panthers were making directly up the railway line. A column of three hundred German infantry were reported from another place. More tanks over to the east. The reports were coming in every minute. They meant only one thing: the Germans were going to counter-attack. They were going to cut off the British column at its base. Worried and uncertain, the officers of the Resistance ran along the streets telling the people to lock their doors and stay inside.

We drove back to the Orange Hotel a little puzzled about what to do. The first British armored brigade had gone straight through to the north. No troops had been left to garrison Eindhoven and the city was pretty well defenseless until the rearward elements caught up on the morrow. It was already dusk. We got back into the jeeps, intending to spend the night outside the town. At that moment a clear golden cluster of parachute flares burst into light above the town. Then another and another. The streets were like day again. The first bombs hit immediately after and one had just time to leap to the ground and run for the nearest house or the nearest shelter.

It was really very easy for the Luftwaffe. The British had not yet had time to move up their anti-aircraft guns. The German pilots were undoubtedly men who had trained and lived at the Eindhoven airfield for many months. They bombed systematically, pinpointing separate buildings and bridges and streets. They dived down to three or four hundred feet so as to make certain of their targets. One wing of the Philips works made a tremendous blaze, one of those fires where all the outward facade of the windows and balconies is silhouetted, detail by detail, against the general body of the flames inside.

Half a dozen trucks carrying shells were hit directly and at once the shells were detonated and began to add a spasmodic stream of horizontal fire to the bombs which were now falling at a steady rhythm every minute. Presently a number of petrol lorries took fire as well and these flames, billowing loudly, reached across to other parts of the convoy which was just then passing through the town, notably the lorries with small-arms ammunition. These bullets exploded and now it seemed that the city was being engulfed by every sort of explosion at once. Each noise came sharply and separately: the shrill whistle of the bombs and then the outrageous shuddering impact of the strike; the windy storm-like noise of the flames taking hold; then the crackle of the small-arms fire punctuated by a heavy double explosion of each shell as it left its burning truck and erupted against the wall of the neighboring house.

My companions had scattered throughout the town. One group was in a house which took a direct hit, but when they tried to run for better cover they found the street impassable because of the passing shells. The roof took fire and fell in. Then the top story, then the first story. This left them with merely one burning floor above their heads. As it collapsed upon them they ran blindly into the open and somehow got away.

In my shelter a Dutch woman lay on the ground with her children, and they sang hymns together. It was a moving little act of faith. Even when some of the bombs fell ten yards away and the shelter was full of mad cyclonic gusts of air and light the family never missed a beat in their song.

The fires now were quite sufficient to enable the German pilots to see, but they continued dropping flares. One of these came down sputtering and sizzling at the entrance to our shelter and beside our jeep. As it subsided the last of the bombers drew away. We ran to our vehicles, hoping to get out of the town at last, but this was impossible. Every entrance was blocked either by fire or by exploding ammunition. We turned one way and another crunching over layers of broken glass, but inevitably found ourselves passing underneath the same burning buildings.

When finally we took refuge with a Dutch family we found them immensely quiet and strong in enduring this, the worst disaster of their lives. They were methodical and practical and brave. When we produced a box of rations the children forgot the raid at once and screamed with delight. Sardines. They had not seen sardines for years. Butter. Jam. Chocolate. One little boy could not bear to eat. He quietly took the things that were given him and put them in his pocket. The shelling continued most of the night.

In the morning one saw with wonder how much of bright Eindhoven was in ruins. Here it was, the whole monstrous unacceptable proposition: an undefended town, a plan in the mind of a commanding officer, a few bombs and then the endless pain stretching ahead indefinitely into the future. This was a microcosm of all Europe. It comprehended all Holland, all Germany, all the coming battlefields. No one here in Eindhoven was ready to confess guilt or admit that they had in any way deserved the bombing. Nor was anyone in any bombed German town going to admit that they had been guilty. That was the last thing they would admit. Whether the inhabitants were German or Dutch, a bombing appeared to them as a blind act of malice on the part of the enemy. A hideous unforgivable thing. And the people of London, who had probably endured as much as anyone, thought that too. The war, in fact, in this sixth year was ending very much as it had begun, in a welter of fear and revenge. All the acts of courage and endurance and technical efficiency were doing nothing to establish an ethic for the war or obtain the acceptance of a moral right for either side.

Gloomily we went off to the head of the column, which was now deep into Holland and well on the way towards relieving the airborne divisions. The prospects seemed good. The fields to the north of Eindhoven were sown with deflated colored parachutes. Gliders in hundreds like monstrous lizards with their heads knocked off were scattered round the landscape. It had been a most successful drop with practically no casualties. Only the weather had turned against us. For two days now no reinforcements or supplies had been dropped to the isolated men. More than ever it was necessary

Arnhem: Gliders like monstrous lizards were scattered about the landscape.

to hasten. And then at once only a few miles north of Eindhoven we
ran into trouble. The reports of the Dutch Resistance had been
true. The Germans had crossed the road. They were shelling it. As
we jumped for the ditch, the motor-cyclist in front of us was
knocked off his bike. The whole column stopped. It stretched back
for fifty miles into Belgium—stationary. The advance brigade
which had gone ahead up the road to Grave was now isolated along
with the parachutists. On top of this, really serious news was coming
in from the Arnhem and Nijmegen sectors. The bridge at Grave
had been taken and held easily enough, but the situation at the two
more northerly bridges was far from good. And now the whole
thrust into Germany was withering away for the lack of vital
supplies.

Horrocks' salient was about forty yards wide. That was all he
needed—just the width of one road. Somehow at all costs it had to
be kept open, and the infantry and tanks fanned out on either side
to do the job. It was not until the next day that we got through. We
paused at Veghel, half-way up, to drop off our kits at a bright little
Dutch hotel, and then ran on through miles of waving villagers,
and then on across the Maas at Grave, where already the stream was
racing with an eight-knot autumn current. A most unusual battle
was going on for the bridge across the Waal at Nijmegen. Horrocks
had got through to the Eighty-second American Airborne Division
there, but the Germans still dominated the bridge. They had

entrenched themselves at a roundabout on a cliff above the river where five roads ran together and descended to the river. The British tanks and the infantry had charged the roundabout with no result. Now they tried again, and while they were fighting through the old streets of the city a few squadrons of British tanks with Americans hanging on the sides slipped downstream unnoticed. On the bank the Americans jumped aground and flung their invasion barges into the water. They crossed through the racing current under fire, and reaching the other side signaled back to the British forces fighting at the roundabout: "Come on: we have reached the end of the bridge. There is no opposition in front of you." This was demonstrably untrue. The British tanks and the American infantry with them were under heavy fire. The bridge itself was certainly deserted, a huge single-span structure which had been saved through the action of some unknown Dutchman who had cut the wires leading to the German explosive charges a few days before. Again the Americans who had crossed the river signaled, "We can't see any opposition here." Maddened by this, the tanks on the southern bank attacked again, swept through the roundabout, then down the cliff and across the bridge. They found no sign of the Americans who had signaled to them, and then it was discovered that an error had occurred. The Americans had captured a different bridge: the railway bridge farther downstream. But that was all to the good. The two forces joined up again and made for their last objective—Arnhem.

The British had dropped at two places in the Arnhem sector. One brigade had parachuted on to the approaches of the bridge itself: the bridge that spans the last of the three streams of the lower Rhine and which the Germans have always regarded as the entrance into the Ruhr. The bigger drop had been made some miles downstream near Osterbeek. Nothing much had been heard from either camp except that they were under heavy counter-attack and unable to hold out much longer unless help arrived. They had been isolated for a week. Some supplies had been dropped at Osterbeek, but in Arnhem the British were holding only a few streets and each time the transports attempted to deliver ammunition and food by parachute the packets were carried away into German hands. Once the British had got on to the bridge, but they had since been driven off and now the structure was dominated by the enemy who were consequently able to demolish it at any moment they chose. For the surviving British it was simply a matter of surviving. The horror and extremity of their position was something that could only be imagined; the untended wounded, the lack of sleep, the black hope-

Arnhem: The British were cut off; it was simply a matter of surviving.

lessness of seeing the garrison grow smaller and weaker hour by hour. Nor were the men at Osterbeek much better off. They were in the open, living in slit trenches under a barrage of anti-personnel shells that split in the air and cast their shrapnel directly downward.

Horrocks put his tanks into the attack once again. They were forced now to travel on roads raised above the flat delta on embankments. Consequently the tanks were silhouetted against the skyline, an admirable target for the German gunners. They could make no headway. Fine rain drizzled down. Mud and cold began to dominate the scene.

The distance between Nijmegen and Arnhem and between Nijmegen and Osterbeek was only ten miles. But now the Germans were rushing reinforcements into the area. Every mile had to be fought for. Supply trucks bogged and slithered off the road. The bridge at Nijmegen was under fire. The Germans even sent a platoon of desperadoes equipped with artificial webbed feet to swim down the river and plant explosives on the piles. The quick current carried the charges away and most of the German swimmers came ashore exhausted to surrender. But still every man and box of supplies had to battle forward under constant shell-fire that grew more and more intense. Worse still the road back to Eindhoven was constantly being cut. Twice my own party drove back to Veghel to try and recover our kit only to be met by heavy artillery fire on the road. When at last we did get through by following an armored patrol we found our hotel half-demolished, the township in ruins. For hours and days the lifeline was cut and the vehicles that might have brought life to Arnhem were drawn up useless and stationary on the road.

Fantastic things were happening in the air. Once I saw about five hundred big transports towing gliders up to the front. They traveled only a few hundred feet above the ground and since the Allied salient was only as wide as the road they came under German small-arms fire from either side. It was a bitter thing to see glider after glider burst into flame from the tracer bullets. The broken helpless machines snapped their tow ropes and crashed in the German lines. Then sometimes we would see squadrons come over and at a given signal their trapdoors opened and the sky was suddenly filled with brilliantly colored parachutes. But many of the bundles floated across to the Germans. And still the rain poured down. Still the enemy made raid upon raid across the road. They even threatened Nijmegen itself.

One night we traveled for hours round the dark streets looking for shelter for the night. The poorer houses were already crammed with refugees. The richer houses did not want us—especially at a moment when the Germans might return. One great castle was inhabited only by an elderly woman and her maid. The war had not touched her. She was determined it should not. "No," she said in English, "you cannot stay here. You have not the right." We were a fairly muddy and desperate-looking crew and rather bad-tempered into the bargain. When at last we were taken in by a roadside cafe one of the Resistance came to wake us in the night with the news that German tanks were coming down the road; by then we were too tired to care. The relief of Arnhem seemed hopeless, we had lost our kit, we were cut off and consequently our messages were not getting through. We were cold and wet and dirty. One of our number had collapsed with malaria. It was one of those recurring moments in the war when one says: "This is enough. I will not put up with anything any longer."

Emotionally and physically we were fed up. Let the tanks come. Our condition was roughly a thousand times better than that of the people cut off at Arnhem, but these things are relative. We got down on the floor and listened to the rain beating outside. In the darkness the mind filled with grotesque fears and imaginings.

A man came along the street whistling the Marseillaise. God

only knew why he should be whistling or walking at that hour in that desolate and dangerous place. He whistled with a peculiarly clear and brilliant phrasing, a disembodied melody in the darkness. We could hear his footsteps coming on one by one and the music poured out of him, sweet and refreshing and triumphant. Once before at Caen and again in Paris I had been uplifted by that hymn. But now, coming so unexpectedly and inexplicably out of the rain, it laid a sudden grace on the world and all one's restless fears. I was asleep before he had gone.

In the morning the infantry got through to the men at Osterbeek. There could be little question of reinforcing them. Boats were launched, but they foundered in the current and were stopped by German fire. The men at Arnhem we had already lost—all of them. The best that could now be done was to retrieve what was left of the defenders of Osterbeek. They came out by night, some swimming, some by barge and boat. In the end about two thousand of the original eight thousand escaped. They were taken to shelter and given food immediately, young men grown old and tired beyond reason. The attempt to make a quick break into Germany had failed.

Could it have succeeded? Never completely, but no doubt we could have done a good deal more than we did. The weather assuredly was a major piece of bad luck. Once a thousand transports set out from England and had to turn back. Yet I could never fully understand why that road up from Eindhoven was not kept open. It is quite true that the Germans were in overwhelming numbers on either side and that it is the easiest thing in the world to dominate a single road by artillery fire.

But there appeared to me to be a fundamental lack of urgency in the rear areas. As soon as the Germans began firing on the road there was a general disposition to say: "Oh, well. It's hopeless trying to get through. We will have to wait for the tanks to clear it up." There was a detour near Veghel which would have taken light traffic but nothing much was done about opening it up. Without doubt there are answers to this criticism; I simply say the answers were not apparent to an observer at the time.

The Germans were certainly taken by surprise at first. At Nijmegen and in the surrounding towns we found great dumps of their supplies. The Nijmegen railway yards contained a train full of presents the German soldiers were sending home to their families. I spent a happy morning going through the parcels. The Germans about this time were seized with an incredible acquisitiveness. They bought anything and everything. It did not matter whether the people at home needed the things or not: if you could buy you bought. I suppose the underlying idea was that the possession of goods was the one fixed thing in a collapsing world. Even so, these parcels, many thousands of them, were almost incomprehensible.

I opened packets containing such things as a gross of curtain rings; sets of spanners and electrical tools; barbers' clippers by the hundred; hundreds of pocket-knives and bottles of varnish. These were addressed to young unmarried girls in Germany. Heaven knows what Fräulein this or that was supposed to do with these cases of false teeth, the coils of fencing-wire and the little boxes each containing a thousand gadgets for fixing pictures on the wall. It was the sentiment I suppose that counted. One lucky girl would have been the happy recipient of ten chisels. Another was being offered forty-six hammers and a nice case of unbleached cardboard. All this stuff was bought by the German soldier with inflated foreign currency. If he wanted to buy hair restorer for his girl he did not restrict himself to one bottle. He sent her fifty. And he added a couple of boxes of horse-shoe nails if they happened to be on sale. There was rarely one pair of shoes in a packet. Usually it was ten pairs all different sizes.

For four years this looting of Europe had been going on. This train, solely comprised of trunks full of soldiers' presents, must have been one of a thousand that had passed that way.

I talked with a number of the Dutch and they agreed that the German lust for possessions was rapidly becoming the dominating matter of their lives. And they added this warning: "Their greatest possession is Germany itself. You will find that once on German soil they will fight very bitterly indeed."

Holland herself was about to enter into the cruelest period of her suffering. Already she had endured hardships much worse than either Belgium or France. Being new to war this century the younger Dutchmen had resisted the Germans very early in the occupation. The Nazis had taken harsh reprisals. Belgium was put under military government which was bearable. Holland got Seyss-Inquart and a civilian Gestapo rule. From his headquarters in The Hague Seyss-Inquart very quickly took control of Holland. The excellent communications and the methodical system of local government helped him greatly. He was able to put out intimate feelers right through the land. Unlike the Belgians and the French the Dutch were not at first skilled in hiding their possessions. Holland was sucked dry. Liquor practically vanished from the country. So did fresh meat. When we arrived the people for the most part were eating potatoes.

The Dutch royal family, Juliana, Bernhard and their children, enthusiastically accepted by their people.

Apart from the awful catastrophe of the war—the flooding and shelling and the hunger—Holland had no considerable political problems for the moment. Prince Bernhard, who was commanding the Dutch Brigade that was entering Holland with the Allies, and Queen Wilhelmina and Princess Juliana were enthusiastically accepted by the people. They wanted their own government back—that was all.

But Holland's material sufferings were possibly the worst in Europe. The Japanese had seized her empire. The homeland itself was about to be partly inundated and a good deal of it was going to be fought over. She had no coal of her own, no petrol, not enough wheat, little timber and stone with which to rebuild. At the end of

1944 one could see little hope for the revival of the country for many years.

For the Allied army now no hopeful alternatives remained. There was only one way—the hard way. Arnhem had failed. The Germans, whether under Hitler or Himmler, had got the necessary breathing space with which to throw up a new Siegfried Line from Switzerland to the North Sea. There was very little we could do through the rest of September and October to prevent them. All hope of a quick end of the war in 1944 had gone. The Allies had to prepare for a winter campaign, the hardest campaign of them all— and possibly for more battles inside Germany in the following spring and summer. The immediate essential for all this was the opening up of Antwerp. Both British armies were now turned to that task. The bitter, freezing battles for the banks of the Scheldt were begun.

Rain, cold and mud dominated the battlefield. The tanks fell back, practically useless in this morass. The infantry came forward. An amphibious warfare developed; first the flooding, then the landings on Walcheren. Then the mopping up on the south bank. This was fighting in conditions which divorced the life of the fighting soldier from anything which the civilian at home could understand or imagine; a business of filth and danger in the mud.

The thing was done at last by November. In that same month Eisenhower finally got his armies in line side by side across France. The railways were beginning to work on an increasing program. The ports were opening up. The supplies were on the ground; the air force ready. Something like two million men were standing by. On November 8th General Patton struck towards Metz. The November battle for Germany had begun.

The Third Quarter

COLLAPSE IN THE WEST:
THE RHINE

14. The Battle of the Ardennes

In November, when one of the hardest winters on record was beginning to set in, the Germans came under an entirely new system of command.

Hitler at last had divided the bulk of his forces into two independent commands; Guderian, the tank expert, with some two hundred divisions in the east, Rundstedt with some sixty or seventy divisions in the west. There existed barely a dozen German divisions inside the Reich itself, but reinforcements were coming in. The German home guard—the Volkssturm—was formed. Sedentary workers, formerly considered unfit, were drafted to the front to meet the crisis. At the same time many thousands of garrison soldiers were withdrawn from Norway, Finland, the Baltic States and the Balkans. All this enabled Hitler to reconstitute an army at least equal in size if not in quality to the army with which he had begun the war.

Of Hitler himself at this time one heard nothing reliable. Some reported him mad, others dead. I was shown one highly circumstantial report of how the Führer spent his day. It was related that he began with a conference at 10 A.M. and then retired alone to his office. For the next five or six hours he could be seen staring at his maps. He sat there without food or drink, entirely alone. Then he called for Model, his chief of staff, and said, "Call Rundstedt" (or Guderian, as the case might be).

Now the story runs that Model, being a shrewd man, would realize that Hitler had taken a decision about something or other and that it would be unwise to brook him over it. And so Model would inquire tactfully if the Führer's meditations had been

217

fruitful. Hitler then would reply, "We must destroy Aachen"—or something of that sort.

At that Model would hurry to Rundstedt and hiss in his ear ("hiss" is my own bit of decoration), "Destroy Aachen," and Rundstedt would pass into the presence.

Hitler: Well, Marshal. What are your plans?

Rundstedt: We must destroy Aachen.

Hitler: Excellent.

The report went on to say that if Rundstedt was not primed beforehand and suggested something quite contrary to what Hitler was thinking, then inevitably a violent scene would ensue.

It is an attractive story and a colorful one. Yet one did not dismiss it entirely as gossip because there was a great deal of outside evidence that something of the sort was actually going on. Mad or sane, the majority of Hitler's decisions and intuitions throughout the war had been remarkably sound, and in any event the generals, having left the presence, were free to carry out the tactics in their own highly professional manner. Then, too, was it not a fact that blind faith and devotion to a leader in warfare could carry out more than all the most cleverly conceived plans? At all events there was nothing very crazy in the way the Reich set about defending its borders in this extreme hour. Himmler as chief executive officer showed immense ability as an organizer and as a stiffener of morale. Guderian and Rundstedt were probably the best possible choices for command in the field.

Moreover, on top of this an entirely new complex was beginning to operate through the German mind. The German began to feel roughly as the Englishman felt in the autumn of 1940: "Very well, I fight alone. Let the whole world come on top of me. I will accept death because that will be a better and an easier thing than occupation by the enemy."

At the roots of this dramatic feeling there was probably a split between the English and the German mind. The Englishman after ten centuries of security never really admitted that he could be beaten. He was emotionally and constitutionally unable to accept such an idea. Against all the facts, he profoundly believed that he would somehow get out of the mess in the end.

The German, on the contrary, accepted the idea of defeat with positive gusto. He was almost in the frame of mind of a Regency gambler: "All right. I have gambled for the highest stakes and won. Now that I am losing I will lose for the highest stakes. I will collapse utterly and heroically."

Both English and Germans loved defeats. Dunkirk will remain in

the English mind long after Tunis is forgotten. The siege of
Stalingrad will rally future generations of German children long
after they have found the 1940 advance into France rather a bore.
But where the Englishman carries this masochistic emotion only a
certain distance the German takes it to the bitter end. Hitler had
taught the people to live for utter victory or utter defeat. Now, at
the end of 1944, he appeared to be in a fair way of winding up the
war by nearly gratifying both those ambitions.

Terrified of the Reds, terrified of the Allied bombing, terrified of
the inevitable suffering ahead, at least a section of the German
people saw themselves as preparing for the greatest act of national
immolation in European history. They would go gloriously and
desperately to their utter defeat.

The Allied November offensive was begun with a series of
staggered attacks. One after another the seven armies were to move
on to the Rhine and endeavor to establish bridgeheads on the other
side. It was hoped that the Ruhr would be pierced.

Setbacks occurred from the very beginning. First Patton and then
Patch (the commander of the Seventh U.S. Army) got ahead only
to find that they had no strategic reserves with which to follow
through. Then when they came to advance again they found the
enemy had closed in before them. One week followed another
through November and still the seven armies, straining forward
together side by side, were measuring their gains only in thousands
of yards.

For Rundstedt in defense the problem was not difficult. If the
Allies were going to maintain an even pressure along the whole line
like this then his difficulties were halved. He had merely to space his
men along the front from Switzerland to the North Sea and let the
Allies come on. So long as we did not mount a definite spearhead he
was perfectly secure. There was no need for him to retire on to the
Rhine and the Siegfried Line. His men were well dug in where they
were and since he was in defense he was obliged to commit far fewer
men than the Allies. Moreover, since his troops were not obliged to
expose themselves they suffered fewer casualties than we did.

All through this unhappy month Rundstedt was building up a
strategic reserve which he called the Sixth Panzer Army. It was kept
out of battle. It was given priorities in the new Panthers and Mark
I and II Tiger tanks. The best of the SS troops and Panzer
Grenadiers were fed into its ranks.

The Sixth Panzer Army was at first designed to counter-attack
any determined Allied break-through; especially in the direction of
Cologne. But when it became clear that the Allies were going to

persist in their policy of mounting no spearhead—of maintaining an even and ineffectual pressure—then Rundstedt began to conceive great plans for the future. His Sixth Panzer Army would attack.

Aachen, the first Germany city, had fallen in ruins, but the Allies had only succeeded in reaching the Rhine at one or two places, and they had no immediate hopes of making a bridgehead anywhere. The Siegfried Line still existed. Clearly the Allies were not going to get anywhere at this rate and the time had come for the Germans to go over to the offensive.

The Rundstedt plan was one of the most imaginative and daring proposals of the war. He resolved to put his fresh and secret Sixth Panzer Army straight through the Ardennes forest and then, having crossed the Meuse, it would proceed straight to Brussels and Antwerp. The possibilities were endless. To begin with, Eisenhower's forces would be cut in half. Four Allied armies—the Canadian, the British, the Ninth U.S. and most of the First U.S.—would be bottled up in Holland and Belgium. With Antwerp taken they had no escape route by the sea. Their only hope would be to fight their way south into France, abandoning their vast system of dumps and many, many thousands of guns, tanks, workshops and men. There was even some doubt as to whether the trapped armies could put up much resistance. Once Antwerp fell they had no other supply port. Within a week (so the German planners argued) we might have exhausted our shells.

This plan, towards which Rundstedt began to move early in December, was not so fantastic as it sounds. His information was excellent. Agents left behind in France, Belgium and Holland were bringing him a constant stream of news. He knew pretty well where every Allied division was placed, and by December it was apparent that in the Ardennes-Luxembourg sector the Americans had put pretty well everything they possessed "into the shop window." They were braced for offensive, they were not expecting a German counter-attack. And so the great bulk of the Americans were either in or immediately behind the front-line. Once break through that line and Rundstedt saw that he would emerge into empty space—an empty space that extended across the Meuse through Brussels to the sea.

Our information about the Germans meanwhile was very bad indeed. We were now up against Germany itself and no news came out of Germany. Hitherto we had always traveled through friendly country where the French and the Belgians and the Dutch had eagerly brought us information of the enemy movements. But now the boot was on the other foot. Rundstedt could be pretty certain of getting surprise.

Then, too, there was the terrain. All his lifetime Rundstedt and many of his senior planners had studied the Ardennes. It was one of the classic gateways in and out of Germany. They knew every mile of the way.

Then again there was the factor of the Allied morale. While the Germans had been growing more and more desperate, something quite different was happening in the British and American ranks. It was apparent to every soldier of reasonable intelligence that the war was going to end in our favor. Why then should one unnecessarily expose oneself on the eve of victory? What was the sense of being killed at the eleventh hour? Already people at home were arguing about the post-war world.

Finally there was the quality and size of Rundstedt's striking force. In addition to the Sixth, he planned also to commit the Fifth Panzer Army which was already in the line opposite Liége. That is to say, he massed together the largest armored spearhead the world had ever known: ten Panzer divisions, plus sixteen or seventeen motorized infantry divisions of the highest caliber. We ourselves had never attempted to gather such a striking force. Certainly we had nothing like it on D Day. It was doubtful if the Russians had ever given or received such a blow in one place. In round figures you might estimate that this terrific hammer blow had behind it nearly two thousand tanks, a quarter of a million men. In addition, two devices new to modern warfare were to be employed. An offensive reconnaissance brigade of Germans, some of them dressed in American uniforms and traveling in American tanks and trucks with American markings; and a flying-bomb barrage.

The Luftwaffe, which had been taking a rest for several months, was regrouped. It planned to put up thousands of aircraft, all to be used tactically in support of the ground troops.

Add all these factors together—the Allies' unpreparedness, the excellence of the German planning and intelligence, the temporary disbalance of the Allied morale, and the size and quality of the German force—and you must concede that Rundstedt had a reasonable hope of so cutting up Eisenhower's armies that they would not recover for many months to come. Once negative the western front and Germany might have good chances of holding off the Russians for another winter. And then with the summer—the V.1 and V.2, the rocket and the jet-propelled fighters in mass production. The prefabricated U-boat in mass production. Yes, anything might happen if the Reich got through intact to the summer of 1945. They might even propose a separate peace to Russia. Hitler might say to Moscow: "Look, you see the Allied position in the west is hopeless. Let us come to an agreement and finish the war."

The whole plan was hatched in the utmost secrecy, and right up to the last moment only Hitler and a handful of the senior generals and politicians knew about it. Outside the Nazi Party Hitler was far from certain that he could command obedience. The July attempt on his life had warned him that he could trust no one implicitly. He lived surrounded by SS guards. He rarely appeared in public.

One day, a week or two before the battle, the German commanders on the front were suddenly summoned to a conference. They were led by circuitous routes to the Führer's headquarters and every care was taken to ensure that they would not be able to fix the place on the map. At the entrance their weapons were taken from them and then the generals entered the conference room in a body. SS men stood round the walls with tommy-guns. Hitler appeared and at once launched into a tirade about the Nazi struggle for power, about the Jewish-Bolshevik menace. While the generals sat there in silence and astonishment the Leader went on and on as though he were addressing a political meeting. Then at last he got down to brass tacks. He outlined the plan. He called for the utmost sacrifice. He said this was Germany's last chance. The Wehrmacht must get through to Antwerp, and he promised three thousand fighter aircraft in support. Model and Rundstedt sat there at the table alongside Hitler nodding agreement. To many in that room the plan seemed crazy. There might have been some way of circumventing a hare-brained scheme of the Führer, but with Model there nodding his head there was nothing more to say. They had to obey. Again they were obliged to swear loyalty to the Führer —and indeed he had shown some of his old fire that day. Then, still under the eyes of the SS, they were led out of the room, given back their weapons and driven away.

All Rundstedt needed now was a clear day for his start and then dark foggy weather for the follow-through, so that the Allied air fleets would be unable to put up. In the middle of December he got what he wanted.

On December 14th and 15th the Fifth Panzer Army was slipped quietly out of the line and sent south through the forest roads to a point opposite Luxembourg round the town of Prum. The Sixth Panzer Army quietly moved into the line in the place vacated by the Fifth. On December 16th both armies struck together on a front less than forty miles wide.

The shock was chaotic. An American division which had just

The Ardennes

landed in France took the first blow around Malmédy and was rolled up in a few hours. An American armored division was caught on its flank and knocked off balance. Three or four other American divisions were either encircled or over-run. Divisional and corps headquarters—even army headquarters—were forced to pack and run. A stream of flying bombs came over, not hitting anything much, but adding to the unreal and frightening savagery of the assault. German parachutists began sniping on bridges far behind the U.S. lines, and then to spread the confusion squadrons of apparently friendly tanks appeared, only to open up murderously when they got within range. No man could trust another in the forward areas. Stavelot fell and the American system of communications broke down. No one—not even at SHAEF—had any clear idea of what was happening. Whole corps of Americans were cut off somewhere in the battle area. It was useless trying to send them orders since one knew nothing definitely of what was going on. With fantastic speed the Germans appeared in one village after another. All through December 17th the battle was out of our control. On the 18th it was serious. Worse still, a fog had settled over the battlefield.

I cannot see anyone disentangling the chaotic history of those two days. Apart from a mass of unrelated detail, only one thing stands out clearly: the American units in the midst of the German flood, being without orders or information, simply took things into their own hands and fought back. This is probably the major imponderable of warfare—to know just when men will suddenly and often of their own free will commit an act of unthinking desperate bravery. Once started, it has a contagious effect and each man tries to outdo the other. But why it should start, and how, is something you can never know for certain beforehand. You can expect the soldiers to fight up to a certain known standard, but here in the Ardennes the Americans rose above themselves, and in the midst of so much confusion and doubt and bloodshed, they held on long after the time when normally all hope would have been lost.

It was this desperate resistance by isolated Americans in the early days—this and nothing else—which saved Belgium and Holland from being over-run. Parts of Belgium might still have been over-run later on had certain dispositions not been taken, like the appointment of Montgomery. But the crises were never again as imperative, and these later moves followed logically and inevitably upon one another. It was here on the battlefield that the issue was really decided when the common American soldier elected to fight up to the point of his death.

Once that decision was taken—and apparently taken almost

The battle of the Ardennes: General Omar Bradley, commander of the American ground forces; and General Patton, leader of the 3rd American Army.

inspirationally by tens of thousands of men—then it was axiomatic that Eisenhower should call on Montgomery and urge Patton and Bradley up from the south. Had the American soldier on the spot not risen immediately to this crisis then nothing Montgomery or Bradley could have done would have altered the situation. They had no reserves to call on quickly enough had the soldiers in the First American Army panicked. But since they did not panic, then plans could be made anew and Montgomery was able to fight what I believe to be his greatest battle.

Montgomery was in bed in Belgium on the night of December 18th when Eisenhower called him on the telephone and asked him to take command of the troops in the main battle area—that is to say the First and Ninth American Armies which were deployed from the neighborhood of Aachen down to the Luxembourg border. Montgomery was living at his tactical headquarters with half a dozen young men who had been trained over many months as his personal liaison officers. Before he went back to bed he ordered them to set out and contact the various American corps wherever they might be, gather their news and then rendezvous with him at General Hodges' First Army headquarters at 1 P.M. the following day. At the same time another batch of liaison officers set off for the neighborhood of the Meuse bridges to gather information down there. News, accurate news above all else, was the vital thing at this moment.

Montgomery went back to bed and slept until his usual hour.

Having breakfasted the following morning, he sat down to make his battle plan.

Already on his own authority he had taken a number of precautionary measures in the past forty-eight hours. He had secretly transferred a British corps down from Holland and it was now moving into positions covering Brussels and Antwerp. The thing now to decide was—what is Rundstedt's plan? Where is he committing his major strength and where is it making for?

Montgomery decided that the Germans, having passed through Stavelot, were going to wheel northward and perform a left hook which would bring them to the Meuse in the neighborhood of Liége. He therefore decided that we must on no account counter-attack. The Americans must regroup and stand in front of this vital thrust. A corps must be formed for this purpose and posted in front of Liége. With this plan in his pocket he set off for General Hodges' headquarters.

Meanwhile the liaison officers were going through a series of wholly unusual adventures. Any trip in a jeep over those icebound foggy roads was a considerable experience, but the chief difficulty occurred when the British officers entered the American lines. They knew no passwords and several of them were promptly arrested as spies and parachutists. Others found that the American corps to which they were assigned had been cut off in the night. Somehow by various means they managed to get themselves out of arrest, to drive on to their destination, to gather the news and then make their way back. All succeeded in making their rendezvous with the commander-in-chief at 1 P.M. and Montgomery at once came in possession of a thing that was of the utmost value: he was the only man on the front who possessed accurate first-hand news of what was going on.

It confirmed his belief that Rundstedt was committing his main striking forces here in the north towards Liége. It had been the American intention on this morning of December 19th to counter-attack and proceed to the rescue of their isolated comrades. This plan was now countermanded. Montgomery instead formed his corps defensively in the path of the German advance with General Collins (who took Cherbourg) in command.

Collins was immediately engaged in battle and his whole corps was drawn into immensely heavy fighting. Montgomery again formed the corps, but again this second corps was sucked into the battle before it had any hope of acting offensively. And so for the third time another American corps was reformed in front of Liége.

By this time—Christmas Day—a series of electric changes had happened over the broad face of the battle area. Rundstedt, seeing that his left hook on Liège was getting nowhere, decided to slip southward and strike again towards Namur and Dinant. It was the same sort of thing—the original break-through, then the holding back of the Allies on either flank while a fresh striking force was passed through up to the pinnacle of the salient. But in order to penetrate in the direction of Dinant and Namur he needed the crossroads town of Bastogne just off the northerly corner of Luxembourg. The 101st U.S. Airborne Division was already surrounded in Bastogne and great pressure was brought to bear upon the garrison to force its collapse. The Germans had even sent in a rather pompous note to the American commander, ordering a surrender, and had received the unusual but lucid reply: "Nuts."

A bitter series of onslaughts upon Bastogne began and the only ray of light for the Allies upon that sector was the fact that General Patton with his Third Army was marching northward through Luxembourg to the rescue.

In the center things were easing slightly. Montgomery's staff—the same staff which planned and fought a dozen other battles from Alamein to Normandy—was working very smoothly with the Americans on the regrouping. It had been found that the Meuse bridges were unmined and practically the only forces between the Meuse and Antwerp were a handful of military policemen. This was being rapidly corrected by the arrival of the British troops, some four divisions in all, including the Sixth Airborne which had been rushed across by sea from England. The German penetration had reached its maximum in front of Dinant, some forty miles, on Christmas Eve. The first enemy tanks and infantry arrived above the defenseless town just at the moment when the first British formation had got itself in position there. A rapid skirmish followed and when, on Christmas Day, the Americans charged in from the northern flank the peak of the German thrust was over-run at Celles.

One other excellent thing for the Allies occurred just about Christmas time. After five days of fog which had grounded most aircraft the weather suddenly broke clear, cold and sunny. An Allied air fleet, some five thousand strong, swept down on the battle area and began to batter the German supply columns along the roads. At places this massacre of vehicles reached the proportions we had known in Normandy. To this effort, which continued right through Christmas, was added the tremendous effect of the isolated Americans holding out behind the German lines.

Nearly every one of Rundstedt's supply roads was coming under cross fire at one point or another from these stranded garrisons. The effect, of course, was to wither up the German supplies, which were needed on the main front many miles away to the west. Heavy snow covered the ground. Soldiers of both sides were dying of frostbite and exposure.

Yet still for the Allies the position was far from secure. If Bastogne fell before it could be relieved then Rundstedt still had the reserves to plunge on again towards and possibly over the Meuse. The crisis could only be said to have passed when at last Patton got through to the 101st Division with a convoy of supply lorries. And thus at the New Year the Allies at last passed to the offensive.

From the north and south immense pressure came down on the German salient; mile after mile the enemy was squeezed back to his original starting line in Germany. This was some of the most grueling fighting of the whole war; the day-long, night-long endless snow, the unremitting cold. Men froze to death in their fox-holes in the night. Petrol, for the first time in my experience, froze in the tanks and the anti-freeze mixture in the radiators froze as well.

There was an other-worldly beauty in the battlefield for those who had the comfort and the leisure to observe. All round Brussels and Liége it was milky fog. But when you drove past the frozen canals and the tobogganing children up to the heights of the Ardennes, the sun broke through and it was like a spotlighted stage, mile upon mile of untrodden snowfields under the clear and frosty lamp of the winter sun. If you turned your back to the ruined villages and forgot the war for a moment, then very easily you could fancy yourself to be alone in this radiant world where everything was reduced to primary whites and blues; a strident, sparkling white among the frosted trees, the deep blue shadows in the valley and then the flawless ice-blue of the sky. Flying Fortresses went by, immensely high, spinning out their vapor trails half-way across Belgium.

All this was an uplifting thing to see and it triumphed for a little in the mind until one came upon a stranded tank threshing madly in a ditch or saw a line of infantry passing over the hill. And then in the villages one met a recurring tragedy as sharp as any in this war. These Belgians had had their outburst of joy at the liberation only to see the Germans come back again. Then the shells as the Allies returned a second time. As the Germans retired they took with them the men of the villages to work in Germany. No wonder that the women stood at their doorways asking over and over again, "Are you sure they have really gone for good?"

No. They had not yet gone entirely. Indeed Rundstedt was

attacking still in other salients, in the Saar, round Strasbourg. But something bigger than all this, bigger even than the battle of the Ardennes, had risen in the east. The Russian offensive was developing wave on wave from the Carpathians to the Baltic. Under that colossal pressure the Germans would never again attack with such power in the west. France and Belgium at last were secure. Having killed and captured and wounded nearly a quarter of a million Germans in this midwinter fighting, the Americans and the British began to muster for their final strike into Germany.

15. The Run Up to the Rhine

The Battle of the Ardennes set back our plans for the final conquest of Germany by about six weeks. On the other hand it probably expedited the end because the morale of the American and British soldiers who had withstood the assault rose sharply, while the Germans now knew at last that their cause was hopeless.

Montgomery's Twenty-first Army Group, composed of the First Canadian, the Second British and the Ninth American armies, was given the job of closing on the Lower Rhine between Nijmegen and the Ruhr, and of eventually crossing the river in great force. It was an ingenious plan. The Canadian and British troops were first to wheel sharply downward from Nijmegen between the Maas and the Rhine, and this operation was to be called "Veritable." Then about a week later General Simpson's Ninth Army was to strike northeastward from Aachen across the Roer river, and this was operation "Grenade." The two forces were to join hands somewhere opposite the Ruhr and thus fill in all the enemy-held territory on the western bank of the Lower Rhine. The battle began on February 8th.

From the first moment the British and Canadians were engaged in a war of mud and cold and water, an amphibious war in which the troops went sailing at the enemy across the floodwaters in their armored boats, and by day and night there was nothing but all-pervading wetness and rain. The Germans rushed to plug the gap in the Reichswald forest, and in the end some eighteen different divisions—or at least parts thereof—were fighting opposite the British. This left the enemy with no adequate defense opposite General Simpson, and so they broke the dams on the Roer river in the hope of holding him back. As a temporary move this was a great success for the enemy. Fifteen days passed, a fortnight of unrewarding battle for the British in the north, before Simpson was able to launch his men. Then on February 23rd, with unbelievable speed, the Americans swept across the river, rushed upon München-Gladbach and Krefeld and reached the banks of the Rhine.

That is the bare bones of the story, and probably it is only of interest now to the historian and the student and the men who fought. But there was something here too for the rest of the world to see and learn. For most of us it was our first experience of Germany itself, the first time we had come into contact with large numbers of German civilians, and seen the way they lived and dressed and carried themselves. It was the beginning of an immensely complicated relationship between ourselves and the defeated, a story that kept changing its plot, so that the farther you went on with it the more it altered its direction and was full of loose ends and contradictions leading nowhere. As soon as you discovered evil and malice in one place you were immediately confronted with kindness and genuine innocence in another, and there was every nuance of these extremes and every kind of character from the villain to the fool. And all this, no matter where you went or what you did, was placed against the unending tragedy and physical ruin of the country.

Everyone went into Germany with a mass of prejudices and a profound ignorance, even those who spoke German and knew Germany before the war. All the older men who had lived through two wars could not think clearly about the Germans. All the young men who had been submitted to five years of propaganda and had perhaps been physically hit at by the Germans were not able to think clearly. And the huge populations of the Empire and the United States were still farther away from understanding, since they had no personal experience, and no means of disentangling or coordinating the popular emotions at home from the actual events inside the Reich.

We had entered Germany in the northwest, the rich Rhineland province, where the border populations were mixed, more subject to outside influences and presumably less overborne by the Nazis. The first thing that struck you in the lush green countryside was the cattle, so numerous, so well fed. Chickens and pigs and horses were running everywhere. The farms were rich, wonderfully well equipped and managed. The farming people and their foreign workers were well dressed, and they looked strong and healthy. One could turn into any house at random and find a cellar lined with glass jars of preserved vegetables and fruits. It was nothing unusual to come on many sides of bacon, and larders of fresh meat and dairy butter. In the better homes there was wine and often French liqueurs.

The villages and smaller towns too had a solid bourgeois comfort which had been unknown in England and France for years. Silk stockings were a commonplace. There was not much leather in the shops, but every house seemed to have a good linen cupboard, and there was always an extraordinary variety of electrical gadgets like radio sets and cookers and vacuum cleaners. On the walls no sign of Nazi flag or pictures of Hitler; these had been snatched down at the last minute before the Allied troops arrived. Whenever you entered a *Gasthaus* or a shop you would always be certain of seeing a discolored patch on the wallpaper where a photograph of one of the Nazi leaders had hung until the previous day. Whenever you approached a farm in a jeep, the German family would remain indoors and send out one of their foreign workers, preferably a Dutchman, in order (they hoped) to make a good impression. Most of their valuables they hid in the cellar or dug into the ground under the chicken runs. As for the eggs and chickens and the other things they could not hide, these they offered almost eagerly, expecting no payment. They expected to lose everything in the way of cattle and horses, and the motor-cars which had been stored away years since under the straw in the barns. That was the first thing we learned inside a week of living with the Germans; they expected to be ill-treated. They had an immense sense, not of guilt, but of defeat. If a man's shop was entered and looted by Allied soldiers he never dreamed of protesting. He expected it. And the reason for this was that he was afraid. Mortally and utterly afraid. And so the German made the ordinary normal reaction of a man overcome by fear; he ran to obey. He was obsequious. And the women turned away their heads. They walked past with wooden despairing expressions on their faces, as though they were being pursued by someone. One saw few tears. For the Germans the catastrophe had gone far beyond that point. Tears were a useless protest in front of the enormity of the shelling and the bombing. And so one was always surrounded by these set wooden faces.

Sometimes our car got stuck in the mud. At a word the Germans ran to push it out. Once a German came up to my driver and said: "The Russian prisoners of war are looting my shop. Will the English soldiers please come and see they do it in an orderly manner?" It never occurred to him to contest the right of the Russians to loot. He was simply anxious to avoid the needless smashing of his windows as well. We lived in farmhouses and small hotels, most of them filled with refugees from the bombed-out towns. We said: "We will require this room and that room in an hour's time." At once the German families rose and left—to live in the cellar probably. They cleaned the rooms, washed our clothes, did our cooking. After the first week in Germany it never occurred to us to mount sentries at night. Often four or five of us would sleep entirely alone in a village filled with hundreds of Germans, most of whom had husbands and brothers who had been killed or captured by the British, and whose houses had been wrecked by the British. Never anywhere did any German civilian attempt to shoot at me or menace me or steal any possession of mine. We could not understand this at first, because in these early weeks in February we did not yet know the depths of the German fear.

We drove one night behind the leading troops into the great industrial town of Krefeld. It was the usual thing; the tramcars stopped in the streets; the military traffic weaving in and out of the bomb craters and the broken electric cables that hung like tropical creepers from the buildings. And the ruins and the half-ruins on either side. It had been an exciting day taking this first big city of the Reich. As the Americans had come up to it they had been astonished to find a number of the factories still working, the furnaces going, the keys in the locks of the safes and offices. And the factory managers had come out saying: "We were told to carry on and hand over to anyone who arrived. What are your orders?" In other words, no sabotage beyond the exploding of the main bridges along the road. And this itself was a strange thing, quite foreign to the Nazi idea of war to the bitter end. Did they then wish to preserve what was left of Germany? Was the end very near now?

The Americans had confined the citizens of Krefeld indoors. It was so eerie and inky dark in the city streets that night that when we proposed to visit one of the underground shelters the Americans judged it necessary for an armed guard to go with us. After all, the city had only been taken a few hours before, and snipers could appear at any moment. No one had any blueprint for the behavior of a captured German town at this stage. Four American doughboys with their tommy-guns piled into a second jeep behind us. We crunched over broken glass and concrete, driving as far as I could see into nothing but blackness. At length there was a faint challenge to the right, and we pulled up before a faint glow coming out of the earth. This was one of Krefeld's huge reinforced shelters, to which a great part of the population had fled as soon as the tanks appeared, and now American sentries were standing at the top of the concrete ramp to ensure no one came out. With the guards following in line abreast, we walked down into the light. A wall of suffocating fetid heat, a tangible thing full of the smell of human bodies, came up the ramp and seemed to close round behind us as we went on. We were in the middle of a great concrete room filled with Germans. Germans sleeping and eating, Germans playing cards, feeding their children, lying and sitting on the concrete floor. Germans talking and crying and whispering and shoving at one another. Mothers washing their children, young men playing a concertina, and the old men and women sitting vacantly in row after row along the benches. And beyond this another room, again filled so densely with humanity that there was no space for everyone to lie down. And beyond that another room and another and another.

As soon as we were seen, the American and the British uniforms, all activity ceased, and for a moment one was only conscious of thousands of pairs of staring eyes. Little groups broke off their conversation on a word to turn and stare. It was an avid and searching kind of staring, something far beyond curiosity. They stared as though some kind of revelation were going to come out of us. We were the first of the enemy they had seen, standing here with guns, having absolute rights of life and death, and we were their first real vision of the men behind Nazi propaganda posters, the actual walking monsters who had flung down bombs on Krefeld. They stared as though we were creatures from another world, sub-humans, capable here and now of some new frightfulness.

As we walked slowly ahead through the rooms towards the central office, German men stood to attention, or stood open-mouthed, or touched their foreheads in salute. The children, affected by the unnatural quietness of their parents, stopped playing their games and fell silent, sensing the general fear about them. Women hastily jumped up and shrank back from our path, fearing perhaps that we would be angered if impeded. And always that wall of faces pressing on us from either side and in front and behind. In that overpowering sickening heat, coming wave on wave from every succeeding room, it was too much to comprehend anything in detail, and presently all faces became one face, a grotesque straining mask expressing first fright, then hatred, then passion and contempt, and then again puzzlement and bitterness and anger and an idiot vacuity underneath the over-riding terror, and then the compression of all these things into one set rigid look.

This was the place, the last refuge, to which the Germans had fled, having lost their relatives in the fight and the confusion, having no longer any possessions, not even a normal hope of living. They had almost no food, no medicines, no breathable air. They were allowed out of the shelter just one hour in twenty-four, and in that hour they had to bury the people who had died in the shelter in the night, especially the children who sickened quickly in that atmosphere. In that hour they had to scrabble quickly through the bomb debris in search of food, and then get back to the shelter again. Families that became separated in the rush to the door became permanently lost in the mob, and women pressed frantically from room to room, in search no doubt of their children. One man made delirious with drink and hysteria, his face livid and working, kept shouting at an American sentry and plucking at his sleeve, until the other Germans drew him back. And now, like dumb herded animals in a cage, the crowd stood still and waited to see what we would do.

We went into a brilliantly lit office, the control room of the shelter where half a dozen men and women were sitting round a large central table. A little Lutheran pastor came forward, a neat little man wearing a white starched shirt, a black frock coat and neat black trousers.

"Please," he said. "Please. . . ." He bowed nervously two or three times. "I speak a little English." He waved his hands vaguely towards the table and the others ran to get chairs for us.

"Tell him," said the American captain, "tell him I got another five hundred refugees coming in. Can he find a place for them tonight?"

A tall young corporal began to translate slowly, and the pastor broke in: "Yes, yes, I understand. Yes, we will find beds."

"Ask him if he's got any food for them—they've had none all day."

"Yes, yes. We will find the food. We have some bean soup."

The American sentries stood round us in a ring, with their guns ready across their forearms. Then we began to move round on an inspection of the rest of the shelter.

"I was in England before the war," the pastor said. "I had many friends there. This is the room for the air raid sirens. We were very much relieved when the bombers came and then passed on to some other place." He was making a big effort to speak English slowly and carefully.

"Here is the first-aid. Here the ventilator room." In each room the attendants jumped up when we entered and stood to attention.

"I must apologize for the lavatories," the pastor said. "Since the Russian prisoners went there has been no one to keep them clean."

I asked why the Germans themselves could not clean their own lavatories, but he apparently did not understand and went on with some other subject. After half an hour I for one could stand no more, and we moved through the lower decks of the shelter towards the entrance.

"There is much damage in London?" the pastor asked.

"Much," I said.

Why argue? I felt suddenly guilty about this shelter, but what was there to say? "You bombed London and this is the result." Or perhaps: "There have sometimes been scenes like this in London in the underground stations." But these things were banal and futile things to say in the presence of the horrible facts around us, and the little pastor knew it and I knew it and we said nothing. In other words, the moral issues of war had simply ceased to have any validity here. This was the pay-off of war, the final inevitable end of war, and in that atmosphere any dispute of who was to blame was ludicrous, academic, absurd. The Nazis were guilty and that was that.

The pastor made no attempt to shake hands. He bowed. "Please," he said. "Please."

At the ramp the new batch of refugees was pushing into the shelter; women with bundles on their shoulders, men wheeling tireless bicycles. We pressed past them into the open air.

This then was one of the first contacts we had with the human mass inside Germany. Looking back on it now across a much more terrible gulf of misery I am astonished to remember what an impression it made on me at the time, and even in writing now the scene comes up before me with the sharpness of a photograph. But probably the impression was too deep. I never went back to Krefeld, but I imagine that the Germans were soon allowed to emerge from the shelter and create some sort of life for themselves among the damaged buildings.

There remains another memory, a peak that soars up equally in the mind from the mist of detail, and this was our first contact with mass physical destruction in Germany—the city of Cologne. All this time the United States First Army was bearing up on the southern flank of the Ninth in the direction of the Rhine, and on March 6th they seized the city of Cologne. At Aachen we had had a foretaste of what high explosive will do to a city, but few people I think were prepared for Cologne. There was something awesome about the ruins of Cologne, something the mind was unwilling to grasp, and the cathedral spires still soaring miraculously to the sky only made the *débâcle* below more difficult to accept and comprehend. A million briquettes burned in the colliery outside the city, a lovely play of light and gold flowing heat; and then we ran down to the

The cathedral in Cologne: the spires still soared to the sky.

suburbs where the sentry stopped the car and said: "You better look out for falling buildings. I'm telling you this on account of the lady." My wife was traveling with me. Then into the city.

A city is a plan on a map. and here. over a great area. there was no plan. A city means movement and noise and people: not silence and emptiness and stillness, a kind of cemetery stillness. A city is life, and when you find instead the negation of life the effect is redoubled.

My friends who traveled with me knew Cologne. but not this Cologne. They remembered that about here they used to take their coffee before the war. and here they used to buy their scent, and over there was the Kaiserhof. which was a very good hotel indeed. But they found themselves looking at disordered rocks. and presently they abandoned any attempt to guide our way by their memory of the city. and instead everyone fixed his eyes on the cathedral spires and used that only landmark as a guide across the rubble. After the first mass raids the Germans had cleared the streets, but lately there had been new raids, and none to clear the wreckage. Under the burden of falling stones the streets grew level with what was left of the buildings, and now there was nothing much left to show you where the street had been.

A fortnight before a master-bomber of the R.A.F. had been telling us in Brussels: "You arrive over the target about ten minutes in advance of the others, and then when you have dropped your target indicators you tell them to 'Bomb the red' or 'Bomb the yellow,' according to what color you have put down. While the raid is on you have to keep going down to make sure the bombs are falling in the right place. If you find that one part of the target is sufficiently covered you drop more indicators in another place and tell them to bomb that."

Jumping from stone to stone over the guts of shops and office buildings in Cologne. one tried to picture the immense play of light and explosion in the raids, the fantastic courage which had put a calm clear brain into the head of the master-bomber in the midst of it all, and then—then this curiously dead result. No sound except the occasional mortar shell whining over the debris on to the opposite bank of the Rhine. Every now and then a German civilian scurried out of a broken doorway into another broken doorway. A group of soldiers backed a truck up to a cellar and began carrying out cases of wine. Someone was saying: "There are forty thousand Germans living underground here, and they have hoards of food and clean tablecloths and flowers on the table."

We went down to the river bank and looked across the broken girders of the bridge at the other bank where the German soldiers were watching us, but no one fired. We ate a cold chicken on the cathedral steps. All that was left of the building opposite was the sign "4711"—the name of the finest Eau de Cologne. Two drunks lurched by. All around us, acre after acre, the rubble lay in the morning sunshine, so real and solid that it seemed that Cologne had always been like that, and that there was no sense or pattern any more in anything. We were glad to leave.

Back at our camp it was a relief to hear that while we had been in Cologne something had been happening farther upstream which was enough to revive anyone's faith in life, even in war. Indeed it was the most romantic story of the whole campaign. A Lieutenant Timmerman, finding himself at the approaches to an unsmashed bridge at Remagen had simply taken a deep breath and led his men across. This was the last bridge across the Rhine, the only one which the Germans had not exploded. No one had dreamed that we could "bounce" a bridge. But here he was on the opposite bank, Lieutenant Timmerman, with half his army pouring across behind him. Timmerman was born and brought up only a few miles from this very place. He went to America and returned as a United States citizen fighting in the line. A round half-dozen of his German relatives were at this moment fighting in the German army. And now the Germans began to wreck the bridge. It shook under the artillery fire. Many people, like my colleague Peter Lawless, were killed there. Little by little the bridge began to crumble, and at last the Germans scored a lucky hit with a V.2 and it subsided into the current. But it was too late. By now other bridges had been built alongside by the American engineers. Many thousands of soldiers were across on the opposite bank. The Rhine was crossed—not effectively perhaps, not with sufficient strength to enable the Americans to push on. But Remagen was to become a running sore in the German lines, a sore that was never to be healed up.

16. The Crossing of the Rhine

March 18th, 1945. General Dempsey perched his map on a wooden bench at his camp near Venlo and explained:

"We will cross the Rhine on the night of the 23rd. Four corps are under my command. Thirty Corps will cross in the north near Rees and continue northward for the capture of Emmerich. Twelve

Corps will cross in the center at Xanten while the Commandos turn south to capture Wesel. On the following morning the Eighteenth United States Airborne Corps with the Sixth British Airborne Division under command will drop near the Issel River on the opposite bank of the Rhine and secure the bridges there. Finally the Eighth Corps will follow through and I cannot yet tell you how far they will go. The Ninth American Army will also attack on my right flank and proceed eastward along the Ruhr."

I asked: "This well might be the last battle?"

"Yes."

Dempsey was an exact and energetic technician. Ever since the landing in Normandy, whenever we met him, one was astonished at the precision with which he elucidated a plan and brought a map to life.

Above and below him were two entirely different commanders; Montgomery with his flair, his processes of instinctive divination, his legendary influence with the generals and the soldiers. Then Horrocks of Thirty Corps, a man with an ascetic, almost an ecclesiastical, face and underneath that more volatility and fire and dash than one could have thought possible in a single man, an ideal break-through general. Both Montgomery (objectively) and Horrocks (subjectively) dealt often in terms of emotion. Between them stood Dempsey the technician, a lean and nervous figure, a manipulator of facts, not so much a popular leader as a remarkable co-ordinator and a planner.

There was a certain greyhound quality about him. Most people spoke too slowly for him and in nearly every meeting I had with him his thoughts were racing impatiently ahead of the conversation. He hated crowds. He hated displays. He avoided the radio and rousing orders of the day. He was unable to relax and talk while his photograph was being taken since that would have meant concentrating on two things at the same time—which is inefficient. For him the emotional and inspirational method of handling things was untidy and imprecise. He had an excellent memory, and every time I went to him he had a neat list of things he wanted to talk about. Fifteen minutes of breakneck conversation and I found myself walking down the step of his caravan, all the things I had asked for granted and a perfectly clear picture of his ideas in my mind. He rarely used slang, even army slang. This arithmetical direction flowed from the commander right through the army staff, leavened a little perhaps by his sense of humor and his genuine burning eagerness. You must list him among the half-dozen really able field commanders thrown up by England in the war.

March 23rd. A black night along the Rhine. A sentry's voice in the darkness. "Don't go down there, sir, that's the river bank, and the enemy are only three hundred yards away and covering us with machine-gun fire."

We felt our way blindly up a side-road looking for the Commando headquarters opposite Wesel. The unbearable whip and lash of the guns started up from the fields around us. Just above the river we found a German holiday villa. Looking out of the second-story window we had Wesel full in view on the opposite bank. As we watched the pathfinder came in, a single hurrying black moth in the air, and he shot his clusters of red flares into the center of the town, which meant—and how acutely one felt it—that Wesel had just about ten minutes to live. Then the Lancasters filling the air with roaring and at last the cataclysmic, unbelievable shock of the strike. Great black stretches of the skyline—buildings and trees and wide acres of city parkland—simply detached themselves from the earth and mounted slowly upward in the formation of a fountain. As the rubble reached its zenith it suddenly filled with bursting light and a violent wind came tearing across the river. The uncontrollable savagery of the bombing went on until all the sky to the east was lit with a red glow spattered here and there with the chandelier light of the flares and the incidental puffs of anti-aircraft shells.

Already the Commandos had launched their armored boats—the buffaloes—and landed on the opposite bank. Then, burglar-like and in single file, the leaders paying out a white tape, the whole brigade crept into the town and demolished its defenders. The German general tried to shoot it out from behind the trees in his garden, but a British sergeant crept into the pantry of the house, took careful aim from ten yards distance and shot the general dead.

From all along the river that night reports poured in of almost bloodless landings.

March 24th. Churchill stood on Xanten hilltop and looked down across the morning battle mist at the place where the troops were still crossing on boats and rafts. "I should have liked," he said, "to have deployed my men in red coats on the plain down there and ordered them to charge." And he added with vim: "But now my armies are too vast."

Suddenly the Prime Minister sprang to his feet, and went coursing wildly for a few steps down the hill.

"They're coming," he shouted, "they're coming!"

It was the first airborne troops. Indeed it was a wonderful sight. They passed only two or three hundreds of feet above our heads, the tow planes drawing sometimes one and sometimes two gliders

The Rhine bridges were smashed.

and flying in tight formation. Then single planes with the parachutists waiting intensely inside for the moment to plunge out through the open hatches. Here and there among all these hundreds of aircraft one would be hit by ack-ack fire, and it was an agonizing thing to see it break formation and start questing vainly back and forth in search of any sort of landing field and then at last plunge headlong to the ground. Within a few minutes nothing would be left but the black pillar of petrol smoke and the unidentifiable scraps of wings and propellers and human beings. Overhead a thousand express trains went screaming heedlessly by.

The Germans were waiting for the landing mainly because there was only one obvious place to drop in the vicinity and this was it. A heavy mist, possibly created by the enemy, covered the dropping zone. Unable to see through it at the last minute, and being full in the face of flying shrapnel, many pilots judged the ground to be either higher or lower than it was. And so many crashed into farmhouses and ditches and others broke up in the air and others again dropped sheer to the earth from thirty or forty feet. At the same time the falling parachutists were picked off during that vital few minutes in the air. In the end the British Airborne division alone had nearly forty per cent casualties. But this was to be no second Arnhem. Barely a mile or two divided our ground troops who had crossed the Rhine overnight from the dropping zone, and they were sending out patrols for the link-up while the drop was still going on.

Crossing the Rhine at that moment was an unreal experience. Temporarily there was complete quiet along the river. Already naval launches flying the ensign were plying to and fro. Already the bridge builders were at work. The buffaloes lay about in the field in the sunshine like prehistoric monsters, their exhausted crews spreadeagled out on the grass asleep after the night's work. One had merely to walk up to the river bank, summon an outboard motor-boat and in three minutes you were stepping out on the opposite bank.

Often immediately behind an assault there is a strange numbness on the battlefield. A kind of vacuum exists between the line of the advancing shock troops and the bulk of the army following behind. Such civilians who have survived are stunned by the barrage so recently ended and the earth itself has a curiously worn-out appearance. But for the tide of aircraft still passing close overhead there would have been nothing but an exhausted silence along the river.

Odd incongruities spring up in this unusual atmosphere. The bargee's wife continues to hang out the washing because that is her normal routine, and not knowing what else to do she clings to this routine as one sane thing in a world gone mad. The house beyond has collapsed like a house of cards a couple of hours back, but a man still digs a vegetable patch in the garden. Little lines of prisoners go by carrying and supporting their wounded, and they walk aimlessly and woodenly since it is too early yet for them to grasp the significance of what has happened in the night and they are still too confused to wonder what their fate might be.

An enterprising Military Government officer had crossed with the assault troops in the night and was distributing General Eisenhower's proclamations in English and German in the first village on the opposite bank. Nazi emblems must be destroyed. All Nazi organizations and courts of law are abolished. Householders must place lists of names of the inmates on the front doors of their houses.

A withered little German civilian has been enlisted to paste up these notices, and he starts off down the street with a bucket of paste in one hand and a bundle of proclamations in the other. He has picked up the proclamations dealing with the financial reforms, but it does not matter much; as yet there is no one to read, and since

Allied trucks and equipment started to pour across the pontoon bridges.

last night money ceased to count for anything any more. He goes to the butcher's shop to paste up his first notice, finds the front of the shop has been bashed in and continues on to the ruins of the baker's next door. Ruins on either side of him. Somewhere every twenty yards or so he finds enough masonry on which to stick a notice. At the top of the street three children come running towards him shouting, "Father . . . father." He quiets them, hands each one a few notices and they too go off to help the work of advising the ruined village that marks at the rate of forty to the pound sterling will henceforth prevail in the Reich.

We climbed into a tracked bren-gun carrier to try and make contact with the airborne troops. No one fires along the roads, and presently at the forward company headquarters we find that the link-up is already accomplished. All round us bright red and yellow parachutes lie over over the fields like enormous poppies.

The assault has been a perfect success. The airborne landing— known by the code word "Varsity"—is complete. The river crossing by the land troops—known by the name "Grenade"—is now continuing over the Issel and eastward into Westphalia and Hanover and Oldenburg. Already American armies are beginning to encircle the Ruhr. Patton and Patch are about to start their great drive past Frankfurt into the hills of southern Germany.

March 26th. General Dempsey's senior intelligence officer stands before a room full of correspondents. He says:

"This is the collapse. The German line is broken. The enemy no longer has a coherent system of defense between the Rhine and the Elbe. It is difficult to see what there is to stop us now."

Many of us in that room—and later many more people at home— were a little chary of that statement. Could it really be the end? So many people had cried "Wolf" so often before. Yet it was right. The end of the war was barely six weeks away. The British and Americans were never again to fight a set battle against the Nazis in Germany. Next morning we set out on a mopping-up operation, a series of headlong skirmishes that were to lead us three-quarters of the way across Germany, and end at last in the junction with the Russians, and the ruination of a modern state.

Eisenhower's plan was nothing less than a series of vast loops and encircling movements on the Russian pattern, the general direction easterly. Seven armies were deployed. At the top of the line the Canadians wheeled northward upon the Zuider Zee and the Dutch coast opposite the Frisian islands. They had three tactical objects, all urgent. First, the isolation of the V.-sites in Holland from their supplies in Germany; then the relief and liberation of the slowly

B17's—the Flying Fortresses—carried up to 10 tons of bombs.

starving Dutch. And finally, the trapping of the German forces
under Seyss-Inquart. On March 30th the Canadians crossed the
Dutch border on the left of the British flank. On April 14th they
reached the North Sea, captured Leeuwarden—and the job was
done, or almost done. The last rocket and flying bomb had fallen
on England. All around on the line of march we came on stranded
trains filled with the V.-weapons: wingless V.1's packed three
abreast in the railway trucks; V.2's paced with rounded wooden
struts and wickerwork, but so large that each projectile overlapped
by half its length into the truck ahead. And in the railway yards
there were many great drums of explosives and strange steel cranes
and scaffoldings for launching the rockets into the air. Often the

trains were latticed over with the branches of trees, and there was evidence that they traveled only by night. But it made no difference. They lay there either broken by the R.A.F. or sabotaged by the retreating Germans themselves, or simply abandoned in the cuttings by the wayside stations, a series of weird tossing shapes among the spring wheat, a brutal warning of what might have happened had the war continued another year.

As for the Seyss-Inquart garrison, it was hopelessly cut off. Most of the men were grouped round the major cities like Amsterdam, Rotterdam, Utrecht and The Hague, on two sides of them the sea, to the south the Rhine and to the east the thickening Canadian army that was now advancing upon the key city of Arnhem. Seyss-Inquart had one last savage gesture to make. "All right," he said in effect, "I will destroy Holland. Every kilometer you advance I will flood a little more of the country. In the end I will smash the dike across the Zuider Zee and that will be the finish of a good many thousands of your Dutch friends." As an example of the use of blackmail in war it was very nearly perfect.

The Canadians halted. Finally Seyss-Inquart was induced to come out to Montgomery's headquarters and parley. He agreed to receive Allied food convoys and doctors and supplies dropped from the air.

At these parleys Seyss-Inquart was reminded that he was regarded by the Allies as a war criminal. He answered curtly "That sort of thing leaves me cold." Someone had the grim wit to reply: "That's exactly how it will leave you."

And so in the end it was not Holland but Seyss-Inquart, the original quisling of the war, who was to die.

The British army came next in the line, and theirs was a north-easterly march of some three hundred miles to Schleswig-Holstein and the Baltic. Again this was a huge encircling movement, designed to isolate and then capture the great ports of Bremen and Hamburg and finally all Denmark. We had four more rivers to cross—the Ems, the Weser, the Aller and the Elbe, and these crossings became progressively easy as we advanced.

At first the march was largely uneventful, since we were plunging into some of the poorest parts of Germany, where there were no great cities or industrial areas. Rheine, Münster and Osnabrück were surrounded and taken in the first ten days after the Rhine crossing. Minden was captured on April 5th. Then the bulk of the British wheeled northeastward across the lonely stretches of Lüneburg Heath for the investment of Bremen and Hamburg and the crossing of the lower Elbe and the last run to the Baltic. Bremen fell on April 26th, and at once the British began handing the city over to the Americans as their major port for occupied Germany. (The British were to use Hamburg.) On April 29th the Elbe was crossed. On May 2nd the soldiers broke through to the Baltic and met the Russians at Wismar; on the 3rd Hamburg fell.

Different divisions at different times got ahead in this race across country. Sometimes we would follow the Eleventh Armored Division (who were usually in the lead) only to find our old friends from the desert, the Seventh, were overhauling them. But the chief honors probably went to the Sixth Airborne Division. Nobody has yet succeeded in explaining satisfactorily how those men, recovering from their dreadful casualties on the Rhine, picked themselves up and, without any military transport to speak of, projected themselves for three hundred miles across Germany to arrive on the Baltic ahead of the tanks and the armor—indeed, ahead of everyone else. I saw only glimpses of the Sixth, and they were surprising enough. Having no vehicles at the outset, they simply seized anything they could get hold of from the Germans—bakers' and butchers' vans, post-office trucks. They did not bother to repaint them. I even saw one man in a steam-roller. Anything to get forward.

When an 88-millimeter gun blocked the road they wasted no time in detours, but ran directly upon it. A spirit of desperate heroism seemed to grip the men in these last days of the war. At one point where they were stopped by a gun they brought a German tradesman's van up to the front, and, judging that the gun would fire directly at the body of the truck, they mounted infantry on the roof. Then wearing their red berets in place of helmets—they never used helmets—they charged the gun. The truck was struck, the men jumped down and killed the gun crew and the whole British column moved on again.

But for the most part there were no spectacular events on the British front until the very end, when the German High Command fled from the Russians on to our front and gave themselves up. It was the two American armies on our immediate right flank—the Ninth and the First—who probably had the best of the early hue and cry. Starting out on March 23rd, General Simpson with the Ninth kept along the north of the Ruhr, heading due east. Then Hodges with the First burst out of his Remagen bridgehead, and wheeling away to the right kept south of the industrial area. Here and there both armies dropped off a division to penetrate the factories and the debris, but the general scheme was to get quickly round the Ruhr and prevent any of the German garrison escaping to the east. It was a brilliant stroke. On April 1st Simpson and Hodges began to link up in the vicinity of Hamm, on the eastern end of the Ruhr. Some twenty German divisions were trapped inside, along with such celebrities as von Papen and Krupp, and the German general promptly gave up. This was the first and one of the greatest of the isolated mass German surrenders, and the first real indication that Hitler had already lost control. From now on individual German commanders were going to act on their own initiative, and the Reich was going to be given up piecemeal to the Allies. There would be no general and instantaneous act of collapse: as soon as the flood raced round an island of German resistance then the island was going to abandon itself to the torrent; and in the end the Third Reich was to be entirely submerged not by the signing of a document or the issuing of an order but by the impetus of *force majeure*.

Without even waiting for the island of the Ruhr to tumble, Simpson and Hodges ran headlong upon the Elbe. On April 10th Hanover was captured. Then Brunswick a few days later, and finally Magdeburg on the Elbe. In one immense stream the Americans poured to the east and occupied all the left bank in the great curve of the river before Berlin.

Farther south Patton with his Third Army was making his last great romp in Europe, with General Patch and his Seventh Army keeping close up to him on his right flank. Having seized Darmstadt (on March 24th) and Mannheim (on the 29th), and having bypassed Frankfurt, it appeared obvious that these southern forces should break out to the north along the traditional route through Kassel and link up with the other United States forces in central Germany. That was the obvious plan. But the military and political map of the Reich at this moment differed very greatly from the ordinary geographical map—and it was the politico-military map that mattered. It resembled a bottle. Its outline was defined not by mountains or territorial frontiers but by the disposition of the German forces. These forces were distributed in a most unusual manner. A minor proportion of them was lining the narrow neck of the bottle, from Norway down through Denmark, past Berlin to Dresden and the borders of Czechoslovakia. Then the bottle widened out. It enveloped Prague, northern Jugoslavia and Italy, and most of the southern mountains. This was the real Germany that took no account of racial groups or borders. This was the famous Southern Redoubt, the existence of which so many people doubted later on because its collapse was so swift and complete. It is only when you look back historically, taking event by event, that

Dresden.

you discover that the Southern Redoubt was a very real issue indeed. It is only when one accepts the fact of the Redoubt that one begins to understand why the Germans resisted so fanatically at Budapest against the Russian drive into the eastern flank; and why after the battle of the Ardennes they committed their only remaining strategic reserve—the Sixth Panzer Army—not for the direct defense of Berlin but in the same southeastern direction. Then, too, one begins to understand why so many German divisions were retained in Italy when they were so urgently needed in the north. They were protecting the base of the bottle.

Several German generals, like Dittmar, pretended after their capture that the Southern Redoubt never existed; but you have only to study the prisoners-of-war figures (Alexander alone accounted for a million prisoners in Italy) to see that the Redoubt was not only a very definite plan of the German High Command but the expression of a last-ditch Nazi hope that they could carry on an underground movement in the mountains after the major operations in Europe were finished.

It seems to me that the plan failed for two main reasons. First, both Eisenhower and the Russians saw it in advance and took steps to destroy it before it became effective. And secondly, Hitler's emotional decision to remain in Berlin. Probably by April it was already too late for his presence in the south to make any difference, but the Berlin gesture certainly hastened the end.

At all events Eisenhower stuck to his declared policy, which was, he said, not to capture landmarks but to destroy the German armies. He knew the Russians were going to assault Berlin frontally. He knew that the neck of the bottle would be snapped under that pressure. And so in early April he diverted the main weight of his striking forces into the south to deal with the bulk of the German army.

This is the main explanation of why the Americans stopped on the Elbe in April. One has not much doubt that the Americans could have advanced into Berlin some days before the Russians reached it. At no time were any German soldiers diverted from the Russian front to hold back the more dangerous menace of the Anglo-American armies. Except for those actually engaged in the mopping-up operations, the run up to the Elbe was largely a joyride. The undercurrent plan in the German mind was already this—let the Anglo-Americans come on and take as much of Germany as possible in order to save the country from the Russians. But the demarcation line agreed upon with the Russians was in the valley of the Elbe, and there Eisenhower waited while he got on with his main job in the south.

Hitler among the ruins.

All that was left of Nüremberg.

Patton was diverted from his northward run. With Patch he wheeled south and east, deep into Bavaria. Nüremberg fell on April 16th. The French joined in and captured Stuttgart on the 22nd. Munich fell on the 29th. On the same day the entire German army in Italy came in to surrender, and Mussolini's body was hanging in the square in Milan. And the Southern Redoubt was no more. With this collapse fell Berchtesgaden, and many a German commander like Rundstedt and Kesselring, who had long foreseen the end and had fled down there in the hope of finding what private salvation they could with the Americans.

Meanwhile the vast Russian wave was breaking loose again. On

April 21st they had entered the Berlin suburbs. On the 26th they linked up with the Americans on the Elbe, near Torgau. On the same day Hitler vanished in the ruins of the Chancellery, and the city was surrendered at 3 P.M. on May 2nd.

All these immense events flowed so quickly—on such a fatalistic and inevitable rhythm—that the end was coming almost as an anti-climax. For days, even weeks, beforehand people at home were saying: "This is it. Tomorrow will see the end." Day after day they were disappointed. The wait for the celebration of V Day became agonizing. Unlike the last war in Europe, this one was ending as a twice-told tale.

For those of us in the field the effect was quite different. We were entirely caught up in the rush and hurry that seemed to take possession of every day after we crossed the Rhine. One's memory of the last six weeks remains in one's mind rather like a fast train journey. The landscape repeats itself infinitely, and is blurred by the speed of the train. Every so often you stop at a wayside station, and suddenly a new world is presented to you, static and isolated from everything that has gone before, and all its details stand out with the vividness of a Flemish primitive. Then abruptly the engine whirls you on again, and stops again and goes on. And in the end it is difficult to relate your stopping places in time and space. They remain simply a series of sharp and disconnected pictures.

Thus on the eastern bank of the Rhine my memory is of great gabled farmhouses where we passed the night, and of the chickens and the eggs brought to us each day by our Italian servant Augusto. When we ourselves went in search of wine and food we always paid in cigarettes or biscuits or sweets, because it is unnatural not to pay unless you happen to be very angry, and one is not angry all the time. Subconsciously, but nevertheless purposely, we never enquired of Augusto how he acquired his stocks for us, until one day the mystery was quite inadvertently explained. We had said to him: "Augusto, why don't you get the people on the farms to pluck and clean the birds before you bring them in?" He paused, and then explained: "It's difficult. You see, there is often only a woman in the place and usually she is in tears." In other words, our brave Augusto was doing what nearly every soldier was doing—looting.

For a few weeks—before it was stopped altogether—the looting was widespread and heavy. German cars by the hundred were dragged out of garages and hiding-places under the straw in the barns, painted khaki and driven away. Cameras and watches and revolvers were taken automatically from prisoners and frequently from civilians. Wine was fair booty for everybody. In nearly every town the shops were broached, the distilleries emptied. Even pictures were stripped from their frames. This was quite different from the German manner. The Germans had looted systematically and officially. They had seized not odd bottles of wine but a whole year's crop. They seized the products of entire factories. They seized rolling stock from the railways, gold from the banks, iron from the mines; and in the end they stole the conquered people themselves.

As soon as we crossed the Rhine we were confronted by a problem almost as big as Germany herself; the millions upon millions of semi-slave workers. With every mile we went into Germany they grew more numerous on the roads: little groups of Frenchmen, then Dutch, then Belgians and Czechs and Poles and Italians, and finally, in overwhelming majority, the Russians in their bright green uniforms with "S.U."—Soviet Union—painted in white on their backs. Half the nationalities of Europe were on the march, all moving blindly westward along the roads, feeling their way by some common instinct towards the British and American lines in the hope of finding food and shelter and transportation there. These millions lived a vagabond existence. At every bend of the road you came on another group, bundles on their shoulders, trudging along

Russians liberated from forced labor in the Belgian mines.

the ditches in order to avoid the passing military traffic. The Germans were terrified of the Russians. Again and again women ran out to us to cry: "Can't you leave a guard with us? The Russians have taken everything. The next lot will smash up the place if they find nothing." More than that the German women feared for themselves. Cases of rape increased. The looting increased. And still that vast moving human frieze kept pouring down the roads, constantly augmenting its numbers with every new town that was captured.

One began to get a new picture of Nazi Germany. What we were seeing was something from the dark ages, the breaking up of a medieval slave state. All the Nazi flags and parades and conquests in the end were based on this one thing—slave labor. There was something monstrous about the wired-in worker's compounds and sentry boxes round each factory, something that was in defiance of all accepted ideas of civilization. As yet, in early April, we had only begun to glimpse the extent and depth of the Nazi terror system, but already one sensed the utter disregard of the value of human life in Germany. And now the Reich was collapsing at its roots because the slaves were melting away.

One saw mostly women in the country towns and in the farms as we passed on; nearly all the German men were either at the front or prisoners or dead. And the slaves were on the road. There was no longer anyone to sow the crop, no one to reap the harvest later on. Here and there a foreigner chose to remain with his German master. Indeed, on the whole the country laborers got sufficient food and they looked healthy enough. But nothing on earth would have kept the industrial workers in the factories and the mines once the Germans had gone. First they rushed out into the streets to loot. Then they took the road to the west until they drifted into hastily made British and American camps where some attempt was made to sort them out and send them home.

Liquor at the moment of liberation caused as much uproar as anything else. The Poles and Russians especially in their first wild moments of freedom would run roaring on the hated factory machines and smash them with crowbars. When they found a distillery or one of the many dumps of wine stolen from France there were scenes to break the heart of the connoisseur.

One day we drove with the Inns of Court, a reconnaissance unit, into a little village, Steyerberg, in the Weser valley. The place was interesting because there was a train carrying fifty flying bombs in the station yard, and much V.2 launching equipment lying about. The villagers and passing refugees, however, were wholly concentrated upon a warehouse in the main street. Inside was a store of the most beautiful wine I have ever seen, all of it cased, and almost certainly loot the Germans had taken from France and brought out here from Bremen to escape the worst of the bombing. Germans and foreigners were milling round among the boxes. An innocent child lurched past carrying a case of Château Yquem of a very good year. Her father and mother and several uncles had gone for the more serious stuff: Margaux 1929 and Haut Brion of the same year, all of it bottled at the Château. These they were loading on to a wheel-barrow, and no one seemed to mind when they dropped a bottle or two on the floor; there was plenty more. The sherries were mostly Amontillado 1911, the Chablis and Rieslings perhaps a little young, but all of it vintage. And now it was all posting down the street on the backs of the villagers, in handcarts and trolleys. Half-demented children were romping among the really great prizes of the place—a Rothschild Château Lafite 1891—and this was in the magnum, the jeroboam and the rehoboam which is the most beautiful kind of bottle in the world and on account of its size very easily dropped and smashed. There was also a fifty-year-old Smith Lafite in bottles and magnums and a rather horrible Barsac which however had great qualities in making the looters drunk.

That evening the floor was awash with the Lafite and the other clarets. A friend of mine who visited the place the following morning said he walked almost ankle deep in slush and nothing remained in the broken cases.

Then again there was the day when the first British prisoner-of-war camps were released. The big one was at a pleasant watering-place called Fallingbostel just beyond the River Aller. As the first of the British army came up they found their comrades the prisoners drawn up in ranks in the compound before the Union Jack, their gaiters and belts whitewashed, their badges shining. Many of these men had spent four or five years in Germany and now on this great day they stood to the salute. To those who came to deliver them it was a moving thing to see this parade which was also a gesture, a determination to show that as prisoners they had not been beaten by imprisonment.

It seemed to many of the prisoners who had been taken years before at Dunkirk and in the desert that an immense gulf divided them from this new army which had rescued them. They felt that their imprisonment was time out of life and that they would never catch up. That was the first reaction. Perhaps the most revealing remark of all was this: "So that's what a jeep looks like." The man who made it had been captured before the days of jeeps, before

Alamein and Stalingrad, before England seemed to have a ghost of a chance in the war.

Another day we drove into Hanover which was still a lovely city despite its ruins, and the car broke down in front of the Rathaus. Two British prisoners of war came up and helped me change the wheel. As they worked they talked. They said: "The Jerries were all right at first, when they were winning. We had last-war guards and there was an inspection every Saturday morning; your kit, and all that. They looked inside the collar of your tunic for lice and you got hell if you were dirty. That camp was a real credit. Then in the last year they began to change. We were marched back here from Poland. When anyone went sick he was beaten by the German sergeant. He beat up a lot of us and killed some. German women used to come out to us while we were on the march with buckets of water, but the guards turned them off. He was a bastard, that German sergeant."

I asked what had happened to him.

"We told the Yanks when they released us about him and they started to beat him up. When our own sergeant-major, who was one of the prisoners, heard about it he sent out word to the Yanks to stop it. But the Yank sergeant just answered that he was in charge and went on with the beating up."

"Well, it's all over now," I said. "You will be home soon. Are you married?"

They said yes, slowly. Then one of them added: "My wife got killed in an air raid and his (indicating the other man) has gone off with an American. She wrote to him about it."

"I'm sorry about that," I said.

They answered: "Well, we've thought about it and we're not sorry. How could we have gone back again after five years? It wouldn't work. No. It's better the way it is."

The Bremen assault came at the very end after a neatly turned operation. For some time the troops had been meeting fanatical resistance from the German marine division, which was composed mostly of boys. They had developed a technique of hiding in the woods with bazookas, a small rocket gun that could be easily man-handled. The crew waited until an Allied tank was within forty yards. Then they fired and ran to a new hiding-place. A direct hit from a bazooka at that range was usually fatal to the tank and most of the crew.

Naval mines were found buried in the roads. Submarine crews fighting as infantry were captured. At times the skirmishing grew so bitter prisoners were being shot. But on April 26th the port suddenly collapsed, and as the British swarmed along the docks they found a dozen U-boats on the stocks, several destroyers and much equipment that was soon to be used in the building of America's biggest supply port in Europe.

All this time we were living away from the cities in the lovely countryside of northern Germany. The spring broke warm and early, and when we passed through Osnabrück we found ourselves among the forests of pine and beech. At every turn of the road there was a half-timbered farmhouse, and between the squares of oak the plaster was tinted pale pink or blue or white. Cattle lived in one end of the house, the family in the other. The great beam across the barn door was decorated with colored scrolls and gothic inscriptions and then the name of the founder of the house: "Johannes Weden. 1781."

As the front advanced we kept moving into the *Gasthaus* in the next convenient village, and we grew used to sleeping under the big white German bolsters filled with down and feathers. The Germans waited on us, cooked our food, and we did not discuss the war.

Each day we drove out along the lanes coming into full leaf and waited perhaps for an hour or more in the traffic blocks at the approaches to the river bridges. At noon we lunched at the forward headquarters. In the evening we drove back to write our dispatches by candlelight while we drank our fine French wine. There were no more battles. For us the war was running down quietly and rather pleasantly. Our only real concern now was with the enemy snipers on the road. It became unsafe to take short cuts through the woods between the main streams of traffic. But many of our friends who had come all the way with us from the desert in Africa would not listen. Five years of reconnaissance had made them unable to resist just one more exploration, and they were ambushed and died now that there was no longer any need to die. The Werewolves and the other last-minute *ad hoc* Nazi formations were never a serious menace. They were merely symptomatic of the general breakup. Here and there a *Gauleiter* who himself was entirely compromised with the Party found he could stir up a little temporary spirit by invoking the Führer and giving the local youth formation a romantic name and a few machine-guns and grenades. But it never lasted. These children, some of them no more than fourteen or fifteen, fought hysterically for a day or a week, and then there was no more ammunition. They came sullenly into the prisoners' cages, their faith in their Nazi gods still high, the problem children of Europe. Prison to them was not the end but merely an interruption of their service for the Führer.

Towards the end we over-ran the German Naval Headquarters for the North Sea outside Hamburg. It was an enormous institution on the edge of the village of Buxtehude, a series of modern barracks planted in the green countryside. Five hundred German Wrens were roaming about, girls barely twenty, some in the usual "gray mouse" uniforms, others not. By the time I arrived the British officer who had captured the place had confined these women into their dining-hall and was rather puzzled about what he ought to do next. They were his first female prisoners of the war. We went into the hall just as the women were being served with their midday meal of hot potatoes. They stood and glared. The commandant came up, a thin waspish little woman in gray overalls, the swastika pinned to her collar, and her eyes snapping and bitter. It is I suppose silly to sum up people on their mere appearance, especially prisoners of war, but this woman, drained almost entirely of sex, was almost frightening. She had made her marriage to the Party and the Führer. That marriage for her was made in a Nazi heaven, and we were her eternal enemies. She snapped her replies in monosyllables. "*Ja.*" "*Nein.*" "*Ja.*" Then she complained that none of the officers could speak German, that the English appeared to have no organization for handling the situation.

At the other end of the barracks compound there was a Nazi chapel. Instead of the usual religious emblems and pictures on the altar and along the walls there were ethereal paintings of Hitler and the other Nazi leaders. Surrounded by the swastika and the Nazi invocations to faith and war one could worship the Führer quietly there.

Another picture comes to mind, and I must place it in counterpoise to this woman and this chapel. It was away back on the Rhine at the Wesel crossing. A German self-propelled gun was shooting into the stream, close beside the bridge which lay like a child's broken meccano set, a tumble of steel girders in the fast current. We set out in a buffalo heading upstream. Underneath the tangled girders the current became too strong for us, and the clumsy armored craft threatened to smash against the stone piers. At this moment shells began dropping round us, and still we could make no headway. One felt very naked and helpless out there in midstream. Those of us who could crouched on the steel floor of the boat and felt the explosions coming through the water. At last we got back to the bank from which we had set out. The gun was still firing haphazardly, killing a man here and there. All round us Wesel lay in utter ruin, a kind of white dust fine as powder, from the battle the night before. A crocodile of German prisoners stumbled by. Two young English officers had dug up an ancient gramophone with a horn from under a broken hen coop, and in that dangerous and horrible place they were playing over the German records: Strauss waltzes, Nazi war songs. "Play that last one again, Bill," one of the officers was saying, "I like it." The German prisoners stared bewildered and hurried on.

Of these two kinds of craziness, the Nazi woman with her passionate faith, the young English officers with their casual approach to life, why is it that one so much prefers the latter?

Again, how do you explain or condone this story? At our last camp near Lüneburg I heard there was a trout hatchery close by, and drove the jeep up there to see what the *Fischmeister* could do about our evening meal.

"*Kaput,*" he said. "Finish."

He was a thin and worried little man wearing gum-boots, and not at all aggressive. He led the way down to the hatcheries, a series of big square pools set pleasantly in the grass. Beside each pool there was a heap of dead trout which were slowly beginning to stink in the sun. At the bottom of each pool more dead fish lay with their white bellies upward. A Dutchman translated for the *Fischmeister*.

"I am unable to understand. I am a Nazi. I did not expect to keep my fish. When the first English soldiers came into the village I was standing ready at the gate with my fish nets. I offered to catch fish for them, as many as they wanted, a thousand if necessary. They did not understand. They rushed past me and started throwing hand-grenades into the pools. This is not a good way to catch fish. For every one you get you destroy a hundred others and make them uneatable."

"Soldiers are always the same," I said. "And fighting soldiers are always in a hurry. They had a right to the fish."

"The officers were worse," the *Fischmeister* went on. "They drew their revolvers and shot them in the water. *Kaput.* Finish."

There is of course no moral excuse for the incident except that the British soldiers were tired and hungry, and heaven knows they had suffered more than the Nazis will ever be able to repay them. But this point does arise: as far as I was able to make out, journeying through Europe, the German soldiers were a good deal better disciplined than ours. They did not loot and destroy in the same way. With them everything was method; a cruel, hard, cold, organized official beating-down of the peoples they conquered. If this *Fischmeister* had been an Englishman his fish would have been meticulously netted, his house seized, himself arrested and his family broken up and sent off methodically to the labor camps. And so I suppose the *Fischmeister* ought to count himself lucky that he received only a few hand-grenades in his hatcheries. I explained all this and the man nodded. I asked him about the concentration camps. He said he knew nothing about them.

During this period we used to ask every German with whom we got into conversation about the camps, and always got the same reply: "We never knew they existed." A German newspaper editor in Hamburg raised the subject himself. "I have been wanting to meet someone who can tell me: are these stories coming out on the radio about Belsen and Nordhausen really true? Everyone here thinks that must be Allied propaganda."

At Schneverdingen I said to the garage proprietor: "How do you explain these fifty Russian bodies in the open grave outside the town?"

"Oh, I know abut that," he said. "It was a train-load of foreigners going through three days ago. It stopped here and the guards dumped off these bodies. I refused to let my wife look. No, I didn't know what it was all about and it was not wise to inquire."

There was also the interesting personality of Herr Gurt Woolf. For generations the Woolf family have been making industrial explosive powder in Germany. When we were in Fallingbostel one day and heard that one of the Woolf family's shadow factories was close by we at once decided to drive there. The place was fascinating, a sort of garden city concealed in the pine forest, with its own roads and railways and a charming network of country walks leading through the trees. Every hundred yards or so a by-path led off into the forest, and there you would come on a half-submerged workshop with grass and trees growing on the roof. I do not pretend to understand machinery, but these shining presses, these corridors of stored tools, the furnaces, the garages and living quarters for thousands of men—all this was very impressive. The plant spread inconspicuously over several square miles of parkland. Many foreign workers were roaming about now that the factory was idle. Presently we found ourselves at the main administrative block, an imposing old home with two large stone statues of wolves on either side of the entrance. It seemed a good idea to interview Herr Woolf, and while one of the servants went off to bring him we filed into his board-room, an agreeable spot well lined with green leather and green baize and electric clocks strewn round about.

Gurt Woolf was wearing an English countryman's tweed jacket, suède shoes, a linen shirt and a lively tie. He was very tall and well-proportioned, and there was a senatorial quality about his fine head—a fringe of gray hair, a clear well-bred profile; in a word, a pre-Nazi German aristocrat.

He was a little nervous and spoke scarcely above a whisper. He admitted at once he was a member of the Nazi Party. (It is necessary to remember that it was not easy to become a member of the Party, and relatively very few Germans were in it.) And then he went on: "Yes, I know you will destroy my plant. It all happened before in 1918. Actually we have been making industrial explosives for over a hundred years, and the new warplant you saw today was ordered by the government in 1934 and completed in 1938. The government supplied the materials for the construction and the workers. I and my brother and cousin were simply ordered to take charge of it. No actual money changed hands. The government supplied us with the raw materials, and we handed back the finished product. Yes, I have heard of the conditions of the workers in other places, and in the concentration camps, but I have no personal knowledge of them since it was not my affair. My own workers were treated very well—you have only to go outside and see whether or not they look healthy. We arranged picnics and outings for them. Naturally the food has not been as good as it ought to have been in the past three months, but that has been the same for everyone. I ate with the workers myself."

And that was that. The government organized all, controlled all. The people obeyed.

Not far away, in the village of Rahden, we discovered several hundred Jugoslav generals and officers who had been left stranded there, foodless and helpless, by the receding Nazi tide. They had been made to march back and forth from camp to camp *by daylight* in the previous few weeks. Daylight marching meant strafing by the Allied air forces. Many had come through five and a half years of imprisonment only to be wiped out by their friends at the end. They could easily have been moved at night, but this the Germans had forbidden. When one asked the Germans about it, the answer was: "We were ordered."

Little by little through this month of April we found that phrase recurring wherever we went: "We were ordered." As yet we were not quite ready to grasp the full significance of it. One glorious spring day followed another. We bowled along the wonderful German autobahns in our cars in the sunshine. Victory was in the air. Lüneburg Heath began to blossom with colors of unbelievable gayness; whole valleys filled with wild flowers and the vivid red trunks of the fallen pines; the dark Hans Andersen fairy-tale gloom in the forests, and in the open places the bright browns and purples of the heath. This region is the home of German folklore, the abode of witches and warlocks and sprites. But now it bloomed and flared with color in the spring. And with the forest fires the rich pungent smell of burning pine needles filled the air.

This was Germany innocent and gay, a country of gabled hamlets and trout streams, a place of wonderful churches and cathedrals like that one in Lüneburg town to which Bach used to come because it had the most beautiful organ in Europe. Pale, sea-green copper spires and a great repose and gentleness in the city square where the old buildings hung together with their curious and lovely façades of twisted stone. High on the wall of the cathedral the coat of arms of the House of Hanover: the English coat of arms. Were the Germans so very different? Had not one seen just such towns as these and just such people back in England?

17. The Germans

Just before you get to the main entrance of Belsen concentration camp—or rather the place where the camp used to be before the British burned it down—you come on a farmhouse. I suggested to the others in my party that we should turn in there and eat lunch before, rather than after, we visited the camp. While the table was being set for us in the dining-room we were interested to know from the farmer what he thought of Belsen. "I don't know very much about it," he said. "Each morning I had to drive up there with a cart full of vegetables, swedes and turnips mostly, and one of the SS guards took the horse and cart from me at the gate. After a bit the cart and horse were returned and I drove away. I was never allowed inside and I didn't want to go in anyway. I knew something horrible was going on, but I didn't ask about it lest I should find myself inside."

We finished the meal and drove up to the gate with a special pass which General Dempsey had given the correspondents; from the first Dempsey was very keen that we should see Belsen and write about it. Although the British had only captured the place from the Germans a few days before they seemed to have things well organized. Hungarian guards were still spaced along the barbed-wire fence, good-looking men who jumped eagerly to attention when an army vehicle came by. At the gate British soldiers were on guard. There were notices in English: "Danger—Typhus." "Car Park." "Powder Room." "Inquiries," and so on. A young army doctor and a captain from the Pioneers were in charge. The captain's job was supervising the counting and burial of bodies. Possibly as a form of immunization from the grisly work he appeared to be in particularly jovial spirits.

"I love doing this," he said, picking up the metal syringe filled with anti-louse powder. "Come on."

A squirt up each sleeve. One down the trousers. Two more squirts down the back and front of the shirt and a final shot on the hair. It was rather pleasant.

"We collected the local burgomasters from the surrounding villages this morning and took them round the camp," the doctor said.

"How did they take it?"

"One of them was sick and another one wouldn't look. They all said they had never dreamed that this was going on."

We were now walking down the main driveway towards the first of the huts and administrative buildings. There were large crowds of civilian prisoners about, both those who strolled about in groups talking many different languages and those who sat silently on the ground. In addition there were many forms lying on the earth partly covered in rags, but it was not possible to say whether they were alive or dead or simply in the process of dying. It would be a day or two before the doctors got round to them for a diagnosis.

"There's quite a different air about the place in the last two days," the doctor said. "They seem much more cheerful now."

"And the burial rate has gone down considerably," the captain added. "I'm handling just under three hundred a day now. It was five hundred to start with. And we are evacuating five hundred every day to the panzer training-school. It has been made into a hospital. Would you like to see the SS boys?"

We saw the women guards first. A British sergeant threw open the cell door and some twenty women wearing dirty gray skirts and tunics were sitting and lying on the floor. "Get up," the sergeant roared in English.

They got up and stood to attention in a semi-circle round the room and we looked at them. Thin ones, fat ones, scraggy ones and muscular ones; all of them ugly and one or two of them distinctly cretinous. I pointed out one, a big woman with bright golden hair and a bright pink complexion.

"She was Kramer's girl friend," the sergeant growled. "Nice lot, aren't they?"

There was another woman in a second room with almost delicate features, but she had the same set staring look in her eyes. The atmosphere of the reformatory school and the prison was inescapable.

Belsen: SS women warders.

Outside in the passageway there was a large blackboard ruled off in squares with white lines. Down the left-hand side of the board was a list of nationalities—"Poles, Dutch, Russians," and so on. Spaced along the top of the board was a list of religions and political faiths—"Communist, Jew, Atheist." From the board one might have seen at a glance just how many prisoners were in the camp from each nation and how they were subdivided politically and religiously. However, most of the numbers appeared to have been rubbed off, and it was difficult to make out the totals exactly. Germans seemed to make up the majority of the prisoners. After them Russians and Poles. A great many were Jews. As far as one could decipher there had been half a dozen British there, one or two Americans. There had been something like fifty thousand prisoners altogether.

As we approached the cells of the SS guards the sergeant's language became ferocious.

"We have had an interrogation this morning," the captain said. "I'm afraid they are not a pretty sight."

"Who does the interrogation?"

"A Frenchman. I believe he was sent up here specially from the French underground to do the job."

The sergeant unbolted the first door and flung it back with a crack like thunder. He strode into the cell jabbing a metal spike in front of him. "Get up," he shouted. "Get up; get up, you dirty bastards."

There were half a dozen men lying or half-lying on the floor. One or two were able to pull themselves erect at once. The man nearest me, his shirt and face spattered with blood, made two attempts before he got on to his knees and then gradually on to his feet. He stood with his arms half stretched out in front of him trembling violently.

"Get up," shouted the sergeant. They were all on their feet now, but supporting themselves against the wall. "Get away from that wall."

They pushed themselves out into space and stood there swaying. Unlike the women they looked not at us but vacantly in front, staring at nothing.

Same thing in the next cell and the next, where the men, who were bleeding and very dirty, were moaning something in German.

"You had better see the doctor," the captain said. "He's a nice specimen. He invented some of the tortures here. He had one trick of injecting creosote and petrol into the prisoners' veins. He used to go round the huts and say: 'Too many people in here. Far too many.' Then he used to loose off his revolver round the hut. The doctor has just finished his interrogation."

The doctor had a cell to himself.

"Come on. Get up," the sergeant shouted. The man was lying in his blood on the floor, a massive figure with a heavy head and a bedraggled beard. He placed his two arms on to the seat of a wooden chair, gave himself a heave and got half-upright. One more heave and he was on his feet. He flung wide his arms towards us.

"Why don't you kill me?" he whispered. "Why don't you kill me? I can't stand any more."

The same phrases dribbled out of his lips over and over again.

"He's been saying that all morning, the dirty bastard," the sergeant said. We went out into the sunshine. A number of other British soldiers were standing about, all with the same hard rigid expressions on their faces, just ordinary English soldiers but changed by this expression of genuine and permanent anger.

The crowds of men and women thickened as we went farther into the camp. The litter of paper and rags and human offal grew thicker, the smell less and less bearable. At the entrance soldiers were unloading trucks filled with wooden latrines, but these had not yet been placed about the camp, so many hundreds of half-naked men and women were squatting together in the open, a scene such as you sometimes see in India—except that here it was not always possible to distinguish men from women, or indeed to determine whether they were human at all.

We drove through the filth in cars and, presently emerging on to an open space of yellow clayey soil, we came on a group of German guards flinging bodies into a pit about a hundred feet square. They brought the bodies up in hand-carts, and as they were flung into the grave a British soldier kept a tally of the numbers. When the total reached five hundred a bulldozer driven by another soldier came up and started nudging the earth into the grave. There was a curious pearly color about the piled-up bodies, and they were small like the bodies of children. The withered skin was sagging over the bones, and all the normal features by which you know a human being had practically disappeared. Having no stomach for this sort of thing I was only able to look for a second or two, but the SS guards and even the British soldiers there appeared to have grown used to the presence of death and to be able to work in it without being sick.

"The doctors are doing a wonderful job," the captain said. "They are in the huts all day sorting out the living bodies from the dead, and it's not easy sometimes to tell the difference. Of course there are many who are just hopeless and they are simply left. But they are saving a lot now. We have got in all the food we want—two meals a day, at ten and six. Come on and have a look at one of the huts. We will go to the women first."

It was a single-story, rectangular wooden building, I suppose about a hundred feet long. Wooden bunks ran in tiers up to the ceiling, and there was a narrow passage just wide enough to allow you to pass through. Since the majority of the women there were too weak to move and had no attention whatever the stench was nauseating. Hurrying through, handkerchief to nose, one saw nothing but livid straining faces and emaciated arms and legs under the filthy bed-clothes on either sides. Many were using their last strength to moan feebly for help. These enforced animals were piled one on top of the other to the ceiling, sometimes two to a bunk.

An old hag somewhat stronger than the others was standing at the farther door. "I'm twenty-one," she whispered. "No, I don't know why they put me in here. My husband is a doctor at the front. I'm German but not Jewish. I said that I did not want to enlist in the women's organization and they put me in here. That was eighteen months ago."

"I've had enough of this," I said to the captain.

"Come on," he said. "You've got to go through one of the men's huts yet. That's what you're here for."

It was if anything more rancid than the one I had seen, but this time I was too sick with the stench to notice much except the sound of the voices: "Doctor—doctor."

As we returned towards the entrance the people round us were noticeably better in health than those at the pits and the huts. As they were able to walk some instinct drew the people away from the charnel houses and up and out towards the entrance and the ordinary sane normal world outside. It was all like a journey down to some Dantesque pit, unreal, leprous and frightening. And now as one emerged into the light again one's first coherent reactions were not of disgust or anger or even, I think, of pity. Something else filled the mind, a frantic desire to ask: "Why? Why? Why? Why had it happened?" With all one's soul one felt: "This is not war. Nor is it anything to do with here and now, with this one place at this one moment. This is timeless and the whole world and all mankind is involved in it. This touches me and I am responsible. Why has it happened? How did we let it happen?"

We stood there in a group, a major from the Commandos, a padre, three or four correspondents, having at first nothing to say, and then gradually and quietly asking one another the unspoken question.

Was it sadism? No, on the whole not. Or if it was sadism, then it was sadism of a very indirect and unusual kind. Relatively little torture was carried out at this camp. The sadist presumably likes to make some direct immediate act which inflicts pain on other people. He could not obtain much satisfaction from the slow, long process of seeing people starve.

Then again the Germans were an efficient people. They needed manpower. Can one imagine anything more inefficient than letting all this valuable labor go to rot? The prisoners in Belsen were not even obliged to work. They were simply dumped in here and left to make what shift they could with a twice-daily diet of turnip stew. Incidentally this lack of work probably led to the break-up of the prisoners' morale as much as anything.

The Germans too had a normal fear of disease spreading among themselves. And yet they let these thousands of bodies lie on the ground. It's true there was not a great deal of typhus in the camp, but it had already broken out when the German commanders approached the British and offered to cede the camp under the terms of a truce.

It was not torture which had killed the prisoners. It was neglect. The sheer indifference of the Nazis. One began to see that the most terrible thing on earth is not positive destruction nor the perverse desire to hurt and destroy. The worst thing that can happen to you is for the master to say: "I do not care about you any more. I am indifferent." Whether you washed or ate or laughed or died—none of this was of any consequence any more, because you as a person had no value. You were a slug on the ground, to be crushed or not to be crushed, it made no difference.

And having become attuned and accustomed to this indifference the guards were increasingly less affected by the suffering of the people around them. It was accepted that they should die. They were Russians. Russians die. Jews die. They were not even enemies. They were disease. Could you mourn or sympathize with the death throes of a germ?

Now here is where the evidence of Kramer, the camp commandant, comes in. To consider Kramer calmly I think we have first got to rid ourselves temporarily of our memory of that published picture of him shuffling across the yard in shackles. And we have to forget for the moment the title he was given through the world: "The Monster of Belsen." A friend of mine, a trained intelligence officer and interrogator in the British army, went into the whole question very carefully with Kramer, and this was Kramer's statement:

"I was swamped. The camp was not really inefficient before you crossed the Rhine. There was running water, regular meals of a kind—I had to accept what food I was given for the camps, and distributed it the best way I could. But then they suddenly began to send me train-loads of new prisoners from all over Germany. It was impossible to cope with them. I appealed for more staff, more food. I was told this was impossible; I had to carry on with what I had. Then as a last straw the Allies bombed the electric plant which pumped our water. Cart-loads of food were unable to reach the camp because of the Allied fighters. Then things got really out of hand. In the last six weeks I have been helpless. I did not even have sufficient staff to bury the dead, let alone segregate the sick."

Thus Kramer.

"But how did you come to accept a job like this?" he was asked.

The reply: "There was no question of my accepting it. I was ordered. I am an officer in the SS and I obey orders. These people were criminals and I was serving my Führer in a crisis by commanding this camp. I tried to get medicines and food for the prisoners and I failed. I was swamped. I may have been hated, but I was doing my duty."

There was some truth in this last. Not only were the prisoners fond of hurling missiles at Kramer since we had arrived but his own guards turned on him as well. Kramer asked the British authorities that he should be segregated. He was told that in this event he would have to be shackled and to this he agreed.

Who then was responsible for Belsen, and for that matter all the other camps? The SS guards? They say they were ordered. They hated the work, but disobedience to Kramer meant death. Kramer says he was in precisely the same position. And so presumably do all the other Kramers above him, until you reach Himmler. What does Himmler say? Himmler says he is serving his Führer. The Führer of course was innocent and knew nothing about the vulgar details. (Quite a number of Germans assured us of that.) But—we can imagine Himmler saying—it was vital to protect the Führer from his declared enemies inside the Reich—the Jewish bolsheviks who would have cheerfully murdered him. At this dire crisis for Germany and the Party one could not be too nice about the details— possibly some people were treated a little too harshly, but one could not afford to take chances. The Nazis were perfectly prepared to treat these prisoners with humanity, but the enemies of Germany made this impossible. They destroyed communications, they blocked the food supply. Naturally the camps suffered.

But the people of Germany? Why had they allowed this thing to be? Why had they not protested? The average German answers: In the first place we did not know these camps existed. Secondly, how could we have protested? What possibly could we have done? The Nazis were too strong.

Very well then, why did you not protest when the Nazis were rising to power?

They answer: How could we foretell that the Nazis would end with this horror? When they first came to power they embarked on a program that was excellent for Germany: new roads, modern buildings and machines. It seemed rational and good at the beginning. When we realized that Hitler was turning to war it was already too late. By then the Nazis had claimed our children. They were Nazified in the schools. A parent would be denounced by his own child if he spoke against the Nazis. Little by little we were overwhelmed and in the end it was too late. There was no point at which we could have effectively protested. Why did not foreign countries which had the power check the Nazis soon enough? If only you had attacked us before the Nazis became strong.

And so the thing is thrown back upon the world. No one anywhere is willing to take responsibility. Not the guard or the torturer. Not Kramer. Not Herr Woolf. They were all ordered. Not Himmler or Hitler (the end justified the means: they were fighting to rid the world of the terrible menace of Jewish bolshevism—they were ordered by their high sense of duty). Not the German people. They too had to obey. And finally, not the world. Is England Germany's keeper?

That is the line of argument which we heard as observers of this eclipse of Germany. We did not accept or reject it because we were still too close to the scene to do much more than report personally and directly.

If I had been compelled to take some sort of direct line at this moment I would have said: Yes, all mankind *is* in some way responsible for Belsen, but in varying degrees. Herr Woolf, for example, is a cultured European. Surely he could have seen a little more clearly than, say, the average German workman what the Nazi Party was going to mean, and have made some protest in time. Clearly too the Germans generally, and the leading Nazis most particularly, are far more embroiled in this monstrosity than anyone else. The Junkers and the Wehrmacht power-through-war class—they too are utterly compromised. But the degree of guilt varies enormously both inside and outside of the Nazi Party, inside and outside of Germany. Probably the least of all to blame is the unpolitical boy who was put into uniform and forced to come here into the German battlefield to support a tardy conscience in the world. And die for it.

There is only one thing possible that one can do for him now: be vigilant to snap the long chains that lead to the future Belsens before they grow too long.

A shudder of horror went round the world when the news of these concentration camps was published, but only I think because of the special interest and the special moment in the war. We were engrossed with Germany, and it is perhaps not too subtle to say that since Germany was manifestly beaten people wanted to have a justification for their fight, a proof that they were engaged against evil. From the German point of view Belsen was perfectly mistimed. Worse camps existed in Poland and we took no notice. Dachau was described in the late nineteen-thirties and we did not want to hear. In the midst of the war three-quarters of a million Indians starved in Bengal because shipping was wanted in other parts, and we were bored.

The last living patient has been evacuated from Belsen. The hateful buildings have been burned down. The physical evidence of all those horrible places will soon have been wiped out. Only the mental danger remains. The danger of indifference.

Total Eclipse

COLLAPSE IN THE CENTRE: GERMANY

18. The Surrender

The surrender of Germany came not with a bang but a whimper, following no precedent in other wars. Indeed the act of surrender—or rather the several acts of surrender—did not do much more than underline a *fait accompli* and give the semblance of authority to a situation that was frankly chaotic.

The Germany in which we found ourselves traveling at the end of April presented a scene that was almost beyond human comprehension. Her capital lost and almost razed, and nothing to give that ash-heap significance beyond a name, a history and the presence of a lunatic who was about to make his last gesture to a colossal vanity—his death. Around us fifty great cities lay in ruins, or at least in partial ruins. Many of them had no electric light or power or gas or running water, and no coherent system of government. Like ants in an ant-heap the people scurried over the ruins, diving furtively into cellars and doorways in search of loot. Like ants you would see women scuttling down a side-track with their bundles only to be blocked by debris and then turn irresolutely back, shoving and bumping against one another. Everyone was on the move, and there was a frantic ant-like quality about their activity. Life was sordid, aimless, leading nowhere. Every house in every unbombed village was stacked to the roof with city refugees living on soup and potatoes. From the Ruhr across Germany an occasional factory chimney smoked, but ninety per cent of the country's industry was at a standstill. No trains ran. Every family was bereaved or broken up. The housing situation was impossible and likely to get worse. A very large part of the population was simply wandering on the roads with the millions of foreigners. And to these was now added the German army itself. A mass flight from the Russians towards the

Elbe and the Anglo-American lines began. Officers stripped off their uniforms and begged or stole civilian clothes from the near-by houses. Mass fear had gripped them so greatly that when aircraft appeared in the sky the shout went up: "The Russians! The Russians!" and the mob would break out in panic across the countryside.

The ports were at a standstill, and such shipping as put out into the Baltic sailed aimlessly for a day or two and then came back to

The Advance on Berlin

the shore for the inevitable surrender. This time the German navy was so disorganized it had not even the will to scuttle. And unlike the last war the naval morale was the highest of the three services. The Luftwaffe had long since been beaten down, much of its personnel drafted haphazardly into the army, where the rot had gone far beyond recall.

The collapse of the Nazi Party was leaving a vacuum; there was no movement, either religious or political or military or dynastic, able to assume control at the last moment. Nowhere in the world was there any sanctuary for a German, and so the average German made a poor man's choice: he decided to surrender to the Anglo-Americans if he could. One had to be in Germany at this moment to appreciate the blind and universal fear of the Russians. In every soldier's mind there was a fixed certainty that if he were taken by the Reds he would be starved, beaten, sent to Siberia and there worked to an early death. In every civilian's mind there was an equal certainty that his women would be seized and raped, his goods impounded or destroyed and himself condemned to some unthinkable inhuman end. Dr. Goebbels had achieved his last success. He had so planted the idea of the terror of the bolshevik hordes that when the hordes actually appeared every German lost hope and the frantic panic to the west began.

By the middle of April there remained only three discernible groups of power in the Reich. First there was the Berlin garrison headed by Hitler, Goebbels, Bormann (the Deputy Führer) and General Krebs. Next there was the OKW—the Ober Kommando der Wehrmacht—which comprised the last active military leaders like Keitel, Jodl, Doenitz and Friedeburg. The OKW was in reality only a name now, but still it had been a mighty name in Germany for the past six years, and it was still the nominal font of orders. In the last fortnight of April this High Command abandoned Hitler in the capital and joined the flight to the west. It moved steadily northwestward until it finally arrived at the port of Flensburg on the Danish frontier. Hamburg was its last remaining big city under control. Finally there was an offshoot of the OKW operating with the armies in the south.

From about April 15th onward Hitler, engrossed in his own Wagnerian night, does not appear to have exercised any overall authority in Germany. Goering was already sacked, and there remained only Himmler capable of acting as an effective liaison with the OKW and the realities of the situation.

One must remember that right up to the last the majority of Germans were quite unable to appreciate that both America and

Soviet tanks enter Berlin.

England (and later France) were determined to honor their alliance with Russia to the bitter end. To the Germans the Reds represented the final barbarity, the final unnamable evil; and it was the German nation alone that was saving Europe. Surely the British and Americans must see it. They must be made to see it. Himmler resolved to make one last desperate attempt.

At this time of writing there is still no positive proof that Hitler was behind Himmler's approach to Britain and America, but it seems probable. Himmler was in contact with both Berlin and the OKW. The OKW at least knew all about his mission. At all events Himmler went down to Hamburg with full power to act about the middle of April. Just outside Hamburg, in the woods opposite the British sector, was Bismarck's ancient castle, the Friedrichsruh; now the headquarters of the International Red Cross, headed by Count Bernadotte, a Swede. He was already known to Himmler, and he seemed to be the obvious man through whom to deal with the British and Americans. Himmler approached him with the project: "Will America and Britain accept our unconditional surrender now, and allow us to concentrate all our remaining forces in warding off the Russians?"

There began a series of comings and goings between Berlin, Friedrichsruh and Stockholm, ending in the Allies' refusal on April 24th.

If there was any hope left in the Nazi Party, and especially in the group in Berlin, it now collapsed. Himmler having failed was at once discredited. He was still nominally Reichsführer and Minister of Defense, but he had never been trusted or liked by the senior generals, especially by those who now had command at the OKW. Not liking the idea of returning to Berlin Himmler hung round the OKW, but he was virtually out of office and without power. Doenitz and the other military leaders were simply waiting their chance to seize control, but this was impossible so long as Hitler continued alive.

On April 25th Hitler was still in the Chancellery in Berlin, and under heavy Russian artillery fire. During the day a Major Friedel, who was the Führer's personal liaison officer, was summoned to the presence. Friedel found Hitler in a highly excited state, but otherwise normal. He did not appear to be unwell. That night the Russians began to put down concentrated artillery fire on individual targets. It was a method greatly used towards the end of the war: three minutes' fire of all guns on one position, three minutes on another, and so on. The Russians began on the Chancellery.

Observers who later got out of the city said that the effect was so awful that people made crazy by the shelling ran through the streets trying to get themselves hit.

The following morning, April 26th, Friedel was again summoned to the damaged Chancellery, where he was met by Krebs and Bormann and told: "The Führer has died in the night. You must proceed at once to the OKW with this information." Another officer was instructed to take the same news to the branch of the OKW in the south; but that command was already disintegrating. It was given out that Hitler had died from shell-fire. The barrage was indeed tremendously heavy, and before he got back to the Air Ministry building Friedel received word that both Bormann and Krebs were dead. Without waiting any longer Friedel took off from the roof of the Air Ministry in a Storch aircraft, and somehow got through to the OKW with the information.

Immediately there was a meeting of Doenitz and the generals. Now at last was their chance. With both the Führer and the Deputy Führer gone, Himmler and Goering both discredited, they could act. Soon too they had the news of Goebbels' suicide. Of all the remaining leaders Doenitz was in the strongest position. He commanded the last coherent German force—the navy—and the OKW was in a naval area. With his rank of Grand Admiral he was the most senior officer in the High Command. It was resolved that he should seize power and make immediate peace—with the British and Americans *only* if that were possible. It was decided that the Allies should be sounded out through Field Marshal Montgomery. Doenitz argued that he himself, as the organizer of the U-boat warfare, could hardly expect to be well received by the British. It was therefore decided that General Admiral Friedeburg should be promoted to command of the navy in place of Doenitz (who was now the new Führer) and act as negotiator.

But first the OKW had to make known these changes, and the best way of doing that was by carrying out a radio *coup d'état*. On May 1st Doenitz hurried to Hamburg and broadcast the news of Hitler's death and his own succession. In order to maintain some sort of discipline through these last hours he added an appeal to the Germans to keep on resisting.

But already the situation was out of control. Generals in command were surrendering piecemeal and of their own accord all along the front, especially opposite the Americans. They clamored to get inside our lines. First divisional commanders, then corps and army and army group commanders, entirely ignoring the OKW, began sending envoys and even coming in themselves under the

Ruins of the Reichstag in Berlin: Red Army soldiers left their autographs.

white flag. The situation was ludicrous. General X would arrive at one of our camps to find that General Y was there too. One can imagine the conversation between them: "How extraordinary finding *you* here." Then to the Allies: "I surrender the Eighteenth Army Group."

"I surrender the Twenty-first Army Group."

"But," it was pointed out to them, "your command is facing the Russians. Your soldiers have already been over-run by the Russians."

The generals: "Then we surrender ourselves."

On May 1st Wolz, the commander of the garrison of Hamburg, now Germany's largest city and the largest port on the continent, came into the British lines. He agreed to everything. The British to walk into the city. The Germans to pull up the mines and road-blocks. A forty-eight hours' curfew for the one or two million people there. German ack-ack gunners to fire on their own aircraft if the Luftwaffe attempted to interfere with the surrender. Wolz himself to lead our troops in as a token of good faith.

The negotiations went on far into the night. In the early hours of the morning the general's senior staff officer asked if he could have a word alone with the British brigadier in charge. When the door was shut and locked behind them the officer said: "This is purely personal. On behalf of General Wolz I want to ask your advice. Will we be sent to Siberia?"

The brigadier said he thought not.

"Then," the German went on, "I want to know if you think we ought to commit suicide?" Finally he ended in tears.

In the midst of this electrical atmosphere General Wolz was desperately anxious that the negotiations should be kept secret until the taking over of Hamburg was an accomplished fact. He did not know how the Nazi leaders in Hamburg would take it, he said. He had disguised from them the real meaning of his visits to the British. Then again, who knew what the OKW was doing? He had had no orders and he was acting on his own initiative.

The general need not have worried. At that moment Blumentritt, a still more senior officer, was having separate dealings with Montgomery. On May 2nd Blumentritt opened up negotiations secretly, and he was told to present himself the following day at Lauenburg, on the Elbe, for the final arrangements. But already the thing had gone even beyond Blumentritt. When Colonel J. O. Ewart, Montgomery's representative, got down to the rendezvous at Lauenburg on the morning of May 3rd he found there only a German staff officer, who said: "There is no point in General Blumentritt dealing individually with you any longer. Field Marshal Busch, the commander of northwest Germany, is trying to contact Montgomery at this moment."

Ewart doubled back to Montgomery's tactical headquarters on Lüneburg Heath to find this was indeed true. Admiral Friedeburg, acting not only for Busch but for the whole OKW, was on his way.

The German delegation was, I must say, an impressive sight coming down the road. Impelled by the urgency of the hour they had simply motored without any formality into our lines outside Hamburg. Realizing that this gang was too hot to handle, the local British commander promptly put an armored car at their head and another at their tail and sent them posthaste off to Montgomery. Sitting waxen-faced, tense and bolt upright in their cars, the German envoys presented a perfect caricature of the Junker officer on parade. Monocles, thin, tight contemptuous lips, jack-boots, long gray belted coats, a general atmosphere of pent-up defiance. All this façade concealed, or perhaps underlined, their most dire misgivings and profound anxiety.

Montgomery met them at the steps of his caravan. "What do you want?" he said.

They said they wanted to surrender three German armies then fleeing from the Russians in Mecklenburg.

"Certainly not," Montgomery said. "Those armies are fighting the Russians, so they must surrender to the Russians. I am not going to have any dealings about anything on my eastern flank. That subject is closed."

There was a hopeless silence among the Germans. They tried again. They said they were most anxious about the needless slaughter of German soldiers by the Russians. They were even more anxious about the slaughter of German civilians in the path of the Red advance. Surely some agreement could be reached with the British by which these millions of lives could be saved. Perhaps the Germans could arrange to fall back step by step and the British move in after them?

Montgomery is a simple man, but shrewd. He looked at this deputation and saw that they were an unusual group of men to come suggesting local surrenders and local arrangements for saving civilians. To begin with it was headed by Friedeburg. Next General Kinsel, chief of staff to Field Marshal Busch of the Northern Command (in whose name the deputation pretended they were operating). Next a Rear Admiral Wagner, chief of staff to Doenitz; and lastly Major Friedel.

No. These were not men who had come to talk about half-measures, truces and temporary arrangements. They had a much bigger game to play. For the moment they were feeling out the ground.

"Will you," Montgomery said suddenly, "surrender to me all the German forces between Lübeck and the Dutch coast, and all supporting troops such as those in Denmark? Also Heligoland and all the German islands?"

Since the field marshal had received no prompting from his intelligence staff, and the meeting was entirely impromptu, it was a not uninteresting flash of inspiration.

The effect was instantaneous. Taken completely aback, Freideburg began to stammer that he had no power.

"I wonder if you really know what the position is," Montgomery broke in, and he sent for a map. Sector by sector he traced the battlefield for them, revealing our positions and, what was much more important, the present state of the German army. This last was information which the Germans simply did not possess, since in the past few days many of their communications had broken down.

They did not even know of many of the individual surrenders along the front.

"You had better go to lunch and think it over," Montgomery said.

Over lunch Friedeburg, overburdened by his responsibility and appalled with the news he had heard, broke down. He wept at the table for five minutes, an embarrassing scene.

In the early afternoon there was another meeting. Montgomery defined his terms clearly. First he wanted the surrender of all the territories along the British front. Next, once this was done, he was willing to work out a plan by which the Germans could surrender. Thirdly, if he got a refusal he would carry on the war, and "would be delighted to do so."

It was finally agreed that Kinsel and Wagner should spend the night in the British camp, while the general admiral and the other went back to get a final reply from Doenitz and the OKW. They were to return the following afternoon with a definite yes or no. Late that night Friedeburg radioed that he was back with Doenitz. The following day he radioed again to say he was returning with the answer.

By now the game was entirely clear. We were dealing, not with a local command but with the entire German forces. It was in fact the end of the war. Doenitz perforce was negotiating the final surrender, and no doubt with a little pressure was ready to hand over Norway and the whole German state to Montgomery. This however was something Montgomery had not the power to accept; it was a matter for General Eisenhower and the Russian representatives at SHAEF. Montgomery had decided to take just his due—which after all included the notable booty of Holland and Denmark and what was left of German Germany—and then pass the negotiators on to SHAEF for the final overall act of surrender.

That this appreciation of the position was correct was amply confirmed later on when one of the field marshal's liaison officers—almost the last of the original ones left alive—went back with Friedeburg and had a talk with Doenitz.

Doenitz was clarity itself. "I took power," he said, "because it is our only chance of saving something of Germany. My sole object in taking command is to conclude a peace as quickly as possible and stop the useless waste of German lives. My generation is never again to see a flourishing Germany. As a nation we have been set back for a thousand years. But we must as quickly as possible do all we can for those millions of Germans who have a chance of going on with life."

All through these conversations both Doenitz and Friedeburg referred to "Occupied Germany" and "Russia." That is to say they regarded Russian-occupied Germany (including Berlin) as permanently Russian, while they had some distant hope that the Anglo-American zones would one day be handed back to the Germans.

In the corridor outside Doenitz's room Montgomery's officer thought he recognized a familiar figure. "Who is that?" he asked: and he was told: "Himmler. He's out of a job."

"What's he doing?"

"Nothing much. He lives quietly at his house here. He has no more authority."

A few days later Himmler, in disguise, tried to slip through the British lines. He was arrested and committed suicide in captivity in Lüneburg by biting on a capsule of cyanide of potassium which he had embedded in his teeth.

About this time we began to understand a little more fully the part being played by Major Friedel, and why the OKW was insisting on including him in all the conversations. Friedel was the last expression of Hitler's dead power. As the Führer's personal aide he still enjoyed influence, and was, incredible as it may seem in the midst of these negotiations, agitating for promotion in rank. He did in fact get himself elevated to colonel on the very day of the armistice, which shows you that the Wehrmacht never really dies, even if it is impotent.

Shortly after five o'clock on May 4th, while the firing died along the front and a tacit truce was being preserved, the war correspondents gathered in a tent at Montgomery's headquarters. It was a wild hill-top on Lüneburg Heath, especially wild in these alternate gusts of cold rain and watery sunshine, and the lovely colors of the countryside spread away for miles, pools of dark green in the clumps of pine, purple in the heather.

Calmly, almost breezily, Montgomery began to tell us of the events leading up to the armistice. The field marshal as a rule did not have the knack of giving good press conferences. But on this day he presented a masterpiece of simplification and condensation. Halfway through his talk Colonel Ewart came in to say that the German delegates had arrived back with their answer, the answer that was to mean whether or not nearly six years of bitterness and death in Europe was at last to end.

"Tell them to wait," Montgomery said, and he went on addressing us for the next half-hour. During this period he did not attempt to learn either by word or sign or message what answer the Germans had brought back. Montgomery was finishing his war exactly as he had begun it—absolutely convinced that he was right and that things were going to go his way.

"And now," he said at last, "we will attend the last act. These German officers have arrived back. We will go and see what their answer is." He led the way to his caravan on the hill-top.

In the night Montgomery's officers had managed to get hold of a copy of the document of surrender which Alexander's headquarters had drawn up in Italy. Based upon this a similar instrument had been written to meet the present situation.

Friedeburg, cigarette in hand, slowly led his delegation across the heath to Montgomery's caravan, where he saluted, mounted the steps and went inside. There followed some discussion as to whether Dunkirk and the Channel Islands might have been included in the surrender, but the subject was dropped as this would have caused delay. The four other envoys, tight-waisted, rigid and silent, stood nervously in a semicircle at the steps of the caravan. Inside, Friedeburg had asked for a German copy of the terms, but he scarcely glanced at them.

Presently he came out, nodded to the others and muttered something as if to say, "It's just as we thought," and the five men walked slowly past us to the conference tent. Its sides had been rolled up, and six chairs had been placed at a trestle table covered with a plain army blanket. An electric light was suspended above the table, and movie cameras were poised ready.

The Germans took their place at the table. Never had I seen Montgomery more sure of himself than at this moment. As he came past us he murmured pleasantly, "This is a great moment," and he proceeded calmly to the tent, the terms of the surrender in his hand. He conducted the proceedings rather like a schoolmaster taking an oral examination. As he went into the tent the Germans rose and saluted. Then sitting at the head of the table, spectacles on nose, Montgomery read the terms slowly, precisely and deliberately in English. The Germans, who spoke hardly a syllable of English, sat there without a word, for the most part staring vacantly at the gray army blanket. Camera lights flicked on and off. The reading took a full three minutes.

At the end Montgomery picked up an unpainted post-office pen, dipped it in the ink-pot and said: "You will now sign the document. First General Admiral Friedeburg," and he handed the pen across.

"Next General Kinsel." Each man leaned over Montgomery's chair to affix his signature. "Next Rear Admiral Wagner. Next Colonel Poleck" (who represented Keitel, the new commander in

General Kinzel signs the surrender on Lüneburg Heath.

chief of the Wehrmacht). "And last Major Friedel" (Montgomery mispronounced it "Freidel").

Finally: "I will now sign for General Eisenhower, the Commander-in-Chief of the Allied Forces," and the field marshal added his signature with the same pen.

Thus, simply, without parade of any kind, Britain's war against

Germany came to an end a few minutes after six o'clock in the evening of May 4th on Lüneburg Heath. Although the armistice did not officially start until eight o'clock the following morning no gun was fired along the British front that night. In the unnatural quiet there was little to assist one to a realization of the moment. Five years and eight months—two thousand days—had passed since Chamberlain as prime minister had broadcast, ". . . and consequently we are at war," and the first air-raid siren had sounded in London. No, it was too much. Too many things had happened. It would be weeks, months, even years before this day found a proper place in one's life.

There was still an immense amount of work to be done. The Germans at once began broadcasting the cease-fire orders; messages began to stream in from OKW, where Doenitz, Keitel and Jodl, the chief of staff, were now in full command. Even now they had hopes that somehow they could force the Russian issue and obtain a separate armistice with Britain and America. It was with this plan in mind that Jodl came to Montgomery's headquarters to join Friedeburg for the signing of the overall armistice at General Eisenhower's headquarters in the champagne town of Rheims in France.

Finally it was made clear to Jodl that he had to sign with all the Allies. He dropped his head in his hands and whispered: "Russia too."

By now Ewart had been through on the telephone to General Bedell Smith, Eisenhower's chief of staff, with the information that the German delegation was on its way with full powers for general unconditional surrender. Negotiations were begun in Rheims on Sunday, May 6th. Signals were routed from Rheims to Flensburg through Montgomery's headquarters, to which the OKW telephone system had been linked up.

At Rheims the Germans were again told: "Unconditional surrender to the Russians as well—and we must have a decision by eleven-thirty tonight."

A message went from Jodl to Doenitz asking for his final authority. This was the moment at which the telephone system to OKW chose to break down, and messages had to pass by radio. At eleven-thirty there was still no reply from Doenitz. And none at midnight. Jodl, made frantic by the delay, came on the telephone to Montgomery's headquarters, where a German officer had been left behind as a liaison. "You have got to get Doenitz at all costs," he cried. "He has got to agree. We've got to get an answer tonight."

Towards twelve-thirty the awaited signal came in from Doenitz,

This to include all naval ships in these areas.

7. The decision of the Allied powers will be final if any doubt or dispute arises as to the meaning or interpretation of the surrender terms.

B. L. Montgomery
Field-Marshal

4 May 1945
1830 hrs

The instrument of surrender.

but it was corrupt to the point of being unreadable. But nothing now was going to stop the Germans from getting the thing finished and done with.

"I can understand it," the liaison officer said. "It states that Doenitz agrees."

"Will you," he was asked, "take the responsibility of advising General Jodl to that effect?"

"Yes. Yes."

At SHAEF they had given up for the night, and there was at first a little difficulty in rousing the envoys. Then the news set the headquarters buzzing. The armistice was signed at forty-one minutes past two A.M. on May 7th. It came into force one minute after midnight on May 8th.

All over broken Europe the war began subsiding fitfully and uneasily to a standstill.

19. The Last Liberation

On Saturday, May 5th, the morning after Montgomery's armistice, a little group of men gathered round the transport aircraft on Lüneburg airfield: a company of airborne troops in their red berets and curious lizard-colored camouflage jackets; a general and an admiral and their staffs; the correspondents.

Nobody seemed to be quite clear about what we were doing except that it was known that the destination was Copenhagen and the general idea was that we should take over Denmark from the Germans.

A pair of gleaming leather top-boots was passed on board. Young officers ran about ticking off names. The sun came down on the red caps and the red tabs, and a Rolls-Royce drove up debouching brigadiers. The ack-ack gunners off duty round the field chewed gum and fell asleep. So this was peace at last, and peace this morning seemed wonderful.

A full three months had passed since we had come into Germany; three months of army rations and no fraternization, three months of refugees and ruined cities, of shuttered shops and no electric light and no hot baths, of lumpish German women and traffic blocks and artillery and mud and the endless dragging knowledge that the war dragged on. All this time we had been promising ourselves Scandinavia. Out through Germany into the light again. One day, we had told each other, we will get back to a place where the people are really glad to see us. This was the day.

While still the cease-fire order was only a few hours old the machines took off—a dozen Dakotas, the fighter escort ranging high and wide on either side. Past Lübeck and Kiel and out over the Baltic. German ships seeing us coming ran up the white flag and turned apprehensively away. Then, one after another, the green Danish islands. Every house on that liberation morning flew the national flag on a pole, the white cross on the red background, and from the air the effect was as if one were looking down on endless fields strewn with poppies.

Over the suburbs of Copenhagen there was at first not much movement in the streets; fearing just possibly this was the final air raid of the war the people ran indoors. But then as we came lower they gathered confidence and poured out into the open. A thickening procession of cars and bicycles and pedestrians came careering down the road to the airfield. One after another the Dakotas slid into a landing between the stationary German aircraft and drew up in line before the airport buildings. The airborne troops jumped down, and with their guns ready advanced upon the hangars. The scene did for a moment look slightly ominous, especially as none of us quite knew what to expect. Armed German guards were spaced along the runways. Two German officers stood stiffly in front of the central office and began to advance towards the landing aircraft. General Dewing, the leader of our mission, met them half-way and in two minutes it was clear: we would have no trouble in Denmark. Lindemann, the German commander, was waiting to receive the British and arrange the formal surrender. All German troops were confined to barracks and the Danish Resistance movement had control. Cars were ready to drive us into the city.

At that moment the Danish crowd burst on to the field, and from then onward I doubt that any of us has a coherent memory of the next two days.

The Danes have a curious staccato bark for use at moments of ecstasy. It sounds like "Wa-wa. . . . Wa-wa." They roared "Wa-wa" at the airborne troops and then threw flowers at them. They danced among the aircraft and sang "Tipperary." The Germans were forgotten. A long line of young Danish soldiers in umbrella-like black steel helmets and armed to the teeth with tommy-guns and hand-grenades were drawn up for Dewing's inspection. While this was going on the two German officers walked back to their staff car only to find it stolen by some enthusiast, and the last I saw of them they were trudging unhappily back towards the city on foot.

Meanwhile our procession of some twenty or thirty cars with Dewing at the head was driving at an alarming speed into a kind of cavern of waving arms and legs and flags and flowers. "Wa-wa." "Wel-kom." "Hello, boys." The general disengaged himself from a wreath of chrysanthemums and we passed on rapidly over the bridge into the lovely city. It seemed to us that we had never seen such pretty girls, such gay dresses, such glistening shops and gardens. The Danes had been celebrating all the previous night, and now the streets—or such of them as you could see through the crowd—were strewn with bits of paper and bunting. Here and there one came on a building or a restaurant with the front smashed in and the furniture tumbled out on the roadway. "German headquarters," my driver explained briefly. The car was now festooned with ribbons and flowers and it was a little difficult to see. Each time the procession stopped the crowd closed in on us, and they had a strange manner of reaching out to touch our sleeves and tunics, apparently to make sure that we were real.

Dewing headed for the Hotel Angleterre, which he intended to make his headquarters, and once we were there the crowd swarmed forward, making it impossible to get in or out of the building. The scene in the lobby bordered on hysteria. One has a disconnected series of recollections, of corks coming out of champagne bottles, of tables laden with smoked salmon and caviar, of grilled steaks and strawberries, of singing and a receding and advancing wall of laughing faces, of bright flowers under the electric light and the sun streaming down on the people chanting in the street outside. "My name's Smith—I've been a prisoner here five years." "Sign your autograph, please—sign, sign, sign."

In the midst of all this a German admiral roamed about the corridors of the hotel vainly trying to find someone—anyone—to whom he could surrender the cruisers *Nürnberg* and *Prinz Eugen*, their attendant destroyers and 600,000 tons of mercantile shipping then lying in the bay. It did not seem of much consequence to anyone at the time, and a good half-hour must have passed before the German tracked down our admiral in his suite.

Then there were the Danish quislings who seemed to be pretty thickly quartered in the Angleterre. They were plucked out of bedrooms and out of the restaurants in the middle of their meals. Flying columns of Resistance boys kept plunging through the lobby with their hand-grenades. One mounted the staircase past the statue of "King Arthur of England" to find a line of people with their hands up on the first landing, their faces to the wall, and a Danish soldier prowling about with a tommy-gun. One was quite likely to be engaged in conversation with a seemingly amiable young man only to see him suddenly snatched away in the middle of the sentence. And outside the crowd kept on with the "Wa-wa-wa" whenever a British uniform appeared.

Those of us who had followed the armies across Africa and Europe knew pretty well the way a liberation went and what happened at the first moments of a city's rejoicing. But here there was a special flavor, a more simple and lighter spirit than usual; fewer shadows under the gaiety. Unwisely one or two of us ventured out of the hotel, hoping to see something of the town. We were seized by the crowd and hoisted shoulder-high around the square. When we pleaded to be put down they dumped us on the roof of a car and began to parade us round the streets. At last we got down and made for the apparent security of the Palace Square, a beautiful courtyard by the canal. At once the guards abandoned their posts and came rushing at us. We bolted into King Christian's rooms and stayed there with the chamberlains until the way back to the hotel was clear again.

Dewing at length was beginning to compose things despite the feverish atmosphere. Indeed his task was much easier than it might have been. We were only a couple of hundred British in the whole country, and separated from our own lines by some two hundred miles of territory then being garrisoned by a hundred thousand Germans or more. But the Danish Underground was better organized than any we had seen before. The Swedes as well as ourselves had poured equipment into them by clandestine routes, and now Swedish officers were openly appearing in the streets in uniform. A brigade of Danish soldiers trained in Sweden arrived and began to take up strategic positions round the city. As for the Germans, they remained strictly in their barracks with the rejoicing going on all round them and made no attempt to interfere. The Danish Resistance were ordered to keep away from the Germans so that no incident should be provoked. But with so many exuberant young men about with so many brand-new weapons which they had been hankering to use for years it was impossible to keep the peace. Shooting continued intermittently all the first night of our arrival and again the next day and night. I was never able to make out precisely who was shooting at whom. One would be sitting in a restaurant when suddenly machine-gun bullets would begin to sail by for no clearly explained reason, and for the next half-hour it would be impossible to go out into the streets.

Most of these skirmishes appeared to be directed against Danish quislings who decided to fight it out from the roof-tops rather than be arrested. The story of Paris again in miniature. I was even at the circus one night when an armed band leaped into the lighted ring and, training their arms on the crowd, demanded that a certain Mr. Ulsen should show himself. Women half-rose to their feet, but no one spoke. "Very well," the leader said, "we will search the audience." Ulsen was sitting in the second row of the stalls when they plucked him out and led him away through the performing dogs and horses.

Anything and everything appeared normal in this madcap atmosphere. In the Tivoli, the pleasure gardens of the city, a brass band was produced to play for us through lunch. People rose and sang their national songs at the mere appearance of a British uniform. We drove out of the city at night to a home on the coast, and looked across the Kattegat to Sweden, only a mile or two away. The sea was still and all the neutral lights of Sweden gleamed and danced across the water as they had done every night all through this war, almost the only lights in Europe. But now tonight the windows were shining in Copenhagen, and beyond that right across the continent as far as the Mediterranean the lights were going up. There was just that dark pool of Germany in the center, where most of the electricity had been smashed by the battle. The Danish radio was saying that peace—total peace (the Danish word for it is *"fred"*) —was going to be signed at General Eisenhower's headquarters on the morrow. Someone was saying a little inanely and drunkenly that total *fred* was going to take a great deal of knowing.

For the Danes the road back would not be difficult. There was still abundant food in Denmark; their only real shortages appeared to be a few things like soap and tobacco. They had their king and a new and acceptable government. Their country was virtually unscarred by war. One could even buy motor cars in the city stores. True, they were worried about the Russian occupation of their island of Bornholm in the Baltic, but that no doubt would be straightened out later on.

As for the Germans in Denmark, they would make no trouble. They showed little inclination to fight. A friend of mine went down to the docks, and when a group of Germans who were playing a concertina on a minesweeper saw his uniform they shouted across to him: "Come on, Tommy. Come and join us." My friend, being interested in the minesweeper, was going on board when a German warrant officer chased him off with a tommy-gun, and the too-amiable crew was sent below decks. There was no scuttling or attempt to scuttle. Since we did not have the guards to spare, Lindemann organized the long march of his own men out of Denmark and down to Germany. As a means of maintaining their discipline and protecting themselves from patriots they carried their arms as far as the German border, and then surrendered them to the British army of occupation. Their heavier equipment was left behind for the Danes.

And now there remained only Norway to set free; Norway, where England had really begun the war. Begun it so badly, with such poor preparation and equipment and so little knowledge of what modern war really meant. Now that we had survived and learned it would be a matter of great pride to go back to Norway and see the country free again.

At Copenhagen no one knew anything at all about the plans for Norway. We were turning over the matter at breakfast in the Hotel Angleterre when we fell in with two air commodores of the R.A.F. Transport Command. They had a plane, a Dakota, they too were thinking of making the two hours' flight northward; it was arranged that we should all go together. Of all the days of the war I can remember none more extraordinary, more buoyant or more inconsequent than this, the day of the signing of the armistice, Monday, May 7th. After so many journeys we were determined to have this, the last and possibly the best.

On arriving at Copenhagen airfield we found we had no maps. This was remedied, not undramatically, by the arrival of a squadron of German fighter aircraft coming in to surrender. Determined to avoid imprisonment by the Russians the pilots had taken off from Courland in Latvia that morning, and they arrived quite unannounced over Copenhagen just as we were about to take off. They were signaled down on to the runway, and one of the Germans in his excitement—or possibly deliberately—half-overturned his machine on landing, without coming to much harm. As each fighter put down an indeterminate crowd of people went coursing across the airfield to grab the pilots prisoner and gather souvenirs. Surprisingly, each machine disgorged a second occupant from its belly—the rush to get away from Courland must have been pretty urgent. Among the piles of leather jackets and flying-suits and other equipment brought out of the machines we found what we wanted: a schoolboy's atlas and a really good flying-map showing the route up over the Kattegat and the Skagerrak to Oslo.

It was brilliant sunshine when we took off, but we had scarcely reached Helsingfors and the coast of Sweden when ten-tenths cloud set in below us, only a few hundred feet above the sea. This was a major problem. We would be perfectly happy flying along in our sunlit sky above for most of the journey, but at the end we were bound to come down into the Norwegian fjords, and this was not a project to be undertaken in heavy cloud, especially as none of us had ever been to Oslo before.

It was resolved that we should continue for another five minutes and then, if the clouds persisted below us, turn back. We were in fact on the point of turning when abruptly the sea appeared again and for the rest of that day we continued in sunshine. It was an odd and beautiful flight. The Danish islands of Anholt and Laso slipped by below. Over to the left Jutland and the northern tip of Denmark; on the right the bright pitted coast of Sweden. Then out over the Skagerrak, northward all the time.

It was at this point, I think, that all of us began to consider some of the more pressing aspects of this flight:

(a) Had any Allied forces at all preceded us into Norway?
(b) Had the German command in Norway in fact surrendered?
(c) If they had not surrendered would they fire on us on arrival? Or possibly—
(d) Would they let us land and then take us prisoner?

Not one of us had a single definite answer to any one of these questions. Gloomily one reflected that this (we were now approaching the Norwegian coast) was the worst possible place and time to debate the matter. As the rocks and pine trees of the shore took shape one noted with surprising clarity the size and complete vulnerability of the Dakota, the absence of parachutes and the fact that we had not been able to contact anyone at all in Oslo on the radio. Two Swedish soldiers who were traveling with us—I do not quite know why, except they seemed to fit in with the general craziness of the whole operation—were wrapped in a world all their own in the tail of the aircraft. They were debating the means by which they would drop a Danish flag on Oslo, and had just decided to pay it out through a hole in the window in such a manner that it was tolerably certain to get caught up in the rudder and prevent us getting down at all.

Watching them uneasily I had the notion of looking down on the first point of Norwegian territory below to see if the houses were celebrating liberation by flying their flags. There were none. There was no ack-ack fire either. One reasoned with some comfort that the entrance to Oslo fjord would have been an admirable place at which to place ack-ack guns and this would have been an admirable moment for the Germans to fire if they were going to do so.

The most uplifting scenery passed below us. Mile after mile of inlets and scattered waterways among the pines, a world of bright lakes and little beaches and gabled hamlets made of timber. Far ahead the eternal snow sat on the great backbone of the country and between it and us nothing but crenelated ridges that rose one upon the other to the skyline. One or two flags began to appear on the buildings. And still no firing. We swooped down towards Oslo. Considerable crowds were scuttling about the streets and open places like black ants. Out went the Danish flag apparently without mishap. Two German Messerschmitt fighters, black and evil, shot by and vanished. A big Junkers transport, crosses on its wings, slid over the mountains to the east. It seemed impossible among all those lakes and forests below that there could be a landing-ground, but the third time round the city we saw it clearly and began to flatten out for the run in. There was much movement of aircraft on the field, and many people standing about. They flashed a red light warning us not to land, but the pilot decided to go ahead anyway. On the point of landing we got into the slipstream of a Junkers just taking off and dropped a sheer thirty feet on to the ground. The bounce seemed to take us higher than the fall, but eventually we settled down in front of the hangars and bundled ourselves outside.

It was a difficult moment. The Germans stood and stared. A major came up and gazed deeply at a group of people definitely new in his experience: the two air commodores and the plane crew in blue, the two Swedes in green, the rest of us in khaki and two photographers setting up their cameras on the tarmac. He saluted a little dazedly. Alexander Clifford, being the most fluent in German, explained, and the major said he felt he ought to get the general. While we waited, the Germans standing round watching us, three R.A.F. officers appeared beaming with delight. They had been shot down in the air battle of Norway, had broken out of their camp that morning and had made their way to the airport.

A German colonel now appeared, festooned with medals, followed by his officers, and made for our two air commodores. The colonel, a dark and muscular man, flung out his Nazi salute and offered his hand. This was rejected. The cameramen had some enjoyment in taking the shot.

"You are British," the colonel said. "Had you been Russians we would have resisted." "Resisted" was pretty good in the circumstances, since our force totaled a dozen men against at least a hundred thousand Germans in Norway.

Then he began a formal speech at the air commodores to open the negotiations. Not understanding German the shorter of the two

British officers lost interest. He whipped a Leica camera out of his pocket and began taking shots of the colonel in action. Baffled by this the colonel drew breath and Clifford rushed into the breach. A long and rapid conversation ensued, during which the answers to nearly all the questions we had been asking ourselves in the aircraft came out:

(*a*) No other Allies had yet arrived;
(*b*) Norway had not surrendered, and—
(*c*) They had not fired at us because they did not know who we were. The question of (*d*) alone remained.

The colonel explained vigorously: "We had no warning of your coming. We were told to expect an Allied mission to discuss terms, flying in a Catalina and a Sunderland painted white. In any event the German capitulation does not take place until midnight to-night." And he was inclined to think he should put us under arrest.

Clifford argued the opposite point of view, against our being arrested, and suggested the colonel should telephone to the German High Command north of Oslo and make it clear that they had to surrender. The colonel demurred. Clifford said he would telephone himself, and the colonel then retracted and said he imagined everything would be all right after all. Clifford then demanded cars to take us into Oslo. The colonel said he had none.

All this time the cameramen were pushing the two of them about so that they should be standing in the right light for the pictures. "Keep him talking, Alex," they shouted. "Make him look at the camera."

A certain glazed look was coming into the colonel's eye as if he found it a little difficult to keep up with the situation. At this point one of the German soldiers sidled up to me and said in French: "I'm frightened."

"What are you frightened about?"

"I'm frightened of the Russians—they'll send me to Siberia."

"Well," I said, "I'm not a Russian," and he saluted and withdrew.

A moment later he was back again, and he said hoarsely: "I'm frightened of you too."

All this time Junkers aircraft were taking off one after another, and the colonel explained vaguely: "They have their duties." In point of fact they were off to collect as many Germans as they could from Courland before the Russians got there, and they were leaving rapidly lest we should forbid the take-off.

On the subject of Oslo, some five miles away, we could get

nothing definite out of the Germans beyond a statement that there was "a carnival air" about the city. No one precisely was in charge. The Norwegian Underground had not risen as far as they knew.

In the end it was agreed that we should have transport, and three battered brown Wehrmacht cars drew up. We had scarcely made five hundred yards towards the city before our leading car with the air commodores inside broke down. Clifford leaped out, stopped another vehicle with two German officers aboard, and we set off again. The corporal driving my vehicle was in a high state of alarm and sweating profusely. He drove abominably. One could hardly blame him. At first the people did not recognize the air-force-blue uniforms, but then seeing the khaki they became lost to all reason. They rushed headlong upon the cars, not caring whether or not they were run over. This was different from Denmark. Different also from France and Belgium and Holland and the other places. There was a convulsive quality about this welcome, something almost religious, deriving from what could one say? The greater hunger here? The Norse temperament? Merely the unexpectedness of our arrival? Or a combination of these things, plus all the subtleties which are displayed at the revealing unconscious moment of a heartfelt mass emotion. But all this we had no time to observe, no precedents with which to check.

All through the war, again and again, one had seen that those who had suffered had the most power to rejoice. But here and there one came on persons or groups and crowds of people who had suffered too much and no longer had the power to rejoice in the ordinary way. And these for the most part had their joy in the passive undemonstrative sensation of release from pain which was beyond shouting or tears, and which, they say, is the greatest happiness of all: the sensation of pain ebbing away.

Here in Oslo this afternoon we were seeing all gradations of the human power to feel happiness. The overall expression was clear enough: spontaneous, explosive, full of contagious color and noise. The people poured themselves into the streets, and once there they took fire from one another, from the flags, from one another's excitement. In this mounting society of emotion, everyone feeling it together and rising with it, loving one another and believing implicitly in the importance and happiness of the moment, they were, for an hour of time, one person and quite unconscious of what they were doing.

And all this mixed up with crazy incidents that made you want—how shall I say?—to laugh with amusement rather than with joy. The crowd became quite uncontrollable. The German soldiers in the streets did the best they could. They tried to keep the people from overwhelming the cars. Then some of the Resistance lads pushed through to help, and, linking arms with their bitter enemies the Germans, they cleared a few more yards along the street. Then the Norwegian mounted police joined in and bumped the people back, and somehow we got through to the Grand Hotel, which was the noted quisling establishment of the town.

My German corporal had by now almost sweated himself away. The only other point I had time to note as I hurried indoors was that the Norwegians, like the Danes, have their own special cry of exaltation. This one sounds like "Hi-yah." "Hi-yah. Hi-yah. Hi-yah." The noise pursued us deep into the hotel.

By this time we were all encrusted with flags and emblems and bunches of flowers, and in this condition we were pushed out on to a balcony overlooking the central square of Oslo. The people flowed out beyond the square, up into the side-streets, a great pink carpet of upturned faces and waving red flags. They hung from the roofs and window-sills. They shouted across from the neighboring buildings. "Hi-yah. Hi-yah. Hi-yah."

Suddenly, under some common impulse, the shouting fell away and they began to sing their national anthem, the men standing stiffly, the women in tears. Then the shouts again. The senior air commodore made a speech. Someone else made a speech. We all made speeches. "Hi-yah. Hi-yah. Hi-yah." Then the national anthem again, the German soldiers standing in the middle of the crowd. And after that for some wholly unexplained reason they sang "Hallelujah." Apparently it passed for an English song.

The suite behind us that led off the balcony was rapidly filling up with people, so that if one left the balcony and turned away from the glare of the mass outside at once one was engulfed in another crowd near at hand. "Sign my book. Sign. Sign. Sign." People pressing forward with flowers, glasses of champagne—anything, so long as they gave us something.

A man with a tiny baby rushed through the room and made an impassioned address from the balcony.

"Who is he?" I asked the *maître d'hôtel.* Things were getting rapidly to a state where we had to find some authority in the city to take the place of the Germans, and this orator seemed to be a likely starter.

"No idea," the *maître d'hôtel* said, "except that he is drunk."

It did not matter. The crowd was with him. Someone rescued the child just as it was slipping perilously over the balustrade and the rejoicing went on.

Two more men suddenly pushed their way into the room. They were wearing canvas jackets with numbers printed in black across the left breast, like most Norwegians lean and strikingly handsome, except that one was lame: the leader of the Resistance movement and his lieutenant. They had just broken out of jail, and now, coming directly from that confinement and torture, they could not speak. They stood holding our hands, and after a little whispered something in Norwegian I could not understand. A girl of incredible beauty in a blue felt hat was jumping up and down by the door, smiling and smiling. Outside the crowd was now cheering in waves of noise, and every now and then this rhythm was broken when one of the British appeared on the balcony.

All this time a delegation of the responsible personages of the town, the governor, the chief of police, the solicitor of the former British Legation, had been waiting across the road at the Bristol Hotel. Clifford now gathered them in so that something could be done in organizing the government of the city to insure that there should be at least no riots that night.

"Quisling," said the governor, "has resigned. He is in his house just outside the city, awaiting his arrest by the Allies. If you would care to go there . . ."

More champagne and another gust of people bursting into the room.

"We have not done too badly," the solicitor said. "We had fish to eat."

Somehow we made it clear that an Allied mission was arriving to accept the official German surrender and gather in such people as Quisling. In the meantime the chief of police volunteered an escort to get us back to the aerodrome. One of the air commodores shouted one last word to the people: "We have all admired the spirit of your resistance."

Then out of the hotel and through the crowds, hands thrusting out at us, and back to the Germans on the airfield. The colonel had vanished. The three R.A.F. boys who had been prisoners jumped aboard. It was a quick take-off. Far down the fjord a Catalina and a Sunderland flying boat, both painted white, were heading past us in the direction of Oslo. Norway was out of the war. Denmark was out of the war. We were flying on to a Europe and to England where there was only peace. So many liberations. So much tragedy between them. The three of us who had made that long march up to Taormina in Sicily so long ago settled back in the plane and fell asleep. It had been a long day.

20. The Day After

May 9th. The peace one day old. For the last time I drove the car out of this, the last of many hundreds of places where we had billeted ourselves behind the front-line; and now for the first time in five and a half years there was no front-line. In twenty countries we had grown used to living with that strange and frightening barrier always a little in front of us, and now that it had gone the mind was either unwilling or unable to comprehend its absence.

I turned the car out on to the Lüneburg-Hanover road, heading westward for the Rhine, for Belgium, for Paris and for England. It was a beautiful morning. We ran quickly past the camps where the prisoners were standing staring through little fences of wire; was that the end of the war? The death of Hitler and Goebbels. The capture of Himmler and Ribbentrop and Goering. The suicides and the shooting squads. All Germany a prison camp and all its people prisoners. No, it did not seem to mean the end, and the more one passed these tens of thousands of beaten people on the roads the less, it seemed, one had the sense of victory.

Even the great cemetery by the river Aller, row after row of crosses in the sunshine, did not disturb the sensation of tiredness and indifference which, I think, lay fairly generally over all the armies on this first full day of peace. We argued in the car: "After all, in this war we—the British and the Americans—developed a way of fighting without taking mass casualties. Sixty thousand men were hit *in a single morning* in the battle of the Somme in the last war, and that is almost as many as the total British deaths in Europe from the landing at Salerno in 1943 until the summer of 1945." But this was no argument for celebration either.

We went by Belsen camp and out on to the autobahn, the long white ribbons of road stretching for mile after mile between green banks of trees. And there just for a moment one had a glimpse of peace. A fleet of British bombers went over carrying our wounded and recaptured prisoners homeward. Suddenly one realized: "There is nothing for them to bomb any longer. In all Europe no single target."

V-E Day.

But then at once we plunged into the fearful wreckage of the
Ruhr and got lost in Essen, where the roads ran into broken bridges
and dry canals or ended abruptly in piled-up debris and bits of steel
and concrete that looked like the tangled litter left behind by a
glacier after the winter is over. And it was impossible here in the
midst of utter destruction to feel any really full satisfaction, even the

satisfaction of gratified revenge. The place was so still. You cannot find victory in a torn-up cemetery. A smashed bridge does not signify triumph; it simply means another boring detour from the main road.

On the Rhine itself we were quite suddenly and unexpectedly touched to see that the Americans had run up a new pontoon bridge at Düsseldorf and they had named it "The Ernie Pyle Bridge." Ernie Pyle, the best-known American correspondent to be thrown up by the war, and one of the kindest and simplest, had been with us so often in Europe until he was killed in the Pacific; one had a feeling of pride to stand on his bridge and know that so many others had known him and liked him as well. A dead soldier, remembered with affection; this was more the feeling that we were, at that moment, trying unconsciously to evoke, and it did in some strange way begin to explain the mystery of the war and this other mystery of its curiously flat ending. We crossed the bridge with a stream of laden refugees.

Liége, in Belgium, was on the spree. The lights up, soldiers everywhere. Colored banners across the streets: *"Bienvenu à nos prisonniers et déposés."* No rooms anywhere. Eventually we slept in a barn over a garage.

In the morning we drove on through the Ardennes and on to Paris. Crowds singing. Dancing in the streets. And yet, and yet: was this really the end? Perhaps we were merely physically tired. Perhaps we were different from other people. But this was not the ending of the war or the explanation of even the *dénouement* of it. And it had no pattern with everything that had gone before.

Then London at last, and still the disillusionment persisted. For the moment many people seemed to be merely grateful that the thing was finished in Europe, and they did not believe—as far as I could make out—that anything had been accomplished beyond the suffocating of the immediate peril of the Nazis. The mass hatred and fears in Europe had been much stronger in this war than last; and now all this appeared to be subsiding not into internationalism but into xenophobia.

Of every hundred men called up for this European war, probably not more than twenty saw the front-line. Both England and America were able to keep the really great tragedies of this struggle away from their own people. By great tragedies I mean the Bengal famine, the mass slaughter of the Jews and others by the Nazis, the furies of the Russian-German front and now our own great slaughter of the Japanese.

And yet that most unlucky generation—the people who were born in the early years of the century—appeared to regard not the last war but this as the greater evil. They said it had been more exhausting, more full of terrors, and they thought it had touched more people more closely than ever before. It was not the front-line but the fish queue and the bus queue and the black-out that did the damage. Not the death in France but the disorganizing and uprooting danger of the bomb and the rocket at home. In the end the continuing absence of the men abroad became more demoralizing than high explosive. The loss of the ordinary little liberties, the unending drab monotony of simply keeping alive—these were the unbearable things, the real punishment on mankind for making war.

Only one thing stood against this depressive tide, and I would like to have it down here in print at the ending of my book. As a correspondent following the armies round the world through ten campaigns one has seen an immense change take hold of the soldier, the ordinary man and woman in the war. The clerk from Manchester and the shopkeeper from Balham seemed to me to gain tremendously in stature. You could almost watch him grow month to month in the early days. He was suddenly projected out of a shallow materialist world into an atmosphere where there really were possibilities of touching the heights, and here and there a man found greatness in himself. The anti-aircraft gunner in a raid and the boy in the landing-barge really did feel at moments that the thing they were doing was a clear and definite good, the best they could do. And at those moments there was a surpassing satisfaction, a sense of exactly and entirely fulfilling one's life, a sense even of purity, the confused adolescent dream of greatness come true.

Not all the cynicism, not all the ugliness and fatigue in the world will take that moment away from the people who experienced it. Five years of watching war have made me personally hate and loathe war, especially the childish wastage of it. But this thing—the brief ennoblement inside himself of the otherwise dreary and materialistic man—kept recurring again and again up to the very end, and it refreshed and lighted the whole heroic and sordid story.

The point perhaps is a little over-mystical, a little too intangible. Yet there it is. Whatever material hardship and monotony lie ahead, the soldier will remember that he made his ultimate gesture, that he did something quite selfless to justify his history, himself and his children. He was, for a moment of time, a complete man, and he had his sublimity in him. If there is one lesson we learned in France and the other occupied countries it was this: it never pays to capitulate. As long as there are things like Belsen camp you must go on protesting. You must protest.

We were indignant. We protested. We won. All mankind advances. And this will be a matter of some lasting strength to those who fought. This, in the end, I saw was the thing I was seeking: the explanation of the war. It was the thought in the mind of the Jugoslav patriot who, knowing he was about to die, wrote to his unborn son:

My child, sleeping now in the dark and gathering strength for the struggle of birth, I wish you well. At present you have no proper shape, and you do not breathe, and you are blind. Yet, when your time comes, your time and the time of your mother, whom I deeply love, there will be something in you that will give you power to fight for air and light. Such is your heritage, such is your destiny as a child born of woman—to fight for light and hold·on—without knowing why. . . .

Keep your love of life, but throw away your fear of death. Life must be loved or it is lost, but it should never be loved too well. . . .

Keep your heart hungry for new knowledge; keep your hatred of a lie; and keep your power of indignation.

Now I know I must die, and you must be born to stand upon the rubbish-heap of my errors. Forgive me for this. I am ashamed to leave you an untidy, uncomfortable world. But so it must be.

In thought, as a last benediction, I kiss your forehead. Good-night to you—and good-morning and a clear dawn.

Index

ing of the Rhine; reports the occupation and collapse of Germany, the
horrors of the concentration camps
there, and the contrasting joys of the
liberation of Denmark and Norway.

It is a work in which personal experiences and historic events are
made both vivid and memorable.
Alan Moorehead combines the best
virtues of war analysis, historical narrative, social comment, and personal
drama in his descriptions of Europe's
cities and their peoples and in his
reports of soldiers under the strain of
battle—GI's spending Christmas in
the Ardennes under attack from Panzers and V. 1 rockets; the Maquis in
Paris; the Dutch civilians in the cellars of Arnhem.

Like *The March to Tunis, Eclipse*
shows the greatest living war reporter
at his most remarkable.

CPSIA information can be obtained
at www.ICGtesting.com
Printed in the USA
BVOW06*1749020717
488347BV00005B/19/P

Disciplines of Grace

Disciplines
of
Grace

R. Kent Hughes

CROSSWAY BOOKS • WHEATON, ILLINOIS
A DIVISION OF GOOD NEWS PUBLISHERS

Art Direction/Design: Mark Schramm

First printing, 1993

Printed in the United States of America

Library of Congress Cataloging-in-Publication Data
Hughes, R. Kent.
   Disciplines of grace : God's ten words for a vital spiritual life /
R. Kent Hughes.
     p.   cm.
   1. Ten commandments—Criticism, interpretation, etc.
2. Spiritual life—Biblical teaching. I. Title.
BS1285.2.H84 1993   241.5'2—dc20   93-5468
ISBN 0-89107-731-6

01	00	99	98	97	96	95	94	93
15	14	13	12	11	10	9 8	7 6	5 4 3 2 1

To
Larry and Susan Fullerton
colleagues in ministry
and treasured friends

TABLE OF CONTENTS

ACKNOWLEDGMENTS

THANKS MUST first be expressed to my wife, Barbara, for her encouragement to open the Decalogue as God's Ten Words of Grace. Next, deepest appreciation goes to my omnicompetent secretary, Mrs. Sharon Fritz, then to Mr. Herb Carlburg for his careful reading of each chapter as it appeared, and to Mrs. Cassandra Niemczyk for her thoughtful interaction and practical suggestions. Lastly, thanks goes to Mr. Ted Griffin, Managing Editor of Crossway Books, for his gentle and cheerful editing.

Disciplines of Grace

And God spoke all these words:
"I am the Lord your God,
who brought you out of Egypt,
out of the land of slavery."

EXODUS 20:1, 2

I N 1980 the United States Supreme Court ruled by a 5-4 decision in *Stone v. Graham* that the schoolchildren of Kentucky
have the constitutional right not to be assaulted by the presence of the Ten Commandments on their classroom walls. The
Court's majority revealed its rationale, in part, with remarkable
secular frankness:

> If the posted copies of the Ten Commandments are to have
> any effect at all it will be to induce the schoolchildren to read,
> meditate upon, perhaps to venerate and obey, the
> Commandments. However desirable this might be as a mat-
> ter of private devotion, it is not a permissible state objective
> under the Establishment Clause.[1]

In short, the passive display of the Ten Commandments was
not permitted because some students might obey them.

The *Wall Street Journal* reported that the Court handed down its decision without hearing oral arguments and despite the fact that the Kentucky statute required that all copies of the Commandments were to be paid for by voluntary contributions and that a footnote was to be imprinted on each document stating it was not intended as a religious guide but as the basis of the secular legal codes of western civilization.[2]

So, in one imperious swoop America's highest court declared that the Decalogue (a document of incalculable influence that has provided the basis for the public morality of western culture, a text which for the first two hundred years of our nation's history was universally used to teach English)[3] was an improper display for impressionable young minds. This is secularism with a vengeance! As the *Wall Street Journal* wryly observed regarding the Court's ruling: "A citizen might be forgiven for suspecting that there is as much long-term danger in this sort of dogma as there is in the Ten Commandments hanging on schoolroom walls."[4]

And indeed there is. Western culture is without a moral compass. The terrible epitaph of the days of Israel's Old Testament judges is being lived out: "[E]very man did what was right in his own eyes." Today it is commonplace to call "evil good, and good evil" (cf. Judges 17:6 and Isaiah 5:20, NASB). Our culture is truly foundering — and may soon be beached on the desolate shores of its own moral emptiness.

WHY STUDY THE TEN COMMANDMENTS?

This moral catastrophe alone ought to provide ample reason for the church to hold the Ten Commandments high. But there are other substantial reasons, not the least of which is the widespread ignorance, among the populace and among Christians themselves, of the Ten Commandments.

Ignorance

A 1988 Gallup Poll revealed that while 85 percent of Americans believe that the Ten Commandments are binding, only 15 percent could name five of them.[5] If the statistics are true, only one out of each six people who say they believe in the Ten Commandments can name even half of them! And if 15 percent can name only five of the Ten Commandments, how many even know where they are found, or have even heard of them? And how many know that the Ten neatly divide into two sections — that Commandments 1–4 teach the *duties we owe to God* and 5–6 the *duties we owe to people?*

There are several parallel ways to state this. Commandments 1–4 teach *love for God* and 5–10 *love for others*; Commandments 1–4 teach *reverence for God* and 5–10 *respect for others*; Commandments 1–4 are *vertical* and 5–10 *horizontal*; Commandments 1–4 are *doctrine* and 5–10 *ethics.*

The painful truth is, although the church can rail about the obtrusive secularism that perpetrates court decisions like *Stone v. Graham*, she hasn't sufficiently taught her own people. And since it is an axiom that *one cannot be profoundly influenced by that which one does not know*, the church can only look to herself for her failure. The pervasive Biblical ignorance of the church, and therefore of culture, ought to be a powerful spur to study the Decalogue (i.e., the Ten Words — *Deca* means ten and *logue* words).

Relativism

Another reason to know the Ten Words is the reign of moral relativism in modern culture. Historian Paul Johnson in his acclaimed *Modern Times* begins with a brilliant discussion of the rise of moral relativism from the 1920s to the present. Johnson notes that with the scientific confirmation of Einstein's theory of relativity in 1919, which established the relativity of time and space, in the 1920s a belief began to circulate for the first time on a popular level that there were no longer any absolutes of good and evil. "Mistakenly," writes Johnson, "but perhaps inevitably, relativity became confused with relativism."[6] Ill-informed people actually thought that moral relativism had a scientific basis rooted in the cosmos and verified by Albert Einstein!

No one was more distressed at this confusion than Einstein himself, who passionately believed in absolute standards of right and wrong. In fact, he believed that moral relativism was a spiritual disease.

But, sadly, Einstein lived to see relativism become a triumphant social epidemic through (among others) three principal intellectual brokers, all atheists — Freud, Marx, and Nietzsche.

Freud psychologized humanity through his arcane system of sexual gnosticism, dismissing conscience and individual guilt as illusions, and rejecting the Judeo-Christian ethic out of hand.[7]

Karl Marx's materialism likewise did away with the concept of individual guilt, teaching instead the collective guilt of society, thereby paving the way for class warfare and genocide. Says Johnson:

> Marxist and Freudian analysis combined to undermine, in their different ways, the highly developed sense of personal responsibility, and of duty towards a settled and objectively true moral code, which was at the center of nineteenth-century European civilization. The impression people derived from Einstein, of a universe in which all measurements of value were relative, served to confirm this vision . . . of moral anarchy.[8]

Marx pictured a world where the controlling dynamic was economic materialism, and Freud a world where the dynamic was sexual. To this was added the philosophy of the other third of the atheistic trio who saw God as a casualty. Nietzsche wrote, "The greatest event of recent times — that 'God is Dead,' that the belief in the Christian God is no longer tenable — is beginning to cast its first shadows over Europe."[9]

Today in twentieth-century America moral relativism is so much in the driver's seat that a Supreme Court Justice can state as the moral basis for his judicial decision, "[O]ne man's vulgarity is another's lyric."[10]

CRISIS IN ETHICS

The result of this combination of ignorance and moral relativism is a colossal ethical crisis that afflicts our society from top to bottom. Lying is pandemic — from the halls of Congress to grade-school classrooms. In tacit recognition of this, law schools have reinstituted courses on ethics. The military has made ethics a major intellectual pillar of its graduate institutions as well.

Public schools are instituting "values education" in which students are encouraged to embrace "positive values" on ostensibly rational grounds. Some of the reasoning is *psychological*: "Such a course of action would benefit your overall well-being." Other rationales are *sociological*: "If you make this choice as opposed to that choice, more people will profit. We'll all be winners." But the successes of such programs are limited — for reasons that are rooted in the very structure of the Ten Commandments themselves. That is, secularists attempt to enact the ethics of the second half of the Decalogue, which have to do with loving others (for example, the prohibitions against stealing and lying), without giving any heed to the first half, which emphasizes loving God. All such attempts to encourage loving man without first loving God are doomed to ultimate failure.

As K. E. Kirk wrote in his book *The Vision of God*, "Ethics, or teaching about man and the conduct proper to him, centers a man's thoughts upon himself; and the end of self-centredness is unethical and unevangelical alike."[11] The point is, ethics will only succeed when God is loved first, because only an authentic love for God can enable a genuine love for man and a successful social ethic.

This is why society's every attempt to elevate itself, while disregarding God, has failed. And this is precisely why the Russian Communist experience was so morally catastrophic. Here an excerpt from a speech delivered in 1991 by David Aikman, senior correspondent for *Time* magazine, in which he recounts an interview with Boris Yeltsin, is most instructive. Aikman writes:

> Yeltsin told me in an interview that he was thinking of ways to get priests into the Russian school system to speak on ethics and morality, which prompted me to observe that it took the United States 200 years of religious freedom to drive Christianity out of the schools and the Soviet Union 70 years of atheism to bring it back.[12]

As Christians, we have the answer to the secularism and relativism and ignorance that have brought on this tragic ethical crisis. That answer involves an understanding and application of God's eternal character and will for His people as contained in the two tables of the Decalogue: *the love of God* first, and then *the love of humanity*. Here is an unfailing ethic that will stand and will bring life and light to a foundering world.

INVITING REASONS FOR THIS STUDY

There are also other inviting reasons to take up a study of the Ten Commandments, reasons that are even more enticing.

Law Invites Grace

Very high among the reasons for this study is that law invites grace. This may sound strange to some ears because salvation is by grace alone, totally apart from the works of the Law. The Apostle Paul is absolutely clear about this: "And if by grace, then it is no longer by works; if it were, grace would no longer be grace" (Romans 11:6). No one has even come close to being saved by the works of the Law. *Sola gratia!*

However, with this truth firmly and forever fixed, we must understand that law and grace are not antithetical or the least bit opposed. In point of fact, the Law was *founded* on God's grace. Significantly, the preamble which introduced the Law in Exodus 20:2 was a reminder of God's grace: "I am the Lord your God, who brought you out of Egypt, out of the land of slavery." Israel was delivered from Egypt for no other reason than God's good pleasure (cf. Deuteronomy 7:7, 8). The Decalogue, the Ten Words that follow the preamble of grace, are the Magna Charta of spiritual freedom given to a divinely redeemed people. Thus the preamble not only underlined their freedom but also the amazing grace that lay behind their deliverance from slavery. And because of this grace, God's people were to live for Him in obedience to the Commandments, not with the idea of attaining salvation by works, but in thanksgiving for what God had done. There was no thought in God's giving the Ten Commandments of providing a way for Israel, or anyone else, to earn salvation. The controlling thought was grace. The Law was, indeed, founded upon grace.

Along with this, the Law also *promised* grace. Jehovah declared to His people, "You yourselves have seen what I did to Egypt, and how I carried you on eagles' wings and brought you to myself. Now if you obey me fully and keep my covenant, then out of all nations you will be my treasured possession" (Exodus 19:4, 5). Thus, implicitly they would be recipients of more grace. So law and grace, rather than opposing one another, go hand in glove.

The compatibility of law and grace was further enhanced by

Jesus, the author and perfecter of salvation by grace, who fulfilled the Law, saying,

> Do not think that I have come to abolish the Law or the Prophets; I have not come to abolish them but to fulfill them. I tell you the truth, until heaven and earth disappear, not the smallest letter, not the least stroke of a pen, will by any means disappear from the Law until everything is accomplished. (Matthew 5:17, 18)

Jesus' "fulfillment" of the Law bears the positive idea of completion.[13] He did not bring a rupture between the Decalogue and His exposition of it, but rather He sustained a continuity between them as He fulfilled the Law in His life and teaching. Jesus' teaching actually harmonized with the old and added to it, completing it!

The significance of this is that when one becomes a Christian and is "in Christ," the source of all grace, the Ten Commandments become for him or her a joyous source of God's will — the way he or she expresses new life in Christ. Practically, the living out of the Law in the life of a child of grace brings more and more grace.

Law Invites Gospel

Next, the Law invites and leads to the gospel, because it slays the non-Christian by showing him how sinful he or she is. As Martin Luther preached:

> The Law must be laid upon those that are to be justified, that they may be shut up in the prison thereof, until the righteousness of faith come — that, when they are cast down and humbled by the Law, they should fly to Christ. The Lord humbles them, not to their destruction, but to their salvation. For God woundeth, that He may heal again. He killeth that He may quicken again.[14]

This was precisely the Apostle Paul's experience:

> Indeed I would not have known what sin was except through the law. For I would not have known what it was to covet if the law had not said, "Do not covet." But sin, seizing the opportunity afforded by the commandment, produced in me every kind of covetous desire. (Romans 7:7, 8; cf. 5:20, 21)

The practical point of all of this is that the authentic preaching of the gospel requires the unvarnished preaching of the Law. Or, put another way, the gospel is not fully preached without the proclamation of the Law. Quite frankly, this is why today there are so many "unsaved evangelicals." Notice I didn't say "unsaved Christians," but unregenerate or unsaved evangelicals. The reason for this tragic situation is that the evangelical presentation of Christ as Savior often centers on His being able to "enrich life" or make one "complete" or, though it is not so crassly stated, to add Christ as a mere religious component of one's self-actualization. Christ is therefore "accepted" with little or no reference to the depth of one's sin and utter lostness. Whatever "repentance" there may be has scant effect on one's lifestyle. Such converts are commonly told that they are now Christians (and that they should countenance no one telling them otherwise), and they are then baptized and received into church membership. Unsaved evangelicals!

What is needed is the preaching of the Law. Such people need to be brought to Sinai, the mount of doom and the consuming fire of God's holiness — "to a mountain that can be touched and that is burning with fire; to darkness, gloom and storm; to a trumpet blast or to such a voice speaking words that those who heard it begged that no further word be spoken to them" (Hebrews 12:18, 19). Having been to the mount of doom, one can then be led to Calvary, the mount of grace and the consuming love of God — "But you have come to Mount Zion, to the heavenly Jerusalem, the city of the living God. You have come to thousands upon thousands of angels in joyful assembly, to the church of the firstborn, whose names are written in heaven" (Hebrews 12:22, 23). It is the two mountains together that make the gospel live and bring life.

My prayer is that these studies will provide a path to the grace of God for many who read this book or for many who are reached by those who read this book.

Law Invites Holiness

Viewed from another perspective, the Law invites holiness because its intrinsic purpose is to help the law-keeper know God better and to enhance fellowship with His divine person.[15] The Law was Jehovah's wedding present to His bride — a call to know and love Him.

The Law reveals God's holiness, that He is a consuming fire. Further, it exposes His moral beauty because in it we see, especially in Commandments 5–10 of the second table, His nature expressed in moral imperatives.[16] Because the Ten Commandments form a unity of love (love for God first, and then love for mankind), they induce a profound internalization of love in the law-keeper. And all of this — the knowledge of God, the fellowship, the holiness, the moral beauty, the love — produces a dynamic holiness.

Law Invites Keeping

Fittingly, meditation upon God's Law invites its keeping by the believer.

It is quite simple: Jesus *authored* the Law, Jesus *kept* the Law, Jesus *indwells* believers, and Jesus *sends* His Holy Spirit to indwell believers and to enhance His life in them. The Spirit then internalizes the Law in His people, and He bestows power to live it. As Paul explained:

Therefore, there is now no condemnation for those who are in Christ Jesus, because through Christ Jesus the law of the

Spirit of life set me free from the law of sin and death . . . in order that the righteous requirements of the law might be fully met in us, who do not live according to the sinful nature but according to the Spirit. (Romans 8:1, 2, 4)

Of course, all believers sin and fall short of the Law. But they keep it in the person of Christ, and their souls long for it and exult in it as they walk in the Spirit.

Law Invites Blessing

David sang about the blessings of the Law in Psalm 19:

The law of the Lord is perfect,
reviving the soul.
The statues of the Lord are trustworthy,
making wise the simple.
The precepts of the Lord are right,
giving joy to the heart.
The commands of the Lord are radiant,
giving light to the eyes.
The fear of the Lord is pure,
enduring forever.
The ordinances of the Lord are sure
and altogether righteous.
They are more precious than gold,
than much pure gold;
they are sweeter than honey,
than honey from the comb.
By them is your servant warned;
in keeping them there is great reward. . . .
May the words of my mouth
and the meditation of my heart
be pleasing in your sight,
O Lord, my Rock and my Redeemer.
                    —vv. 7-14

Such a prayer and such a graced life has the smile of God. We know His smile is upon us when we live within the parameters He has given us: loving Him with all our heart and soul and mind, and loving our neighbor as ourself (cf. Deuteronomy 6:5; Leviticus 19:18; Matthew 22:37-40).

What more could we desire than his smile?

I am convinced that for the Christian, the understanding of God's Ten Words, the Decalogue, coupled with a determination to live them out by God's Spirit, will invite God's grace and will free his children to soar above the ignorance, moral relativism, and ethical desolation of our culture. Therefore, what follows in later chapters are ten disciplines that will, if taken to heart, enhance the flow of grace in our lives.

DISCIPLINES OF GRACE

As we begin our ten-point journey, I would like to ask you to commit yourself to some initial disciplines.

• First, *read the Ten Commandments* as they are given initially in Exodus 20 and again in Deuteronomy 5.

• Second, *memorize the Ten Words* from Exodus 20. (Note: you need not memorize all of Commandments 2, 3, 4, 5, and 10 but only the opening line.)

    I. You shall have no other gods before me.
    II. You shall not make for yourself an idol in the form of anything.
    III. You shall not misuse the name of the Lord your God.
    IV. Remember the Sabbath day by keeping it holy.
    V. Honor your father and your mother.
    VI. You shall not murder.
    VII. You shall not commit adultery.
    VIII. You shall not steal.

    IX. You shall not give false testimony against your
        neighbor.

    X. You shall not covet.

• Third, if you have a family, *teach your children one Commandment per week* so they will be able to recite all ten. As you do this, remember God's Word to parents:

> Hear, O Israel: The Lord our God, the Lord is one. Love the Lord your God with all your heart and with all your soul and with all your strength. These commandments that I give you today are to be upon your hearts. Impress them on your children. Talk about them when you sit at home and when you walk along the road, when you lie down and when you get up. Tie them as symbols on your hands and bind them on your foreheads. Write them on the doorframes of your houses and on your gates. (Deuteronomy 6:4-9)

• Fourth, *pray weekly for God's blessing* upon yourself, your family, and your church as you study the Ten Words.

Discipline yourself, for these are Ten Words of Grace!

PART I

Loving God

1

The First Word of Grace

Loving God:
His *Primacy*

You shall have no other
gods before me.
EXODUS 20:3

THE UTTER moral wretchedness of the philosopher Jean-Jacques Rousseau shocks even our twentieth-century sensibilities. He was a sexual adventurer, a champion voyeur,[1] and a shameless advocate of onanism. Incapable of lasting friendships, any attempts at such ended in Rousseau's spewing acrimony and abuse. Rousseau fathered five illegitimate children, gave them no names, and abandoned them to the *Hôpital des Enfants-trouvés,* where they surely died. Despite this, he claimed that no one enjoyed playing with children more than himself.[2] In a grotesque outpouring of unparalleled egoism he wrote:

> The person who can love me as I can love is still to be born.
> No one ever had more talent for loving. I was born to be the

best friend that ever existed. I would leave this life with apprehension if I knew a better man than me. Show me a better
man than me, a heart more loving, more tender, more sensi-
tive. . . . Posterity will honour me . . . because it is my due.[3]

Astonishingly, future generations have done just that. Upon his
death he was buried in the lake on the *Île des Peupliers* at
Ermononville, which immediately became a shrine for secular pil-
grimage. The outlandish religious display of his devotees rivaled
that for a saint in the Middle Ages. Said one admirer, "I dropped
to my knees . . . pressed my lips to the cold stone of the monument
. . . and kissed it repeatedly."[4] Rousseau's tobacco pouch and jar
were carefully preserved as relics at "the Sanctuary," as his tomb
was called. In Immanuel Kant's judgment, Rousseau had "a sensibility of soul of unequaled perfection." The poet Schiller proclaimed him "a Christ-like soul for whom only Heaven's angels are
fit company."[5]

So we see that the eighteenth century's Enlightenment and its
proud commitment to reason did nothing to liberate modern man
from idolatry — and it is certainly alive and well today as well!
Significantly, when the atheistic French philosopher Jean-Paul
Sartre died 202 years later in 1980, secular Paris — almost fifty
thousand mourners, most of them young — followed his body to
the Montparnasse Cemetery. The veneration was so intense that his
followers climbed trees along the way, and one came crashing
down onto his coffin.[6]

In more recent times, the embalmed bodies of Stalin and Lenin
(their brains carefully removed) were viewed in lugubrious religious
silence by perpetual lines of pilgrims. Malcolm Muggeridge once
quipped that the brainless bodies of communism's saints were
splendid metaphors for the reasoning and soul of dialectical
materialism!

Today in the English-speaking West John Lennon's sainthood

is perpetuated by the syrupy, cinematic hagiography of Yoko Ono and others from the Sergeant Pepper era. And of course, we must not forget the prevailing "Elvis-olatry" of our day by groupies such as Dennis Wise who had his face lifted by a plastic surgeon and his hair contoured so that he came to look remarkably similar to Elvis. Mr. Wise told the *Boston Globe*, "Yes sir, Presley's been an idol of mine ever since I was 5 years old. I have every record he ever made, twice over. Pictures in the thousands. I have books, magazines, pillows, even a couple of books in Chinese and Japanese about him. I even have tree leaves from the front of his house." The truth is, transgression of the First Commandment, "You shall have no other gods before me," is as frequent today as ever, perhaps more so.

And yet today 76 percent of all Americans consider themselves "completely true to the first commandment." According to *The Barna Report 1992-93*, 81 percent of women claimed fidelity to the First Commandment as compared to 69 percent of men[7], and thus the composite 76 percent. This is an extraordinary assertion since only 15 percent of the same people can name even half of the Ten Commandments.[8]

Something is wrong here. The figures simply don't jibe. The reason, as Barna points out, is that the question assumes people are able to identify the idols in their lives.[9] And, he adds, "Denial of sin is rampant in America. The probability is that a great many people who claimed to be completely satisfying any given commandment were fooling themselves."[10] Barna is right. Further, the sin of idolatry can be far more subtle than "Elvis-olatry" and often takes unseen, even unconscious forms that, though not as crude, are nevertheless just as deadly.

Make no mistake though — idolatry, both subtle and overt, is on the rise in our land — including pagan idolatry. If you doubt this, consider *Earth's Ten Commandments* by Ernest Callenbach and illustrated by Berkeley's famed poster artist David Goines.

I. Thou shalt love and honor the earth for it blesses thy life and governs thy survival.

II. Thou shalt keep each day sacred to the earth and celebrate the turning of its seasons.

III. Thou shalt not hold thyself above other living things nor drive them to extinction.

IV. Thou shalt give thanks for thy food to the creatures and plants that nourish thee.

V. Thou shalt limit thy offspring as multitudes of people are a burden unto the earth.

VI. Thou shalt not kill nor waste earth's riches upon weapons of war.

VII. Thou shalt not pursue profit at the earth's expense but strive to restore its damaged majesty.

VIII. Thou shalt not hide from thyself or others the consequences of thy actions upon the earth.

IX. Thou shalt not steal from future generations by impoverishing or poisoning the earth.

X. Thou shalt consume material goods in moderation so all may share earth's bounty.

This rise of neo-paganism has been accompanied by a strident pagan and secular Christophobia that is so entrenched that one major U.S. daily, as a matter of policy, will not print the two words "Jesus Christ" together, because the editor says that *Jesus* coupled with *Christ* is an editorial judgment.[11]

All the above present inescapable consequences for the church and her attempts at upholding the First Commandment. Humanity's tendency to long for other gods, the seductive Siren appeal and arcane subtleties of idolatry, and the aggressive oppressiveness of secular and neo-pagan culture all make it very difficult to keep God's First Word — "You shall have no other gods before me." In addition, the stakes for believers are spiritually incalculable because the First Command is the key to fulfilling the First Table of the Law (the first four Commandments) — loving God with all our hearts — which then makes it possible to love others as ourselves.

The First Commandment is meant to unlock the floodgates of God's grace. As such, it has everything to do with one's spiritual health and, if one has children, their spiritual destiny. As Christians we must excel in this initial discipline of grace!

A PREAMBLE OF GRACE (vv. 1, 2)

The setting of the Ten Words was without parallel. Israel, while camped at the side of Mount Sinai, saw a thick cloud cover the top of the mountain illumined by gold veins of flashing lightning, with accompanying thunder rolling down the slopes. This display was accompanied by a deafening trumpet blast that reduced everyone to trembling (Exodus 19:16). Whether the trumpet sound was natural or supernatural cannot be absolutely determined. Very likely it was the latter because it was heard by all the million plus in the camp and because the giving of the Law was attended by "myriads of holy ones" (Deuteronomy 33:2). There were hundreds of thousands of angels hovering invisibly around and over Sinai, and some probably were blowing celestial horns.

Moses then led his people from their tents to the foot of the mountain, and this is what they saw:

> Mount Sinai was covered with smoke, because the Lord descended on it in fire. The smoke billowed up from it like smoke from a furnace, the whole mountain trembled violently, and the sound of the trumpet grew louder and louder. Then Moses spoke and the voice of God answered him. (Exodus 19:18, 19)

Imagine yourself there! The ground is unsteady under your feet due to continual seismic tremors. The sky is in deep darkness except for the radiating forks of lightning in the gloom and the fire blazing from the top of Sinai "to the very heavens" (Deuteronomy 4:11). Celestial shofars blare louder and louder in primal moans, and then Moses speaks, and God answers him with a voice like thunder: "I am the Lord your God, who brought you out of Egypt, out of the land of slavery" (Exodus 20:2). This is the preamble of grace, spelling out gracious revelations before pronouncing the Ten Commandments.

God's Gracious Nature

The initial six words in English, "I am the Lord your God," provided a dynamic communication of God's gracious nature. He was "I," not "it." And they were "you," not "them."[12] The very phrasing of this opening line is reminiscent of Moses' initial encounter with God at the burning bush over forty years earlier when God instructed Moses to inform the Israelites of His name, saying, "This is what you are to say to the Israelites: 'I AM has sent me to you'" (Exodus 3:14). This was God's personal name, given so God's people would know He was with them in intimate relationship. "I am" coupled with "the Lord your God" is an announcement of the closest intimacy. This is, of course, an abiding statement of the grace which, happily, every child of God today enjoys through Jesus Christ.

God's Gracious Actions

Next, this description of God's gracious nature and His relationship with His people is coupled with the declaration of His gracious actions on their behalf — "who brought you out of Egypt, out of the land of slavery" (v. 2b). This declaration summarized Israel's experience during the preceding several months when God had progressively pried open Pharaoh's iron grip with the ten plagues, finally slaying Egypt's firstborn while passing over Israel's sons as they kept the Passover. Moreover, the declaration further called to mind their deliverance through God's rolling back the Red Sea and His providing quail in the evening and manna in the morning and water from the smitten rock. God's grace was all there in living color in their memory bank and ready for instant replay.

This all came solely by grace, as Moses clearly reminded Israel at the second giving of the Law: "The Lord did not set his affection on you and choose you because you were more numerous than other peoples, for you were the fewest of all peoples. But it was because the Lord loved you . . ." (Deuteronomy 7:7, 8). The psalmist would sing, "I am the Lord your God, who brought you up out of Egypt. Open wide your mouth and I will fill it" (81:10).

We celebrate the marvels of God's grace — His lovingkindness given so freely without any cost to us! God did for the Israelites what they could not rightfully demand from Him or compel Him to do and what he had no apparent good reason to do.

Fellow-Christians, this gracious preamble to Israel is a prophecy and parable of our own experience of grace. We were in the slavemarket of sin, in such bondage that there was no way of escape. We could not earn our way out. We could never make ourselves worthy of deliverance. But God reached down with unmerited love and saved us, as John so clearly explained: "This is love: not that we loved God, but that he loved us and sent his Son as an atoning sacrifice for our sins" (1 John 4:10).

Gratitude for Grace

This thundering preamble rolling down from Mount Sinai — "I am the Lord your God, who brought you out of Egypt, out of the land of slavery" — was meant to kindle in God's people a deep love and gratitude and to motivate them to keep his Ten gracious Words. Appropriately, therefore, the *Heidelberg Catechism* includes the discussion of the Ten Commandments under its third part, entitled "Of Thankfulness."[13]

This appeal for gratitude as a motivation for keeping the

Commandments is an *individual* appeal, and thus each
Commandment is expressed in the second person singular, for God
is addressing each person by name.[14] "You, *Kent Hughes*, shall ..."
Thus, it is of the greatest importance that we individually receive
each of the Ten Words as words of grace, as gifts of God's love, and
that we respond with thanksgiving. May we daily thank God for
his Ten Words.

A PROHIBITING GRACE

The First Commandment is also a forthright and emphatic prohibition:[15] "You shall have no other gods before me." And its meaning is unequivocal: *nothing* is to be placed before God — no person,
thing, ideology, or purpose.

The depth of this prohibition is apparent when we understand
that every human being has a god. There is no man or woman, no
humanist, no atheist, no Marxist materialist who does not have
somewhere inside his being a shrine that houses a deity whom he
worships. G. Campbell Morgan insightfully observed:

> It is as impossible for a man to live without having an object
> of worship as it is for a bird to fly if it is taken out of the air.
> The very composition of human life, the mystery of man's
> being, demands a center of worship as a necessity of exis-
> tence. All life is worship. ... The question is whether the life
> and powers of man are devoted to the worship of the true
> God or to that of a false one.[16]

So we must understand that there is no middle ground. There
are only two categories of people: true worshipers or true idolaters,
for all have a god.

Martin Luther similarly defined an idol as that upon which one relies. In the *Large Catechism* Luther asks, "What is it to have a god?" or "What is God?" And he answers:

> A god is that to which we look for all good and in which we find refuge in every time of need. To have a god is nothing else than to trust and believe him with our whole heart. As I have often said, the trust and faith of the heart alone make both God and an idol. . . . That to which your heart clings and entrusts itself is, I say, really your God.[17]

So if we understand idolatry merely in terms of "Elvis-olatry" or obeisance to Mother Earth, we miss the point. And that, frankly, is why 76 percent of Americans in 1992 can say that they are "completely true to the First Commandment." Their moral ignorance places the point beyond their reach.

What, then, are the gods that humanity places before the true God?

Technology

Some have technology for their god, especially those who exploit others. Habakkuk, likening humanity to fish in the sea, poetically describes those who use their technology to control others:

> The wicked foe pulls all of them up with hooks, he catches them in his net, he gathers them up in his dragnet; and so he rejoices and is glad. Therefore he sacrifices to his net and burns incense to his dragnet, for by his net he lives in luxury and enjoys the choicest food. (1:15, 16)

Men worship their dragnets, the technology that brings them, either licitly or illicitly, what they consider to be "the good life." Some even pray, "Give us this day our daily bread," but in their deepest heart they worship the means by which they get it.

Appetites

Paul described the Philippians as a people "whose God is their belly" (3:19, KJV). What a repulsive description — worshiping one's own digestive tract! In this vein, Clement of Alexandria wrote of a fish that had its heart in its belly — an apt description of the Epicureans.[18] Paul further described such people to the Romans by saying, "They that are such serve not our Lord Jesus Christ, but their own belly" (Romans 16:18, KJV). And, of course, there are people who think of nothing but how they are going to sauté some culinary delight, sauce it, and present it to their palates with the proper vintage. Whole magazines are exclusively devoted to this.

Of course, there is nothing wrong with pleasure per se. Christians ought to be free to enjoy life's pleasures. Good food, recreations, and diversions are important parts of life — in proper perspective. We all know that "All work and no play makes Jack a dull boy." But we must remember, too, that all play and no work makes Jack an idolater!

Besides, as Joy Davidman has said, "Living for his own pleasure is the least pleasurable thing a man can do; if his neighbors don't kill him in disgust, he will die slowly of boredom and lovelessness."[19] Today's idolized bellies can be ample or trim. In fact, some of the trimmest are the most demanding of all the gods.

Sex

After a night before the Tube a visitor from another planet would have to conclude that earthlings worship lithe, muscular male and female bodies. Indeed, as our popular culture has it, anyone "who is not continually fizzing like champagne with sexual excitement is . . . a failure in life."[20] The images of modern culture's gods are everywhere, in various stages of undress and sexual arousal. Perhaps more smoke goes up to Baal from the altars of passion than from any other.

Money

Our coins read, "In God we trust." But someone has suggested that we should alter today's inscription to read, "In *this* god we trust."[21] Job wisely said, "If I have put my trust in gold or said to pure gold, 'You are my security,' if I have rejoiced over my great wealth, the fortune my hands had gained . . . then these also would be sins to be judged, for I would have been unfaithful to God on high" (Job 31:24, 25, 28). This is idolatry! Jesus put it with supreme simplicity: "You cannot serve both God and Money" (Matthew 6:24). In what, then, do we really trust?

Self

Perhaps the most common thing given priority over God is self. There are many today who worship themselves with all their heart and strength and mind and serve only themselves. Consider actress Shirley MacLaine:

> The most pleasurable journey you take is through yourself . . . the only sustaining love involvement is with yourself. . . . When you look back on your life and try to figure out where you've been and where you're going, when you look at your work, your love affairs, your marriages, your children, your pain, your happiness — when you examine all that closely, what you really find out is that the only person you really go to bed with is yourself. . . . The only thing you have is working to the consummation of your own identity. And that's what I've been trying to do all my life.[22]

These are but a few of the things people place before God. But whatever it is — technology, appetites, pleasure, sex, money, self, or something else — whatever we love, whatever we desire, whatever we rely upon, whatever we make the center of our lives will be "Dead Sea fruit in our mouths unless we remember God comes first."[23] And if we err in that way, we will surely not drink from the river of grace.

A POSITIVE GRACE

Possessing God

The other side of this relentless negative — "You shall have no other gods before me" — is the sublime positive, "You shall have *Me*!" This is the grace of the First Commandment! The New Testament metaphor, foreshadowed in God's corporate relationship to Israel, is that of a groom to the bride. We are the bride of Christ, and he has a holy *eros* for us! Hear the *eros* in these sublime words:

> Christ loved the church and gave himself up for her to make her holy, cleansing her by the washing with water through the word, and to present her to himself as a radiant church, without stain or wrinkle or any other blemish, but holy and blameless. (Ephesians 5:25-27)

We must respond by letting Him possess our bodies and souls and thus coming to possess Him. This will bring grace upon grace!

Loving God

The positive side of "You shall have no other gods before me" is not only "You shall have Me" but "You shall *love* me!" Israel's *Shema* puts it memorably: "Love the Lord your God with all your heart and with all your soul and with all your strength. These commandments that I give you today are to be upon your hearts" (Deuteronomy 6:5, 6). Recognizing that the heart is the wellspring of our being, our deepest innermost self, we understand that the entire core of what we are and all our energy must be devoted to loving God. And this is what we ought to inculcate in those we love — especially our children. King David's love song sets the example for our hearts' love:

O God, you are my God,
earnestly I seek you;
my soul thirsts for you,
my body longs for you. . . .
Because your love is better than life,
my lips will glorify you.
I will praise you as long as I live,
and in your name I will lift up my hands.
My soul will be satisfied as with the richest of foods;
with singing lips my mouth will praise you.
On my bed I remember you;
I think of you through the watches of the night.
Because you are my help,
I sing in the shadow of your wings.
—Psalm 63:1-7

We need to learn to say to God, "I love you," because doing so will confirm and elevate our love.

Loving God is the greatest thing we can do, as Jesus solemnly affirmed: "Love the Lord your God with all your heart and with all your soul and with all your mind. This is the first and greatest commandment" (Matthew 22:37, 38).

Loving God will suspend our souls in a sea of grace, and the tide will bear the souls of our children up to Heaven.

DISCIPLINES OF GRACE

As we further commit ourselves to the disciplines of grace, we must keep in mind that such disciplines are not legalism, but rather a matter of grace from beginning to end. Consider slowly and carefully Paul's words: "But by the *grace* of God I am what I am, and his *grace* to me was not without effect. No, I worked harder than all of them — yet not I, but the *grace* of God that was with me" (1 Corinthians 15:10, italics added). There is no contradiction between grace and hard work. In fact, grace produces discipline. Discipline is a means of grace.

• *Pray* for yourself, your family members by name, and your church — first, for the *negative*, that you will have no other gods before Him, and second, for the *positive*, to love Him with all you are and have.

• *Memorize* the First Commandment. And if you have a family, help your children to do so.

• *Reflect*. Take some time alone to shut everything out and stand alone with God.

This can be terrifying, but it is absolutely necessary. First reflect on the question, "Who or what is *my* God? What is the center of my life? What do I rely on?" Second, imagine yourself before God and His asking you, just as God the risen Son asked Peter on the shores of Galilee, "Do you truly love Me more than these? . . . Do you truly love Me? . . . Do you love Me?"

• *Meditate and pray* through the two great love psalms, Psalm 63:1-7 and Psalm 18:1, 2.

• *Talk about loving God with others* — your friends, your spouse, your children. Take advantage of special occasions to express love for God — a sunset, a birthday, a funeral, a drive.

• *Sing love songs to God*, songs such as:

"My Jesus, I Love Thee"
"Fairest Lord Jesus"
"Jesus, the Very Thought of Thee"
"When I Survey the Wondrous Cross"
"May the Mind of Christ My Savior"
"O Lord, You're Beautiful"
"I Love You, Lord"
"Worthy Is the Lamb"

This is the First Word of Grace!

The Second Word of Grace

Loving God:
His *Person*

*You shall not make for
yourself an idol in the form
of anything.*
EXODUS 20:4–6

A S WE HAVE SEEN, God's Ten Words were launched on a sea of grace. The divine preamble that echoed down the slopes of Mt. Sinai in God's thunderous voice conveyed in concise terms God's *gracious nature* — "who brought you out of Egypt, out of the land of slavery" (Exodus 20:2). Then the divine voice boomed the *First Word of Grace* — "You shall have no other gods before me" (v. 3) — followed by the *Second Word,* upon which this chapter focuses.

> You shall not make for yourself an idol in the form of anything in heaven above or on the earth beneath or in the waters below. You shall not bow down to them or worship them; for

I, the Lord your God, am a jealous God, punishing the children for the sin of the fathers to the third and fourth generation of those who hate me, but showing love to thousands who love me and keep my commandments. (vv. 4-6)

As the Second Word's echo faded, it was revived by the distinct divine roar of each of the subsequent eight Commandments.

Exodus 20 concludes the story of the giving of the Law, informing us that when God ceased speaking, the people remained at a distance while Moses approached the thick darkness where God was. Very significantly, God solemnly reiterated the importance of the first two words for His people: "Tell the Israelites this: 'You have seen for yourselves that I have spoken to you from heaven: Do not make any gods to be alongside me; do not make for yourselves gods of silver or gods of gold'" (vv. 22, 23). The prohibition of idolatry could scarcely be given greater emphasis!

This memorable event was followed by God's giving to Moses the specific details of the social and civil laws of Israel, as recorded in Exodus 21 — 23, which culminated in the grand day of the confirming of the Covenant of the Law (Exodus 24). Moses set up twelve stone pillars at the foot of Sinai, representing the tribes of Israel. Beside them he sacrificed young bulls, sprinkling half of the blood on the altar. Next he took up the Book of the Covenant and read aloud beginning, of course, with the first two Words prohibiting idolatry. The people responded, "We will do everything the Lord has said; we will obey" (Exodus 24:7).

Then Moses solemnly raised the bowl containing the remaining half of the blood and doused the book of the Law and the surrounding people (cf. Hebrews 9:18-22). It was not a pretty sight, except in its supreme symbolism. The altar, the Law, and the people dripped with blood; the Covenant had its crimson seal.

This done, Moses ascended to the top of Sinai and into the cloud of glory that looked like a "consuming fire," and there he remained for forty days while God instructed him and then presented him with the Law engraved on stone with His own finger (Exodus 24:15-18; 31:18).

What a colossal spiritual landmark this was for God's people. There had never been anything like it in the history of the world — and there never would be again. One would think that the glow of those sacred moments would hold those present to be faithful for the rest of their lives — that they would never come close to the faintest hint of breaking the first two Words. But that was not to be.

When the people saw that Moses was long in returning, they mocked the gracious preamble God had thundered from Heaven — "I am the Lord your God, who brought you out of Egypt, out of the land of slavery." Their mocking made snide, contemptuous reference to "this fellow Moses who brought us up out of Egypt" (Exodus 32:1), thereby attributing their divine deliverance to a man!

This brazen contempt for God and His servant Moses was coupled with a demand that Aaron make them new gods. Astonishingly, Aaron, Moses' brother, responded with enthusiasm, enlisting everyone in the act. Parents and children contributed their gold earrings for the idol. Aaron cast a golden calf (the image of a bull) and then worked it over artistically with a tool into a "graven image." And then he himself blasphemed God, aping God's words again as he proclaimed, "These are your gods, O Israel, who brought you up out of Egypt" (Exodus 32:4). And if that wasn't enough, an altar was constructed before the golden calf, "a festival to the Lord" was announced (32:5), blood sacrifices were made to the calf, and the people said again, "These are your gods, O Israel, who brought you up out of Egypt" (32:8).

Astounding! Israel's descent to idolatry after hearing God's voice proclaim the Law from the flaming pinnacle of Sinai — less than forty days after proclaiming, "We will do everything the Lord has said" — taxes our credulity. But it happened. And the Holy Spirit has chronicled it for our instruction.

Fellow-Christians, Israel's debacle establishes for all time the abysmally infinite tendency and capacity of the human heart for idolatry — even among fresh recipients of God's grace. This was just the beginning for Israel who, despite divine judgment, did it again and again. And through the millennia since, idolatry has likewise proved to be the bane of the Christian church. A London preacher, writing from "Christian" England in 1901, noted that "In Westminster Abbey, to-day, there may be seen a great many vacant niches where images once stood. They were removed not because they were statues, but because lamps were burned in front of them, and worshippers knelt before them."[1]

Today idolatry is alive and well. In fact, "Jesus can be yours by calling [toll-free number]." Callers can purchase a Jesus doll who bends at the waist and is machine-washable. He looks friendly and is nearly two feet tall; he wears a white tunic under a red robe, which sets off his red heart emblazoned on the front of his tunic. His creator sees the doll as a special help to children because "it's hard to hug air," but it can also provide solace to the elderly and infirm and those under emotional duress. Jesus is only the first in a line of dolls called "Firstfruits." He can be yours for $29.95 — and would make a fine companion for the soon-to-be-introduced God doll.[2]

Make no mistake — the Second Commandment, "You shall not make for yourself an idol," is broken today as frequently and flagrantly as any time in history. And it is broken by recipients of God's grace, Christians who have been long or recently delivered from "Egypt."

As we take up this Second Commandment we must understand that it is by no means a duplication of the first. The First Commandment forbids the *existence* of other gods. The second forbids the *making* of other gods — idols. The first could be broken *unconsciously*, whereas the second references a *conscious* breaking — the volitional making of an idol.

This Second Commandment, the *Second Word of Grace*, has

everything to do with our spiritual well-being because, if obeyed, it further assures a perpetual stream of God's grace in our lives.

THE GRACIOUS PROHIBITION

Fully stated, the Second Word's prohibition is, "You shall not make for yourself an idol in the form of anything in heaven above or on the earth beneath or in the waters below. You shall not bow down to them or worship them" (Exodus 20:4, 5a). As to its precise meaning, it does not forbid the sculpturing and painting of images of living things, as some have supposed. If that were the case, then one has to account for God directing that cherubim be sculpted to preside over the Ark of the Covenant and also be woven into the veil of the Holy of Holies, as well as commanding the embroidery of lilies and pomegranates. Likewise, Solomon's Temple displayed lions, bulls, and cherubim (cf. 1 Kings 7:18-20).

Rather, what is explicitly forbidden is the making of figures or objects representative of God as objects or aids to worship. It rules out the use of pictorial and sculptured images that depict God as an animal or an object. And furthermore, as J. I. Packer has said:

> This categorical statement rules out . . . also the use of pictures and statues which depict Him as the highest created thing we know — a man. It also rules out the use of pictures and statues of Jesus Christ as a man, although Jesus Himself was and remains Man; for all pictures and statues are necessarily made after the "likeness" of ideal manhood as we conceive it, and therefore come under the ban which the commandment imposes.[3]

Church history reveals that Christians have disagreed as to whether the Second Command disallows the use of pictures of Jesus as an aid to teaching, as is common in Sunday school materials. The

general consensus is that they do not. But one thing is sure — the
Second Commandment forbids the use of such objects (pictures
and statues of Christ and/or His Father) *in private and public
worship*.[4]

The reasons we must not make or use man-made images in
worship are trenchant and penetrating.

Limiting

God's later instruction to Israel against making images was that
God is limitless and images are confining. He said:

> You saw no form of any kind the day the Lord spoke to you
> at Horeb out of the fire. Therefore watch yourselves very
> carefully, so that you do not become corrupt and make for
> yourselves an idol, an image of any shape, whether formed
> like a man or a woman, or like any animal on earth or any
> bird that flies in the air, or like any creature that moves along
> the ground or any fish in the water below. (Deuteronomy
> 4:15-18; cf. vv. 19, 20)

Since God is limitless, whenever man makes an image, he limits and thus denies God. We chain and warp our thoughts of Deity
when we shut them up in marble and paint.

Obscuring

In a similar way, images obscure God's glory. The problem with
images of God is that while they are ostensibly made to reveal
aspects of God, they end up hiding the real God. For example,
when Aaron made the golden calf (the bull image), he no doubt
thought he was honoring God by using such a symbol of power —
"Here is the bull who charged before you to bring you out of
Egypt." But Aaron was unwittingly masking and degrading God,
for how could a bull reveal God's moral excellence, gentleness, and
loving grace?

In fact, it may well be that the orgy that ignited in front of the golden bull image happened because the bull was not only a symbol of strength but of virility and sexual power. *Our human tendency is to become like the gods we worship.* That is, if we perpetually tailor our thoughts and prayers to fit an idolatrous image, we will begin to mentally ape that image.

Localizing

When we imagine that God is represented in a statue or painting, it naturally follows to subtly imagine that He is localized. Those who have been to countries such as Guatemala and have seen penitents on their bleeding knees approaching the steps of the Black Christ of Esquipulas will understand how an image can delude us into imagining a localized God.

Projecting

The Hebrews rightly believed that man was created in God's image (Genesis 1:26), but they also emphatically understood that God was not like man (Isaiah 55:8, 9). But through the delusion of idolatry, many of God's people began to create gods in their own images as they unconsciously projected their own weaknesses back onto Him. This was the essence of pagan idolatry — capricious, sensual deities that were projected magnifications of human weakness.

Controlling

Further, through an image, the great sovereign God of the universe, who is by definition limitless, infinite, and eternal, becomes to the worshiper a god imprisoned in plaster or wax or acrylic — and He is therefore controllable. Through images, then, one can own God and run one's universe to maximize need fulfillment. This is so attractive and comfortable for the sinful heart.

The makers of the forthcoming God doll say that the prototype is a white-haired, white-bearded, white man in a long rainbow-colored robe with all the animals of creation flowing from it. He's also about two feet tall. But a local Chicago talk show host says he's got an even better idea for the God doll. Why not simply market bags of clay? Then we could mold God into any image we wanted. Now there's an idea that will sell!

Subtracting

Lastly, in the words of Joy Davidman, "The real horror of idols is not merely that they give us nothing, but that they take away from us even that which we have."[5] Idols subvert what precious revelation we have of God through nature, conscience, and Scripture, thereby effectively burgling the knowledge of God from our very souls!

So we see that we have some very penetrating reasons why we must at all costs avoid making images. Namely, images are limiting, obscuring, localizing, projecting, controlling, and subtracting. Here we may be tempted to say, "I'm clean. For once in my life I'm home free. Lay it on me!" Well hold on — there's a bit more to the Second Commandment.

THE GRACIOUS DEPTH

The proper understanding of the Second Word requires that the prohibition against making material images of God also forbids dreaming up *mental* images. Imagining God in our heads can be a massive breach of the Commandment.

This is very much a "Christian sin." Our untaught, unthinking, unreading, self-absorbed, sentimental evangelical subculture houses thousands of idolaters. Christian idolatry is betrayed in this telltale phrase: "I like to think of God as _____."[6] What's used to fill in the blank can take many directions. "I like to think of God as a loving Father — as a mother — as an artist — as forgiving — as an architect."

Indeed, God is any one or all of these. But the problem is that such musings are often coupled with a denial of something else the Scriptures teach about God — for example, that He is Judge. We've all heard this line of reasoning: "I don't like to think of Him as a Judge, but as a loving Savior." Such subjectivism can inject just as much idolatrous limiting and projecting and controlling and subtracting as the grossest devotion to material images.

Negatively, we must avoid all subjective image-making of God. Positively, we must understand that God is totally transcendent, wholly other, infinite, and eternal — and thus beyond any human grasp. Further, while His being and power are revealed in His creation, we cannot know Him except by special revelation.

But in His grace, He has also spoken in His holy Word. What we need to do, rather than subjectively muse about His being, is to scour His Word — embracing both the things we *like* to think and do *not like* to think about God. This requires reading, thinking, meditation, prayer, and great humility as we ask God to reveal Himself. This demands a willingness to balance seemingly opposing truths in our minds in blessed theological tension. For example, God the Son is the submissive "Lamb of God, who takes away the sin of the world" (John 1:29) *and* the wrathful Lamb from whom men will attempt to hide (Revelation 6:16).

Happily, there is yet another great source of knowledge of God revealed in His Word — and that is that He has spoken in His Son, Jesus Christ (Hebrews 1:1, 2). John declared, "No one has ever seen God, but God the Only Son, who is at the Father's side, has made him known" (John 1:18). Jesus said, "I and the Father are one" (John 10:30), and, "Anyone who has seen me has seen the Father" (John 14:9). Paul said that God has "made his light shine in our hearts to give us the light of the knowledge of the glory of God in the face of Christ" (2 Corinthians 4:6). We need to comb the Gospels and the Epistles, drinking in everything we can find of Jesus because "In the past God spoke to our fore-fathers through the prophets at many times and in various ways, but in these last days he has spoken to us by his Son" (Hebrews 1:1, 2).

Now we begin to understand why this Commandment is the Second Word of Grace, because when you keep it *negatively*, you cleanse and protect your soul of every wrong thought of God. And when you keep it *positively*, you fill your soul with the knowledge of God through His Word and His Son. And if you do this, you see God more and more for what He is. And in so doing you will be able to love Him more and more and will thus worship Him better and better.

THE GRACIOUS WARNING

Understanding God's gracious prohibition, the gracious warning that concludes His Second Word makes ultimate sense — "for I, the Lord your God, am a jealous God, punishing the children for the sin of the fathers to the third and fourth generation of those who hate me" (Exodus 20:5b).

Divine Jealousy

That God is jealous may not ring properly in our ears because the word over the years has acquired an exclusively bad meaning. "Zealous" might be a better translation because the word is very close to that idea. God is zealous for His people to remain pure and devoted to Him. Even if we keep the jealous idea, if we think of God's love as marital love (which it is!), then it is a virtue, and its absence a sin. Here again is the divine *eros* of our loving God.

Divine Punishment

God's zeal will carry Him to great extremes to keep us faithful — "punishing," as he explains, "the children for the sin of the fathers to the third and fourth generations of those who hate me." A generational curse will extend for idolaters virtually as far as man can see in his life.[7] This means, essentially, that God leaves a man's off-spring as it is. He simply just lets go — as the idolaters wish — and the curse goes on. This can sometimes be a "negative grace" because the wretchedness that follows can, in God's mercy, become a springboard for an upward thrust into the atmosphere of His unmerited love!

THE GRACIOUS PROMISE

We need to note that the Second Word ends on a towering note of grace: "but showing love to thousands who love me and keep my commandments" (v. 6). I like the math here — four to one thousand — a curse for a human life span followed by a blessing of infinite grace. John Calvin says:

> Now by that he shows what is still better explained in other texts of Scripture, that he is slow to anger, inclined toward mercy, patient, and that, if his anger burns for a minute, his loving-kindness is for life and permanent. Thus there you have the true character of God; that he only wants to draw men in all gentleness and does so through his goodness. When he punishes them it is almost against his nature. Not that it is any more improper for God to punish than it is for him to be gracious, but he wishes to show us that his goodness is much greater, and, in brief, that he is not harsh; rather he only wants to open his heart to us if we will [but] permit him. In fact, he wills to be known as good and merciful; and it is in that that his glory principally shines.[8]

Judgment is God's "strange work," whereas grace is His natural work (cf. Isaiah 28:21; Psalm 103:8).

Oh, the blessing of a life that rejects idolatrous images both *material* and *mental*; which strives to know God through both His written Word, the Bible, and His ultimate Word, the Son; and which then loves and worships God with everything and keeps His Commandments. The divine inclination is to bless the "thousandth generation."[9] Think of it! This is indeed "grace for grace" (John 1:16, KJV).

DISCIPLINES OF GRACE

Seeing the stakes for what they are ought to motivate us to pursue the disciplines of grace with all we have.

• *Covenant to learn and be able to recite* the first two Words of Grace in sequence, remembering that the First forbids the *existence* of other gods, and the Second the *making* of other gods. Those of you who have children must take pains to help your children learn these, perhaps reciting them before meals and at bedtimes.

• *Reflect* as to whether you have *material* images that are serving as idols in your life and worship. Further reflect as to what extent you are a *mental* idolater. Have you limited your knowledge of God by confining thoughts to what you *like to think* about God?

• *Covenant to think about what the Scripture says about God*, whether you like it or not. This requires reading all His Word, and also giving special focus to Christ.

• *Pray for an idol-free life*, and ask for blessing to the thousandth generation for you and your church.

• *Discipline yourself*, for this is the Second Word of Grace!

> *Help me to discard*
>   *all false images of*
> *Thee, whatever the cost*
>   *to my comfort.*
>   —Anthony Bloom
>   *Living Prayer*

3

The Third Word of Grace

Loving God:
His *Reverence*

You shall not misuse the name
of the Lord your God.
EXODUS 20:7

THE DEMISE of civility in everyday language is a fact of American culture. Language has become increasingly vulgar and irreverent both to man and God precisely because there has been a devaluation of both man and God.

Paul Galloway, writing for the Fall 1992 *Chicago Tribune*, made a striking linguistic comparison between William Shakespeare's *Julius Caesar* and Chicago playwright David Mamet's *Glengarry Glen Ross*, noting that while both treat human greed and ambition, they are exactly 232 obscenities apart. Shakespeare managed to muddle his way through without a single blankety-blank, while Mamet managed his herculean 232 blankety-blanks with an astonishing 152 variations of his favorite vulgarity.[1]

Movie critic Michael Medved says, however, that on this point the record belongs to the 1990 Martin Scorsese film *Goodfellas*, which disgorged 272 expletives, 246 of which were variations of one single word. There was a major obscenity every 32.2 seconds![2] Of course, we all know that these "artistic" accomplishments have been eclipsed by the linguistic abyss of Two Live Crew and by some of America's most popular disc jockeys.

Interestingly, no one seems to be counting the blasphemous abuse of God's name — the number of times "God" and "O God!" are used as fillers for absent syntax and "Jesus" and "Christ" as divine exclamation points. Perhaps it is because the profaning of God's name is so commonplace that it attracts less notice — especially if the profanity is witty or "cute."

The fact is, today blasphemy is no longer considered *déclassé* but rather, if done smartly, a way of showing that one is urbane and "with it." A male blasphemer can employ the name "God" in such a way as to effect swagger and élan. And a skillful female blasphemer can find God's name, fashionably intoned, a marvelous way to communicate a worldly-wise, attractively-bored air. Today God is debased on every side and in ways so subtle that, as we shall see, they even entangle some believers.

But God's Word still stands: "You shall not misuse the name of the Lord your God, for the Lord will not hold anyone guiltless who misuses his name" (Exodus 20:7). This is the *Third Word of Grace*, and as we shall see, it is a third way that, if properly understood and observed, will open our lives further to the streams of God's grace.

THE MISUSE OF GOD'S NAME

To comprehend what is required for one not to misuse the name of the Lord our God, we must first understand what is meant by "name," and then by "misuse." "Name," as it is used here, is not a mere designation but a description of *character* — which here is the character "of the Lord your God" — literally, "Jehovah your God."

Jehovah (YHWH) is God's Old Testament name *par excellence*. It is the *redemptive* name of the God who chose His people and delivered them from bondage. It is the *covenantal* name of the God who keeps His promises to His people. As such, *Jehovah* is redolent with faithfulness. It is also the name of *relationship*, as Geoffrey Bromiley says: "the God who establishes a relationship of faithfulness and obedience, the God of mutual relationships of love."[3] *Jehovah* is an unutterably precious name.

This name was held so sacred that it was pronounced only once a year by the priest when giving the blessing on the great Day of Atonement (Leviticus 23:27). Israel came to value the name so much that when Scribes copied the manuscripts and came to the name Jehovah, they would stop, ceremonially bathe all over, and then go back to the scroll with an unused pen! Jehovah was the awesome personal, covenantal, promise-keeping name of God that must not be misused.

The idea of "misuse" (which the *King James Version* renders "take . . . in vain") means "unreal, empty, frivolous, insincere."[4] The idea is that you must not use the name of your God (who is utterly faithful and promise-keeping) insincerely or in an empty way.

Oaths

The primary application of this Command was in swearing an oath or a promise. When a believer swore by God that such-and-such was true, or made a promise by God's name to do a thing, it was to be done with utter sincerity — and such a promise must *never* be broken. Breaking one's promise was flagrant misuse of God's name.

Interestingly, in the Old Testament such oaths in God's name were actually encouraged. Deuteronomy 10:20 admonished the people, "Fear the Lord your God and serve him. Hold fast to him and take your oaths in his name." God even instructed them through Jeremiah that swearing in God's name was a sign of spiritual vitality: "And if they learn well the ways of my people and swear by my name, saying, 'As surely as the Lord lives' — even as they once taught my people to swear by Baal — then they will be established among my people" (Jeremiah 12:16). So in the Old Testament, oaths were assumed to be part of a committed life.

But once made, such oaths were not to be broken under any circumstance. Moses' writings repeatedly emphasize this: "Do not swear falsely by my name and so profane the name of your God. I am the Lord" (Leviticus 19:12). "When a man makes a vow to the Lord or takes an oath to obligate himself by a pledge, he must not break his word but must do everything he said" (Numbers 30:2). "If you make a vow to the Lord your God, do not be slow to pay it, for the Lord your God will certainly demand it of you and you will be guilty of sin" (Deuteronomy 23:21). God's teaching regarding keeping oaths was crystal-clear.

Tragically but predictably (human nature being what it is), by New Testament times the traditional, Biblical teaching regarding vows had come under amazing abuse. For example, some rabbis had begun to teach that an oath was not binding if it omitted God's name or did not imply it. Therefore, if you swore by your own life or someone else's life or the life of the king (as Abner did in 1 Samuel 17:55) or by your health (Psalm 15:4, KJV) or by some object, but avoided mentioning or alluding to the name of God, you were not bound. The *Mishnah* devotes one whole section called "*Shebuoth*" ("Oaths") to an elaborate discussion of when oaths are binding and when they are not.[5] In effect, the swearing of oaths had degenerated to a system that indicated when a man could lie and when not.

The results were disgraceful. There was a virulent epidemic of frivolous swearing. Oaths were continually mingled with everyday speech: "By your life" — "By my beard" — "May I never see the comfort of Israel if . . ." There was a trivialization of everyday language and a devaluation of integrity. Evasive swearing became a fine art. The height of accomplishment was, while lying, to convince another you were telling the truth by bringing some person or eminent object into reference. For instance, one rabbi taught that if one swore *by* Jerusalem, one was not bound; but if one swore *toward* Jerusalem, it was binding — evidently because the latter in some way implied the divine name. All of this produced a moral schizophrenia: "I'm really not lying, but I'm also not telling the truth." The use of oaths had become like children's "I had my fingers crossed!"

Recognizing the absurdity of the situation, Jesus gave them a piece of His divine mind as recorded in Matthew 5:34-36: "But I tell you, Do not swear at all: either by heaven, for it is God's throne; or by the earth, for it is his footstool; or by Jerusalem, for it is the city of the Great King. And do not swear by your head, for you cannot make even one hair white or black." Jesus ruled out making vows that used references to people or objects as backup. The reason for this is, *God stands behind everything*. The entire creation is God's, and you and I cannot call up a part of it without ultimately referring to Him. All oath-taking that calls into witness people or items of God's creation as witness is thus a grievous sin. If there is anything in our speech that even approaches swearing by something else, we must drop it at once.

Oath-taking is popular because people are liars. It's that simple. We all know that when someone says, "I mean it, swear to God" or "As God is my witness . . ." we had better watch out. Such a person is marking out an area of his life as true in distinction to the rest of his life. Thus, when we hear oaths in everyday speech, we can expect to be lied to.[6]

What are the implications of this radical teaching for our lives?

Are we never to take personal oaths? What about the public oaths we are asked to take in court? Some — for example, the Reformation's Anabaptists and later the Moravians and Quakers — have taken this as a prohibition against taking oaths in any circumstance. But this sets the standard higher than Christ did for Himself, because it is a fact that Jesus honored the official oath put upon him by Caiaphas before the Sanhedrin, as recorded in Matthew 26:63, 64a: "But Jesus remained silent. The high priest said to him, 'I charge you under oath by the living God: Tell us if you are the Christ, the Son of God.' 'Yes, it is as you say,' Jesus replied." In addition to Jesus' clear example, we have the repeated examples of Paul swearing that he is telling the truth: "I call God as my witness that it was in order to spare you that I did not return to Corinth" (2 Corinthians 1:23). "God, whom I serve with my whole heart in preaching the gospel of his Son, is my witness how constantly I remember you in my prayers at all times . . ." (Romans 1:9). Paul would never have called God a witness that he was telling the truth if he thought such a practice was wrong.

How does this translate into our lives today? Oath-taking is permitted. In civil life — for example, in a courtroom — oath-taking is proper. And when one is put under oath, he or she is not sinning against either the Third Commandment or Christ's teaching by answering. Moreover, there are very positive religious oaths for us all. For example, when a man and woman stand before me and make their wedding vows, I solemnly abjure them saying, "These vows are for life; they may never be broken. God, this congregation, your family, and your friends are witness." And later, if the Lord gives them children, the mutual promise they make to God at the baptism or dedication of their children is to bring them up in "the nurture and admonition of the Lord" (Ephesians 6:4, KJV).

But (and this is the great point), vows, oaths, and promises made before God are *never* to be broken. Willful breach is a gross misuse of God's name and thus a grievous breaking of the Third Commandment. Any promise we make, whether we call God as a witness or not, is made in the presence of God and must be kept, because as Christians (indwelt by the Holy Spirit) God's name is automatically inserted whether we verbalize it or not. Any Christian life other than one which is radically sincere and truthful misuses the name of the Lord our God! The call is exhilaratingly high!

But this is just one way God's name is misused. There are several others, a few of which call for specific mention.

Irreverence

There is the common irreverence we have alluded to that is constantly saying "God" and "O God" like a cocktail party groupie in a Neal Simon play. Some begin half their *positive* sentences by using the name of Jesus in a disrespectful way. And when they hit their thumb with a hammer, they hit a *negative* nadir, spitting out both names of our Lord, along with some blue curses. Some consider such use of Jesus' name as fashionable, but it is mindless and wrong. As Lord Byron, an accomplished blasphemer himself, observed of a friend, "He knew not what to say, and so he swore." As someone so aptly put it, "Profanity is the linguistical crutch of the inarticulate."

Such speech may be fashionable in the circles of men, but with God it is eternally unfashionable — unless one likes the style of Hell.

Contempt

A step below irreverence is contempt for God, calculated malice, like that of the older waiter in Ernest Hemingway's "A Clean, Well-Lighted Place," who parodies the Lord's Prayer: "Our nada who art in nada, nada be thy name thy name thy kingdom nada thy will be nada in nada as it is in nada...." But perhaps more people today are familiar with Bart Simpson's "grace": "We made all this stuff. So thanks for nothing! Amen." This is an affront to God.

Cursing

The ultimate depth is using God's name to curse others. Some scholars believe this is what Goliath did when he "cursed David by his gods" — that is, he may have used David's God's name, Jehovah, to curse David (cf. 1 Samuel 17:43). To damn someone in God's name is a monstrous misuse of God's name. The tongue that descends to such abuse houses a hideous mouth and soul. "'Their throats are open graves; their tongues practice deceit.' 'The poison of vipers is on their lips.' 'Their mouths are full of cursing and bitterness'" (Romans 3:13, 14).

These are a few of the principal ways men misuse God's name: insincere, unkept *oaths*; casual *irreverence*; blatant *contempt*; and employing God's name as a *curse*. These forms of speech all have this in common: they are wretched abuses of God's name. And all have a common effect: to stop up the free flow of grace in a believer's life. The misuse of God's name will leave one high and dry on a horizonless spiritual Sahara.

Besides this, there are other profound reasons why we must not misuse or abuse God's name.

What Misuse Does to God

In one sense, on the ultimate level, misuse of God's name cannot hurt God — puny men cannot harm the transcendent God. But there is also a sense in which He has made Himself vulnerable to us by electing to deliver us from our "Egypts" and then adopting us as His children. And because our awesome God, whose name we are not even worthy to take on our lips, has become our Father, it is an incalculable outrage and slap at God to abuse His name. Further, what a horrific thing it is to misuse the name of Jesus — for the lips of those He has saved to dishonor Him. John Calvin put it with unusual poignancy:

Now this applies to us today. For when the Son of God, who is ordained the judge of the world, shall come in the last day, he will be able to say to us: "What? You have carried my name, you have been baptized in memory and testimony that I was your Redeemer; I drew you out of the pit into which you had plunged. I delivered you from eternal death by means of the cruel death which I suffered. And for this cause I was made man. I submitted myself to the punishment of God my Father in order that you might benefit by my grace and way, and here is the reward which you have paid me, that I am torn to pieces by you, that I am thrown there in opprobrium, that the death which I endured for you is [held] in mockery, that my blood which is the washing and purging of your soul is trodden under foot; in brief that you have taken the occasion to blaspheme and vilify against me as if I were a poor detestable creature."[7]

Beloved in Christ, if we truly understand who God is, and who God the Son is, our hair will stand on end at the very thought of abusing His name!

What Misuse Does to Us

But the verbal misuse of God's name is not only an assault on Him, but also an attack by ourselves on our own persons. It is a fact that the way we verbally reference another person has a profound effect on how we regard and treat that person. For example, if I consistently tell my wife that I love her — "Barbara, I love you. My dear, I love you with all my heart" — I will love her better! The reason is, of course, that verbalizing my love for her elevates and substantiates my love. Conversely, if I never verbally say, "I love you" and in fact verbally deride her, my love will be further crippled. It is similarly true that just imagining I love my wife, even concentrating on thoughts of love, will not elevate my love as much as verbalizing it will.

Just so with God. The proper use of His name will elevate and substantiate my love. But the misuse of His name through insincere *vows* or *irreverence* or *contempt* or *cursing* will stunt my capacity for relating to Him. Verbal reverence for God's name is of incalculable importance to my soul.

What Misuse Does to Others

The misuse and abuse of God's name can have dire effects on the lives of others, especially those closest to us. Children who grow up where God's name is not properly reverenced and even abused through, say, flippancy and occasional contempt by their parents will often draw some tragic deductions about God's worth and relevance. Too many children have been damned by their church-attending parents' abuse of God's name!

What reverence we are called to by this Third Word of Grace! The positive corollary is: "You shall always properly use and reverence the name of the Lord your God."

PUNISHMENT FOR MISUSING GOD'S NAME

The penalty for misusing God's name receives powerful emphasis in the final phrase of the command: "for the Lord will not hold anyone guiltless who misuses his name" (v.7b). Everyone — no exceptions — will pay a great price for abusing God's name.

Punishment in This Life

We have already alluded to this because, as we know, the misuse of God's name can curse the lives of those we love most. In addition, the abuse of His name snaps open an umbrella that deflects the showers of grace God desires to give us!

Punishment in the Life to Come

The fact is, in the life to come we will be evaluated and judged by our words. Our Lord gave a mighty discourse on this in which He said, "But I tell you that men will have to give account on the day of judgment for every careless word they have spoken. For by your words you will be acquitted, and by your words you will be condemned" (Matthew 12:36, 37).

Speech is the sacred vehicle of the invisible soul, the most spiritual, non-material function of the body. Jesus said, "For out of the overflow of the heart the mouth speaks" (Matthew 12:34). Speech diagrams the unseen soul. In this respect the ancient Hebrews viewed words as quasi-material, almost palpable. This is why they were so careful with what they said. How this wisdom is needed for today's believers who are inundated with a constant flow of insincere media verbiage almost all their waking hours. We need to cultivate our speech — especially as to how our mouths relate to God.

THE PROPER USE OF GOD'S NAME

I am convinced beyond a shadow of a doubt that the key for a proper use of God's name, or steeling ourselves against its misuse, is a proper understanding of God. If we truly know who God is, we will never come close to abusing His name! If we could really see God's *eternity* (that He is without beginning and end), if we could see His *limitlessness* (that the entire universe cannot contain Him), if we could see His *power* (that every throb of power originates from Him), if we could see His *holiness* (that He is so awesomely pure that even the unfallen angels cover themselves in His presence), if we could see all this and let it penetrate our souls, we would never come close to misusing His name! In other words, if we could allow the Scriptures to liberate us from our idolatrous, limited views of God, we would never foul His name, ever!

This Third Word of Grace says positively, "You shall lift up the name of the Lord your God." Here we must take careful notice that this is precisely what Jesus prayed for in the opening petition of the Lord's Prayer, for Jesus began His great pattern for prayer with a positive petition that the Third Commandment be upheld, saying: "Our Father in heaven, hallowed be your name" (Matthew 6:9). In other words, "Heavenly Father, let Your name be lifted up as holy by Your children! Let everything in the universe declare You as holy. Hallowed be Your name!"

The positive thrust of the Third Commandment against the misuse of God's name is a powerful admonition to make every effort to reverence His name. This calls, first, for one to purpose to *personally reverence* God's name through reflecting on the majesty of His name, which includes His infinitude (His utter limitlessness), His stunning holiness, and His astounding condescension in effecting a relationship with us built on His promise. His name must reverently be on our lips in personal prayer and song.

Our personal reverence is meant to produce a *domestic reverence* for His name, so that our spouses and children never hear His name abused in any way within the home — not even in jest. Within the home God's name must be recalled in unaffected reverence so that all naturally give Him the deepest respect.

When one reverences God privately and domestically, *public reverence* will follow most naturally, so that regardless of what happens (embarrassment, pain, surprise, humiliation, horror, anger) God's name will never be abused or used as a curse.

Lastly, there is the *corporate reverencing* of God's name in divine worship, which is the primary place to instill respect for God's name. The corporate ethos of God's people, the way they speak His name and lift it up with reverent lips in prayer, song, and preaching, will be massively influential on our children and new converts in instilling wholesome reverence. How we conduct ourselves, how God's name falls from our lips, and how we sing of Him in our hymns will bear eternal consequences in building up a people who shrink from the slightest misuse of God's name.

DISCIPLINES OF GRACE

• Recognizing that we live in a culture that regularly misuses God's name, *we must check our lives* to see if we are participants in any or even all the common abuses.

Take a few minutes to quietly reflect and evaluate yourself in the following areas:

- Oaths
- Irreverence
- Contempt
- Curses

• *Covenant to reverence God's name verbally.*

Realizing that verbalizing one's love for God elevates and substantiates it, take some time alone to tell God out loud that you love him.

• If you are a parent, *consciously see to it that you reverence God's name with your children.*

Speak of God, not in affected pious tones but with honest reverence.

• *Ask God to take away your idolatrous mental images of Him,* so that in seeing Him as he reveals Himself, you will not be inclined to ever misuse His name. Then flesh out this prayer as appropriate to your own life:

Hallowed be Your name *personally* in my interior life.

Hallowed be Your name *domestically* in my private home life.

Hallowed be Your name *publicly* in my life in the world.

Hallowed be Your name *corporately* in my worship within the Body of Christ.

The proper use of God's name — this is the way to keep the gates of grace wide open.

This is the Third Word of Grace!

4

The Fourth Word of Grace

Loving God:
His *Time*

*Remember the Sabbath day
by keeping it holy.*
EXODUS 20:8–11

B Y THE TIME of Christ, the Fourth Commandment —
"Remember the Sabbath day by keeping it holy" — had
become the unintended basis for exotic legalisms. To ensure
that no work be performed on the Sabbath, thirty-nine clarifica-
tions of work were devised, with each category capable of endless
subdivision. One category forbade the carrying of *burdens* and
hedged it with minute prohibitions for every situation. Anything
equal to, or heavier than, a dried fig was declared a burden. So it
was permissible to carry half a fig on the Sabbath, unless one put
it down and picked it up, thus doubling the weight to a full fig and
so breaking the Sabbath!

Similarly, if a person was in one place and extended his or her
hand, which was holding a piece of fruit, into another place, and

the Sabbath began at that moment, the person would have to drop it that instant. Otherwise he or she would be breaking the Sabbath by transporting a burden from one locality to another.

Happily, one could pick up a child on the Sabbath, provided the child's hands were first examined to make sure they had nothing in them, for otherwise that would involve lifting a burden. Less happily, false teeth were not permitted on the Sabbath because they might fall out, and the poor denture-wearer would be tempted to pick them up, thus sinning against the Sabbath.

Another category prohibited *travel* on the Sabbath. So the rabbis defined a permissible Sabbath day's journey as two thousand cubits (one thousand yards). To walk one inch further was an egregious breach of the Sabbath. However, if a rope was tied across the end of one's street creating an *eruv*, then the legal fiction was that the whole street became a single house, and so one could walk one thousand yards beyond the rope. Interestingly, present-day Orthodox Jews have perpetuated the *eruv* by marking off areas of modern cities with symbolic "gateways" of thin wire stretched between tall, slender poles. Today there are *eruvim* in such cities as Los Angeles, Toronto, and Miami. The *eruv* that contains the White House dates from 1990.[1]

One of the largest of the thirty-nine categories dealt with guarding one against *labor*. Here, women were forbidden to gaze into a mirror on the Sabbath, because they might discover a white hair and be tempted to pluck it, which would be a grievous sin. While eating, a radish could be dipped in salt, but not left too long, since one would then be performing the labor of pickling the radish. Spitting was allowed on the Sabbath, provided one spit into his handkerchief or on the rocks. But it was unlawful to spit on the ground, because one might inadvertently scuff the spittle and the earth with his sandal, thereby plowing and cultivating the earth. So being a righteous person under this system depended more or less on which way a person spit![2] And so went the legalisms and abstruse rules *ad infinitum* — all to hedge the Sabbath.

Thus, the *Fourth Word of Grace*, which was meant to enhance God's people's love for Him and open them further to the flow of His favor, became a relentless burden. Israel's great Sabbath day became a "day of don'ts." To be sure, some souls, due to their deep devotion, managed a day of joyous worship. But for many, legalism had murdered the Sabbath. Seeing this, our goal is to uncover the Sabbath for what it was, see how it related to the Christian church's radically new Lord's Day, and then consider how to enhance the flow of God's grace in our lives today.

THE SABBATH

The Sabbath's Newness

The command to keep the Sabbath holy was a new law, a *lex nova* for God's people. There had never been a law like it before this giving of the Fourth Commandment to Israel. Interestingly, God, in creation, had celebrated a divine Sabbath for Himself at the consummation of his six days of work, as Genesis 2:2, 3 informs us: "By the seventh day God had finished the work he had been doing; so on the seventh day he rested from all his work. And God blessed the seventh day and made it holy, because on it he rested from all the work of creating that he had done." But His divine Sabbath celebration was not a "creation ordinance" (a law directing humankind to observe the Sabbath), as some have alleged. There is no command in Genesis 2:2, 3 and in fact no mention of humanity. Everything is focused on God.[3]

But even more telling is the fact that there is no evidence whatsoever that the Sabbath was observed by Israel before her being commanded to do so in the Ten Commandments. For example, the history of the pre-diluvians, including Noah, and then of the patriarchs beginning with Abraham, mentions many things — prayers, sacrifices, even circumcision — but *no* Sabbath-keeping! The only reference to such is in the prelude to the giving of the Fourth Commandment, which occurred in God's giving Israel manna exactly one week prior to Sinai (cf. Exodus 16:1 and 19:1). As the account goes, Moses ordered them to gather a double portion of manna on the sixth day saying:

> This is what the Lord commanded: "Tomorrow is to be a day of rest, a holy Sabbath to the Lord. . . . Bear in mind that the Lord has given you the Sabbath; that is why on the sixth day he gives you bread for two days. Everyone is to stay where he is on the seventh day." (Exodus 16:23, 29)

Thus, they were prepared for the *lex nova*, the great new Sabbath law which was about to come!

The Sabbath's Requirement

When God's voice rolled down the slopes of Mt. Sinai, the command was most explicit as to its requirements:

> Remember the Sabbath day by keeping it holy. Six days you shall labor and do all your work, but the seventh day is a Sabbath to the Lord your God. On it you shall not do any work, neither you, nor your son or daughter, nor your manservant or maidservant, nor your animals, nor the alien within your gates. (Exodus 20:8-10)

The grand emphasis of the Command is total *rest*. Significantly, nothing is said about worship or religious observances, though such were implicit. But the emphasis on rest made the Command a foundational piece of social and humanitarian legislation. Everyone and everything was entitled to rest — even one's donkey! As the renowned Jewish scholar Abraham Heschel wrote: "The

Sabbath is a day for the sake of life. Man is not a beast of burden, and the Sabbath is not for the purpose of enhancing work."[4] The Sabbath also instructed all humankind that there is more to life than work. For these reasons the Sabbath's unexceptionable demand of rest was a great grace.

The Sabbath's Function

When God gave this Fourth Commandment, He alluded to the memory of His own divine Sabbath: "For in six days the Lord made the heavens and the earth, the sea, and all that is in them, but he rested on the seventh day. Therefore the Lord blessed the Sabbath day and made it holy" (v. 11). The Sabbath became a remembrance of God's own rest from the work of creation — a remembrance of His own genesis rhythm. Being omnipotent, God did not have to rest after creation. Regardless of how great the outflow of His power, He was not depleted one whit. But He delighted to rest, and He blessed and sanctified the seventh day — and the sabbatic pattern. The Mosaic Sabbath built on this creational rhythm. As we know, the year is made up of twelve lunar months, each having twenty-eight days, which then gives us four seven-day phases. The Sabbath rides on these rhythms.[5]

Physically, then, the created order is such that humankind needs a rest — in the pattern of the seven-day cycle. This has been proven repeatedly in history. During the French Revolution, radicals abolished Sunday, but they found that the health of the nation suffered, and they had to reinstitute it.[6] The Russian Communists, on the theory that they had created a new man, instituted a much-ballyhooed ten-day week. But despite its superworkers (*stakonovites*), the new social order miserably failed. God's rhythm is best for men and women because God created them.

Spiritually, the seven-day pattern is best for the soul, for properly observed in worship it brings Heaven's cadence to all of life.

Thus, the memory of the divine pattern enlightens us to the wisdom of the Sabbath rest. But there was also a second memory demanded of the Israelites as they obeyed the Sabbath law, and it is given in Deuteronomy 5:15's version of the Fourth Commandment: "Remember that you were slaves in Egypt and that the Lord your God brought you out of there with a mighty hand and an outstretched arm. Therefore the Lord your God has commanded you to observe the Sabbath day." While in Egypt they had no rest. But with their divinely wrought redemption came the rest that had eluded them for hundreds of years. Therefore on the Sabbath they were not only to rest but to celebrate their redemption and liberation.

How beautiful and revelatory the Sabbath Command was. Though it did not come out of nothing, it was a *lex nova*, a brand-new, first-time Command. Its positive thrust commanded rest on the seventh day. The Sabbath's purpose was to grace God's people — to grace their bodies with rest of the genesis rhythm — to grace their souls with Heaven's rhythm, providing Israel with respite from their labors so they could focus on God and gratefully commemorate their gracious liberation. It was, indeed, the *Fourth Word of Grace*. And what joy it was to the righteous soul, as Isaiah sang:

> *"If you keep your feet from breaking the Sabbath*
> *and from doing as you please on my holy day,*
> *if you call the Sabbath a delight*
> *and the Lord's holy day honorable,*
> *and if you honor it by not going your own way*
> *and not doing as you please or speaking idle words*
> *then you will find your joy in the Lord,*
> *and I will cause you to ride on the heights of the land*
> *and to feast on the inheritance of your father Jacob."*
> *The mouth of the Lord has spoken.*
>
> —Isaiah 58:13, 14

THE SABBATH AND JESUS

As we have noted, in Christ's time the Sabbath and its gracious flow had been strangled for many by the volumes of relentless legalisms written to protect the Sabbath. It was time for a new day to rise.

Jesus' Sabbath

When we consider Jesus' relationship to the Sabbath, we must keep in mind that the Mosaic Sabbath with its demand for cessation from work was not designed to promote inactivity so much as to promote total abstention from one's daily work. Thus understood, we can categorically state that Jesus never broke the Sabbath. For example, when on the Sabbath His disciples picked ears of corn and ate them, they were not breaking the Law (cf. Mark 2:23-28). Likewise Jesus' healings were not a part of the daily work of a medical practitioner (cf. Matthew 12:9-14; John 5:9-16). Jesus and His disciples broke the rabbinical extension of the Law, but not the Biblical Law.[7]

In respect to the Fourth Commandment, Jesus' declaration, "Do not think that I have come to abolish the Law or the Prophets; I have not come to abolish them but to fulfill them" (Matthew 5:17), is most helpful. The fact that He did not come to "abolish" the Law emphasizes His *continuity* with the Fourth Commandment, while His intention to "fulfill" it emphasizes His *discontinuity*. He superseded the Sabbath Commandment by establishing the Lord's Day.[8]

THE LORD'S DAY

The Sabbath Superseded

Christ's advent eventuated the prominence of a new day, "the first day" of the week, Sunday, which became the church's "Lord's Day." The evidence for this is as follows:

Resurrection. The first day of the week was certainly the day Christ rose from the dead, for many references mention "the first day" (Matthew 28:1; Mark 16:1, 2; Luke 24:1; John 20:1).

Emmaus. On the first day Jesus appeared to some of His followers and broke bread with them on the road to Emmaus (Luke 24:13-35).

Thomas. One week after the resurrection, Christ appeared to Thomas and the disciples on the first day (John 20:26; cf. v. 19).

Pentecost? It is possible, though not certain, that the outpouring of the Holy Spirit at Pentecost took place on the first day (this is dependent on Sadducean chronology).

Worship. The New Testament indicates that early Christian worship took place on the first day. Acts 20:7, which describes Christians as gathering together "on the first day of the week . . . to break bread," is a decided reference to Sunday and not Saturday. The language suggests this was a regular occurrence. 1 Corinthians 16:2 — "On the first day of every week, each one of you should set aside a sum of money in keeping with his income, saving it up, so that when I come no collections will have to be made" — has implicit reference to taking an offering on the first day.

"Lord's Day." In the Revelation, John records, "On the Lord's Day I was in the Spirit" (1:10), thus providing evidence that the first day was so established that it was titled the "Lord's Day."

So by the beginning of the second century the Lord's Day was universally understood to be the Christian day of worship. The *Didache* (the first worship manual of the church), written just after A.D. 100, instructed believers, "On the Lord's Day come together, break bread, and hold Eucharist" (14:1). Ignatius, writing about

110, states that Christians have come to a new hope — "no longer living for the Sabbath, but for the Lord's Day" (*To the Magnesians*, 9:1).

Significantly, when the Lord's Day replaced the Sabbath it was not a day of rest. A day of rest was impossible at first — especially for the poor and the slaves. Because Christians worked on the Lord's Day, they met either early in the morning or in the evening after work. It was in such an evening meeting that poor Eutychus fell sound asleep, as the Apostle Paul talked on and on, and fell out of a third-story window (cf. Acts 20:7-12). Even in cases where it was possible not to work on the Lord's Day, people still worked. Jerome tells in his *Letters* (108:20) of a fifth-century religious order proceeding to church and then, upon returning home, devoting themselves to their tasks as garment makers. Worship and work went together on the Lord's Day.[9]

The fact is, the post-apostolic church hardly references the Fourth Commandment. New Testament scholar Andrew Lincoln observes, "It is almost as if the Sabbath commandment were not a part of the Decalogue."[10]

Actually, it wasn't until Constantine that the Lord's Day received political and social prominence. And from there a theology developed in the church, culminating in the eighth century, which identified Sunday with Sabbath. This was the received position at the time of the Reformation — except that there was a great laxity in matters of Sunday pleasure.

When the Reformation began, the Reformers were unanimous that the Lord's Day and the Sabbath were not the same, and they were equally of one opinion that the Fourth Commandment had been superseded. Luther's *Large Catechism* directs that the common people must have a day of rest and refreshment, a day on which they may assemble to "hear and desire God's Word and then praise God with song and prayer." That day could be any day, but from ancient times Sunday has been designated for this purpose, and there is no reason to change it.[11]

Calvin's *Institutes of the Christian Religion* states: "For because it was expedient to overthrow superstition, the day sacred to the Jews was set aside; because it was necessary to maintain decorum, order, and peace in the church, another was appointed for that purpose" (2.8.33). Calvin concludes: "For those of them who cling to their constitutions surpass the Jews three times over in crass carnal Sabbatarian superstition" (2.8.34).[12] Calvin's translator remarks: "It is clear from this passage . . . that for Calvin the Christian Sunday is not . . . a simple continuation of the Jewish Sabbath 'changed into the first day of the week,' but a distinctively Christian institution adopted on the abrogation of the former one, as a means of church order and spiritual health."[13] Calvin's position is consciously anti-Sabbatarian.[14]

The *Second Helvetic Confession* summarizes regarding the Lord's Day:

> In regard hereof, we see that in the ancient churches there were not only certain set hours in the week appointed for meetings, but that also the Lord's Day itself, ever since the apostles' time, was consecrated to religious exercises and to a holy rest; which also is now very well observed by our churches, for the worship of God and the increase of charity. . . . Yet herein we give no place unto the Jewish observation of the day, or in any superstitions. For we do not account one day to be holier than another, nor think that mere rest is of itself acceptable to God. Besides, we do celebrate and keep the Lord's Day, and not the Jewish Sabbath, and that with a free observation. (chapter 24)[15]

So the Reformers were in concert in not identifying the Sabbath with the Lord's Day.

But in the English Puritan branch of the Reformation it was quite another matter because they developed a highly-refined "Sabbath transference theology" that carried the day in the mid-seventeenth century and was given monumental expression in the 1648 *Westminster Confession*. This wrongly termed the Lord's Day the Sabbath and affirmed:

> As it is the law of nature, that, in general, a due proportion of time be set apart for the worship of God; so, in his work, by a positive, moral and perpetual commandment, binding all men in all ages, he hath particularly appointed one day in seven for a sabbath, to be kept holy unto him; which, from the beginning of the world to the resurrection of Christ, was the last day of the week; and, from the resurrection of Christ, was called the Lord's Day, and is to be continued to the end of the world, as the Christian Sabbath. This Sabbath is then kept holy unto the Lord, when men, after due preparing of their hearts, and ordering of their common affairs beforehand, do not only observe a holy rest all the day from their own works, words and thoughts about their worldly employment and recreations: but also are taken up the whole time in the public and private exercises of his worship, and in the duties of necessity and mercy. (21, 7, 8)

This is to my mind a position that cannot be supported from the Scriptures, from the history of the apostolic and post-apostolic church, or from the original leaders of the Reformation. I say this carefully and with respect because I rarely disagree with the magisterial *Confession*.

Days Compared[16]

There are, of course, similarities between the Sabbath and the Lord's Day.

Weekly

The most obvious similarity is that both are weekly, recognizing a distinction for one day in seven. Both stand on the genesis rhythm stamped in the weekly cycle of our cosmos.

Redemption

Both have an emphasis on redemption. The Sabbath memorialized God's redemption of His people from Egypt (cf. Deuteronomy 5:15). The Lord's Day celebrates redemption through the triumph of Jesus' resurrection.

Worship

Sabbath and Sunday are linked by their provision for worship. Though worship was not a primary feature of the Mosaic Sabbath, it did develop as an emphasis, especially with the rise of the synagogue.

Lordship

Both days emphasize God's Lordship. On the Sabbath His Lordship was elevated by one's ceasing from work for a whole day. But on the first day of the week, the Lord's Day, His Lordship is held up as believers meet for worship. The fundamental focus of the Sabbath was on abstaining from work, but the focus of the Lord's Day centers on worship of the living Lord.

These similarities are important, for in the superseding Lord's Day, the Sabbath similarities inform and enrich our worship. Having seen this, the grand transcending distinctions of each are these: The Sabbath's distinctive is *rest*, in cessation from labor; and the Lord's Day distinctive is *worship* of the risen Lord. As Christians, worship is absolutely binding upon us as a matter of regular Lord's Day observance (cf. Hebrews 10:25). As Christians, *rest* (cessation from labor), while it is not demanded, must be a matter for prayerful and humble application, as we shall see.

LORD'S DAY WORSHIP

The Lord's Day is Resurrection Day. Every Sunday when we assemble, we commemorate the resurrection of our Lord Jesus Christ. I'm in sympathy with the great nineteenth-century English preacher R. W. Dale, who was so taken with this reality that he demanded that a resurrection hymn be sung every Sunday morning. There is a sense in which every Sunday is Easter Sunday. We serve a risen Savior. That's why it is the *Lord's* Day!

When we assemble for worship, we are gathered to offer *praise* to our risen Redeemer who, the Revelation reveals, walks by and around the flickering candle of His church as the awesome "son of man" (cf. Revelation 1:12ff.). We do not come to worship in order to rest or relax, but for a heightened awareness that focuses on Jesus and His saving, healing power.

Our praise is wedded with corporate *prayer* that mutually focuses and elevates our souls. We *hear* God's Word and are instructed in truths immemorial. We learn how to love God, and we learn how to live under his ethic. We *give*, we *fellowship*, and we depart for *service.*

Joy is the medium of the Lord's Day, contrary to popular myth and sometimes, sadly, reality. The minister of a Scottish congregation had to travel some distance from his home to the church where he was to conduct the worship service. It was winter, and the river that flowed past both his home and the church was completely frozen over. Being an excellent ice skater, the minister decided to skate to the church. Church members gathering outside the building were surprised to see their preacher on skates — flushed but ready for divine worship!

The incident spawned debate as to whether the minister should have skated on the Sabbath. The elders then met and discussed the matter at great length. The argument raged back and forth on the question of whether the practicality of getting to church or the keeping of the Sabbath should be the prime consideration.

At last came the vital question to the minister: "Did you enjoy skating up the river?"[17] You see, pleasure and the Lord's Day were thought to be mutually exclusive!

Sunday is indeed a day of joy, but it ought also to be a day of feasting, though not necessarily at an elaborate meal. As Ignatius well said, "To fast on the Lord's day is to kill Christ; but to rejoice in the Lord this day, and to rejoice in all the duties of this day, and to rejoice in that redemption that was wrought for us on this day, this is to crown Christ, this is to lift up Christ."[18] The Lord's Day is the day for a joyous table with family and friends and the needy and the searching.

Finally, Sunday is a day for action rather than inaction. It is not a day for idleness. We do not honor the Lord's Day by doing nothing. It is a day to serve in the church, to teach, to counsel, to reach out to others, to evangelize. All this and more is to be part of Lord's Day worship!

LORD'S DAY REST

As we have seen, although the Sabbath's command to cease from all menial labor is not binding upon us, we nevertheless ought to submit our lives to the divine rhythm. Our bodies and souls need the genesis rhythm of regular rest one day a week. If we can't get it on Sunday, we must find it elsewhere. Ironically, rest on the Lord's Day is a near impossibility for a preacher. Normally, I rise at 4 A.M. on the Lord's Day, preach twice in the morning, doctor some needy souls late in the afternoon, preside at evening worship, and often, along with my wife, meet again with others after the service to offer counsel and prayer. My rest has to come another day.

But for most people, the perfect day for rest *is* the Lord's Day. And if so, wise Christians will carefully plan to joyfully embrace

God's gracious rhythm. Sometimes what we need most physically and spiritually is sleep, as Eugene Peterson imaginatively puts it:

> While we sleep, great and marvelous things, far beyond our capacities to invent or engineer, are in process — the moon marking the seasons, the lion roaring for its prey, the earthworms aerating the earth, the stars turning in their courses, the proteins repairing our muscles, our dreaming brains restoring a deeper sanity beneath the gossip and scheming of our waking hours.[19]

We must also understand that rest and relaxation are not mutually exclusive. John Calvin knew how to pray and play. His reputation for humorless austerity doesn't square with the facts. He led his congregation in worship in the morning and in the afternoon went among the people of Geneva and played skittles, an ancient version of bowling![20]

Having put the Lord's Day in Biblical perspective, it must also be said that whether one is a Sabbatarian or holds that the Lord's Day and Sabbath are separate institutions, all must mourn the immense tragedy of the demise of the observance of the Lord's Day in the second half of the twentieth century. Christianity has come to a sorry state when one can attend church on Saturday night and give a convenient "nod to God" so that the Lord's Day can be a full day of play! What a travesty to choose the early service because it won't interfere with the next ten hours of hedonism. Quick, get home from church, change, stuff the kids in the car, hoist in the cooler, shove in a Beach Boys tape, head for the beach, eat, watch the air show, eat, play a little football until someone gets banged up, eat, return home exhausted, and drift off into a brain-dead stupor, dreading Monday morning. Praise the Lord!

This is a tragedy of immense proportions. The Lord's Day has been lost to millions of professing Christians — to the impoverishment of their own souls, for they have abandoned a major path to loving God.

What is the answer? Certainly it is not a draconian legalism which hedges the Lord's Day about with little rules. But it must begin with two things: an acknowledgment, first, that we ought to do our best to make the Lord's Day holy, and second, that if we don't plan to have a great Lord's Day, we won't — it will be more like a Chevy Chase vacation! I will now risk being interpreted as "legalistic" by suggesting some personal disciplines.

DISCIPLINES OF GRACE

• *Preparation.* To begin with, we ought to prepare for the Lord's Day. Edith Schaeffer tells how, when living in Villars, Switzerland, the church bells would toll every Saturday at 4:30 P.M. as a reminder to prepare for the Lord's Day. The bells were ignored by most but were a poignant reminder of a more enlightened day. My point is, we need to begin thinking about the Lord's Day *before* Saturday night.

Parents, and I mean both men and women, how much more meaningful the day would be if clothing were laid out and food decided upon and if everyone headed to bed at a reasonable time. How much better the Lord's Day would be if Christian families took just two minutes on Saturday evening to pray for God's blessing on the worship and events of the day. How much better if we fasted from TV in preparation. And on Sunday morning, how far better it would be if a wife never heard, "Honey, you got the kids ready yet? I'm going to be late," but instead something like, "Dear, the boys are ready, and so am I."

• *Participation.* Lord's Day participation could be made so much more meaningful by arriving a few minutes early, getting the kids situated, and slipping into church to read the text and hymns and offer some prayer.

• *Preservation.* Then there's the matter of preserving what has happened. Here I am compelled to say that there is no better way to erase worship than to turn on the TV when you walk in the house after church. Sunday afternoon football, and sports in general, with the incessant beer commercials and inane chatter, is a sure-fire way to flatten out one's spiritual brain waves. And the whole family will suffer — "You want daddy to look at your Sunday school paper? In a moment, son . . . at half-time maybe." Men, if you're the kind who sits in church fretting because you've already missed the first quarter of the game and wondering when the preacher is going to end, you will rarely get anything out of the service! Indeed, the cultivation and preservation of the spiritual benefits of the Lord's Day demands thoughtful discipline and sacrifice.

• And, of course, there is the matter of *rest*. For most of us, the Lord's Day is the best day to rest, because Christianity's past influence has made it the day most people have off. And Christians ought to make use of the day for rest — not legalistically, but in thankful observance of the genesis rhythm. For some, that rest may be sleep. For some, it may include some activity. If so, we must keep in mind the distinction between the older understanding of recreation as *re-creation* and the modern pursuit of recreation. In broad strokes, today's idea of recreation is a hedonistic pursuit of pleasure. It's not re-creative but destructive.

The older, wiser way of re-creating is the way to go. Forget your regular labors, and re-create with *conversation* with family and friends. A common, unrushed meal around a table is so important. Especially re-creative are *picnics, walks, swims,* or *playing* with the kids, wrestling on the floor, shooting baskets with the boys. Listening to *good music* is also a marvelous way to re-create. A great *"read"* in one of the Christian classics is a time-proven way to restore the soul as well.

Think of it — the Lord's Day, a day to show love for Him —

a day to break your frantic rhythm and allow Him to recharge you — *a day of grace*!

This is the Fourth Word of Grace!

The First Four
Words of Grace

NOWHERE is the breath-taking intelligence of Jesus more brilliantly showcased than in His verbal exchange with His religious adversaries as reported in the twenty-second chapter of St. Matthew's Gospel. Jesus rendered His detractors frustrated and speechless when they put the deadly question to Him, "Is it right to pay taxes to Caesar or not?" (v. 17). With the ease of cosmic genius, Jesus simply held up a coin, forced them to identify the portrait and inscription as "Caesar's," and then replied, "Give to Caesar what is Caesar's, and to God what is God's" (v. 21).

Next, Jesus' incredibly dexterous mind silenced the resurrection-doubting Sadducees by pointing them to the present tense of "I am" in Exodus 3:6 where Jehovah says, "I am the God . . . of Abraham, the God of Isaac and the God of Jacob" — the unanswerable argument being that if God is *presently* the patriarchs' God, they must be alive and there must be a resurrection. Then came embarrassed silence. It was not wise to go one-on-one with Jesus.

Fortunately for us and for all of history, yet another had the temerity to interrogate Jesus. One of their legal experts asked Him the question, "Teacher, which is the greatest commandment in the

Law?" (Matthew 22:36). The question sprang from the common scribal mind-game of attempting to reduce their religion to a single maxim, as, for example, when a Gentile supposedly promised Rabbi Hillel that he would convert if Hillel could give him the whole Law while he stood on one foot. Hillel nimbly balanced and answered with a version of the Golden Rule: "What is hateful to you, do not to your neighbour: that is the whole Torah, while the rest is the commentary thereof; go and learn it."[1] Presumably Hillel's facile but inadequate answer carried the day. This was the kind of answer the scribe anticipated from Jesus when he asked, "Teacher, which is the greatest commandment in the Law?"

He was not to be disappointed, for Jesus, without any rabbinical sophistry, gave a definitive summation of the Law, beginning with these words: "Love the Lord your God with all your heart and with all your soul and with all your mind. This is the first and greatest commandment" (Matthew 22:37, 38). As a point of fact, this opening part of our Lord's answer was known to everyone, for it was from the *Shema Israel*,[2] based on Deuteronomy 6:4, 5. These were the initial words of every synagogue service, words that were repeated in full by every pious Jew morning and evening, every day. The *Shema* was deemed so essential that the words were worn by the devout in a tiny leather box, called a *phylactery*, on the forehead and on the wrist while in prayer. Godly households also hung the *Shema* on their doors in a small round box called a *mezuzah*. Everyone knew this part of Jesus' answer by heart. It was the creed of Israel! And everyone understood what it meant: heart, mind, soul (the sum of human personality) — *everything* — was to be devoted to loving God.

The second part of Jesus' answer was taken from Leviticus 19:18 — "love your neighbor as yourself" — a phrase that was also very familiar to all Jews. So where, then, was the genius in Jesus' answer? It was in this: though the thoughts of loving God and loving humankind had been earlier voiced together by other rabbis and scribes, *this was the first time any rabbi had fused these two* Scripture references together! There had never been anything like it. Jesus' answer was *sui generis*, in a class by itself.

The brilliance of our Lord's summation lay not only in its formulation but in its extent and implications. It was a comprehensive summary. The first part of Jesus' answer summarized the first four commandments, which demand love for God (Exodus 20:1-11). The second part of his answer summarized the final six, which enjoin love for humankind (vv. 12-17). Jesus' answer is comprehensive to the *nth* degree!

Not only was His double answer comprehensive, but it declared that love for God and love for humankind cannot be separated. Jesus' coupling of the loves had a profound impact on the teaching of the Apostolic Church, so that John would later write, "Whoever loves God must also love his brother" (1 John 4:21; cf. Romans 13:8, 9; Galatians 5:14; James 2:8). Ultimately Jesus' answer formed the basis for Christian ethics and was given extended treatment by the Scholastics and Reformers — a subject we will consider when we take up the last Six Words.

But now, in respect to the first Four Words, our thought is this: if the *Shema* (which teaches that we must love God with everything) summarizes the first four commandments, then the first four commands must provide a divine précis for loving God. Therefore, if we carefully cultivate them, they, in bouquet, will produce a profound love for God in us. And ultimately this love will open us wide to the rivers of divine grace. So in what follows, we will arrange and hopefully breathe the sweet bouquet of love for God.

THE FIRST WORD OF GRACE

The First Word — "You shall have no other gods before me" — falls today upon a profoundly idolatrous world that, ironically, has worshiped the fathers of the Enlightenment (for example,

Rousseau) who were heralded as deliverers from superstition and idolatry! Subsequently, the modern world has bowed before a pantheon of successive gods — parading past the brainless, embalmed bodies of Lenin and Stalin — spacing-out before Yoko Ono's filmland hagiography of John Lennon — descending to the absurdity of "Elvis-olatry" that has been given the national imprimatur of Elvis's own postage stamp — and now, especially, succumbing to New Age neo-paganism with its *Earth's Ten Commandments* and the worship of self as god.

Thus the First Word is supremely gracious, because its prohibition protects God's people from worshiping people and philosophies. Going yet deeper, "You shall have no other gods before me" forbids worshiping *technology*, the burning of incense before the science that provides our comforts, as the ancients did before their dragnets. It also forbids worshiping one's *appetite*, one's digestive tract. It forbids worshiping *sex*, making an idol of another's body and demanding the worship of one's own body and passions. It forbids the worship of *money*, the lifestyle which announces, "In *this* god we trust." And, again, it forbids the worship of *self*, outlawing the twentieth-century man — arms wrapped around his own torso in loving embrace, lips passionately pressed against his own mirror image.

In all of this, the prohibition "You shall have no other gods before me" is a sublimely positive grace, because at bottom line God says, "*You shall have Me!*" This is an exquisite declaration of heavenly *eros*. God wants to have us, and He wants us to have Him.

So, then, the First Word of Grace calls us to take inventory of our lives in order to see what we are placing ahead of Him. This demands total honesty — like that of Peter who answered the Lord's probing by saying, "Lord, you know all things." This demands a conscientious conscience, to tune in to the serpentine ways of our hearts, for we all tend toward unconscious idolatries.

But what grace such self-examination brings, because when there is nothing between us and God, we will be better able to respond to His divine love — and to have greater love for Him. When God moves from fourth place to first, we will love Him more. And when He moves beyond first to a new first — and beyond that to a greater first — we will love Him yet more!

THE SECOND WORD OF GRACE

The Second Word in the divine bouquet sounds very much like the first because it says, "You shall not make for yourself an idol in the form of anything . . ." (v. 4). But there is an important distinction, because it is possible to break the first commandment *unconsciously*, whereas the breaking of the second is *conscious* and volitional — the willful making of idols. The First forbids the *existence* of other gods, and the Second the *making* of other gods.

The prohibition here against making material idols for worship, or as aids to worship, is easily understandable. God is utterly limitless, wholly transcendent, and eternal and infinite, but idols are *limiting* to the human concept of God. Idols are also *obscuring*, for invariably they inadequately emphasize an aspect of God and effectively distort the overall vision of God — just as Aaron's calf did for Israel. Likewise images are *localizing* as to one's concept of deity. They also promote the *projecting* of one's ideas about God back onto the idol, which inevitably reflects human attempts at *controlling* God. In all of this, idols are *subtracting* because they not only give us nothing, but they take away what we have.

Happily, most of us are free from the tyranny of *material* idols. But the fuller understanding of the Second Word also forbids the dreaming up of *mental* images. Many Christians succumb to this, and their delusion is revealed in the telling phrase, "I like to think of God as _____." The blanks are many: a loving Father — a nurturing mother — an artist — a forgiving judge — an architect. And,

indeed, God is any one or all of these. But the problem is, such musings are often coupled with the denial of something else that the
Scriptures teach about God — for example, that He is Judge. Such
subjectivism can inject just as much idolatrous subtraction as the
grossest material images; unabated, it reinvents God.

The antidote to this lies in two sources: the written Word of
God, and the living Word of God. Rather than subjectively muse
about God's being, we must scour the Bible, embracing both the
things we *like* to think about God and the things we do *not like* to
think about Him. This demands prayer, reading, thinking, and
humility. And it demands the willingness to take what we find and
hold it together in blessed tension, for then we shall begin to see
God. Then, of course, we need to meditate on Jesus, for God spoke
His final word in His Son (Hebrews 1:1, 2). Jesus is the exegesis of
God (John 1:18).

This takes some holy sweat, but here's the boon: the more
clearly you see God, the more you will love Him. The greater your
vision, the greater your love! Remember Lucy's experience in *The
Chronicles of Narnia*? Lucy, amidst her spiritual quest, sees the lion
Aslan — Christ — shining white and huge in the moonlight. In a
burst of emotion Lucy rushes to him, burying her face in the rich
silkiness of his mane, whereupon the great beast rolls over on his
side so that Lucy falls, half-sitting and half-lying between his front
paws. He bends forward and touches her nose with his tongue. His
warm breath encompasses her. She gazes into the large wise face.

"Welcome, child," he says.
"Aslan," says Lucy, "you're bigger."
"That is because you are older, little one."
"Not because you are?"
"I am not. But every year you grow, you will find me
bigger."[3]

As we grow in the knowledge of God, we will find Him bigger and bigger and will love Him more and more and more.

What grace there is in these first two Words in the bouquet. The First Word calls us to put God first, before all else, and thus to have Him. Giving utter primacy to God is the path to great love. The Second Word calls us to go beyond our subjective material and mental images and truly see God and embrace Him as He is revealed in His Word. The clearer our vision, the freer it is of idolatry, and the greater our love.

THE THIRD WORD OF GRACE

We observed in our study of the Third Word that not only do we live in a culture where language has become increasingly vulgar and scatological, but today blasphemy is no longer considered *déclassé*, but rather, if done smartly, a way of showing that one is urbane and "with it." We also saw that God's Word still stands — "You shall not misuse the name of the Lord your God" — and that this Command is, indeed, a Word of Grace.

The Third Command has primary reference to the breaking of *oaths* — that is, making a promise in God's name and then failing to keep it. Because of the wholesale abuse of this commandment in Jesus' day, Jesus prohibited the casual everyday use of oaths. The overall application of this is that any promise we make, whether we call God as a witness or not, is made in the presence of God and must be kept, because as Christians, indwelt by the Holy Spirit, God's name is automatically binding upon us, whether we verbalize it or not. Any Christian life that is not radically sincere and truthful misuses the name of the Lord our God.

This command bans *irreverence*, the use of "O God" and "Jesus" as an exclamation point or as a chic expression that apparently fears not even the divine. Likewise, *contempt* for God is a flagrant abuse of His name, as in Hemingway's parody of the Lord's

Prayer. And, of course, *cursing* others with God's name is perhaps the very bottom of a deep, deep sin.

The great grace in the Third Word's prohibition comes from the fact that the misuse of God's name and growth in our love of God are mutually exclusive. The truth is, the way we verbally reference another person or being has a profound effect on our regard for and ultimate treatment of that person. Positively, if we are constantly telling our spouses we love them, our telling will elevate and substantiate our love. The same principle, negatively invoked, works a tragic disintegration of love.

So, in the development of our love for God, how we use His name is of greatest importance. Jesus gave first place to this in the opening line of the Lord's Prayer by directing us to pray, "Our Father in heaven, hallowed be your name" (Matthew 6:9). If we wish to love God more, we must *personally* reverence His name in our thoughts and prayers. Such reverence rests on volitional determination. Reverence must permeate the *domestic* circle of our closest relationships in the home, so that His name is given unaffected and sincere respect. Of course, in *public* it is also incumbent that we make His name holy. And as the Body of Christ, the *corporate* ethos of God's people, the way we lift His name in conversation, prayers, song, and preaching is of incalculable importance in elevating the church's love for God.

Reverencing God's name is a divinely ordained verbal path to loving Him and being filled with His grace. As we consciously do it, we will love Him more!

THE FOURTH WORD OF GRACE

In our study of the Fourth Word — "Remember the Sabbath day by keeping it holy" — we drew some distinctions, some of which were: 1) the Mosaic Sabbath day was superseded by the "Lord's Day" (the day Jesus was resurrected, Sunday), the church's day of worship; 2) the Lord's Day is not simply a "Christian Sabbath"; 3) the distinctive of the Lord's Day is worship — and the day ought to be observed as such; 4) it is not incumbent upon Christians to follow the Mosaic Sabbath's stringent command to desist from labor and to rest, because that command is not transferred to the Lord's Day; 5) but at the same time, wise Christians will incorporate the Sabbath rest principle into their observance of the Lord's Day as best they can, because the rest principle is rooted in our cosmos, so that there is a genesis rhythm to life which, if observed, will benefit us *physically* and *spiritually*.

THE FIRST FOUR WORDS

What a remarkable enabling bouquet we have in the first four words — to help us live out the *Shema* — loving God with all we have. Each of the words is magisterial and foundational, and each is uniquely powerful. But like a floral bouquet, their maximum effect comes when they are held together, for then comes the sweet power to love God. Consider the bouquet:

The First Word of Grace — *the primacy of God*: "You shall have no other gods before me." That is, "You shall have Me! I must be in first place." If God is first, if there is nothing before Him, you will love him more and more! Is He truly first in your life?

The Second Word of Grace — *the person of God*: "You shall not make for yourself an idol in the form of anything. . . ." That is, you shall not make a *material* image or dream up a *mental* image of God according to your own design. God wants you to see Himself in His Word and in His Son, because if you do, you will love Him more. The clearer your vision, the greater your love. How is your vision?

The Third Word of Grace — *reverence for God*: "You shall not misuse the name of the Lord your God." That is, "you shall reverence God's name." Reverently loving Him in your mind and with your mouth will elevate and substantiate your love. Honestly, do you misuse or reverence His name?

The Fourth Word of Grace — the time for God: "Remember the Sabbath day by keeping it holy." This tells us to keep holy the Lord's Day. Are you week by week offering it up in love to Him?

This is a divine bouquet, a recipe for loving God and offering a sweet aroma to Him.

> Love the Lord your God with all your heart and with all your soul and with all your strength. These commandments that I give you today are to be upon your hearts. Impress them on your children. Talk about them when you sit at home and when you walk along the road, when you lie down and when you get up. Tie them as symbols on your hands and bind them on your foreheads. Write them on the doorframes of your houses and on your gates. (Deuteronomy 6:5-9)

These are the first Four Words of Grace!

PART II

Loving Others

5

The Fifth Word of Grace

Parents and
Loving Others

*Honor your father and
your mother.*
EXODUS 20:12

C S. LEWIS concluded a lengthy letter to a searching friend
with these wise words:

> When I have learnt to love God better than my earthly dearest,
> I shall love my earthly dearest better than I do now. In so far
> as I learn to love my earthly dearest at the expense of God and
> *instead* of God, I shall be moving towards the state in which I
> shall not love my earthly dearest at all. When first things are
> put first, second things are not suppressed but increased.[1]

Lewis's great mind was referencing the logic embedded in the
structure of the Ten Commandments. The first four
Commandments, when obeyed, grace us with a deep love for God,
so we can love God with all our heart and soul and strength. The

dynamism of this vertical love for God then makes it possible to love others with a greater love. So it follows that the deeper our love for God, the greater our capacity to love others.

This principle was well expressed by the celebrated missionary Hudson Taylor when he encountered the suggestion that he had given his life to the Orient because he loved the Chinese, whom he indeed did love. In response, Hudson Taylor shook his head slowly and answered reflectively, "No, not because I loved the Chinese, but because I loved God."

Loving God is the key to loving others and, in fact, the key to all proper ethics and conduct. This has been the ancient understanding of the church, summarized by St. Augustine in his famous epigram, "Love, and do what thou wilt" (Homily 7.8 on 1 John 4:4-12).[2] Augustine had every confidence that if one truly loved God, one would do the right thing in the rest of his life. And the truth is so broadly practical that a child can understand it, as when the imposing Lewis tenderly wrote a little girl, "If you continue to love Jesus, nothing much can go wrong with you, and I hope you may always do so."[3]

So now, riding high on the vertical love instilled by the first four Commandments, we come to the Fifth Word of Grace, which commands that we love our nearest and dearest — "Honor your father and your mother, so that you may live long in the land the Lord your God is giving you" (Exodus 21:12). This is the divine, unchanging formula for domestic blessing, which, if obeyed, will guide one's family in the paths of grace. As such, it contains indispensable advice to both growing children and mature adults. This is God's message for young and old.

THE FIFTH WORD: ITS MEANING

Here the Hebrew word for "honor" is most informative because it comes from a verb that means "to be heavy," so that we "give weight," so to speak, to the person who is honored.[4] We therefore hold the honored in high esteem, elevating them to a place of importance and reverence. Surface actions such as offering one's chair and saying "Yes, sir," while important, do not fulfill the word. "Honor" demands a profound respect that governs all relations with the honored. The command to honor one's father and mother and all it entails is an enduring command that extends through the growing and into the mature years.

"Honor" — the Growing Years

"Honor" during the growing years is largely manifested through obedience. New Testament references to the Fifth Commandment emphasize this. Paul tells the young Ephesians, "Children, obey your parents in the Lord, for this is right. 'Honor your father and mother' — which is the first commandment with a promise — 'that it may go well with you and that you may enjoy long life on the earth'"(6:1-3). More succinctly, he commands the Colossians, "Children, obey your parents in everything, for this pleases the Lord" (3:20). The *Heidelberg Catechism* summarizes, in Question 104, "What does God require in the fifth commandment? That I show all honor, love, and faithfulness to my father and mother, and to all in authority over me; submit myself with due obedience to all their good instruction and correction, and also bear patiently with their infirmities, since it is God's will to govern us by their hand."[5]

Today this kind of obedience is not in vogue. To talk up obedience today is to be profoundly countercultural. Our culture-shapers are determined to lower the age of autonomy for the young so that teenagers and earlier can pursue unbridled freedom. Society's restraints (unless, ironically, they are against smoking) are viewed as assaults on individual freedom. Obedience, in the mind of popular culture, suggests mindless conformity. The problem is further inflamed by the many television sitcoms that portray parents as dull-witted incompetents and their children as dispensers of logic and good sense. Of course, as we know, society is "paying the piper" and thus in some schools teachers have found they simply can't teach.

Significantly, there is nothing mindless in the New Testament command to obey because it literally means "to listen under" — conscious listening. The idea is to listen under with the intent to understand and obey. This does not mean that a son or a daughter is to obey if the parents ask him or her to do something that is morally wrong or goes against Scripture or Christian conscience. Children are to obey parents "in the Lord" (Ephesians 6:1) — that is, in those things that are consistent with Christ and His Word. Obedience is really an exercise of freedom to choose to do the right thing and then do it! A disobedient spirit is intrinsically enslaving.

Along with this understanding of obedience, there are substantial reasons for a child to choose to obey. Children ought to obey because parents stand in the place of God to their children. Of course, they do not take the place of God, but they do function as vice-regents of God for one's childhood. From birth, parents, by virtue of their office, perform the God-like functions of loving, providing, and law-giving. Shakespeare wrote, "The voice of parents is the voice of gods, for to their children they are Heaven's lieutenants." Thus, a reflexively rebellious spirit intrinsically fights against God.

Children ought to obey because parents (unless mentally deranged) generally have their children's best interests at heart. Most of us would not be here today if we had been allowed to disobey — to run across the street during rush hour or drink the paint thinner or paddle out beyond the breakers or run with the wrong crowd. With few exceptions, no one cares for us more than our parents. Virtually all would have given their lives for us had the occasion come to make such a sacrifice.

Children ought to obey because the growing-up years are short. For a teenager, growing up seems interminable, but just yesterday he or she was a tiny child riding on Daddy's shoulders, heels bouncing in his heart, and in another day or two the teenager will be grown up and his heart will be still.[6] Annie Dillard has described how fast her male childhood companions grew up: "Those froggy little beasts had elongated and transformed into princes and gods. When it happened, I must have been out of the room. Suddenly here they all were, Richie and Rickie and Dan and all, diverse in their varied splendors, each powerful and mysterious, immense."[7] Growing up happens, and it happens fast.

Children also ought to obey their parents because Jesus did. Our Lord passed through all the stages of childhood — from total dependence to responsible manhood. Like any other newborn human, He focused His uncomprehending eyes on His baby hand. He learned speech just as we did. Jesus became a teenager, a young man, and an adult. Significantly, when He was entering His teens and was coming into fuller awareness of His powers and who He was as He discoursed with Israel's teachers in the Jerusalem Temple, He chose to obey His parents' uninformed pleas and returned with them to Nazareth, where He continued to obey His parents (cf. Luke 2:51). Though He was God of the universe, He obeyed His earthly, fallible parents. The Scriptures add, "And Jesus grew in wisdom and stature, and in favor with God and men" (Luke 2:52).

Lastly, children ought to obey their parents because it opens them up to God's grace. When children and teens allow the logic behind obedience to penetrate their thinking — when they recognize that parents stand in God's place, that their parents have their best interests at heart, that their growing up will happen faster than they realize, that Jesus, though God, obeyed His parents, that obedience invites grace — they will be strengthened *to listen under* and to exercise the freedom of obedience.

The one thing a son or daughter must not, and indeed cannot, plead as an excuse for disobedience is his or her youth, because being young focuses the Fifth Command's spotlight directly upon him or her. Besides, some of God's most used servants — for example, the famed missionary Rachel Saint — chose to become deeply obedient to both God and man as preteenagers. No young person can plead exemption from the call to obey because he or she fancies himself or herself young and immature. God does not accept such self-serving excuses.

"Honor" — the Mature Years

Time passes, and the honoring of one's parents takes on a distinctly different emphasis. It isn't totally different or new, but the old emphasis on obedience naturally recedes, and *reverence* rises to become the dominant way the mature child honors his father and mother. As a mature adult, reverencing one's parents must not be confused with obedience, or even feeling we must always have their approval. Nevertheless, reverence for one's parents has wholly positive factors.

Respect

Reverence requires respect. In the Old Testament economy, respect for one's parents was considered so important that it was linked with the Sabbath and thus was seen as essential for living: "Each of you must respect his mother and father, and you must observe my Sabbaths. I am the Lord your God" (Leviticus 19:3). Respect always involves speaking kindly *to* one's parents. Such speech is affectionate and intimate; it is always properly toned and never patronizing. Winston Churchill's biographers record that the famous family all had affectionate animal nicknames for one another, so that, for example, when the renowned prime minister returned to Chartwell, they would all proceed to address one another with silly names like Kitten, Mary Mouse, and Duckadilly.[8] "Corny and sentimental," some may think, and that it was. But I believe it also modeled the kind of sweet respect and mutual affection that has the smile of Heaven.

Respect also involves speaking kindly *of* one's parents.

Recently I came across a novel by a well-known son in one of America's most prominent evangelical families, a book which is, to say the least, unkind to his parents' reputation. The book is a well-written, titillating mixture of truth and fiction that effectively casts a shadow over the interior life of his family. The book has achieved some acclaim, but whatever its literary merits, it is a woeful breach of the Fifth Commandment.

Provision

Next, reverence for one's parents involves making provision for their material needs. Jesus noted that the religious leaders of His day had exempted themselves from providing for their aged parents. The method was to piously inform their parents, "Whatever help you might otherwise have received from me is a gift devoted to God [literally, *Corban*]" (Matthew 15:5). Jesus condemned this ethical sleight-of-hand, saying, "And why do you break the command of God for the sake of your tradition? For God said, 'Honor your father and mother'" (Matthew 15:3, 4). Therefore, we understand that any Christian who neglects his or her needy parents is guilty of a grievous breach of the Fifth Word and is living under the disapproval of God.

Consideration

It follows that respect and provision for one's parents must be linked with consideration — namely, remembering them, taking time to be with them, including them, doing them acts of kindness. Here our modern culture's sin is of scandalous proportions. As a pastor, I see this regularly in my visits to convalescent hospitals where many elderly men and women who have prosperous surviving children endure months and even years without a visit. This is a grievous sin!

Instruction

Reverence is, of course, enhanced when one's children are instructed to love one's parents. My former pastor and colleague

Verl Lindley and his wife, Lois, tell how their little grandson, whose parents are missionaries in Taiwan, kept asking his parents if he could go over and visit another of his little friends. Finally they asked him, "Why?" He answered, "Because they say they have grandparents over there." His experience with his own grandparents was so positive, he couldn't wait to get in on other grandparents — even if they were someone else's! Such wonderful attitudes don't just happen. They are a family affair.

Character

Lastly, one brings honor to one's parents by one's character and reputation. Proverbs tells us, "The father of a righteous man has great joy; he who has a wise son delights in him. May your father and mother be glad; may she who gave you birth rejoice!" (23:24, 25). Upright children become a precious crown to an old, gray head.

The dimensions of Biblical honor and reverence are beautiful to see written together on the page of a Christian's life — *respect, provision, consideration, instruction,* and *character* — because together they form a recipe for grace for oneself and the community of faith.

THE FIFTH WORD: ITS GRACE

The Fifth Commandment is explicit about the grace that comes from honoring one's parents — "so that you may live long in the land the Lord your God is giving you."

National Grace

To begin with, honoring one's father and mother would bring national/corporate grace to Israel in the form of extended prosperity in the land. Obedient children were, and are, a national treasure. Today's children are tomorrow's politicians and teachers and scientists and preachers. And when they honor their parents in both the growth years and mature years, they effect a strength of character that diffuses grace and prosperity to all.

Getting down to where we live, the longevity and health of a given church can be monitored by its fidelity to and appropriation of the Fifth Commandment. How I treat my parents, how you treat yours, how my children treat me, and how yours treat you affects us all. The Fifth Commandment obeyed is a Word of corporate grace!

Individual Grace

The rich individual grace of this Fifth Word is glimpsed in its reference to long life, which is also emphasized in its parallel expression in Deuteronomy 5:16 ("so that you may live long") and in its exposition in Ephesians 6:3 ("that it may go well with you and that you may enjoy long life on the earth"). The truth is that nature and life itself, without the direct intervention of God, will bestow longevity upon the life of a loving and obedient child.

There are always exceptions, but the general rule is that unruly children who have rejected natural affection will lead shortened lives. The grace-impeding spiral of disobedience is easy to trace. *Spiritually*, disobedience to parents may unwittingly slay the desire to obey God, our Father in Heaven. Spiritual rebellion may then produce *psychological* aberrations — complexes, phobias, compulsive desires. This, in turn, can have devastating effects on one's *social* habits and friendships. Finally, *physical* trauma often results from rebellion — bad habits, drugs, violence, and illicit desires.

Proverbs 4:10-13 presents this principle in positive summary: "Listen, my son, accept what I say, and the years of your life will be many. I guide you in the way of wisdom and lead you along straight paths. When you walk, your steps will not be hampered; when you run, you will not stumble. Hold on to instruction, do not let it go; guard it well, for it is your life."

Not only is there longevity, but well-being also comes to the obedient: "My son, keep your father's commands and do not forsake your mother's teaching. Bind them upon your heart forever; fasten them around your neck. When you walk, they will guide you; when you sleep, they will watch over you; when you awake, they will speak to you. For these commands are a lamp, this teaching is a light, and the corrections of discipline are the way to life" (Proverbs 6:20-23).

So we see that the Fifth Word is a monumental Word of Grace. If obeyed, it will bring a flood of grace upon the church, her families, and her children. And today, in the final decade of the twentieth century, as the nuclear family is taking direct hits from the academe, from politics, and from pop culture, there can scarcely be a more relevant life-and-death call. It will not go well with us if we neglect this Word. This Commandment is the bridge in the Decalogue. If we have heeded the first four words, loving our nearest and dearest must come next.

The greatest force of this command falls on those in the growing years — preteenagers (eight to twelve), teenagers, and young collegians. The unadorned truth is this: "Honor your father and your mother, so that you may live long in the land the Lord your God is giving you" (Exodus 20:12). But in the widest sense this command is binding on us all.

It is also true that some may have what they consider to be super-strict parents; others may have unbelieving, disordered parents. And there may be times some cannot in good conscience obey them, situations in which Biblical teaching and moral principle are at stake. But believers must have obedient spirits which *will* to honor their parents.

Most of us have godly parents who, despite their infirmities and faults, are trying their best. And God's Word comes to us in the Fifth Commandment, one of the ten most important Words given to the people He loved — "Honor your father and your mother."

DISCIPLINES OF GRACE

Perhaps you've been failing miserably, but God has been convicting you about breaking His Fifth Word. If so, some practical disciplines of grace are in order.

Disciplines for *Growing* Children

- A child should *honestly answer*, "Am I a truly obedient child?"
- If he or she is disobedient, he or she should *make a specific list* of offenses.
- He or she should then *pray* over the list, *repenting* of each offense.
- He or she should *go to his or her parents*, confess his or her sin, and state his or her resolve to repent.
- Then he or she should *change!* He or she may rest assured that if he or she does that which God asks him or her to do, he or she will receive supernatural help to do it.
- Then he or she can *expect God's blessing* in his or her life, because He has promised that "it will go well" with those who obey.

Disciplines for *Mature* Children

- *Honestly answer*, "Do I truly reverence my parents? Specifically, do I *reverence* them in the way I speak *to* them and *of* them? Do I make *provision* for them? Do I give them *consideration*? Does my *character* honor them?"
- If you answered in the negative, *list* your offenses.
- Then *pray* over the list, *repenting* of each offense.
- *Go to your parents*, confess your sin, and state your resolve to repent.
- *Change!* You may rest assured that if you do that which God asks you to do, you will receive supernatural help to do it.

• *Expect God's blessing* in your life, because He has promised that "it will go well" with you.

This is the Fifth Word of Grace!

6

The Sixth Word of Grace

Life and
Loving Others

You shall not murder.
EXODUS 20:13

*T*HE FACTS are in — the evidence is conclusive: the modern state has proven itself the greatest killer of all time. By 1990, state violence (war, collectivist pogroms, revolutions, and "ethnic cleansing") had been responsible for the unnatural deaths of 125 million people during this century, which is more than the state had succeeded in destroying in all of human history up to 1900.[1]

Not surprisingly, violence has had its academic godfathers — for example, the philosopher Jean-Paul Sartre and writer Norman Mailer. Sartre invented the verbal technique of identifying the existing order as "institutional violence," thereby justifying murder to overthrow it. He was the direct intellectual father to most of the terrorist movements that began during and after the 1960s, especially those with a French language connection in Africa and

Southeast Asia. The "killing fields" of Cambodia, which orchestrated the deaths of one-fifth to one-third of the population, were organized by eight French-speaking, middle-class Cambodian intellectuals who had all studied in France in the 1950s, where they had been schooled in Sartre's doctrine of "necessary violence."[2]

Just before the dawn of the sixties, American writer Norman Mailer published a thesis, *The White Negro*, which became his most influential piece of writing. It was a brilliantly written attempt to legitimize personal, individual violence. Mailer referenced a real murder in which two young men beat to death a candy shop owner, and Mailer then argued that their action was actually a beneficial act of violence: "One murders not only a weak, fifty-year-old man, but an institution as well, one violates private property, one enters into a new relation with the police and introduces a dangerous element into one's life."[3]

The logic of Mailer's thesis was capsulized by historian Paul Johnson: "Since rage, when turned inwards, was a danger to creativity, was not violence, when used, externalized and vented, itself creative?"[4] Mailer's reasoning, morally gruesome and depraved as it is, was just what the counterculture was looking for, because it gave intellectual respectability to acts that had previously been considered beyond the range of civilized behavior.

Thus, the twentieth century has become a very good century for murder. Terrorist organizations have demonstrated a deadly solidarity. Basque killers who had been trained in Cuba and South Yemen by East Germans, Palestinians, and Cubans used explosives acquired from IRA gangsters whom they met in Algiers to kill a Spanish admiral. In Chicago, the heartland of America, violence is at its creative best. Citywide, according to the lead article in the March 1993 issue of *Chicago* Magazine, 936 people were murdered in 1992, the highest total since 1974, when the city's population was almost one-half million more. The murder rate was the highest ever — 33 per 100,000.[5]

The future for murder in America is excellent! All the leading indicators are up. Homicide is at a new height. Suicide is up too — especially among teenagers — triple what it was in 1960.[6] More children than ever are dying at the hands of their abusive parents. Feticide is booming, with over thirty million abortions since 1973. John Wayne Gacy and Jeffrey Dahmer are part of our national vocabulary.

Of course, we are appalled. Our politicians, educators, and preachers all decry the violence. No previous age has equalled our horror of killing; but then, no previous age ever killed so much! As a people, we have become richer and better informed, but homicide's dark atavism stalks our relationships.

Where are we to turn? For the Christian, it is to God's Word and the healing light of the Sixth Word of Grace — "You shall not murder" (Exodus 20:13). This is a Word which, if understood in Scriptural depth and applied, will bring grace to one's soul and healing to the world around us.

MURDER FORBIDDEN

The Sixth Commandment in Hebrew consists of only two words, giving a very blunt imperative: "No killing" — the idea being the prohibition of the violent erasure of a personal enemy. "Murder" is an excellent translation and thus appears in most modern versions (Moffatt, NEB, NASB, NIV, NKJV, TLB)[7]: "You shall not murder" — "no murder!"

Capital Punishment

Some have ignored this sense and have argued that the Commandment really forbids *all* taking of human life under any circumstance. But this is not possible because corresponding Jewish law lists eighteen crimes liable to the death penalty, including murder, child sacrifice, kidnaping, incest, adultery, and witchcraft. In

Biblical times, therefore, capital punishment was an accepted means of law enforcement, though it was rarely carried out.

Moreover, capital punishment was commended by God long before Moses, when God said to Noah, "Whoever sheds the blood of man, by man shall his blood be shed; for in the image of God has God made man" (Genesis 9:6). Later Mosaic legislation confirmed and refined the application of the penalty by distinguishing between accidental and premeditated killing, and by providing cities of refuge for those who accidentally killed a neighbor (cf. Deuteronomy 19:1-21). Significantly, Christ nowhere set aside the death penalty, though He did intervene on behalf of a woman who deserved to be stoned.

In light of this, we conclude that capital punishment ought to be viewed as an *option* of human government. But as such it ought to be used sparingly, and then "only in cases of premeditated murder with no mitigating factors and [with] certain proof."[8]

Law and Order

In addition to capital punishment, human government has been vested by God with the right to use appropriate force, which may at times involve killing to uphold its laws. In Romans 13, where Paul develops the relationship between church and state, the governing authorities are given the right to use the sword: "But if you do wrong, be afraid, for he does not bear the sword for nothing. He is God's servant, an agent of wrath to bring punishment on the wrongdoer" (v. 4). "The sword" refers to a government's power over life and death. As the New Testament lexicographer Marvin Vincent says, the sword is "borne as the symbol of the magistrate's right to inflict capital punishment."[9]

War

There is no doubt that war is terrible and degenerating. When the First World War began, it was the most popular war in history. A

French soldier wrote that he "loved life at the front, the bath in the elemental, the annihilation of the intelligence of the heart." Rupert Brooke, the Cambridge (and soon to be dead) poet, found it "the only life . . . a fine thrill, like nothing else in the world."[10]

But then the joy evaporated amidst the mud and mustard gas of the Western Front, and young Winston Churchill, the Secretary of State for War, jotted his thoughts on a sheet of War Office stationery:

> All the horrors of all the ages were brought together, and not only armies but whole populations were thrust into the midst of them. The mighty educated States involved conceived — not without reason — that their very existence was at stake. Neither peoples nor rulers drew the line at any deed which they thought could help them to win. Germany, having let Hell loose, kept well in the van of terror; but she was followed step by step by the desperate and ultimately avenging nations she had assailed. Every outrage against humanity or international law was repaid by reprisals. . . . The wounded died between the lines. . . . Merchant ships and neutral ships and hospital ships were sunk on the seas and all on board left to their fate, or killed as they swam. . . . Bombs from the air were cast down indiscriminately. Poison gas in many forms stifled or seared the soldiers. Liquid fire was projected upon their bodies. . . . When all was over, Torture and Cannibalism were the only two expedients that the civilized, scientific, Christian States had been able to deny themselves: and they were of doubtful utility.[11]

No one can gainsay the evils of war.

Yet war is sometimes valid for the Christian, for though there are few just wars, some are justifiable. The "just war" is, in a word, *defensive*. It includes at least seven distinctions: 1) just cause, 2) just intention, 3) last resort, 4) formal declaration, 5) limited objectives,

6) proportionate means, and 7) noncombatant immunity.[12] Here retired army colonel Alexander Shine states the Christian soldier's duty:

> Bearing the sword, in order to execute justice, is a proper duty of human governments. The soldier does not, of course, have blanket license to hate or kill. As an individual sinner, prone to avenge and resist personal abuse, he must, like all other believers, restrain himself. He should, I believe, examine himself. He should, I believe, examine the cause for which his nation fights, and if he concludes that it is evil and unjust he should refuse to participate. Even when he finds the cause acceptable, he may at times feel led to disobey certain orders that he feels abuse the proper use of force.[13]

So we conclude that there are at least four areas where the taking of human life is sometimes justifiable: *capital punishment*, maintaining *law and order*, *self-defense*, and the so-called "*just war.*"

Now, if we were to stop here, having merely noted the instances in which the Commandment "You shall not murder" allows the taking of life, we would miss the main thrust of the Sixth Word, which is *the preciousness of human life*. The original Genesis call for capital punishment alluded to this in its assertion that man is made in God's image — "Whoever sheds the blood of man, by man shall his blood be shed; for in the image of God has God made man" (Genesis 9:6).

I recall fishing at the mouth of the Sea of Cortez — the cloudless, windless day — the perfect sunlight dancing rhythmically on the water in platinum and blue. I remember gliding into an emerald cove surrounded by a cactus desert, donning a snorkel, and slipping over the side into a world of green and turquoise and yellow and pink — another world of slower, gentler rhythm. I recall, too, the sunset with its Pacific fire as we sat on the sand and gazed at the summer stars. There I saw God through His handiwork. But in all those wonders I did not see His chief work!

Consider something far beyond that — a newborn human baby, eyes and mouth wide-open, arms reaching for life — the apex of God's creation. Why do we say this? The baby is, of course, a physical wonder. Its mind is an amazing computer, recording virtually everything it experiences. Its eyes pass on incredible amounts of data — first through the cornea, then through the focusing lens where the image strikes the retina, stimulating 125 million nerve endings simultaneously. This is processed by millions of microswitches and funneled down the optic nerve, which contains one million separate insulated fibers (so there are no short circuits). When the information reaches the brain, an equally complex process begins — all of which takes place in a millisecond! Likewise, the infant's ears are so tuned to the vibrating around her that one day she will make music.

But far beyond this wonder is the fact that the baby is made in the image of God — *imago Dei*. "So God created man in his own image, in the image of God he created him; male and female he created them" (Genesis 1:27). He or she has not only a body but *an eternal soul*. That newborn child has, despite its sin nature, a delicate moral sensibility and mind-boggling possibilities of achievement. *Man* is without a doubt the apex of God's creation. No angel can rival him, for no angel is made in the image of God. Thus murder is, in the most intense sense of the word, a sacrilege. It is not only a crime against mankind — it is a crime against God, in whose image men and women are made.

John Calvin gave the positive implications of the Sixth Commandment for human relationships in this sublime expression in his *Institutes*:

> This commandment rests upon a twofold basis: man is both the image of God, and our flesh. Now if we do not wish to

violate the image of God, we ought to hold our neighbors sacred. And if we do not wish to renounce all humanity, we ought to cherish him as our flesh. (2:8.40)[14]

There's the ethic! This is exactly what Jesus said when He taught that the second table of the Law, which includes this Command, is summarized by, "Love your neighbor as yourself" (Matthew 22:39; cf. Leviticus 19:18). We are under divine obligation to cherish our neighbor's life as much as we cherish our own flesh. Your life is sacred! My life is sacred! Your parking attendant's life is sacred! Your President's life is sacred! The sacredness of life is at the root of the Christian ethic. The serious Christian must be a committed humanist, in the most exalted sense of the word.

That is why *homicide* and all other "cides" (patricide, matricide, fratricide, sororicide, parricide, genocide, regicide) are wrong and forbidden.

That is why *suicide* is forbidden as well. Now, this is as forgivable as any other sin, and "the redeemed suicide, crashing uninvited into God's presence, is acceptable to the Father because of One who deliberately gave his own life a sacrifice" (Robertson McQuilkin).[15] Nevertheless, suicide is violence against one made in the image of God — and perhaps even more violent emotionally to the survivors than to oneself. Those who present suicide as an option are guilty of great sin, because some depressed minds will seize upon the suggestion and act it out.

Lastly, because humans are in the image of God, *feticide* (abortion) is a direct sin against God and the preciousness of humankind. Dr. Jerome LeJeune, professor of fundamental genetics at the University of Rene Descartes in Paris and discoverer of the genetic basis for Down's syndrome, says: "Life has a very, very long history, but each individual has a very neat beginning — the moment of conception."[16] And, "To accept the fact that after fertilization has taken place a new human has come into being is no longer a matter of taste or of opinion. The human nature of the human being from conception to old age is not a metaphysical contention, it is plain experimental evidence."[17] Dr. Micheline Matthews-Roth, principal research associate in the Department of Medicine at Harvard, agrees: "It is an accepted fact that the life of any individual organism reproducing by sexual reproduction begins at conception, or fertilization — the time when the egg cell from the female and the sperm cell from the male join to form a single new cell, the zygote."[18]

Today virtually all scientists agree that zygotes (fertilized eggs), embryos, and fetuses are individuals of the same human species. Thus the controversy has moved from the question of *when* life begins to the question of the *value* of the various stages of life.

Here a page from Luke's birth narrative gives us vital information. When Jesus, a zygote in the womb of His mother, enters a room, John the Baptist, a six-month-old fetus in Elizabeth's womb, leaps for joy. Elizabeth addresses Mary as "the mother of my Lord" (Luke 1:43, 44). From that exchange we pose this question: if young Mary had gotten an abortion, what would she have aborted — a potential human being or the eternal Son of God?[19] There can be only one answer!

The Sixth Commandment — "You shall not murder" — is a profound Word of Grace because it is a call to be a great lover of all humanity from conception to the grave — ovoids and octogenarians. It has ranging ethical implications, not only about the unlawful taking of life, but in regard to existing conditions that threaten life such as harmful pleasures, careless laws, unsafe environments, and insufficient health care. Consistent Christian commitment demands an informed activism aimed at preserving human life from all forms of killing.

Nevertheless, Christian ethics aside, the future for murder in America is excellent. Homicide, suicide, and feticide are up. Our culture is killing us. What to do? Certainly we ought to mourn over the world's misery. We must also set ourselves to pray for our death-dealing world. And we must show mercy — compassion that leads to action. But where to begin? The answer is, *in the heart*.

During the last century a dispute erupted between Reverend Newman Smith and the great Baptist preacher Robert Hall. In a controversy with Hall on some religious point, Smith wrote a bitter pamphlet, denouncing Hall and his doctrine. Unable to select what he thought was just the appropriate title, he sent the pamphlet to a friend on whose judgment he relied and asked him to suggest a suitable title. Some time before, Newman Smith had written a widely read and very helpful pamphlet, *Come to Jesus*. When his friend read this bitter tirade against Hall, he sent the pamphlet back to Smith with this personal note: "The title which I suggest for your pamphlet is this, 'Go to Hell' by the Author of 'Come to Jesus.'"[20]

There is no hate so hateful as that exercised in the name of Christian love. Christians can nurse murderous hearts to which there is no appeal because in their twisted thinking Christ has validated or even produced their hatred. The fact is, many Christians have become unwitting spiritual accomplices to making this the century of death. Their hateful ethos has enhanced the murderous spirit of the age.

MURDEROUS THOUGHTS FORBIDDEN

To such thinking and to such people, Jesus gives no quarter in His exposition of the Sixth Commandment:

> "You have heard that it was said to the people long ago, 'Do not murder, and anyone who murders will be subject to judgment.' But I tell you that anyone who is angry with his brother will be subject to judgment. Again, anyone who says to his brother, 'Raca,' is answerable to the Sanhedrin. But

anyone who says, 'You fool!' will be in danger of the fire of hell." (Matthew 5:21, 22)

This is an unusually emotive "in your face" statement. It forthrightly proclaims that those guilty of contemptuous anger are guilty enough to go to Hell. Jesus says in effect, "The Old Testament Law condemns murder, but I say that contemptuous anger will get you a fiery Hell just as surely." He means what He says, and we need to let this truth sink in with all its absoluteness.

Jesus is speaking of unrighteous anger, and His graphic words leave no doubt about what He means. To call someone the Aramaic word *Raca* is literally to call him "emptyhead." The commentators suggest a number of more contemporary substitutes such as "numbskull" or "nitwit" or "blockhead" or "bonehead" or "jerk" or "idiot." *Raca* used in deadly earnest demotes another person to the level of a nothing — a nobody. It is a fiercely contemptuous word.

The term "fool" has behind it the Greek word *moros*, from which we derive *moron*. But its meaning had nothing to do with one's IQ but rather one's moral condition. It was applied to those who denied God's existence and as a result fell to further evil. The Psalmist's phrase, "The fool says in his heart, 'There is no God'" bears this idea (14:1).

Summarizing the two words, we see that "*Raca*" expresses contempt for a man's head — "You idiot!" "Fool" expresses contempt for his heart and character — "You moral moron!"[21] These were not "terms of endearment," but of malignant, sulphurous contempt. Jesus condemns angry contempt and all its doleful cousins — animosity, malice, hostility, malevolence. He is not suggesting a ladder of offenses that result in progressively sterner judgments (i.e., "anger" gets a minor judgment, "*Raca*" a stiffer penalty, and "fool" gets Hell). He is simply multiplying examples to make His point, as any good rabbi does. And the point is, such murderous attitudes can land one in Hell.

Jesus is saying that we mustn't think we are safe just because we haven't shed blood; we are guilty enough to receive punishment if we have harbored anger and contempt. He says, "You may think you are removed from murder, morally. But you're wrong. Have you ever wished someone were dead? Listen, your heart has known murder!" Heard like this, we cannot escape the truth that we are all murderers. We have all murdered others in mind and heart. We have treasured thoughts about others that are as foul as murder.

This is powerful, painful, confrontational teaching. But it is eminently loving because it is meant to drive us to grace. Not one of us perfectly measures up. We are lawbreakers. We are secret murderers. But by God's grace we can be forgiven and then, by the indwelling power of His Holy Spirit, begin to live out the Sixth Commandment in all its depth.

What this murderous century needs first and foremost are Christians who truly love God and the rest of mankind. Their acquaintances will sense that they cherish them and are truly committed to their best interests. Other associates and friends will find the authentic love of their hearts to be ineluctably inviting — like a cool drink in a parched desert — and will seek the same God-given elixir for their hearts. Christians who truly live out the love of the Sixth Commandment will become fountains of the grace of God.

IMMEDIATE ACTION!

When one is truly a believer, but is guilty of inwardly transgressing the Sixth Commandment, our Lord encourages immediate action. The picture Christ gives in the subsequent vignette is meant to stick in our memories. A worshiper has entered the great Temple of Herod with his sacrifice and has passed through the concentric courts (the Court of the Gentiles, the Court of Women, the Court of Men), and now beyond him lies the Court of the Priests, into which only priests could pass. The worshiper is standing at the threshold of the court. His hands are on the sacrifice, and he is ready to confess his sins. But then he remembers that he has wronged his brother, and his conscience throbs. He whirls and retreats through the great courts. He must first go to his brother!

Jesus' point is so clear — it is far more important to be reconciled to our brother than to fulfill a worship duty: "Leave your gift there in front of the altar. First go and be reconciled to your brother; then come and offer your gift" (Matthew 5:24). The immediacy of Jesus' demand to make things right must be heeded. If we put it off, we'll likely never do it. Moreover, our dark century needs graced hearts now. If God is speaking to you, tell Him right now, "I will do it!"

DISCIPLINES OF GRACE

- "You shall not murder" is positively a call to cherish our neighbors because they are made in the image of God. Do we cherish our neighbors? If not, it may be that we do not love God as we ought, for loving God is the key to loving others (cf. 1 John 4:19). Perhaps you need to *ask God, with all your heart, to increase your love for Him — and then for others.* Frankly, this is a prayer I find myself praying with increased frequency.

- "You shall not murder" forbids the taking of life through homicide, suicide, and infanticide — to name the primary paths of murder. *Have you taken public responsibility for doing what you can to prevent their occurrence?* Perhaps you need to get out in the community and be salt and light. Perhaps you need to open your home to an expectant single mother, or to consider adoption. Perhaps you need to consciously befriend a lonely person.

- "You shall not murder" forbids hateful thoughts. We cannot invite some people to Jesus while entertaining hatred for others. Do you have malignant thoughts about certain people? If so, privately list them. Then, with eyes wide-open to the list, *ask God to forgive you — and to enable you to love them.* Also, if you have wronged anyone in word or deed, go to them, privately confess your sin, and ask their forgiveness. The decision to make things right can be your watershed for the grace of God.

This is the Sixth Word of Grace!

7

The Seventh Word of Grace

Sexuality and
Loving Others

*You shall not
commit adultery.*
EXODUS 20:14

N O ONE with any sense of history would argue that adultery, fornication, and sexual deviation have come suddenly to the vogue they now enjoy. Social historians know there has always been a gap between what people profess and what they practice, even in the most Christian environments. At times the dissonance has been scandalously blatant, but mostly it has been quietly subterranean.

Characteristically, adultery has been an aristocratic sin — as a glance at Europe's royal houses invariably reveals. In our own century, England's Edward VII turned his private digs into mini-seraglios in which he entertained famous ladies. At one of his well-equipped residences the king could, at the touch of his royal finger, conveniently rotate a bed into the dining room. When Edward died, his mistresses paid him public tribute at what became known as "Black Ascot" when Jennie Churchill, Lillie Langtry, and the others stood in their own box at the racecourse wearing black feathers and ribbons on enormous black hats — symbols of their perverse pride. More recently, in far-off Zaire the elite proclivity resurfaced when Joseph Mobutu banned Christian names and renamed himself Monutu Ses Seko Kuku Ngbendu Wa Za Banga — "the cock that leaves no hens alone." Edward VII and Mobutu are "birds of a feather," in barnyard solidarity.

Popular adoption of such behavior gained momentum during the twenties and thirties in Weimar, Germany, and in Paris through the lives and writings of such people as playwright and director Bertolt Brecht and American expatriates, left-bank intellectuals and writers including Gertrude Stein and Ernest Hemingway. Meanwhile, as their groupies in America began to imitate their style, intellectual undergirding came not only from philosophers but from the social sciences and from prominent persons such as Margaret Mead and her *Coming of Age in Samoa*.

But it wasn't until the 1960s and 1970s that the sexual revolution kicked in. It was then that monogamous, one-man/one-woman marriage came under direct fire for stunting emotions and fanning conjugal frustration and resentment. Sociologist Morton Hunt, quoting leading psychiatrists and sociologists, wrote in 1969:

> The disapproved model (polygamy) seems better suited to the emotional capacities and requirements of many people, particularly men; it offers renewal, excitement and continuance of expressions of personal rediscovery; it is an answer to the boredom of lifelong monogamy. We are by nature polygamous.[1]

The logical outcome of this was an epidemic of wife-swapping in which one's spouse was shared with others, with the one proviso that the shared spouse did not "fall in love." Such sharing was said, of course, to require men and women who are emotionally "mature." Thus, in our century western culture's view of adultery underwent an astounding descent. Originally adultery was considered illicit; then it was justified if there was "love" between the lovers; next adultery was declared natural on the grounds that humankind is innately polygamous; and finally it was pronounced good as long as there was, ironically, no "love"![2]

In all fairness it must be said that not everyone in popular culture agrees that adultery is good. There are eloquent public voices saying otherwise — for example, Barbara Dafoe Whitehead in the cover article in the April 1993 *The Atlantic*.[3] Nevertheless, the ethos of popular culture is increasingly sensual, as we see in advertising, best-selling books, and the cataract of sensuality that nightly bursts from our televisions. The icons of youth culture — Prince, Madonna, Michael Jackson — crusade for unbound lust.

Even the church is prey. For example, a major denomination recently rejected a proposal from a committee of seventeen of its ministers, academics, and health professionals that, according to *Newsweek*, read "like a sermon on Eros prepared in the heat of politically correct passion." *Newsweek* summarized the committee's major points as follows:

> *On ethics*: A Christian ethic of sexuality is needed that honors but does not restrict sexual activity to marriage. *On homosexuality*: The fundamental moral problem is not gay men and lesbians but rather heterosexism, the oppression of this sexual minority by the privileged majority. *On fornication*: No longer will the church insist that celibacy is the only moral option for single persons. The moral norm of Christians ought not to be marriage but "justice-love."[4]

The moral philistines of our day are relentless. They take no prisoners. Recently in DeFuniak Springs, Florida, lawyers for a man charged with child abuse asked the trial judge to remove a plaque of the Ten Commandments from outside a courtroom because it prejudiced the jurors. (Presumably the Seventh Commandment was the prejudicial statement.) At first, the circuit court judge ordered the plaque covered. But after a publicity campaign by local clergy and a politician, the judge granted a change of venue. Subsequent rulings both in Florida and in Georgia have ruled the displays unconstitutional.[5]

The bottom line is, the Seventh Commandment — "You shall not commit adultery" — has fallen to increasing disfavor. Even more, the church has not escaped its devaluation, as the now famous 1988 *Christianity Today* survey so painfully demonstrated: 23 percent of its readers had had extramarital intercourse, and 45 percent had done something they themselves had deemed sexually inappropriate.[6] For the population of *CT* readers, one in four Christian men are unfaithful, and nearly one half have behaved unbecomingly. How sad if these trends are representative of American evangelicals. As to the women, the count could likewise be intoned, only with less frequency — but the statistical margin is shrinking.

A sensual plague has struck the church, and I see it firsthand. In my wife's and my travels we have met evangelical pastors who have confessed to serial adultery in successive pastorates, child molestation, bestiality, and even some who subsequently died of AIDS. We can no longer be shocked. If this be the shape of the generals, how much more the troops? Only God knows!

This is why the Seventh Commandment is a luminous Word of Grace. God's prohibition of adultery, properly set in the corpus of Scripture, is a radiant jewel that flashes light and life on human existence. Taken to heart, it can revive a dying relationship with God. Taken to heart, it can resurrect a marriage. Taken to heart, it can energize a church.

As we take up the Seventh Word, we must understand and own

that the proper attitude for expounding this subject comes from an awareness of one's own sinfulness. Martin Luther coined a classic Latin phrase for this: *simul justus et peccator*: "at the same time righteous and a sinner." The phrase perfectly combined what he knew himself to be — righteous by God's gift from above, but in himself a sinner. Such an awareness will foster humility and even tears. Anyone who can discuss this topic lightly or with condescension is self-disqualified.

This attitude must also be matched with a confidence in the gracious forgiveness God extends to repentant sinners. No one, regardless of how many times he or she has flagrantly transgressed God's Commandment, is beyond God's grace. I have seen God do bona fide miracles of healing and restoration. The Seventh Word is an invitation to God's grace!

ADULTERY FORBIDDEN

The most scandalous misprint in all of Bible-making came in the year 1631 when someone discovered a word missing in the hot-off-the-press *King James Version*. It was the word "not" in the Seventh Commandment — which then made the Authorized Version to read, "Thou shalt commit adultery." Archbishop Laud was so enraged that he fined the printers £300 — easily a lifetime's income! Thereafter the 1631 edition became known as the "Wicked Bible."[7]

One wonders, was this a conscious omission or a pre-Freudian slip? But there is no doubt whatsoever about what the full Commandment prohibits: sexual relations between a husband and someone else's wife, or of a wife with the husband of another. Adultery in the strictest sense was and is a sin possible only for the married. Ultimately, however, it became the basis for the prohibition of a whole range of sexual sins, which Christ expanded to the wide range forbidden in the New Testament (cf. Matthew 5:27-32).[8]

The frequency of the prohibition of adultery is second only to idolatry in the Old Testament, and second to none in the New Testament. It was considered to be a heinous sin, not only against another person, but against God, as expressed by King David's pitiful cry, "Against you, you only, have I sinned" (Psalm 51:4; cf. Genesis 20:6; 39:9).

Great Sin

The immensity of this offense rose from several factors. First was the *sacredness* of marriage, a view which has suffered in recent years, a prime example being pop poet Rod McKuen's wedding "vows." To get the proper feel for this, we must imagine a groovy couple wearing bellbottoms, standing barefoot before the minister, and saying to each other, "I believe in love. I believe the person I will walk away with today to start another lifetime with to be someone I wish to comfort and I will expect comfort in return. I will share everything I have to share, and I will always expect the sharing and the giving to be returned." The pastor then says his piece: "This is a vow for forever. If forever should end for the two of you, or one of you, tomorrow, or next year, stay together only as long as you need each other. Go only when your need for the other ends."[9]

The Bible owns no such linguistic and moral hocus-pocus. Marriage forms a sacred, indissoluble bond between a man and a woman before God, for the duration of life on earth. To transgress the marriage bond is a grievous sin (cf. Matthew 19:4-6).

Secondly, adultery was a huge sin because of the *sacredness* of the human body, and ultimately of Christ Himself. A living human is innately connected with both the material and spiritual world. That body, first committed to a sacred trust and then prostituted from its commitment, inflicts a sacrilege upon itself.

In the New Testament, Paul calls adultery a sin against the body: "Flee from sexual immorality. All other sins a man commits are outside his body, but he who sins sexually sins against his own body" (1 Corinthians 6:18). Clearly, the apostle puts sexual sin in a category by itself, apart and distinct from other sins. Why? Because a Christian's body is a member of Christ, as Paul had explained in the immediately preceding verses:

> Do you not know that your bodies are members of Christ himself? Shall I then take the members of Christ and unite them with a prostitute? Never! Do you not know that he who unites himself with a prostitute is one with her in body? For it is said, "The two will become one flesh." But he who unites himself with the Lord is one with him in spirit. (vv. 15-17)

Paul's assertion is that sexual sin by the Christian is directed against the Lord, with whom he is in union.

New Testament scholar Gordon Fee explains:

> In fornicating . . . a man removes his body (which is a temple of the Spirit, purchased by God and destined for resurrection) from union with Christ and makes it a member of her body, thereby putting it under her "mastery" (v. 12b; cf. 7:4). Every other sin is apart from (i.e., not "in") the body in this singular sense. . . . Thus the unique nature of sexual sin is not so much that one sins against one's own self, but against one's own body as *viewed in terms of its place in redemptive history.*[10]

Therefore, Paul follows immediately with this explanation and charge: "Do you not know that your body is a temple of the Holy Spirit, who is in you, whom you have received from God? You are not your own; you were bought at a price. Therefore honor God with your body" (vv. 19, 20).

So we see that adultery and its kin are unique in their sacrilege and spiritual devastation. Adultery is a sin against the sacredness of *marriage*, the sacredness of *one's own body*, and the "*body of Christ*" — not just against the church, but against Christ Himself. Calvin bluntly portrays sexual sin as a "rape" of the body of Christ.[11]

One does not have to be a therapist to know the miseries that attend adultery — the harm to *self*: the ego disintegration that takes place from multiple illicit unions, the Willy Loman type of guilt, the disease, the disgust and self-hatred; the harm to *marriage*: the betrayal, the destruction to one's spouse, the possibility of divorce; the harm to *children*. Infidelity tells a child, "Your mother is not worth much, and your father is a liar and a cheat. Furthermore, honor is not nearly as important as pleasure. In fact, my child, my own satisfaction is more important than you."[12] This, of course, is followed by the harm to the *church* as it is evacuated of power and authenticity; and harm to the *world*, for if the gospel cannot give Christians the power to control their sexuality, how can it save the world?

Great Grace

But we must also see the other side of the coin — the immense grace that floods from fidelity to the Seventh Word. I can testify that faithfulness has enhanced my intimacy with God. The divine analogy between human marriage and our union with Christ is only an analogy, and yet it is the most far-reaching of all types of the mystical union between Christ and His church. Faithfulness to the earthly analogy cannot help but enrich one's experience of the heavenly.

Faithfulness has also been the soul of my marriage for thirty-plus years. Marital love plus absolute commitment and trust builds a sweet intimacy that is sublime. My wife is my soulmate, and I am hers. She is my confidant, my best friend, my excitement, my dream. Robert Browning's words say it well:

Grow old along with me!
  The best is yet to be. . . .

My sons and daughters know I love and respect their mother
— and that is more important than the knowledge that I love them.
For if I love her so, I will surely love them. They know that I am
no poseur. And because of my integrity I can call them and their
spouses to the same fidelity.

The Seventh Word is the way of grace: grace with God — grace
in marriage — grace in family — and grace in the church and
world.

ADULTEROUS THOUGHTS FORBIDDEN

We all know there is much more to adultery than the *physical* act,
and Jesus addressed that with unparalleled eloquence. But before
we ascend to the Master's thoughts, one other thing must be said:
do not succumb to the untidy reasoning that there is no difference
between *physical* and *mental* adultery. It is true that lust, lascivi-
ousness, and adulterous thoughts are damning sins that, unfor-
given, will send one to Hell as surely as adultery. Nevertheless,
adultery is a greater sin. Adultery breaks the marriage covenant,
whereas adulterous thoughts do not. Adultery provides the ground
for divorce, whereas mental adultery does not. Adultery violates
and defiles another's body, whereas its mental counterpart does
not. Adultery invites abortion, whereas the other does not.
Adultery is the vehicle for sexually transmitted diseases, whereas
the mind is not. There are vast, substantive differences between
mental adultery and the act of adultery. Never fall to the "If you've
thought it, you've done it!" fallacy. However, this is not to say that
mental adultery ("adultery . . . in his heart," Matthew 5:27) is not
a serious matter.

Now, having made that point, it must be said that to regard

immorality as only one thing, sexual sin, is to err greatly. For example, grasping, unscrupulous people are certainly immoral. Similarly, the mentally adulterous man or woman (who has never committed sexual sin) is an immoral man or woman.

Jesus' exposition of the Seventh Commandment raises the standard to its spiritual conclusion: "You have heard that it was said, 'Do not commit adultery.' But I tell you that anyone who looks at a woman lustfully has already committed adultery with her in his heart" (Matthew 5:27, 28). This, then, is a call to radical purity.

Tragically, Abigail Van Buren ("Dear Abby"), counselor for millions, regularly tells her correspondents that sexual fantasy is normal and harmless — and even beneficial so long as the imagined illicit relationships are not carried out. She goes even further, blasphemously saying that the teaching of Christ on lust is one of the most damaging religious teachings ever put upon the human race.[13] But what she ignores is that faithfulness is an act of the mind, not merely the body. Intimacy, commitment, and mutual trust are first violated in the mind. To imagine intimacy with someone else is to break unity and assault the divine metaphor — and to begin to erode one's marriage.

Jesus forbids the second look. Generally, one is not responsible for the first look. But culpability begins with the repeated look, the stare, the libidinous leer. This is why Job said, "I made a covenant with my eyes not to look lustfully at a girl" (Job 31:1).

Jesus' command forbids fantasizing. Of course, He is not condemning the normal curiosity that goes along with growing up and naturally involves the imagination. Rather, He forbids mental musings that would be immoral if acted out. Jesus' teaching condemns sexual fantasizing and voyeurism out of hand, as well as all pornography and indeed anything that leads one to sinfully sensual thoughts.

Our Lord couched His demand in the most drastic of terms: "If your right eye causes you to sin, gouge it out and throw it away. It is better for you to lose one part of your body than for your whole body to be thrown into hell. And if your right hand causes you to sin, cut it off and throw it away. It is better for you to lose one part of your body than for your whole body to go into hell" (Matthew 5:29, 30). Elsewhere Jesus includes the foot: "And if your foot causes you to sin, cut it off. It is better for you to enter life crippled than to have two feet and be thrown into hell" (Mark 9:45).

Predictably, there have been some who have taken this literally, as did the brilliant theological student who went crazy one night and cut off his hand with a razor. When his friends found him, he was laughing exultantly, saying, "I did right. . . . I can look Jesus in the face."[14] The most famous case of crass literalism was Origen of Alexandria, who had himself emasculated in an attempt to overcome sexual desires. It is significant that not long after that, the Council of Nicea outlawed this practice. Such mutilation is not only contrary to the Scripture, but it is possible to be minus hands, feet, and eyes and to be neutered and still be the most libidinous, proud person in town!

Jesus is not calling for physical mutilation but spiritual mortification, cutting off spiritually harmful practices from one's life.

The gory metaphors tell us that halfway measures just will not do it. There must be a severing, a gouging out of sin, if there is to be victory. This must be decisive and complete — as serious and final as a hand or foot or eye cast upon the floor.

The metaphorical language here further suggests that you alone must do it. It is "*your* hand," "*your* foot," "*your* eye" that you must cast away. It is a delusion to think that anyone else can or should do it for you.

Christ's compelling logic demands some answers. Are there places where your feet carry you that you have no business being — perhaps a social establishment you visit after-hours? Are there events you attend that involve temptations you cannot handle? Regarding the hand, are there hidden activities or habits that occupy you, things perhaps which if someone else knew about, you would be most embarrassed?

Finally, and importantly, Jesus' metaphors recommend that we be willing to endure pain in order to conquer our sinful habits. It hurts to sever your foot or to tear out an eye, and it hurts to give up wrong things in our lives. But better your blood on the ground than your life on the rubbish heap for eternity!

If God is speaking to you to do this, *do His bidding now.*

DISCIPLINES OF GRACE

God's Seventh Word, however restrictive and out-of-date popular culture holds it to be, is a supreme Word of Grace, and it calls for a gracious response on our part — some disciplines of grace.

• *Seek God.* The greatest motivation for purity is one's desire for God Himself. Sexual sins and impure thoughts are impediments to intimacy with God. Jesus said, "Blessed are the pure in heart, for they will see God" (Matthew 5:8). Your purity will enhance your vision of God; impurity will impede it. Therefore, the best thing you can do to overcome sexual sin is to seek God with all you have. Paul wisely advised:

> Since, then, you have been raised with Christ, set your hearts on things above, where Christ is seated at the right hand of God. Set your minds on things above, not on earthly things. For you died, and your life is now hidden with Christ in God. When Christ, who is your life, appears, then you also will appear with him in glory. (Colossians 3:1-4)

• *Pray.* Along with this comes the discipline of prayer. Pray daily and specifically for your own purity. Amazingly, many men and women who are concerned about their sexual proclivities do not pray about it. Enlist the prayers of your spouse and friends, and pray for others in this respect. Do not wait to be asked. Your friends need prayer, and so do you.

• *Divine awareness.* Next, there is the discipline of divine awareness. This is what sustained Joseph through the temptations by Potiphar's wife. "How then could I do such a wicked thing," he said, "and sin against God?" (Genesis 39:9), and he fled. "Flee the evil desires of youth, and pursue righteousness, faith, love and peace, along with those who call on the Lord out of a pure heart" (2 Timothy 2:22). Many believers are practically ignorant of God's presence, like Jacob who suddenly saw it and cried out, "Surely the Lord is in this place, and I was not aware of it" (Genesis 28:16). We must discipline ourselves to the fact of the numinous, the presence of God and His angels, because that will steel us against our lower natures.

• *Memorization.* Next, fill yourself with God's Word through the discipline of memorization. Our Lord set the example *par excellence* in rebuffing Satan's temptations with four precise quotations from the Old Testament Scriptures (cf. Matthew 4:1-11). The Psalmist said, "How can a young man keep his way pure? By living according to your word" (119:9). And, "I have hidden your word in my heart that I might not sin against you" (119:11). Of course, he was referring to all of God's Word, not just the passages that deal with sensuality. Nevertheless, I have seen the disciplined memorization of 1 Thessalonians 4:3-8 change a Christian's life.

> It is God's will that you should be holy; that you should avoid sexual immorality; that each of you should learn to control his own body in a way that is holy and honorable, not in passionate lust like the heathen, who do not know God; and that in this matter no one should wrong his brother or take advantage of him. The Lord will punish men for all such sins, as we have already told you and warned you.

Other helpful passages include Job 31:1, Proverbs 6:27-29, Mark 9:42ff., Ephesians 5:3-7, and 2 Timothy 2:22.

• *Accountability.* An important place to begin our training is with the discipline of accountability. This is to be done with someone who will regularly hold you accountable for your moral life, asking you hard questions. If you are married, ideally you should use your spouse, but I also recommend another person, one who will give you no quarter in sensual matters. You need someone of the same gender who will understand your sensuality from the inside out — someone you can be completely honest with, to whom you can confess temptations and attractions. You need someone who will help you toe the mark and keep your soul faithful to God. Mutual accountability is the ideal. In this connection I think of a certain salesman who regularly maintains accountability via phone contact with other Christian salesmen and even works at scheduling trips to cities at the same time they will be there.

• *Church.* The discipline of regular church attendance is a must. Those struggling with sensuality and its attendant guilt must resist the urge to absent themselves from divine worship and the fellowship of the Body of Christ. The writer of Hebrews wisely charged his congregation, "Let us not give up meeting together, as some are in the habit of doing, but let us encourage one another — and all the more as you see the Day approaching" (10:25). He knew it is virtually impossible to lead a healthy Christian life if one is willfully separated from the church. You need the elevation of soul that comes from corporate worship. You need the regular teaching of the Word. You need the discipline of the church. The desire to bolt in guilt is all the more reason to be there!

• *Modesty.* The discipline of modest dress and deportment is essential. It is one thing to dress attractively and with good style; it is quite another to be given to preening in order to catch the admiring eye of the opposite sex — especially if one is married. Moreover, husbands especially, and occasionally wives as well, who encourage their spouses to dress so others will ogle their mate are toying with an explosive vanity. Additionally, chaste, modest speech will help preserve one's integrity, for it is but a small step from word to deed (cf. Ephesians 5:3, 4).

• *Eye to eye.* Lastly, there is the discipline of the eyes. It is true that the eyes of a sensual man will excite a sensual woman, and vice versa. The opposite sex knows what you do with your eyes. Learn to look the opposite sex in the eye. You will be amazed how it puts the other at ease. The other will feel respected and ultimately comfortable.

Let us discipline ourselves for the purpose of godliness.

This is the Seventh Word of Grace!

8

The Eighth Word of Grace

Property and Loving Others

You shall not steal.
EXODUS 20:15

MY WIFE, Barbara, who helps in the teaching of the four-year-olds in the Sunday school at the church I pastor, witnessed a revelation of human nature. It came at story-time when the Story Lady, Mrs. Teune, donned her hand puppet, Ladi, and told the children the story of Ladi's visit to the family doctor for a checkup. While there, Ladi spied a big red pencil just like the one she had always wanted.

As Mrs. Teune dramatized at some length Ladi's fixation on the wondrous red pencil, the entire group of forty-five preschoolers assumed an unnatural quiet — especially as she described Ladi's inching closer and closer to the scarlet pen while the doctor's back was turned — and then reaching out and touching it — and finally grasping the pencil, which she then quickly hid under her dress! But, alas, the doctor had seen the theft, for in a deep voice he said, "You must not take what doesn't belong to you."

Mrs. Teune was connecting because one of the four-year-olds, who happens to be my grandson, raised his hand, waving it insistently, and said, "Mrs. Teune, will you tell the story again?" And she did! — in exact detail, line by line until the fatal filch, while every child again sat motionless.

Their sweet little hearts were with Ladi in her every larcenous move because in their own brief time on earth my grandson and his peers had experienced the same little larcenies — and the same results! Covetousness and thievery are endemic to the human race. We all catch it, and we all, hopefully, get caught. Actually, it is in our family blood. One of my clearest memories of being that age is dreaming of a box of caps at Eddie's Ace Market, and then going to the market, creeping up to the counter while Eddie's back was turned, stealing two boxes, taking them home, shooting them in my cap gun, and never being caught — not by man, anyway.

Thievery is not only natural to the human condition, it presently rages through modern culture. I've had both my home and my car burglarized, the latter while it was parked (ironically, as I thought afterwards) in the underground parking lot of the Notre Dame Cathedral in Paris.

An ethical mist hangs over our national life, as a recent *New Yorker* cartoon drove home. It pictures two clean-shaven, middle-aged men sitting together in a jail cell. They are obviously politicians. One is saying to the other, "All along, I thought our lives of corruption fell well within community standards."

The media have reported that scores of members of Congress regularly abuse their banking privileges, some writing hundreds of bad checks. And almost all say they are not guilty of any wrongdoing. Schiller's cynicism is sadly appropriate: "It is criminal to steal a purse, daring to steal a fortune, a mark of greatness to steal a crown. The blame diminishes as the guilt increases."[1]

The ethical mist has become a killer fog in everyday life. It is estimated that employee theft accounts for 60 percent of all inventory losses. One drugstore chain, Super D Drugs, began integrity testing after what they termed a dramatic rise in "shrinkage." The testing centers on screening out would-be thieves. Super D's vice president for loss prevention says they have saved $400,000 in employee theft.[2] Indeed, dishonesty is so pervasive that some prominent voices are saying that if everyone would pay what they truly owe in income tax, the national debt would quickly disappear. This is, of course, presuming that the added income is not pilfered from the top.

In light of the undeniable immensity of the problem, are people concerned? As public policy, yes. But personally, no. You see, people have an endless capacity to condemn others while they excuse themselves for the same practice. This has huge implications for the future of our nation if it is true, say, that respect for property is foundational for society. For if such respect dissolves, life as we now know it will disappear.

This is also why the Eighth Commandment is a Word of Grace. If it is fully lived out in its profound implications, it will grace the church and, ultimately, society.

STEALING'S PROHIBITION

The Eighth Word couldn't be clearer — "You shall not steal" (Exodus 20:15). Calvin said of its clarity:

> He [God] could have easily put it in other ways. He could have said: "Be careful lest you take any of your neighbor's goods from him. Look out that you don't gain your profit at your fellowman's expenses. Beware not to engage in any violence." But in one word he said: *Don't steal.* And why? In order that we might regard fraudulent activity, robbery, graft, and all wrong with the greatest abhorrence, and be ashamed

of cheating anyone and be horrified (I say), seeing that we are guilty of stealing before God.[3]

The Command plainly forbids robbery and extortion — the taking of another's possessions by force or threat of force. And it also forbids similar crimes of stealth such as embezzlement, graft, and bribery.

Significantly, the prohibition against all theft is an implicit statement of the right to have personal property. It underlines the wrong-headedness of Marxist or collectivist ideas that would relegate all ownership to the state. At the same time, it is not a mandate for the self-centered, acquisitional materialism pursued by so many today.

Stealing was severely penalized in the Old Testament, primarily through stiff restitution. If one stole and disposed of a sheep or an ox, the required restitution was four sheep or five oxen! If the original animal was recovered, the restitution was double (Exodus 22:1-4). Fraud required full restitution plus one fifth of the full value of what was taken (Numbers 5:7). If one stole another human being, restitution was to be made with the kidnapper's life (Exodus 21:16; Deuteronomy 24:7). The purpose behind the Eighth Commandment was readily apparent — a well-regulated society that respected and protected one another's property. As such, the Commandment was a substantial societal grace.

STEALING'S ESSENCE

What lies at the heart of stealing? The answer is best seen if we reflect on the impulse that faith, especially faith in Christ, brings — namely, *giving*. C. S. Lewis wrote: "God loves us; not because we are loveable but because he is love, not because he needs to receive but because he delights to give." This truth received eloquent statement from St. Paul in 2 Corinthians 8:9 — "For you know the grace of our Lord Jesus Christ, that though he was rich, yet for your sakes he became poor, so that you through his poverty might become rich." Jesus was the giver nonpareil! Interestingly, this wonderful statement concerning Christ is lodged in a chapter that repeatedly asserts the astounding giving of the early church. The connection is clear: God gives, and His children give. It is a family trait — a grace trait. Christianity sees the needs of others and denies itself, even forgoing personal comfort in order to help others.

In marked contrast, stealing contradicts the generous, giving essence of Christianity and enthrones self as the center of one's universe. One's "needs" become the driving force behind life. The thief says, "I am first, and nothing will stand in the way of my pleasure and self-gratification." The essence of true Christian living then, is *giving*, as compared to the essence of thievery, which is *getting*.

We have drawn this emphasis in order to point out that the modern focus on materialism provides a toxic lure toward the descent into thievery. As Donald Hagner has written, the credo of American Society is, "to get is to live," and the on-the-street version of Christ's words is, "Truly, truly a man's life *does* consist in the abundance of his possessions."[4] The old Jack Benny skit used to bring the point home. Mr. Benny is walking along when suddenly an armed robber approaches him and demands, "Your money or your life!" Benny pauses and does nothing. The robber impatiently shouts, "Well?" And Jack Benny replies, "Don't rush me. I'm thinking about it."

Today's advertising inflames the living is getting delusion by its promotion of the idea that what we possess is what we are. Consider the Cadillac commercial that abandons all subtlety and urges us to buy with the repeated jingle, "Whose Cadillac is that? Whose Cadillac is that?" The idea is that when people look at the car, they will be transfixed by its automotive elegance and will wonder what empyrean being will float down the street and slide in behind the wheel — "Whose Cadillac is that?" The further suggestion is that if you buy a Cadillac, *you* will be one of those celestial persons who forever hears, "Whose Cadillac is that?," intoned by the worshiping masses of Chevrolet owners, for example.

The Siren song has numerous versions: "great people have great things," "inferior people have inferior things," "the best people have the best things." Spending for identification . . . Buying significance.

Ridiculous! we think. But this takes its toxic toll not only on our credit cards but in the creation of a society of thieves. Because if living is getting, and if one does not make enough to get and live, then one is entitled to steal. Theft becomes the avenue to a meaningful *persona* — and thus is a perverse moral imperative. Theft is, then, the great leveler.

STEALING'S SUBTLETIES

Of course, relatively few of us become felons, but the sin of stealing is indulged in by millions who would be insulted were they ever to be called, "Thief!" Martin Luther said, "If all thieves — who nevertheless do not wish to be considered such — were to be hanged to the gallows, the world would soon be desolate, and would be without both executioners and gallows."[5]

The common rationalization seems to be that if theft occurs against an impersonal institution or against the rich, it is okay — or, at least, not so bad. Such thinking is often inconsistent and confused, as the teacher learned when she was attempting to impress her students with the importance of honesty. She had asked her class, "Suppose you found a briefcase with half a million dollars in it. What would you do?" Johnny raised his hand immediately and replied, "If it belonged to a poor family I'd return it!"

Common Thefts

Thievery's subtleties insinuate themselves into everyday conduct, so that they are scarcely noticeable. Life becomes "larceny as usual."

Tax theft is at the top. Omissions of hidden income, fudging, and falsification are epidemic. *Customs theft* is right up there with it. A United States Customs officer told me personally that he is appalled by the number of Christians he apprehends. There is also *debt theft*. Those who refuse to pay their debts effectively rob another. Not a few small businessmen have been put out of business by customers who would not pay up. Similar stealing takes place through *borrowing theft* that is inflicted by chronic borrowers who subconsciously have no intention to return the eggs, the saw, the book, or the money. Akin to this is the petty larceny of the parsimonious church elder who would never steal anything — except a daily read of the newsstand's paper, which he neatly replaces without parting with a cent of "the Lord's money." *Welfare theft* has become an institution for some who would rather let the government support them than do it themselves. And now, most recently, we have *computer theft* that takes place on the netherworld of a luminous screen behind closed doors where copyrighted software is pilfered, and, the thieves think, no one will ever know.

Employee Theft

As the 1990s began, James Patterson and Peter Kim conducted the largest survey of morals ever taken anywhere and published the results in the 1991 best-seller, *The Day America Told the Truth*. This is their conclusion about workers in America:

> The so-called Protestant ethic is long gone from today's American workplace.
>
> Workers around America frankly admit that they spend more than 20 percent of their time at work totally goofing off. That amounts to a four-day work week across the nation.
>
> Almost half of us admit to chronic malingering, calling in sick when we are not sick, and doing it regularly.
>
> One in six Americans regularly drink or use drugs on the job.

Only one in four give work their best effort; only one in
four work to realize their human potential rather than merely
to keep the wolf from the door.[6]

Employee theft has many faces: *Time theft* — coming in late
and leaving early and, while there, taking extended breaks and loaf-
ing whenever possible. *Work theft* — doing shoddy, substandard
work. *Phone theft* — using the company phone for personal calls.
Expense account theft — taking friends to lunch and reporting it
as "business," or using company funds to make personal purchases. *Supply pilfering* — filching stamps, envelopes, copy
machine and other company products, etc.

Management Theft

This occurs through abusing employees by paying inadequate
wages for services rendered or by allowing unsafe working conditions to exist. Businesses can also steal by the deception of con-
sumers, unfair profit-taking, marketing inferior products, or
building obsolescence into goods. John Calvin, the theological
father of modern capitalism, has strong words for such conduct,
excoriating the manufacturer or entrepreneur who takes advantage
of an unwilling customer. He warns that withering judgment will
be pronounced on such persons.[7] It will be a fearful thing when
some of our leading economic moguls stand before God. Much will
be required of them.

Subtler Thefts

But the sin of stealing has even broader, more subtle application. For
example, *plagiarius* means "kidnapper" in Latin, so we understand
that the plagiarist is someone who snatches a writer's brainchildren.[8]
Plagiarism is a shabby theft. It is a distressing experience to have
one's hard-earned paragraphs served up as another person's off-
spring. This is literary fornication! Lance Morrow describes his vic-
timization this way: "The words mocked me across the distance, like

an ex-wife who shows up years later looking much the same but married to a gangster."⁹ Such a theft can be immensely hurtful to the original writer and to the plagiarist (consider Senator Joseph Biden).

Cheating — that is, taking unfair advantage, whether in business or in a classroom — steals from the others involved. Academic cheating steals the time spent in study by one's fellow students, for it diminishes the outward results of their work when compared with that of the cheater. Cheating is a palpable theft and is as damning as stealing another's savings.

Reputations can also be pilfered, through a devilish subtraction of one's esteem through jealousy and gossip. Shakespeare wrote in *Othello*:

> *Good name in man and woman, dear my lord,*
> *Is the immediate jewel of their souls.*
> > *Who steals my purse, steals trash; 'tis*
> > *something, nothing;*
> *'Twas mine, 'tis his and has been slave to*
> > *thousands;*
> *But he that filches from me my good name*
> *Robs me of that which not enriches him*
> *And makes me poor indeed.*
> > —Scene III, 156

Perhaps the subtlest theft is the patently Christian sin of failing to give from what God has given you. However one regards the tithe, the principle obtains: "Will a man rob God? Yet you rob me. But you ask, 'How do we rob you?' In tithes and offerings" (Malachi 3:8).

STEALING'S TOLL

We may or may not be thieving felons, but few, if any of us, have escaped the subtle thefts of life. We all have fallen short. And most of us continue to fall short. The materialistic "to get is to live" poisons our existence. So we find ourselves stealing: a tax deduction — our company's time — our customers' trusting dollar — an author's brainchild — a reputation. It seems no "big thing." But it is. That is because every theft, even the most hidden and subtle of them, takes its toll on who we are. Such sins extinguish the sparkle in the eye, inject distance where there ought to be engagement, and smother our souls. And because we are members of each other, the smallest thefts leave unholy fingerprints on our brothers' and sisters' souls.

Besides, small thefts often lead to bigger thefts. William Hendricks explains in *Keeping Your Ethical Edge Sharp*: "What we do in the small issues of life sets the stage for bigger issues. What we do at the copier, on the phone, in front of the mail machine are important and set the stage for how we will respond to greater temptations that *will come!* It is also true that once we violate our conscience in an area it is easier to do it the next time. Before long, our heart becomes callous."[10] Hendricks goes on to relate how after speaking on the radio about ethics, he received a letter from an inmate in a federal prison that detailed how he and three other men had been leading executives in a defense contracting company that had won acclaim from President Reagan himself. The letter further chronicled how the man had become a Christian as a boy. But early in his twenties he had began to compromise his integrity in so-called "little" things — with increasing ease as time went on. His company grew, but the growth came through his participation in a scam that illegally stole thousands of dollars of taxpayers' money. The story was made even more poignant for Hendricks when during the same week that he received that tragic letter, he happened to have lunch with a Justice Department prosecutor. The prosecutor was the one who had won the man's conviction! Says Hendricks, "He [the prosecutor] was astounded that the prisoner knew Christ. Compromise is habit forming."[11]

We may think "little" sins do not count. But they are being counted in our character. *God, give us the humility and grace to receive and believe this.*

STEALING'S REMEDY

What is the answer in this world raging with theft?

Regeneration

It must begin with conversion. When the wealthy materialist Zacchaeus came to Christ, he brought with him a thieving past. The Jews hated him for his legalized tax thefts. But when he met Christ, this was his regenerated life's vow: "Look, Lord! Here and now I give half of my possessions to the poor, and if I have cheated anybody out of anything, I will pay back four times the amount" (Luke 19:8). Zacchaeus' example tells us that you may be presently so grasping that you cannot imagine letting go of what you've gotten. But Christ can open your grip like an unfolding flower.

Restitution

Next, give back everything you have stolen. If it is God's will to do so (and it is!), He will make it possible for you to do this.

Most of all, you need Christ. The question is, Is your life truly His? Do you know beyond a shadow of a doubt that your sins are forgiven and that He is the captain of your soul? Are you assured of the power within to change? If not, do not go any further. Confess your belief that Jesus is God's Son, who died for your sins. Repent of your sins and ask Him to remove your guilt. Thank Him for the faith to believe, and for your salvation.

DISCIPLINES OF GRACE

If you are a believer, it will do your soul immense good to *undergo careful self-examination* in regard to subtle theft in your life. Your life in Christ demands moral meticulousness right down to the paper clips in your desk. So honestly respond to these suggestive terms. How do you measure up?

Are you a good citizen?

- Tax theft
- Customs theft
- Debt theft
- Borrower theft
- Welfare theft
- Computer theft
- Literary theft
- Academic theft
- Reputation theft
- Giving theft

Are you a good employee?

- Time theft
- Work theft
- Phone theft
- Expense theft
- Supply theft

Next *repent* specifically and in detail of any thefts. Then, wherever possible, *make restitution.*

Finally, *rest in God's grace.* Grace will help you love others as yourself. Grace will help you to give. Grace will produce more grace.

This is the Eighth Word of Grace!

9

The Ninth Word of Grace

Truth and
Loving Others

*You shall not give false
testimony against your neighbor.*
EXODUS 20:16

TODAY IT IS understood that Immanuel Kant's philosophy was the continental divide for modern thinking — the turning point from truth to ideology. Christians believe his work was one of the greatest philosophical mistakes of all time. Kant taught that no one could ever know objective truth, that all one could ever do was impose one's personal, subjective mental categories onto reality.[1] Therefore, according to Kant, truth is relative to the mind. Kantian thinking has become so pervasive that professor Allan Bloom began his celebrated book *The Closing of the American Mind* with these words:

> There is one thing a professor can be absolutely certain of: almost every student entering the university believes, or says he believes, that truth is relative. If this belief is put to the test,

one can count on the students' reaction: they will be uncomprehending. That anyone should regard the proposition as not self-evident astonishes them, as though he were calling into question $2 + 2 = 4$.[2]

This, of course, has had a doleful effect on the virtue of truth-telling. If you cannot know the truth, if truth is only what you subjectively think, how can you tell the truth? Besides, lying is of little consequence if all knowledge is subjective opinion.

Of course, lying is not new. People have always managed very well in its practice. But the prevailing skepticism regarding truth has made it so much easier and acceptable.

Thus, the post-Kantian twentieth century has become the century of the great lie. Slogans and propaganda (which bypass reason) have become the tool for intellectual and political dominance. The Communist movement lived on this, even arguing at times that "reason is the tool of the bourgeoisie" as they refused rational discourse and shouted their slogans over and over again. And western democracies have not escaped, because today, in politics and in other arenas, image is everything. Images transcend reason, and politicians are often elected, not for what they think, but rather for their putative "image."

During the last decade, lying as a necessary part of human nature has received support from the scientific community as well. To be sure, Biblical theology teaches that lying is endemic to human personality, that we are by nature liars. But it is quite another thing to view it as a necessity, or even as a socially adaptive virtue. However, that is precisely what researchers recently told the annual meeting of the American Association for the Advancement of Science when they argued that "proficiency at lying may be the best measure of advancement, with primates much more adept at it than other mammals and human beings the most masterful deceivers on the planet."[3] Thus, the evolutionary hypothesis presents a moral proclivity as a necessary virtue. Some speakers at the conference went even further, arguing that the human capacity for lying to self by creating religion (i.e., "culturally determined perceptions of nature") aided in man's survival. So there we have it: lying is an indispensable, socially adaptive virtue. We couldn't survive without it!

Very significantly, this is also what some child psychologists are saying. A case in point is *Child* magazine's April 1990 article "The Truth About Lying," which is captioned:

> *The Old View:* Lying, like other issues of morality, was seen only in black and white. Children were taught that all lying was bad, deserving of strict punishment, and frequently reminded that "lying will make your nose grow as long as Pinocchio's." *The New View:* Today, some lying is considered normal. In fact, a child's first few lies are seen as an important step in the development of the self.[4]

Again, we would agree that lying is certainly normal, and further that parents need not overreact to their children's lies. (By the way, the article does contain some helpful advice for dealing with a child's lies.) But to see your child's first few lies as important to the development of self is problematic, to say the least. If this is so, then Jesus Christ never attained a healthy development of self! The implicit message of such articles is that lying in general is no big thing unless it's "pathological."

So here we are in the last decade of the twentieth century in a post-Kantian smog of relativism and agnosticism, where *Pinocchio* is reactionary, where lying is intellectually defended and propaganda *de rigueur* with our politicians and media. The result? We are a culture of liars.

According to the research data for *The Day America Told the Truth*:

Americans lie. They lie more than we had ever thought possible before the study. But they told us the truth about how much they lie.

JUST ABOUT EVERYONE LIES — 91 PERCENT OF US LIE REGULARLY.

The majority of us find it hard to get through a week without lying. One in five can't make it through a single day — and we're talking about conscious, premeditated lies. . . .

When we refrain from lying, it's less often because we think it's wrong (only 45 percent) than for a variety of other reasons, among them the fear of being caught (17 percent). . . .

We lie to just about everyone, and the better we know someone, the likelier we are to have told them a serious lie. . . . 36 percent of Americans confess to telling that kind of darker lie. . . .[5]

As to the question, who lies most in America?, the studies tell us:

- Men lie more than women.
- Young men lie more than older men.
- Gays and bisexuals lie more than heterosexuals.
- Blacks lie more than whites.
- Catholics lie a bit more than Protestants, and both lie more than Jews.
- Unemployed people lie more than those with jobs.
- The poor lie more than the rich.
- Liberals lie more than conservatives.

Among the authors' conclusions were these startling statements:

- There are more serious liars right now (liars who do harm) than at any time in our nation's past.

- Lying has become a cultural trait in America. Lying is embedded in our national character. That hasn't really been understood around the world. Americans lie about everything — and usually for no good reason.

- The majority of Americans today (two out of every three) believe there is nothing wrong with telling a lie. Only 31 percent of us believe honesty is the best policy.[6]

Honesty requires that we Christians admit that lying has also been a problem for the church, so that even the Apostle Paul had to exhort believers, "Do not lie to each other, since you have taken off your old self with its practices" (Colossians 3:9). But, candidly, we have to confess that today the disease flourishes in the Body of Christ. So widespread is it that 32 percent of Americans think they've been lied to by a clergyman.[7]

What is needed is a healing word, and none is more salving than the Ninth Word of Grace — "You shall not give false testimony against your neighbor" (Exodus 20:16; cf. Deuteronomy 5:20). This great Word gives us the basis for a singularly graced life. Lived out, it will bring grace in your relationship with God, your family, your church, and the world.

LYING: THE PROHIBITION

Strictly speaking, this Commandment was originally focused against perjuring oneself in a judicial trial, not against other forms of lying and deception. But just as with the previous Commandment against adultery, which was expanded by Christ to include adulterous thoughts, and likewise with the Commandment against murder, which was expanded to forbid hatred, so here the very serious sin of lying/perjury will be broadened to include the whole spectrum of lying — sins of the tongue.[8] Leviticus 19:11, which comments on the Ten Commandments, says simply, "Do not lie. Do not deceive one another" — giving us the gist of the Command.

The Scriptures are explicit that God hates lying in any form. "The Lord detests lying lips, but he delights in men who are truthful" (Proverbs 12:22). The famous divine diatribe in Proverbs, "There are six things the Lord hates, seven that are detestable to him," begins by listing "haughty eyes, a lying tongue" and ends with, "a false witness who pours out lies and a man who stirs up dissension among brothers" (Proverbs 6:16-19).

God's inveterate hatred of lying is embedded in the fact that He is *emeth*, true and faithful. It is therefore "impossible for God to lie" (Hebrews 6:18). His Son said simply, "I am the . . . truth" (John 14:6), and God's written Word bears the dominical seal, "Your word is truth" (John 17:17).

God hates falsehood because he is the Father of truth and, further, because Satan "is a liar and the father of lies" (John 8:44). Thus, lying so contradicts and outrages the character of God that it incurs his withering, unrelenting hatred. Moreover, lying as it is originally laid out here in the Ninth Commandment as perjury is a singular act of hatred toward another human being. This kind of lying is doubly loathsome because it attacks both God and man.

God's Word is most graphic about the coming punishment for those who practice lying and deceit. The Father warns, "No one who practices deceit will dwell in my house; no one who speaks falsely will stand in my presence" (Psalm 101:7). The Son warns, "But I tell you that men will have to give account on the day of judgment for every careless word they have spoken. For by your words you will be acquitted, and by your words you will be condemned" (Matthew 12:36, 37). This is sobering grist for reflection.

But the reverse is sublime, for telling the truth is an unfailing act of love to God and man. In fact, the truth-teller, according to Jesus, is actually fulfilling the second table of the Law — loving your neighbor just as you love yourself (Matthew 22:39; cf.

Leviticus 19:18). And God rewards those who so love. This is sweet substance for reflection!

LYING: THE MOTIVATIONS

The Kantian intellectual reasons aside, have you ever mused as to why we lie? There are many reasons, but some are more common than others.

Malevolence

The most grievous lies come from sheer malice and hatred. Unlike sword thrusts and bullet wounds, the tongue's wounds are more deadly, for words do not die. The book of Proverbs attests to the tongue's lethal power: "A gentle tongue can break a bone" (Proverbs 25:15). "Reckless words pierce like a sword" (Proverbs 12:18).

Have you ever been impaled by the sable shaft of a lying tongue? A dark missile comes flying from the night and lodges deep within your being. It cannot be pulled out, and so it remains, producing shooting pain with every attempted movement. Jeremiah the prophet wrote of his enemies, "Their tongue is a deadly arrow" (9:8), and "They make ready their tongue like a bow, to shoot lies" (9:3). Jeremiah's metaphor sees the tongue arch like a taut bow, flexed with incredible power, and then released, sending an unseen arrow into his soul. David, who had often been used for target practice, sang these dark lyrics: "[They] sharpen their tongues like swords and aim their words like deadly arrows. They shoot from ambush at the innocent man; they shoot at him suddenly, without fear" (Psalm 64:3, 4).

The bloody shafts of lies about oneself are relentlessly painful, because there is no way they can be removed or rendered powerless. Time and God's grace are the only healers, for lies diminish only as they rot and fall away.

Fear

Perhaps even more lies are told out of fear. This may be the root of most children's lies — fear of consequences. And the result is usually quite harmless. But in adults deception can have monstrous effects — Watergates, Irangates, Pearly Gates.

Embarrassment

Many lie to avoid embarrassment or to keep from hurting others' feelings. In 1987 the *Washington Post Magazine* devoted its year-end issue to "1987: The Year of the Big Lie." The *Post's* respondents said they lied 92 percent of the time to save face and 98 percent of the time to keep from offending someone else.[9] The latter reason often finds a congenial reception in the church, because concern for others' feelings is so purely "Christian."

Money

Some otherwise honest people find their Achilles' heel to be money. The rationalization is so reasonable: "Business is tough. The margin between success and failure is fractional. All my competitors 'fudge' on their accounting procedures. If I don't do what everyone else is doing I'll fail! And then what will my investors say? They all know that I'm a Christian. I can't let them down. God will understand." Of course, God *does* understand — all too well!

Culture

Some people lie because they see the application of the Scriptures' prohibition against lying as culturally conditioned. Robertson McQuilkin, past president of Columbia Bible College, recounts his encounter with this kind of thinking while a missionary in Japan:

> We were striving to achieve accreditation for our Christian theological school in Japan, surely a good end pursued for the glory of God. But the professor in charge of the project constantly brought for my signature documents that were not

factual. Finally in exasperation, he exclaimed, "A lie may become the cross you must bear!" It fit well with the Japanese proverb, "A lie also is a useful thing." When I still declined to sign, the professor gave up in disgust: "Your problem is that you haven't become accustomed to the Japanese way of doing things." Was this a mere clash of culture? Was God to be served best by deception in this cultural format? (I should add that he was the only Japanese colleague who held this position.)[10]

McQuilkin's clash points to a specter that looms large in much Christian thinking, even though it is rarely given such forthright articulation. So many succumb to the "that's the way things get done around here" delusion.

LYING: THE WAYS

The human mind seemingly knows no end to its creativity when it comes to rationalizing conduct. This capacity is only exceeded by the creation of deceptions and lies.

Slander

The most forthright is slander itself — lying about another's character or conduct. Thomas Watson, the Puritan divine, wrote: "The scorpion carries his poison in his tail, the slanderer carries his in his tongue."[11] Christ suffered such slander when He was called "a friend of sinners" — the implication being that He was a sinner Himself. And good John the Baptist was said to have a devil.

Slander is a sin to which the religious are particularly susceptible. So often when Christians learn to shed the obvious "big" sins, they become particularly vulnerable to dishing out pious slander. For while they are careful to avoid adultery, drunkenness, or stealing and are enviable examples of the upright life, they indulge a perverse delight in assaulting the character of others.

Gossip

Gossip is the unnecessary bearing of information that may or may not be true and is harmful to the subject. It isn't so much the things that "go in one ear and out the other" that hurt, as the things that go in one ear, get all mixed up, and then slip out of the mouth.

Here God's Word must be taken to heart.

- "Do not go about spreading slander among your people. . . . I am the Lord" (Leviticus 19:16).
- ". . . a gossip separates close friends" (Proverbs 16:28).
- "He who covers over an offense promotes love, but whoever repeats the matter separates close friends" (Proverbs 17:9).
- "The words of a gossip are like choice morsels; they go down to a man's inmost parts" (Proverbs 18:8).
- "Without wood a fire goes out; without gossip a quarrel dies down" (Proverbs 26:20).

Tale-bearing may be rationalized as a kind of Christian obligation — even a duty. But such reasoning ignores the straightforward teaching of Scripture.

Flattery

Among the subtlest forms of deceit is flattery, which someone has piquantly defined as "saying things to a person's face that you would never say behind his back!" Flattery does not come from love for that person, but rather from a love for self that wants to be noticed or perhaps ingratiated to the one being flattered. Elihu ominously spoke against this when he said, "I will show partiality to no one, nor will I flatter any man; for if I were skilled in flattery, my Maker would soon take me away" (Job 32:21, 22). God's people must avoid flattery just as the Apostle Paul and the writer of Proverbs averred: "You know we never used flattery" (1 Thessalonians 2:5); "do not associate with one who flatters with his lips" (Proverbs 20:19, NKJV).

Exaggeration

Playful exaggeration in story-telling — embellishing a story to entertain others — is not forbidden. But exaggerating one's work, as is so common in Christian ministry — making God's work more glorious or more "successful" than it is — is sin. Pretending that something is more wonderful than it is falls under the same condemnation.

Carelessness

Many people become "chronically inaccurate" in what they say. They do not lie deliberately but carelessly. For this reason Dr. Samuel Johnson, the great man of letters, advised: "Accustom your children . . . constantly to this; if a thing happened at one window and they, when relating it, say that it happened at another, do not let it pass, but instantly check them; you do not know where deviation from the truth will end."[12] The lazy lie is a sign of moral stagnation.

True Words

Even true statements can be employed to deceive others — as a ship's first mate so well understood. It seems that the first mate had been derelict in his duties and had been disciplined by the ship's captain. But a few days later he got his revenge when the captain became ill, and the first mate assumed running the ship — and the keeping of the ship's log. His opening entry that day began, "Captain sober today . . ." Perfectly true — and a perfect deception in what it implied!

Insinuation

Satan's slander of Job is instructive. His method involved an insinuating question: "Does Job fear God for nothing?" (Job 1:9). The enemy did not plainly slander Job as a believer who followed God for what he could get. He slyly raised the question — a grievous slander. This is so easy to do. "Is John really that smart?" "Why would Joe do that?" "Would Jane qualify for that position?" Insinuating questions are slippery libels on others. Those attacked are defenseless and the attackers unassailable — in this world.

Silence

The breaking of the Ninth Commandment need not be active, and in fact is very often done through passive silence. In the quick exchange of conversation, something untrue may be said about another, and instead of correcting it you let it pass. Slander by silence. Complicity by passivity.

It is better to be like David's friend Jonathan, who defended David regarding the slanders issued by his erratic, homicidal father Saul: "Let not the king do wrong to his servant David; he has not wronged you, and what he has done has benefited you greatly. . . . Why then would you do wrong to an innocent man like David by killing him for no reason?" (1 Samuel 19:4, 5b).

Because we are sinners, lying subtleties come naturally — *slander, gossip, flattery, exaggeration, carelessness, true words wrongly used, insinuation*, and *silence*, to name a few. The subtleties are so penetrating that any of us with an ounce of self-honesty feel interior conviction. Frankly, such tension is a sign of spiritual health.

LYING: THE DESTRUCTION

If we feel stirrings in our soul to do something about this, one further negative motivation is necessary — namely, an understanding of the destruction lying and deceit bring.

Character Destruction

Dr. McQuilkin eloquently states: "Falsehood is the basic faultline in the foundation of the soul, putting all the superstructure in jeopardy. All the believability a person has, his very integrity, totters on the shifting sand of one lie. Deceit holds hostage all other virtues."[13] There is no more effective way to destroy your character than deceit. Deceit removes the soul from reality. The self-deceived can become like Samson, who "did not know that the Lord had left him" (Judges 16:20).

Relationship Destruction

Inject lying and deceit into a relationship, and it will never be quite the same. Adultery is damning to one's relationship, not just because of the physical unfaithfulness, but because of the labyrinthine deceit. Lies are compounded with lies, and the lies are held together by the futile adhesive of more lies, which are then stapled together with additional lies, which are layered and paper-clipped to further falsehoods. Lie to your colleagues, your elders, your friends, or your family and life will never be what it was. Deceit eats relationships.

Church Destruction

Have you ever wondered why God so grievously punished Achan's deception? All he did was hide for himself a few of the spoils of battle. The answer is, his lie came at a crucial time in the formation of Israel. God deemed honesty and integrity so important to the future health of His people that Achan and his whole family had to forfeit their lives (Joshua 7). The same was true of the deaths of Ananias and Sapphira. All they did was claim that their giving was a greater sacrifice than it was. But God knew that the baby church could stand no such deception. Such lying would harm the Body, so both shamefully paid with their lives (Acts 5).

Any church can survive only on truth. Deceit will sink us.

Soul Destruction

Liars — unrepentant, self-deceived liars whose lives are characterized by deceit — will not know Heaven. God's Word is firm: "But the cowardly, the unbelieving, the vile, the murderers, the sexually immoral, those who practice magic arts, the idolaters and all liars — their place will be in the fiery lake of burning sulfur. This is the second death" (Revelation 21:8). Jesus explained more exactly, "But I tell you that men will have to give account on the day of judgment for every careless word they have spoken. For by your words you will be acquitted, and by your words you will be condemned" (Matthew 12:36, 37).

Oh, if we could truly grasp the horror of deceit — that it is a libel against God whose image we bear, that it destroys our *character*, our *relationships*, our *church*, and our *souls* — we would do all in our power to put it away! Do we really understand the horrific effects of deceit? Even more, do we *believe* it?

RADICAL TRUTHFULNESS

On the other hand, the truthful tongue can also be a mighty instrument of grace. It can be used to love others as we love ourselves. It can be the medium for fulfilling the second table of the Law. Job's righteous tongue foreshadowed the ideal, for Eliphaz extolled him, saying, "Your words have supported those who stumbled; you have strengthened faltering knees" (Job 4:4). "The tongue of the wise," said Solomon, "brings healing" (Proverbs 12:18b).

The New Testament gives the idea full expression: "speaking the truth in love, we will in all things grow up into him who is the Head, that is, Christ" (Ephesians 4:15). We see here that the medium of growth — this is exquisitely beautiful — is literally, "*truthing in love.*" This is the medium through which growth is maximized. When there is "truthing in love," when our tongues are married to love, the Spirit is free to do His work, and the result is wonderful. "Instead, speaking the truth in love, we will in all things grow up into him who is the Head, that is, Christ. From him the whole body, joined and held together by every supporting ligament, grows and builds itself up in love, as each part does its work" (vv. 15, 16). The tongue can help put others, and the church, together!

It's hard to tell the truth in this post-Kantian, self-deceived world that has substituted ideology for truth and feeling for facts — that believes that truth is relative. It's hard to be an honest person when lying has become a cultural trait in America — when we Americans lie about everything. But we must be honest for the sake of our character, our relationships, our church, and our souls. We must do this so grace will have free course in our lives and so our lives will grace a lost world.

DISCIPLINES OF GRACE

This calls not for petty verbal legalisms, but interior disciplines of grace.

Prayer

Ask God to watch over your mouth and to help you speak the truth. Candidly, this is a part of my regular prayers for myself because I naturally gravitate to falsehood and misuse of the tongue. Sometimes I exaggerate, sometimes I find myself delighting in passing on a delicious morsel of gossip, and there are terrible times that I flex my tongue and send a vicious dark arrow flying deep into another. The verse I keep next to my self-petition is Proverbs 24:26 — "An honest answer is like a kiss on the lips." As you pray for yourself, utilize some of the psalmist's prayers: "Keep me from deceitful ways" (Psalm 119:29). "Set a guard over my mouth, O Lord; keep watch over the door of my lips" (Psalm 141:3). Another good verse is, "Keep falsehood and lies far from me" (Proverbs 30:8).

Meditate

Meditate on Scriptures that specifically address lying, deceit, and truth. These include:

- "He who conceals his hatred has lying lips, and whoever spreads slander is a fool" (Proverbs 10:18).

- "With his mouth the godless destroys his neighbor, but through knowledge the righteous escape" (Proverbs 11:9).
- "A gossip betrays a confidence, but a trustworthy man keeps a secret" (Proverbs 11:13).
- "The words of the wicked lie in wait for blood, but the speech of the upright rescues them" (Proverbs 12:6).
- "The Lord detests lying lips, but he delights in men who are truthful" (Proverbs 12:22).
- "He who covers over an offense promotes love, but whoever repeats the matter separates close friends" (Proverbs 17:9).
- "The words of a gossip are like choice morsels; they go down to a man's inmost parts" (Proverbs 18:8).
- "Better a poor man whose walk is blameless than a fool whose lips are perverse" (Proverbs 19:1).
- "A false witness will not go unpunished, and he who pours out lies will not go free" (Proverbs 19:5).
- "He who guards his mouth and his tongue keeps himself from calamity" (Proverbs 21:23).
- "Like a coating of glaze over earthenware are fervent lips with an evil heart" (Proverbs 26:23).

Examination

Prayerfully examine your life in respect to lying, slowly utilizing the following list of the subtleties of deceit:
- Slander
- Gossip
- Flattery
- Exaggeration
- Carelessness
- True words
- Insinuation

- Silence

Amends

Whenever possible make amends for past deception.

Vows

Vow that by God's grace you will be lovingly truthful in all your dealings. "I said, 'I will watch my ways and keep my tongue from sin'" (Psalm 39:1).

10

The Tenth Word of Grace

Attitude and Loving Others

You shall not covet.

Exodus 20:17

*T*HE PEASANT Pahóm in Leo Tolstoy's short story "How Much Land Does a Man Need?" had become a man of property, and his ownership inflamed him with a desire for more land. As fortune would have it, through "chance" meetings, first with another peasant who came from beyond the Volga, and then with a traveling merchant, Pahóm learned of vast lands that could be obtained for a relative pittance from a far-off nomadic people called the Bashkírs. So Pahóm traveled to this distant land. It was all virgin soil, as flat as the palm of one's hand and as black as the seed of a poppy, with grasses chest high.

"And what will be the price?" asked Pahóm.
"Our price is always the same: one thousand rubles a day."
Pahóm did not understand.

"A day? What measure is that? How many acres would that be?"

"We do not know how to reckon it out," said the Chief. "We sell it by the day. As much as you can go round on your feet in a day is yours, and the price is one thousand rubles a day."

Pahóm was surprised.

"But in a day you can get round a large tract of land," he said.

The Chief laughed.

"It will all be yours!" said he. "But there is one condition: If you don't return on the same day to the spot whence you started, your money is lost."

That night Pahóm could not sleep. But shortly before dawn he drifted off, and he began to dream. He dreamt he was in his own tent and heard laughing from outside. Venturing forth he saw the Bashkir chief sitting in front of the tent holding his sides and rolling about in laughter. As he came closer, he saw that it was no longer the chief but the traveling merchant, and on further inspection it was instead the peasant from beyond the Volga. And then it was neither, for it was the Devil himself with horns and cloven hoofs, chuckling away. Before the Devil lay a barefoot man wearing only trousers and a shirt.

As Pahóm dreamt on he looked closer to see what sort of man it was, and he saw that the man was dead — and that the man was himself! Pahóm awoke in horror. "What things one does dream," he thought.

Pahóm reached the plain as the morning red was beginning to kindle. Placing his thousand rubles in the fur hat the chieftain had set on the ground, he began. His pace was neither slow nor quick, but as he walked through the land, he picked up his stride because with each step the land seemed better. In an effort to include a particularly inviting field, he went much too far before he set his marker and turned. Such was Pahóm's procedure as he hurried along ever faster under the hot sun, which then began to wester.

Exhausted after circling such a huge tract, Pahóm turned back toward the starting hill, walking with difficulty, and his legs began to drag. His chest was working like a blacksmith's bellows, his heart beat like a hammer, his legs sometimes failed him. Pahóm could see the hill with the Bashkírs cheering him on.

Tolstoy closes:

> Pahóm looked at the sun, which had reached the earth: one side of it had already disappeared. With all his remaining strength he rushed on, bending his body forward so that his legs could hardly follow fast enough to keep him from falling. Just as he reached the hillock it suddenly grew dark. He looked up — the sun had already set! He gave a cry: "All my labor has been in vain," thought he, and was about to stop, but he heard the Bashkírs still shouting, and remembered that though to him, from below, the sun seemed to have set, they on the hillock could still see it. He took a long breath and ran up the hillock. It was still light there. He reached the top and saw the cap. Before it sat the Chief laughing and holding his sides. Again Pahóm remembered his dream, and he uttered a cry: his legs gave way beneath him, he fell forward and reached the cap with his hands. . . .
>
> His servant picked up the spade and dug a grave long enough for Pahóm to lie in, and buried him in it. Six feet from his head to his heels was all he needed.[1]

"How Much Land Does a Man Need?" is a tale of immense power and universal appeal because covetous greed diseases the soul of humanity. Pahóm's race is being run right now through the streets of Tokyo and New York and along the tree-lined avenues of suburbia — with the same tragic ending.

We, of course, reject the disease as sub-Christian. But the fact is, every day a preacher somewhere presides over the grave of a but-toned-down brother or well-coiffed sister who has neurotically and compulsively sacrificed everything, including family, in the head-long charge up the elusive hilltop.

This is why God's Tenth Word is such a monumental Word of Grace — "You shall not covet your neighbor's house. You shall not covet your neighbor's wife, or his manservant or maidservant, his ox or donkey, or anything that belongs to your neighbor" (Exodus 20:17). Understood and lived out, the Tenth Word will silence Hell's amusement and invite the laughter of Heaven to grace one's footsteps. The Tenth Word applies to the world, of course. But we must remember that it was given to God's people, as a Word of Grace. It is for all of us — no exceptions.

COVETOUSNESS

The word for "covet" is the Hebrew *hāmad*, which is not a bad word by itself, because it simply means "desire." But, of course, here in the Tenth Commandment it is evil, so that the ancient trans-lators of the Old Testament into Greek used a word that means "lust" or "passionate longing." Paul uses the same word in the New Testament in direct reference to the Tenth Commandment (Romans 7:7). So we understand that the Commandment means we are not to lust after what is our neighbor's.

Specifically, we must not lust for his "house," which means his *possessions* and his *people*. Lusting after another's things, be they next door or across the street or in another city, is strictly forbid-den. Interestingly, the parallel version of this commandment in Deuteronomy 5:21 places lusting after another's spouse as the first thing forbidden — "You shall not covet your neighbor's wife" — for one's spouse is the crowning possession of any man or woman (cf. Proverbs 12:4).

Here we must be quick to add what the Commandment does not say, because it does not forbid desiring to have a wife or a husband or a home. It forbids desiring Mrs. or Mr. Jones or their cars, their furniture, their clothing, their landscaping, their ski-boat, their appliances, their lawnmower, even their style. It also forbids jealousy because they have these things; it forbids "poor me" bitterness and an attitude of ungratefulness toward God.

If you haven't yet noticed, the Tenth Word differs from the preceding Commandments because instead of forbidding an action, it forbids a *state of mind*. The Tenth Commandment goes right to where no other human being can see. You can be living out an orgy of covetousness, and no one will know it. You may have a conventional, congenial face and wear a conventional haircut, you may not have a single tell-tale extravagance in your life (no panache), you may be an elder in your church — and yet be seething with angry covetousness! No one would come even close to dreaming that you are covetous. It is an easily camouflaged interior sin.

We must also take notice that covetousness is in direct antithesis to the main thrust of the second table of the Law — namely, to "love your neighbor as yourself." Covetousness is self-serving and self-loving. Covetousness promotes breaking the second table, commandment by commandment. The Fifth Word — "Honor your father and your mother" — falls to the covetousness that says my possessions are "Corban" (devoted to God) and therefore I cannot help my parents. The Sixth Word — "You shall not murder" — is regularly transgressed by coveting for something that is another's. The Seventh Word — "You shall not commit adultery" — is always broken first by coveting another person. It is likewise with the Eighth Word — "You shall not steal." The Ninth Word — "You shall not give false testimony" — is often broken because of covetous desires.

Covetousness, then, is at the heart of assaults on fellow humans and the breaking of the Commandments. A covetous man or woman cannot love others as himself or herself!

This makes the Tenth Word so important because if we, by God's grace, can get this teaching in our hearts and minds, a whole dictionary of sins will go uncommitted by us!

AN INSIDIOUS SIN

Covetousness is excoriated by the Scriptures. The prophet Micah saw it as the source of iniquity and oppression,

> *Woe to those who plan iniquity,*
> *   to those who plot evil on their beds!*
> *At morning's light they carry it out*
> *   because it is in their power to do it.*
> *They covet fields and seize them,*
> *   and houses, and take them.*
> *They defraud a man of his home,*
> *   a fellowman of his inheritance.*
>   —Micah 2:1, 2

Proverbs views covetousness as the dividing line between righteous and evil people: "All day long he craves for more, but the righteous give without sparing" (21:26). Jesus warned a covetous young man who requested Him to make his brother divide the family inheritance, saying, "Watch out! Be on your guard against all kinds of greed; a man's life does not consist in the abundance of his possessions" (Luke 12:15). Then Jesus went on to teach the parable of the rich fool who planned out his full-barned early retirement, only to die the very night the plan was complete. Early retirement indeed! (See Luke 12:16-21.)

The Apostle Paul repeatedly assaulted covetousness. He told the Ephesian church, "But among you there must not be even a hint of sexual immorality, or of any kind of impurity, or of greed, because these are improper for God's holy people" (Ephesians 5:3). To the Ephesian elders he proclaimed, "I have not coveted anyone's silver or gold or clothing" (Acts 20:33). Paul exhorted the Colossians, "Put to death, therefore, whatever belongs to your earthly nature: sexual immorality, impurity, lust, evil desires and greed, which is idolatry" (Colossians 3:5). John the Apostle lovingly warned his flock, "Do not love the world or anything in the world. If anyone loves the world, the love of the Father is not in him. For everything in the world — the cravings of sinful man, the lust of his eyes and the boasting of what he has and does — comes not from the Father but from the world. The world and its desires pass away, but the man who does the will of God lives forever" (1 John 2:15-17).

In assessing the spiritual significance of the sin of covetousness, we inevitably are taken very deep into the interior of our souls. This is where the battles are won or lost. The Scriptures are calling us to do all we can to root out this deadly desire.

Let us now consider the various forms of coveting so we can better understand its uprooting.

Possessions

Notwithstanding the proverbial cliché that "things cannot make you happy," people (including many Christians) actually believe otherwise in their heart of hearts. Elvis had three jets, two Cadillacs, a Rolls, a Lincoln Continental, two station wagons, a Jeep, a custom touring bus, and three motorcycles. His favorite car was his 1960 Cadillac limousine. The top was covered with pearl-white Naugahyde, and the body was sprayed with forty coats of a specially prepared paint that included crushed diamonds. Nearly all the metal trim was plated with 18-karat gold. There were two gold-flake telephones. There was a gold vanity case containing a gold electric razor and gold hair clippers, an electric shoe buffer, a gold-plated television, a record player, an amplifier, an air conditioner, an electrical system for operating any kind of household appliance, and a refrigerator that was capable of making ice in precisely two minutes. But he died a lonely and unhappy man.

When Diet Coke was available only in the United States, Christina Onassis would monthly dispatch a jet to the U.S. at the cost of $30,000 round trip to pick up fresh cases of "the real thing." Friends who were too busy to spend all their time with her were paid $20,000 to $30,000 per month to be her pals. Yet, Christina Onassis died an unfulfilled and profoundly unhappy woman.[2]

Everyone knows why the lives of these super-rich celebrities ended so miserably — because money can't buy happiness. Yet as a society, we're like the two men who watched a wealthy friend be buried as he wished — sitting behind the steering wheel of his luxury convertible. As a crane lowered the car into the grave with the corpse propped behind the wheel, one said to the other, "Now that's really living!"

Clichés aside, we somehow believe that if we had lots of money, we would be the exception. But the Bible is clear: "Whoever loves money never has money enough; whoever loves wealth is never satisfied with his income. This too is meaningless" (Ecclesiastes 5:10). Moreover, Paul would later say, "The love of money is a root of all kinds of evil" (1 Timothy 6:10). There is no problem with what the Bible says. The problem is *us*. We need to believe the Bible!

People

The Tenth Word also specifically forbids coveting people — namely, other people's people. I recall an older Christian leader recounting to me the self-pitying complaint of another Christian leader whose career had soured late in life. His complaint? If only God had given him Ruth Graham for a wife instead of the one he had, then he would have been successful! Think of the inevitable imagined adultery with the other's wife. Perhaps this even included a death wish toward her spouse, for how otherwise could she be his? Using the man's own logic, did he ever think of what Ruth Graham might *not* have become if she'd been tethered to his ignoble soul?

This coveting of people may also involve coveting family. "If only I'd been born into that family . . . I would have been a better daughter than her." "Oh, to be a part of a dynasty — to have a *name*."

Position

A similar common covetousness is for position and status. Jesus saw this firsthand among the scribes and Pharisees who loved the places of prominence (cf. Matthew 23:5-7). Sadly, He saw it only too closely in His disciples when they argued about who would be the greatest in the Kingdom (cf. Mark 10:35-45; Luke 22:24-27). We're so prone to covet another's place.

> *We people on the pavement looked at him*
> *He was a gentleman from soul to crown,*
> *Clean favored, and imperially slim.*
> *And he was always quietly arrayed,*
>
> *And he was always human when he talked;*
> *But still he fluttered pulses when he said,*
> *"Good morning," and he glittered when he walked.*
> *And he was rich — yes, richer than a king —*
>
> *And admirably schooled in every grace:*
> *In fine, we thought that he was everything*
> *To make us wish that we were in his place.*
> —"Richard Cory" (Edwin Arlington Robinson)

Accomplishments

Some fall to coveting other's educational and professional accomplishments. That Ph.D. should have been yours. Your friend writes a book, and it becomes "the book you ought to have written," because you would have done it better. This is often accompanied by a "people are getting ahead of me" malaise. When you're at your desk, people are working out at the gym and getting ahead of you. When a friend gets a promotion, he's getting ahead of you. If a colleague reads a book you haven't read, he's getting ahead of you. When you're sitting in church listening to a sermon, your unchurched golfing partner is getting ahead of you![3]

Spirituality

A particularly insidious form of this sin is coveting another's spirituality. St. John of the Cross put it this way: "Many experience displeasure when they see others in possession of spiritual goods. They feel sensibly hurt because others surpass them on this road, and they resent it when others are praised."[4] The Apostle Paul was the object of such coveting when he languished in prison as his colleagues engaged in sinful competition for his spot (cf. Philippians 1:12-18). It also spurred John the Baptist's disciples to warn John of Jesus' rising ministry and the danger of eclipse as they told him "everyone is going to him" (John 3:26).

So we see that coveting can have many flash points (coveting *possessions*, coveting *people*, coveting *position*, coveting *accomplishments*, coveting *spirituality*), but it reaches its nadir in the damning sins of envy and jealousy by which one actually feels wounded by the prosperity and success of another. The French have a word for this, *ressentiment*, a word that describes the longing to do harm to the one envied. But since that is unacceptable, this attitude manifests itself in one's saying things that detract from the other's worth, and also in rejoicing at the other's misfortune. *Ressentiment* festers with the desire to do harm.[5] It "whispers continually: 'I can forgive everything, but not what you *are* — that you are *what* you are — that I am not what you are — indeed that I am not *you*.'"[6] This cannot be forgiven!

This hybrid envy can take very subtle forms. For example, "When hatred does not dare to come out into the open it can be easily expressed in the form of ostensible love — love for something that has features that are the opposite of those of the hated object. This can happen in such a way that the hatred remains secret."[7] This covetousness-turned-envy secretly assaults the person who is its object. It is the interior demonic opposite of the law of love.

Further, where covetousness breaks out, there is relational mayhem. A Greek fable captured the essence of this when it told of a covetous man to whom the gods granted any wish he liked — on the condition that his neighbor would get twice as much of it. Unable to bear the thought of his neighbor coming out better than he, he wished to lose one eye![8]

Coveting, unchecked, precipitates the breaking of the second table of the Law, bringing about unfilial acts — murder, adultery, theft, and lying. No wonder God crowned the Decalogue with the prohibition against coveting; no wonder both the Old and New Testaments repeatedly shout covetousness down.

The fact is, we are all covetous. It was precisely this Tenth Commandment that convicted the Apostle Paul he was a breaker of the Law. As Paul relates in Romans 7, in his initial superficial understanding of the Law he thought he was doing quite well. But then he seriously considered the Tenth Commandment, and this was the outcome, in his famous words:

> Indeed! I would not have known what sin was except through the law. For I would not have known what it was to covet if the law had not said, "Do not covet." But sin, seizing the opportunity afforded by the commandment, produced in me every kind of covetous desire. For apart from law, sin is dead. Once I was alive apart from law; but when the commandment came, sin sprang to life and I died. (Romans 7:7-9)

Spiritually illuminated, Paul saw that his entire interior life was filled with coveting. And when he tried to abstain from coveting, he coveted all the more. The Law killed — it condemned him! He then knew what he was. He felt the sentence of death.

But it was this despair that gloriously opened him to grace. And today the same honest realization will do the same for us. None of us can keep the Law. I'm guilty! You're guilty! I can't do it! You can't do it! There is only one way to turn — and that is to God's grace.

Perhaps you've never seen yourself in this light before, but now your sinfulness is painfully clear. If so, you may be ready for your own Damascus Road experience because you realize that your only hope is for God to bestow His righteousness upon you through Christ. To employ Paul's terminology again, "But now a righteousness from God, apart from law, has been made known, to which the Law and the Prophets testify. This righteousness from God comes through faith in Jesus Christ to all who believe" (Romans 3:21, 22). If you see it, and if you believe it, Christ is now your righteousness because this righteousness comes by faith. Do you truly believe it? Then you are a soulmate with Paul and indeed all the saints of the ages.

DISCIPLINES OF GRACE

If one has through faith become an heir of God's forgiving grace, the ultimate remedy for a covetous heart is in place. This, along with some common-sense disciplines, will enable you to live within the parameters of grace and beyond the Devil's laughter.

Loving

First John 4:19 instructs us that "We love because he first loved us." That is, His love from Heaven enables us to love Him back, and then to love others. This is precisely the structure of the Ten Words, because the first four instruct us in loving God and the second six in loving others. So we understand that the way to love others is to intensely love God. Do this truly, and you will love your neighbor as yourself and will thus be liberated from sinful coveting.

Seeking

Jesus said, "But seek first his kingdom and his righteousness, and all these things will be given to you as well" (Matthew 6:33). His explicit meaning is that He will provide everything necessary for a rich, full life to His children who seek His sovereign reign. Therefore, if we are Kingdom seekers and as such have everything, we will have no need to covet anything. Kingdom seekers are *ipso facto* not coveters. Tempted to covet? Seek His Kingdom and His righteousness.

Feeding

Jesus also said to his own, "I am the bread of life. He who comes to me will never go hungry, and he who believes in me will never be thirsty" (John 6:35). To be full of Jesus is to be in the state where covetousness is out of mind.

Contenting

We must make sure we are actively contenting our souls with Christ. Content souls do not covet. Jesus said, "But whoever drinks the water I give him will never thirst. Indeed, the water I give him will become in him a spring of water welling up to eternal life" (John 4:14). Those, like Paul, who have learned Jesus' way testify, "For I have learned to be content whatever the circumstances" (Philippians 4:11). Further, they assure us, "And my God will meet all your needs according to his glorious riches in Christ Jesus" (Philippians 4:19). And finally, they state categorically, "But godliness with contentment is great gain" (1 Timothy 6:6). Royal contentment is the fare of God's children.

My crown is in my heart, not on my head;
  Not deck'd with diamonds and Indian stones,
Nor to be seen: My crown is call'd content;
  A crown it is that seldom kings enjoy.
                    —*King Henry the* VI (William Shakespeare)

Coveting

A proper coveting is the answer to sinful coveting. First there is the proper coveting for *self* that Paul enjoins: "But eagerly desire the greater gifts" (1 Corinthians 12:31). We must covet, not for others' gifts, but to grow in the gifts that God has given us, and to long for even greater gifts. St. Augustine wisely instructs, "Be always displeased with what thou art . . . . Always add, always walk, always proceed. Neither stand still, nor go back, nor deviate."

Second, we must covet the best for *others* through our prayers. We ought to prayerfully covet for others blessings in regard to *possessions, people, position, accomplishments,* and *spirituality.* Pray for the prosperity of your brothers and sisters — pray that their marriages will be blessed — pray that their position and influence will increase — pray that they will accomplish great things — pray that they will grow in grace.

Such sublime coveting will free you from all sinful covetousness.

"You shall not covet your neighbor's house. You shall not covet your neighbor's wife, or his manservant or maidservant, his ox or donkey, or anything that belongs to your neighbor" (Exodus 20:17).

This is the Tenth Word of Grace!

PART III

Loving God and Loving Others

The Ten Words of Grace

Norman Maclean's lyrical remembrance *A River Runs Through It* begins whimsically:

In our family, there was no clear line between religion and fly fishing. We lived at the junction of great trout rivers in western Montana, and our father was a Presbyterian minister and a fly fisherman who tied his own flies and taught others. He told us about Christ's disciples being fishermen, and we were left to assume, as my brother and I did, that all first-class fishermen on the Sea of Galilee were fly fishermen and that John, the favorite, was a dry-fly fisherman.[1]

Of course, there was a distinction in the Maclean family between the *Westminster Catechism* and fly fishing, but their father catechized his boys in both. In respect to the latter, Reverend Maclean would summon his two sons, button on his casting glove, and hold his rod straight out in front of him, where it "trembled with the beating of his heart."[2] Having the boys' dutiful attention, he would instruct them in the discipline of fly-casting using the four-count rhythm. The one count lifts the line, leader, and fly off the water; the two count raises them straight up into the sky; the three count is a pause, just *before* two o'clock in which the leader and fly are given time to trail out behind the line; the four count is when the rod is powered forward to the ten o'clock position where

fly and leader then go ahead of the line and coast to a perfect landing. "Remember," their father would say, "it is an art that is performed on a four count rhythm between ten and two o'clock."

So the Maclean boys learned to fly-cast Presbyterian-style, by
the discipline of their mother's metronome — one . . . two . . . three
. . . four . . .[3] And this disciplined pedagogy provided the ground
for Norman and especially Paul Maclean to become master fly
fishermen.

That wise father understood that *discipline is the key to becoming proficient at anything*, whether it be painting, music, writing,
calculus, basketball, golf, chess or the sublimest of arts — fly fishing. Discipline is what separates the achievers from the also-rans.
And this is doubly true in spiritual matters, because man's sinful
nature naturally gravitates to foot-dragging in things spiritual.
This is why the Apostle Paul unabashedly admonished his young
disciple, Timothy, to "train yourself to be godly" (1 Timothy 4:7).
The very word "train" has the smell of a good workout.
"Gymnasticize (exercise, work out, train) yourself for the purpose
of godliness." Spiritual sweat is a major component to leading a
godly life. No man or woman has ever become godly without it.

Moreover, discipline is not antithetical to grace. Paul, as the
preeminent apostle of grace, wrote, "But by the grace of God I am
what I am, and his grace to me was not without effect. No, I
worked harder than all of them — yet not I, but the grace of God
that was with me" (1 Corinthians 15:10). He was saved by God's
grace, not by works (Ephesians 2:8, 9). But the effect of God's free
grace was to make him sweat more in his labors for Christ than all
the rest.

This does not suggest, of course, that human discipline in and
of itself can empower anyone to please God, much less keep the
Law. As we have seen, Paul, who had the equivalent of a couple of
Ph.D.s in the Mosaic Law and who, in his own words, was "in
regard to the law, a Pharisee . . . as for legalistic righteousness, fault-

less" (Philippians 3:5, 6), was actually a great transgressor of the Law.

Later in fact, as he came to understand what covetousness was, he saw that his whole life was filled with coveting. His testimony was that the more he set himself (unaided by grace) not to covet, the more he coveted (Romans 7:7-11). This insight further helped him see the interior substance of the Law and ultimately led to the realization that he was constantly breaking the other laws in his heart. The Law killed his spiritual presumption. He knew he couldn't live out the Law, and that in fact no one could.

However, if one knows Christ, it is possible, through discipline, to live within the spiritual parameters, the borders, of the Law. How so? Because Jesus Christ fulfilled the Law (Matthew 5:17).

- Jesus never put any god or indeed anything before His Father.
- Jesus never constructed materially or mentally an idol in the form of anything; He worshiped God, as He taught others, "in spirit and in truth."
- Jesus never misused the Father's name but instead "hallowed" it.
- Jesus kept the Sabbath day holy.
- Jesus unfailingly honored His earthly father and mother.
- Jesus never indulged in a murderous, hateful thought.
- Jesus never engaged in mental adultery, much less physical adultery.
- Jesus never stole, or even had a larcenous thought.
- Jesus never once bore false testimony — no slander or gossip or flattery or untrue words — only perpetual truth.
- Jesus never coveted anything except another's spiritual well-being.

Therefore, because Jesus Christ fulfilled the Law, and because we are in Christ and He is in us (cf. 2 Corinthians 5:21; Colossians 1:27), we can live within the blessed borders of the Law. Jesus' indwelling puts our souls in spiritual sympathy with the Law. We resonate with it — and we want to live it out. The indwelling Christ also sends the Holy Spirit as "another Counselor," one like Himself, to empower us to live out His life (John 14:16). Admittedly, no Christian ever perfectly lives out the Law, but hosts of believers live within its borders.

To so live is to live in grace, because it is to live by the divine pattern. To so live is to "Love the Lord your God with all your heart and with all your soul and with all your mind." To so live is to "Love your neighbor as yourself." To so live is to live with a passionate *upward* love for God and a passionate *outward* love for humanity. To so live is to live as we were created to live. This is a great grace!

LOVING GOD

As we come to the end of our study of the Ten Commandments, let us again draw them together in tight bouquet, for greater pungency and to enhance their ongoing aroma in our lives.

The Primacy of God

The First Word of Grace — "You shall have no other gods before me" — thunders today across a deeply idolatrous world that has bowed before a pantheon of false gods — from statist deities like Lenin and Stalin to Hollywood's "Elvis-olatry" to New Age neo-paganism's earth worship. Given thoughtful application, the First Commandment forbids the worship of technology, appetites, sex, money, and self. But far from being negative, it is a deep grace, because it positively commands "You shall have *Me*!" It is a declaration of heavenly *eros*. God wants to have us, and He wants us to have Him. The First Word graciously demands that we ask ourselves, is God first? First place is the place of love!

The Person of God

The Second Word of Grace — "You shall not make for yourself an idol in the form of anything" — is distinct from the First Word in that while the First forbids the *existence* of other gods, the Second forbids the *making* of other gods. Material idols are forbidden because in respect to understanding who God is, they are limiting, obscuring, localizing, projecting, controlling, and subtracting. Most moderns do not succumb to the making of *material* images of God, but the dreaming up of idolatrous *mental* images of God is rampant. Many like to imagine a God of their own liking, which then diminishes or obviates God as revealed in Scripture.

The antidote is twofold: the *written Word* of God, and the *living Word* of God. We must scour the Bible — embracing the things we *like* to think about God as well as the things we do *not like* to think about Him — and then humbly meld them together in blessed tension. Then, of course, we must focus on Jesus, because God spoke His final word in His Son. This takes some discipline, but the reward is great, for the more clearly you see God, the more you will love Him!

The Reverence of God

The Third Word of Grace — "You shall not misuse the name of the Lord your God" — is particularly relevant in a day in which irreverence and blasphemy are increasingly sophisticated and culturally cachet. It forbids making insincere oaths; it prohibits the abuse of God's name through irreverence, contempt, and cursing. The Command demands the opposite — the hallowing of God's name, just as Jesus instructed His disciples to pray: "Our Father in heaven, hallowed be your name" (Matthew 6:9). The great grace here is that the verbal reverencing of God's name will elevate and ground our love for Him. Reverencing God's name is the divinely ordained path for loving Him and being filled with His grace. Consciously hallow His name, and you will love Him more and more!

The Time for God

The Fourth Word of Grace — "Remember the Sabbath day by keeping it holy" — invites some Christian distinctions. First, the Mosaic Sabbath day was superseded in the New Testament church by the "Lord's Day" (the day Jesus was resurrected — Sunday). The Lord's Day is not simply a "Christian Sabbath," but a day set aside for worship, and Christians ought to observe it as such. Second, it is not incumbent upon Christians to follow the Mosaic Sabbath's stringent command to desist from labor and to rest, because that Command is not transferred to the Lord's Day. However, wise Christians will incorporate the Sabbath rest principle into their observance of the Lord's Day as best they can, because the rest principle is rooted in our cosmos. There is a genesis rhythm to life which, if observed, will benefit us greatly. The benefit, of course, is that it will enhance our love for God. Time spent with the object of our love, especially in corporate worship and restful communion, will unfailingly elevate our love.

What an effective bouquet these four words are! Do you want to love God? Then give Him *primacy*, focus on His *person*, *reverence* Him with your words, and invest your *time* with Him. As a result, you will grow more and more to live out life's highest priority: loving God with your all! Your life will then be a sweet aroma to Him.

LOVING OTHERS

Turning now to the second table of the Law, moving from upward love of God to outward love for others, we observe the logic: *love God and then love others.* But this is not what culture would have us believe. The modern world and indeed much of Christianity have reversed the order of the two tables of the Law and have scrambled their clauses, so that Jesus' summation is twisted to read: "Thou shalt love thy neighbor with all thy heart, soul, mind, and strength. This is the first and great commandment. And the second is like unto it, namely, thou shalt love God as thyself."[4]

This inversion is precisely why the modern attempt at social ethics fails so miserably. By making man the center and measure of everything, the ethical center is always changing. Truth, goodness, right, and wrong are no more than what human opinion currently holds them to be. Modern floating ethics! The impotence of this system is further sealed by demoting one's love for God to second place, which is really to give it no place at all. This effectively removes the power to love others, because God's Word tells us, "We love because he first loved us" (1 John 4:19). There is simply no power to love in secular ethics.

On the other hand, what amazing power there is in God's love order! Love for God is the reason missionaries have gone to the ends of the earth. Love for God is why Wilberforce fought and succeeded in ending Britain's slave trade. Love for God is why Charles Colson has given his life to prison ministry. Love for God brings grace to this needy world.

Parents and Loving Others

The Fifth Word of Grace — "Honor your father and your mother" — enjoins *obedience* to one's parents during the growing years and *reverence* during one's mature years as demonstrated by respect, provision, consideration, and character. Such honoring of parents is regularly followed by the individual grace of longer life and greater well-being for the child. And it also produces, of course, rich national grace, because obedient children become a societal treasure.

Life and Loving Others

The Sixth Word of Grace — "You shall not murder" — resounds over a world bent on homicide, suicide, and feticide. Correctly understood, it addresses the source of man's murderous spirit, as Jesus explained:

> You have heard that it was said to the people long ago, "Do not murder, and anyone who murders will be subject to judgment." But I tell you that anyone who is angry with his brother will be subject to judgment. . . . Therefore, if you are offering your gift at the altar and there remember that your brother has something against you, leave your gift there in front of the altar. First go and be reconciled to your brother; then come and offer your gift. (Matthew 5:21-24)

The immediacy of Jesus' demand to make things right must be obeyed. We must heed His word, for if we put it off, we will not do it. Our dark century needs graced hearts now.

Sexuality and Loving Others

The Seventh Word of Grace — "You shall not commit adultery" — comes to a culture raging with adultery and sensuality and increasingly barnyard ethics. Adultery and its kin are great sins. But the other side of the coin, fidelity, is the way of grace: grace with God — grace in marriage — grace in family — and grace to the church and world. Again Jesus goes to the heart of the Law:

> You have heard that it was said, "Do not commit adultery." But I tell you that anyone who looks at a woman lustfully has already committed adultery with her in his heart. If your right eye causes you to sin, gouge it out and throw it away. It is better for you to lose one part of your body than for your whole body to be thrown into hell. And if your right hand causes you to sin, cut it off and throw it away. It is better for you to lose one part of your body than for your whole body to go into hell. (Matthew 5:27-30)

All mental sin, all fantasizing, all voyeurism are to be radically dealt with through stringent discipline. The purity thus attained is a gift of love to others.

Property and Loving Others

The Eighth Word of Grace — "You shall not steal" — addresses today's larceny-ridden culture. "How do I steal from thee? Let me count the ways: tax theft, customs theft, debt theft, borrowing theft, welfare theft, time theft, work theft, phone theft, computer theft, account theft, supply theft, plagiarism, the theft of another's reputation. How do I love thee? By respecting your property as the Eighth Word so clearly commands."

Truth and Loving Others

The Ninth Word of Grace — "You shall not give false testimony against your neighbor" — cuts through the post-Kantian fog of relativism that blankets modern life so that 91 percent of all Americans lie regularly. "Americans," say the analysts, "lie about everything — and usually for no good reason." But God's people, living under the authority of His Word, are to avoid every kind of lie — slander, gossip, flattery, exaggeration, carelessness, deceptive true words, insinuation, and silence. Radical truthfulness brings grace and love to one's character, one's relationships, and the church.

Attitude and Loving Others

The Tenth Word of Grace — "You shall not covet" — crowns the Decalogue because, though Jesus explains the inward application of some of the preceding Commandments, such as murder and adultery, this final Commandment specifically forbids the inner proclivity of desiring that which belongs to others. It shows up everyone as guilty. Moreover, covetousness lies at the root of one's breaking all the other Commandments. It therefore slays us. We cry, "Woe is me!" and we are driven to grace. And that is, of course, wonderful. But the positive side is even more wondrous, because it calls us to lovingly covet blessing for others — to pray that God will bless them with possessions, fulfilling relationships, position, spirituality, and everything that will make for their well-being.

Now think of the Ten Words. What a way to live! First by *loving God* through loving His *primacy*, loving His *person*, loving His *reverence*, and loving *time* with Him. Then comes *loving others* through *parents*, *life*, *sexuality*, *property*, *truth*, and *attitude*.

This is a life of grace, because this is the way God meant us to live. It is the proper life. And we all want it.

But, fellow-Christians, it requires discipline. Remember the boys learning to fly-cast Presbyterian-style on a metronome? Well, it paid off. In a passage of poignant eloquence, Norman Maclean, who was William Rainey Harper Professor of English at the University of Chicago, describes his brother at the height of his power:

> He shook himself duck-dog fashion, flopping. Then he steadied himself and began to cast and the whole world turned to water.
>
> Below him was the multitudinous river, and, where the rock had parted it around him, big-grained vapor rose. The mini-molecules of water left in the wake of his line made momentary loops of gossamer, disappearing so rapidly in the rising big-grained vapor that they had to be retained in memory to be visualized as loops. The spray emanating from him was finer-grained still and enclosed him in a halo of himself. The halo of himself was always there and always disappearing, as if he were candlelight flickering.[5]

Through discipline young Paul Maclean became, in his father's words, "beautiful" in his practice of the art of fly-casting. Sadly, however, as the story chronicles, he failed to learn the disciplines of grace — which resulted in his untimely death.

DISCIPLINES OF GRACE

The Ten Words call us to divinely-shaped discipline, because they provide us the architecture God would have for every soul. The foundation is loving Him with everything; the superstructure is loving others as we love ourselves.

In respect to the discipline required, much has been said at the end of each of the ten chapters, and the reader is encouraged to refer to those specific disciplines as is appropriate. At the same time, concluding advice about the essential outline of disciplining oneself in the Ten Words is in order. This falls under three simple, coordinated headings.

Knowing the Ten Words

In a culture in which most Christians cannot even name the Ten Words, it remains our task to know them well. If they are to serve as a moral *aide mémoire*, they must be in your mind. You must know what the two divisions are — the significance of the first four Words and then the second six. You must work at being able to describe the essence of each one. It would be most helpful to be able to refer to each by number. "The seventh? . . . Adultery. The third? . . . God's name."

Praying the Ten Words

Next, you ought to regularly pray the Ten Words for yourself.

> *Gracious Lord, enable me to so live that nothing comes*
>   *before You.*
> *Cleanse my life of all idols, material and mental.*
> *Help me, God, to never misuse Your holy name.*
> *May the Sabbath's genesis rhythm order my spiritual life.*

Empower me to honor my parents through obedience
*   and reverence.*
*   Save me from the anger and hatred of a homicidal heart.*
Deliver me from the sensuality of an adulterous heart.
*   May I never steal anything.*
Empower me to be truthful.
*   Mighty God, liberate me from covetousness.*

Living the Ten Words

Perfectly living out the Ten Words is, of course, an impossibility. But living within their gracious borders is quite within the Christian's reach. This is because Jesus lived the Ten Words to perfection, and because all believers can say with Paul, "I have been crucified with Christ and I no longer live, but Christ lives in me. The life I live in the body, I live by faith in the Son of God, who loved me and gave himself for me" (Galatians 2:20).

These are the Ten Words of Grace. Amen!

NOTES

INTRODUCTION: *Disciplines of Grace*

1. *Stone v. Graham*, 449 U.S. 39, 42 (1980).
2. "Godless in Kentucky," *Wall Street Journal* (Thursday, November 20, 1980), p. 26.
3. Paul Leicester Ford, ed., *The New England Primer, a History of Its Origin and Development* (New York: Dodd, Mead and Company, 1967), p. 61, which repeats questions like: "Which is the fifth commandment?"
4. "Godless in Kentucky," p. 26.
5. Gallup Poll, 1988.
6. Paul Johnson, *Modern Times* (New York: HarperCollins, 1991), p. 4.
7. *Ibid.*, p. 11.
8. *Ibid.*
9. *Ibid.*, p. 48.
10. Robert H. Bork, *The Tempting of America* (New York: The Free Press, 1990), pp. 248, 249.
11. K. E. Kirk, *The Vision of God* (Harrisburg, PA: Morehouse Publishing, 1991), p. 46.
12. David Aikman, "The New Revelation, Russia's Spiritual Awakening," *Religious Broadcasting* (December 1991), p. 41.
13. Alan Johnson, "Jesus and Moses: Rabbinic Backgrounds and Exegetical Concerns in Matthew 5 as Crucial to the Theological Foundations of Christian Ethics," Chapter 7 in Morris Inch and Ronald Youngblood, eds., *The Living and Active Word of God: Studies in Honor of Samuel J. Schultz* (Winona Lake, IN: Eisenbrauns, 1983), p. 89.
14. Ernest C. Reisinger, *Today's Evangelism: Its Message and Methods* (Phillipsburg, NJ: Craig Press, 1982), p. 17.
15. Knox Chamberlain, "The Law of Moses and the Law of Christ" in John S. Feinberg, ed., *Continuity and Discontinuity* (Wheaton, IL: Crossway Books, 1988), p. 182 writes: "God *always* gives his law to his covenant-people for the sake of this personal bond — whether to establish it, deepen it, or restore it: see, e.g., Lev 26:12; Jer 31:33-34."
16 R. Alan Cole, *Exodus* (Downers Grove, IL: InterVarsity Press, 1973), p. 152.

CHAPTER ONE: *The First Word of Grace*

1. Paul Johnson, *Intellectuals* (New York: Harper and Row, 1988), p. 17.

2. *Ibid.*, p. 21.
3. *Ibid.*, p. 27.
4. *Ibid.*
5. *Ibid.*
6. *Ibid.*, p. 251.
7. George Barna, *The Barna Report 1992-93, an Annual Survey of Lifestyles, Values and Religious Views* (Carol Steam, IL: Christianity Today, Inc., 1993), p. 113.
8. Gallup Poll, 1988.
9. Barna, p. 114.
10. *Ibid.*, p. 120.
11. Charles Colson, *Kingdoms in Conflict* (New York/Grand Rapids, MI: William Morrow/Zondervan, 1987), p. 216.
12. David Field, *God's Good Life* (Leicester, England: Inter-Varsity, 1992), p. 46.
13. Philip Schaff, *The Creeds of Christendom*, Vol. 2 (Grand Rapids, MI: Baker, 1969), pp. 338-341.
14. J. Philip Hyatt, *Exodus* (Grand Rapids, MI: Eerdmans, 1971), p. 209. See also Thomas Watson, *The Ten Commandments* (Edinburgh: The Banner of Truth Trust, 1981), p. 49 who writes:

Though we are forward to take privileges to ourselves, yet we are apt to shift off duties from ourselves to others; therefore the commandment is in the second person, *Thou and Thou,* that every one may know that it is spoken to him, as it were, by name.

15. W. H. Gispen, *Exodus*, trans. Ed van der Maas (Grand Rapids, MI: Zondervan, 1982), p. 189 says:

Eight of the commandments are negative: "you shall not." The Hebrew *lo* makes the prohibitions emphatic: God absolutely did not want the Israelite to do this, and He fully expected that he would not do it.

16. G. Campbell Morgan, *The Ten Commandments* (New York: Revell, 1901), pp. 18, 19.
17. Robert H. Fischer, *The Large Catechism of Martin Luther* (Philadelphia: Fortress Press, 1959), p. 9.
18. Thomas Watson, *The Ten Commandments* (Carlisle, PA: The Banner of Truth Trust, 1965), p. 57.
19. Joy Davidman, *Smoke on the Mountain* (Philadelphia: Westminster, 1954), p. 24.
20. *Ibid.*
21. Lehman Strauss, *The Eleven Commandments* (Neptune, NJ: Loizeaux, 1979), p. 30.
22. Charles Colson, *Loving God* (Grand Rapids, MI: Zondervan, 1983), p. 11, which quotes Shirley MacLaine, *Washington Post* interview, 1977.
23. Davidman, p. 29.

CHAPTER TWO: *The Second Word of Grace*

1. G. Campbell Morgan, *The Ten Commandments* (New York: Revell, 1901), p. 26.
2. T. M. Shine, "A Savior You Can Hug," *Chicago Tribune* (January 1, 1993), Section 5, Tempo, p. 1.
3. J. I. Packer, *Knowing God* (Downers Grove, IL: InterVarsity Press, 1973), p. 39.
4. *Ibid.,* p. 40.
5. Joy Davidman, *Smoke on the Mountain* (Philadelphia: Westminster, 1954), p. 24.
6. Packer, p. 42 writes:

   How often do we hear this sort of thing: "I *like to think* of God as the great Architect or, Mathematician, or Artist." "I don't think of God as a Judge; I *like to think* of Him simply as a Father." We know from experience how often remarks of this kind serve as the prelude to a denial of something that the Bible tells us about God. It needs to be said with the greatest possible emphasis that those who hold themselves free to think of God *as they like* are breaking the second commandment.

7. Alan F. Johnson, ed., *God Speaks to an X-Rated Society* (Chicago: Moody Press, 1973), p. 27:

   The phrase "to the third and fourth generations" indicates that God's judgment extends virtually as far as a man can see. The contrast to this is the term "thousands" referring to His infinite mercy, His lovingkindness, and His faithfulness. A comparison of this reference to God's mercy with the statement about His wrath extending to the third and fourth generations shows the phrase does not literally mean "three or four generations" but the entire length of a man's life.

8. Benjamin W. Farley, trans., *John Calvin's Sermons on the Ten Commandments* (Grand Rapids, MI: Baker Book House, 1980), pp. 78, 79.
9. C. F. Keil and F. Delitsch, *Biblical Commentary on the Old Testament*, Vol. II, *The Pentateuch* (Grand Rapids, MI: Eerdmans, n.d.), p. 116: "On the other hand He shows mercy to the thousandths, ie, to the thousandth generation (cf. Deut. vii9)."

CHAPTER THREE: *The Third Word of Grace*

1. Paul Galloway, "Blank Verse Versus [blank] verse," *Chicago Tribune*, Tempo (October 12, 1992).
2. Michael Medved, *Hollywood vs. America* (New York: HarperCollins, 1992), p. 179.
3. Geoffrey W. Bromiley, ed., *The International Standard Bible Encyclopedia*, Vol. 2 (Grand Rapids, MI: 1982), p. 497.
4. J. Philip Hyatt, *Exodus* (Grand Rapids, MI: Eerdmans, 1971), p. 212.
5. Herbert Danby, trans., *The Mishnah* (London: Oxford, 1974), pp. 408-421.

6. Helmut Thielicke, *Life Can Begin Again* (Philadelphia: Westminster, 1980), p. 55.
7. Benjamin W. Farley, *John Calvin's Sermons on the Ten Commandments* (Grand Rapids, MI: Baker Book House, 1980), p. 89.

CHAPTER FOUR: *The Fourth Word of Grace*

1. "Drawing the Jewish line," *The Economist*, February 6, 1993, p. 64.
2. Alfred Edersheim, *The Life and Times of Jesus the Messiah*, Vol. 2 (Grand Rapids, MI: Eerdmans, 1967), pp. 777-787, provides the examples of the legalisms listed above.
3. D. A. Carson, ed., *From Sabbath to Lord's Day: A Biblical, Historical, and Theological Investigation* (Grand Rapids, MI: Zondervan, 1982), p. 348 explains:

How then do the biblical writers relate the seventh day to God's activity in creation? Genesis 2:2-3 concludes the creation account, and does so in terms of God's resting on the seventh day and blessing and hallowing that day. Elsewhere in Genesis 1 and 2 there are explicit commands for the first pair to follow. Not only is there no explicit command and no use of the term "sabbath," there is also no mention of humanity. The depiction of the seventh day in the schema is solely in terms of God.

4. Abraham Heschel, *The Sabbath: Its Meaning for Modern Man* (New York: Farrar, Straus & Giroux, 1951), p. 14.
5. Eugene H. Peterson, *Working the Angles* (Grand Rapids, MI: Eerdmans, 1989), pp. 48, 49, writes:

Sabbath extrapolates this basic, daily rhythm into the larger context of the month. The turning of the earth on its axis gives us the basic two-beat rhythm, evening/morning. The moon in its orbit introduces another rhythm, the twenty-eight-day month, marked by four phases of seven days each.

6. William Barclay, *The Ten Commandments for Today* (New York: Harper & Row, 1973), p. 40.
7. Carson, p. 361.
8. *Ibid.*, pp. 373, 374.
9. Barclay, p. 32.
10. Carson, p. 378.
11. Robert H. Fischer, *The Large Catechism of Martin Luther* (Philadelphia: Fortress, 1959), p. 20.
12. Ford Lewis Battles, trans., John Calvin, *Institutes of the Christian Religion*, Vol. 1 (Philadelphia: Westminster, 1960), pp. 399, 400.
13. *Ibid.*, p. 399.
14. *Ibid.*, p. 400.
15. John H. Leith, *Creeds of the Churches* (Richmond, VA: John Knox, 1973), pp. 179,180.
16. Carson, pp. 398-400.
17. John W. Drakeford, *Humor in Preaching* (Grand Rapids, MI: Zondervan, 1986), pp. 17, 18.

18. Alexander B. Grosart, ed., *The Complete Works of Thomas Brooks*, Vol. 6 (Edinburgh: Banner of Truth, 1980, reprint of 6 volumes, 1861-1867), p. 299.
19. Peterson, p. 48.
20. *Ibid.*, p. 52.

SUMMARY: *The First Four Words of Grace*

1. I. Epstein, ed., *The Babylonian Talmud, Seder Moed*, Vol. 1 (London: Soncino, 1938), p. 140.
2. The full *Shema* consisted of quotations from Deuteronomy 6:4-9, 11:13-21, and Numbers 16:37-41.
3. C. S. Lewis, *Prince Caspian* (London: Fontana, 1980), pp. 122-124.

CHAPTER FIVE: *The Fifth Word of Grace*

1. W. H. Lewis, ed., *Letters of C. S. Lewis* (New York: Harcourt, Brace & World, 1966), p. 248.
2. Philip Schaff, ed., *Nicene and Post-Nicene Fathers*, Vol. 7, *St. Augustine: Homilies on the Gospel of John, Homilies on the First Epistle of John Soliloquies* (Grand Rapids, MI: Eerdmans, 1974), p. 504:

This we have said in the case where the things done are similar. In the case where they are diverse, we find a man by charity made fierce; and by iniquity made winningly gentle. A father beats a boy, and a boy-stealer caresses. If thou name the two things, blows and caresses, who would not choose the caresses, and decline the blows? If thou mark the persons, it is charity that beats, iniquity that caresses. See what we are insisting upon; that the deeds of men are only discerned by the root of charity. For many things may be done that have a good appearance, and yet proceed not from the root of charity. For thorns also have flowers: some actions truly seem rough, seem savage; howbeit they are done for discipline at the bidding of charity. Once for all, then, a short precept is given thee: Love, and do what thou wilt: whether thou hold thy peace, through love hold thy peace; whether thou cry out, through love cry out; whether thou correct, through love correct; whether thou spare, through love do thou spare: let the root of love be within, of this root can nothing spring but what is good.

3. Lyle W. Dorsett and Marjorie Lamp Mead, eds., *C. S. Lewis Letters to Children* (New York: Macmillan, 1985), p. 111.
4. W. H. Gispen, *Exodus*, trans. Ed van der Maas (Grand Rapids, MI: Zondervan, 1982), p. 196.
5. Philip Schaff, ed., *The Creeds of Christendom* (Grand Rapids, MI: Baker, 1969), p. 345.
6. Annie Dillard, *The Living* (New York: HarperCollins, 1992), p. 182, writes, "His wife laughed at his jokes; his mother waited on him; his red-haired daughter rode on his shoulders, and bounced her heels in his heart."

7. Annie Dillard, *An American Childhood* (New York: Harper & Row, 1987), p. 196.
8. William Manchester, *The Last Lion* (Boston: Little & Brown, 1983), pp. 36, 37, 643, 644.

CHAPTER SIX: *The Sixth Word of Grace*

1. Paul Johnson, *Modern Times: From the Twenties to the Nineties* (New York: HarperCollins, 1991), p. 783.
2. Paul Johnson, *Intellectuals* (New York: Harper & Row, 1988), pp. 245, 246.
3. *Ibid*, p. 322.
4. *Ibid*.
5. Rich Soll, "The Killing Fields," *Chicago* Magazine (March 1993), pp. 56, 57.
6. David Elkind, *The Hurried Child* (Reading, MA: Addison-Wesley, 1931), p. 18 says:

   In 1988, suicide is the second leading cause of death for Americans aged fifteen to twenty-four, after accidents. Accidents account for some ten thousand young lives each year, while suicide takes five thousand. Both accidents and suicide are often substance-abuse related, and some accidents are probably suicidal. Although the suicide rate has leveled off in the last few years, it is still triple what it was in 1960.

7. R. Alan Cole, *Exodus* (Downers Grove, IL: InterVarsity Press, 1973), p. 159.
8. Robertson McQuilkin, *An Introduction to Biblical Ethics* (Wheaton, IL: Tyndale House, 1989), p. 367.
9. Marvin R. Vincent, *Word Studies in the New Testament* (Wilmington, DE: Associate Publishers and Authors, 1972), p. 746.
10. Johnson, *Modern Times*, p. 19.
11. *Ibid*, pp. 13, 14.
12. Arthur F. Holmes, "The Just War," *War: Four Christian Views*, ed. Robert G. Clouse (Downers Grove, IL: InterVarsity Press, 1981), pp. 120, 121.
13. Col. Alexander Shine, *Command* (Spring 1980), pp. 9, 10.
14. Ford Lewis Battles, trans., John Calvin, *Institutes of the Christian Religion*, Vol. 1 (Philadelphia: Westminster, 1960), pp. 404, 405.
15. McQuilkin, p. 331.
16. Hearings before the Subcommittee on Separation of Powers of the Committee on the Judiciary United States Senate, Ninety-seventh Congress, First Session on S. 158, a Bill to Provide That Human Life Shall Be Deemed to Exist from Conception, April 23, 24; May 20, 21; June 1, 10, 12, and 18, Serial No. J-97-16, p. 8.
17. *Ibid.*, p. 10.
18. *Ibid.*, p. 14.
19. McQuilkin, p. 320.
20. Clarence Edward Macartney, *The Woman of Tekoah* (New York/Nashville: Abingdon, 1945), pp. 128, 129.

21. Alexander Balmain Bruce, "Matthew," *The Expositor's Bible*, Vol. 1 (Grand Rapids MI: Eerdmans, 1970), p. 107.

CHAPTER SEVEN: *The Seventh Word of Grace*

1. Robertson McQuilkin, *Biblical Ethics* (Wheaton, IL: Tyndale House, 1989), p. 206, quoting Morton Hunt, *The Affair* (New York: World, 1969), pp. 22, 23, 41.
2. *Ibid.*
3. Barbara Dafoe Whitehead, "Dan Quayle Was Right," *The Atlantic* (April 1993), pp. 47-84.
4. Kenneth L. Woodward with Alden Cohen, "Roll Over John Calvin," *Newsweek* (May 6, 1991), p. 59.
5. Mark Curriden, "Ten Commandments Ruling," *ABA Journal* (March 1993), p. 37.
6. "How Common Is Pastoral Indiscretion?," *Leadership* (Winter 1988), p. 12, says:

   The survey probed the frequency of behavior that pastors themselves feel is inappropriate. *Since you have been in local church ministry, have you ever done anything with someone (not your spouse) that you feel was sexually inappropriate?* The responses: 23 percent yes; 77 percent no. The "inappropriate" behavior was left undefined — possibly ranging from unguarded words to flirtation to adultery. Subsequent questions were more specific. *Have you ever had sexual intercourse with someone other than your spouse since you have been in local-church ministry?* Yes: 12 percent. No: 88 percent. And of that 88 percent, many indicated their purity had not come easily.

   To lend some perspective to these figures, CTi researchers also surveyed almost one thousand subscribers of *Christianity Today* magazine who are *not* pastors. Incidences of immorality were nearly double: 45 percent indicated having done something they considered sexually inappropriate, 23 percent said they had had extramarital intercourse, and 28 percent said they had engaged in other forms of extramarital sexual contact.

7. F. F. Bruce, *History of the English Bible* (New York: Oxford, 1978), p. 108.
8. W. H. Gispen, *Exodus*, trans., Ed van der Maas (Grand Rapids, MI: Zondervan, 1982), p. 198.
9. David Field, *God's Good Life* (Leicester, England: Inter-Varsity, 1992), p. 159.
10. Gordon D. Fee, *The First Epistle to the Corinthians* (Grand Rapids, MI: Eerdmans, 1987), pp. 262, 263.
11. Benjamin W. Farley, *John Calvin's Sermons on the Ten Commandments* (Grand Rapids, MI: Baker, 1980), p. 172.
12. McQuilkin, p. 209.
13. *Ibid.*, p. 228.
14. A. J. Gossip, *The Hero in Thy Soul* (New York: Scribners, 1930), p. 140.

CHAPTER EIGHT: *The Eighth Word of Grace*

1. W. H. Auden and Louis Kronenberger, *The Viking Book of Aphorisms* (New York: Dorset Press, 1981), p. 210.
2. James Patterson and Peter Kim, *The Day America Told the Truth* (New York: Prentice-Hall, 1991), p. 157.
3. Benjamin W. Farley, trans., *John Calvin's Sermons on the Ten Commandments* (Grand Rapids, MI: Baker, 1980), p. 186.
4. Alan F. Johnson, ed., *God Speaks to an X-Rated Society* (Chicago: Moody Press, 1973), p. 72.
5. Lehman Strauss, *The Eleven Commandments* (Neptune, NJ: Loizeaux, 1979), p. 23.
6. James Patterson and Peter Kim, *The Day America Told the Truth*, p. 155.
7. *John Calvin's Sermons on the Ten Commandments*, p. 188.
8. Lance Morrow, "Kidnapping the Brain Children," *Time* (December 3, 1990), Vol. 136, No. 24, p. 126.
9. *Ibid.*
10. Doug Sherman and William Hendricks, *Keeping Your Ethical Edge Sharp* (Colorado Springs, CO: NavPress, 1990), pp. 71, 72.
11. *Ibid.*

CHAPTER NINE: *The Ninth Word of Grace*

1. Peter Kreeft, *Making Choices: Practical Wisdom for Everyday Moral Decisions* (Ann Arbor, MI: Servant Books, 1990), pp. 127, 128.
2. Allan Bloom, *The Closing of the American Mind* (New York: Simon and Schuster, 1987), p. 25.
3. Jon Van, "Scholars Say It's True: Lying is Part of Human Nature," *Chicago Tribune* (February 17, 1991), Section 1, p. 22.
4. Franny Shuker-Haines, "The Truth About Lying," *Child* (April 1990), p. 30.
5. James Patterson and Peter Kim, *The Day America Told the Truth* (New York: Prentice-Hall, 1991), pp. 45, 46.
6. *Ibid.*, pp. 45, 49.
7. *Ibid.*, p. 49.
8. W. H. Gispen, *Exodus,* trans. Ed van der Maas (Grand Rapids, MI: Zondervan, 1982), p. 159.
9. Doug Sherman and William Hendricks, *Keeping Your Ethical Edge Sharp* (Colorado Springs, CO: NavPress, 1990), p. 91.
10. Robertson McQuilkin, *An Introduction to Biblical Ethics* (Wheaton, IL: Tyndale House, 1989), p. 427.
11. Thomas Watson, *The Ten Commandments* (Edinburgh: The Banner of Truth Trust, 1981), p. 169.
12. William Barclay, *The Ten Commandments for Today* (New York: Harper & Row, 1971), p. 191.
13. McQuilkin, pp. 425, 426.

CHAPTER TEN: *The Tenth Word of Grace*

1. Carl E. Bain, ed., *The Norton Introduction to Literature*, Fifth Edition (New York: Norton, 1991, pp. 208-218.
2. Lynn Van Matre, "Onassis Wealth Was Christina's Bane," *Chicago Tribune* (March 11, 1991), Section 5, Tempo, p. 3.
3. Doug Sherman and William Hendricks, *Your Work Matters to God* (Colorado Springs, CO: NavPress, 1987), pp. 37, 38.
4. Henry Fairlie, *The Seven Deadly Sins* (South Bend, IN: University of Notre Dame Press, 1979), p. 79.
5. Herbert Schlossberg, *Idols for Destruction* (Washington, D.C.: Regnery Gateway, 1990), pp. 51, 52.
6. *Ibid.*, p. 51, quoted from Max Scheler, *Ressentiment*, ed. Lewis A. Coser, trans. William W. Holdheim (Glencoe, IL: Free Press, 1961), p. 52.
7. *Ibid.*, p. 53, referencing Scheler, p. 96.
8. Joy Davidman, *Smoke on the Mountain* (Philadelphia: Westminster, 1954), p. 120.
9. William Shakespeare, *King Henry the VI*, Part II, Act III, sc. i, l. 62.

SUMMARY: *The Ten Words of Grace*

1. Norman Maclean, *A River Runs through It and Other Stories* (Chicago: The University of Chicago Press, 1976), p. 1.
2. *Ibid.*, p. 2.
3. *Ibid.*, p. 4.
4. Philip Turner, "To Students of Divinity: A Convocation Address," *First Things* (October 1992), Number 26, p. 26.
5. Maclean, p. 20.

SCRIPTURE INDEX

GENERAL INDEX